For

with much love

Mom + Dad

September 26, 2007

PRAYERFULLY

Creating the Bond Between Man and His Maker

RABBI ABRAHAM J. TWERSKI, M.D.

We acknowledge the graciousness
of our dear friend JUDAH SEPTIMUS who,
among others,
made available to us his collection of
antique *siddurim* and *machzorim*.
Facsimile pages from these works
grace and enhance this book.

First edition – First impression / September 2001

Published by SHAAR PRESS
and Distributed by MESORAH PUBLICATIONS, LTD.
4401 Second Avenue / Brooklyn, N.Y 11232 / (718) 921-9000 / www.artscroll.com

Distributed in Israel by SIFRIATI / A. GITLER
6 Hayarkon Street / Bnei Brak 51127 / Israel

Distributed in Europe by LEHMANNS
Unit E, Viking Industrial Park, Rolling Mill Road / Jarrow, Tyne and Wear, NE32 3DP / England

Distributed in Australia and New Zealand by GOLDS WORLD OF JUDAICA
3-13 William Street / Balaclava, Melbourne 3183, Victoria / Australia

Distributed in South Africa by KOLLEL BOOKSHOP
Shop 8A Norwood Hypermarket/ Norwood 2196 / Johannesburg, South Africa

ISBN: 1-57819-488-1

Printed in the United States of America by Noble Book Press
Custom bound by Sefercraft, Inc. / 4401 Second Avenue / Brooklyn N.Y. 11232

Table of Contents

Acknowledgments

Writing this book on "the service of the heart" was a labor of love that vastly enriched my own life. I would like to express my gratitude to several of the people who helped make it a reality:

RABBI MEIR ZLOTOWITZ has been a friend and source of inspiration for many years. The idea for this book – and the encouragement to undertake it – were his.

MRS. JUDI DICK masterfully and caringly edited my manuscript. Her perceptiveness and insight have immeasurably enhanced this work, as well as the many other books I have published with Mesorah Publications and Shaar Press.

That this volume is a work of beauty is a tribute to ELI KROEN who designed both the book and its cover.

To paraphrase the words of Moses after the *Mishkan* was completed: "*Yehi ratzon she'tishreh Shechinah b'maasei yadeinu* – May the Divine Presence rest in the work of our hands."

Abraham J. Twerksi

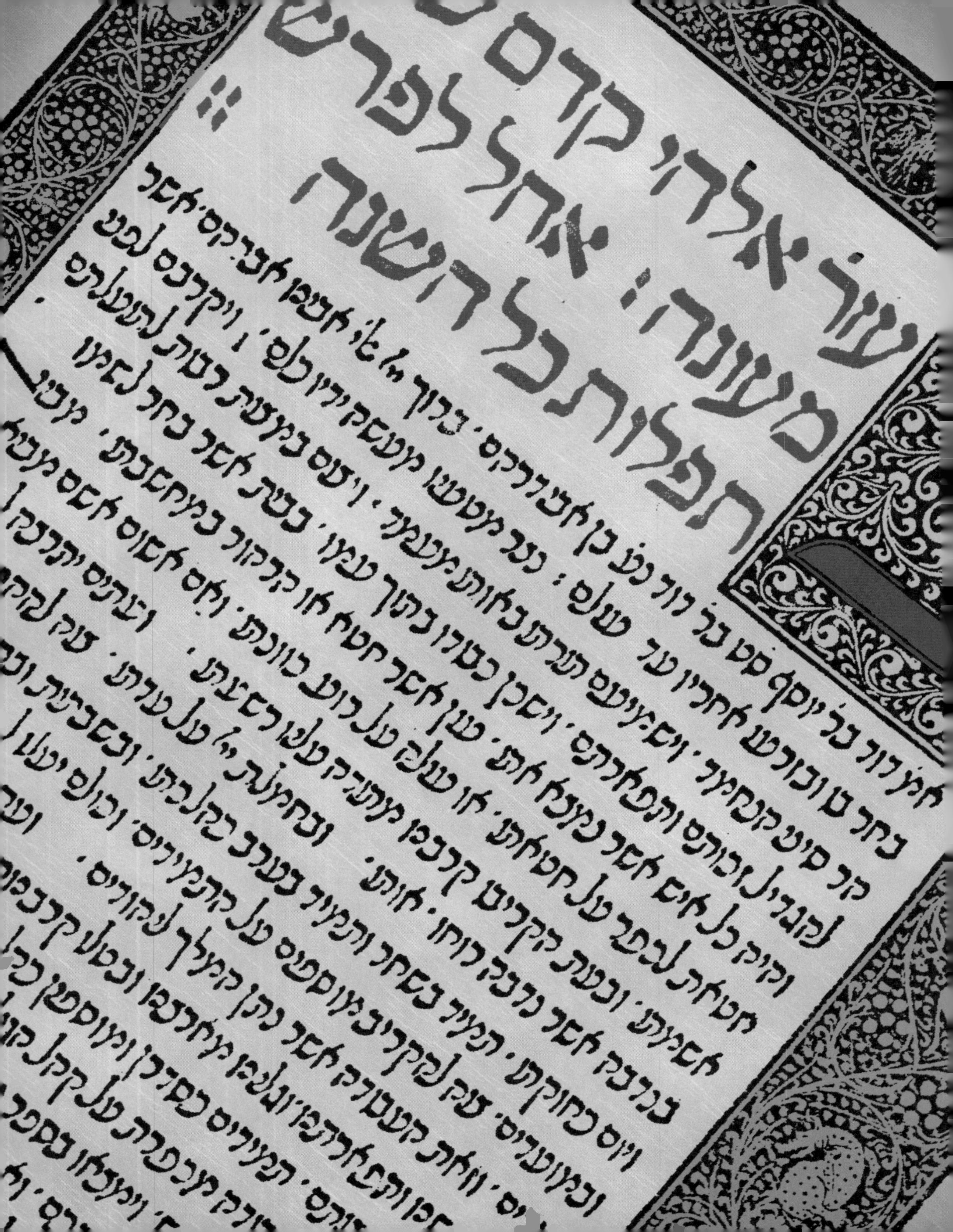

שער אלהי קדם מעונה: אחל לפרש תפלות כל השנה:

אמ׳ דוד בר׳ יוסף ספ׳ בר׳ דוד נע׳ בן אבודרהם. ברוך יי׳ א׳ אשר בחר באברהם. אשר
נטע טו ובורשו אחריו עד שלש. נגד מקטשו מעשיו. בחק ירין כלם. ויקרבם לפניו
קרא שמו קנטמא׳. וים מיוחם תורתו באותו מעשיו. וישם במצות רבות להשלים
לבוגדיל ובורתם והפלאותם. ויסכן כבודו בתוך עמו. כשר במעשה נחר לכמו
והיה כל איש אשר נמצא אתו. שין אשר חטא או נקדר. ואם במחשבתו. מנו
חטאתו. ובעת נדבה רוחו. או שלם על רוע כוונתו. ואם אחום אשם מעה
אשמתו. אשר נדבה הקדים קרבן מתנה קרבנו. ונרעים יקריב
בגל נחוקתו. לבנו לכפר על חטאתו. ונחמלה על עלו רם צנתו. עד לגו
ויום כחוקתו. תמיד בשחר והמיד בערב באלהיו. ובשנויות ועו
ובמועדים. עד לקריב אשר נתן על הקמיים. ובכס יתלו
...ים. וזאת העטרה ואשר מאחריו המלך להודיות.
...כן והתאחרונו ובאו מאחריו כסדרן ומוספין.
...ים. התמידים מכפרת על קהל
...רים. וחרק מכפרת על קהל כפר
...ים. וימנגלו נספר. וי

Introduction

Introduction

"There are three things that support the world: Torah, *avodah* (the Divine service) and *gemillas chasadim* (acts of kindness) (*Ethics of the Fathers* 1:2). Our people are without peer in *tzedakah* and *gemillas chasadim*. We have many fine Torah institutions, and there is an increasing interest in Torah study and formation of adult education classes in synagogues. We might think that two out of three is pretty good, but of what use is a three-legged table which is lacking one of the legs?

For whatever reason, *avodah*, which essentially is prayer, has not received its due. We do have *siddurim* with fine translations and commentaries, but it would be less than truthful to state that the quality of our prayer is of the same magnitude as our devotion to Torah and to *gemillas chasadim*.

Even if we regularly attend the daily morning *minyan*, the pressure of the pace of the service and the rush to leave for work indicate that our prayer is essentially perfunctory. This is precisely what the Talmud cautions us to avoid (ibid. 2:18). The word *avodah* means "work, " but the character of our prayer bears little resemblance to hard labor. Proper concentration on prayer is indeed "work." Even on Shabbos, when we spend more time in the synagogue, the mundane conversation that is so often scattered throughout the service betrays a lack of appreciation of the importance of prayer.

Much of the riches in Judaism can be found in our heritage, of which we may be justly proud. Turning to this treasure house of wisdom, we may find guidelines that can help us gain a better perspective on *avodah*.

The prophets compare the blundering of sin to intoxication with alcohol (*Isaiah* 5:11; 28:1,3,7; 29:9; *Joel* 1:5; *Job* 12:25). I, therefore, beg the reader's indulgence as I take the liberty of applying what I have learned from people attempting to emerge from the addiction to alcohol. In the same vein, R' Moshe Leib of Sassov said that he did not fully grasp what *ahavas Yisrael* (love of a fellow Jew) means until he learned it from a drunkard.

> *Passing a tavern, R' Moshe Leib overheard a conversation between two drunken men. The first man said, "I love you, Ivan."*
>
> *"No, Stefan," Ivan responded. "You do not love me."*
>
> *"Yes, I do love you, Ivan. I swear to it," Stefan protested.*
>
> *"No, no, Stefan. I know that you do not love me," Ivan said.*
>
> *Again Stefan tearfully swore that he loved Ivan more than anything in the world. Whereupon Ivan said, "If you really love me as you say, Stefan, then tell me if you feel my suffering as if it were yours."*
>
> *R' Moshe Leib said, "That was when I learned that to truly love another person, you must feel his pain as if it were your own."*

I allow myself to follow in the footsteps of R' Moshe Leib.

> *A recovering man who had over twenty-five years of sobriety told me that he was having much difficulty with a newcomer to the recovery program who was unable to abstain from drinking. "I cannot believe that you haven't had a single drink in twenty-five years," the novice said. "I can't put together one week. What's your secret?"*
>
> *"There is no special trick," the veteran said. "Every morning upon arising I ask God to please give me another day of sobriety. Every night before going to bed I thank God for having given me another day of sobriety. That's all there is to it."*
>
> *"Well, how do you know it was God Who gave you the day of sobriety?" the novice asked.*
>
> *The veteran looked at him as if in disbelief. "You fool!" he said. "I didn't ask anyone else!"*

The simplicity of this logic is refreshing. I trust you will understand why I take advantage of things I have learned this way and share them with you.

There is much interest today in the role of Judaism in *tikkun olam*, rectification of the world. This is, after all, the charge we were given at Sinai. Inasmuch as prayer is one-third of the support upon which the *olam* is dependent, we will strengthen the world by improving the quality of our prayer.

Although we may think of prayer as being separate from Torah, this is not accurate. Torah means "teaching," and just as Torah texts are guides for proper living, so can we also gain valuable guidelines for life from a proper understanding of prayer. It is to this end that this book is dedicated.

This book is not intended to be a running commentary on the *siddur*. Rather, it focuses on excerpts from the *siddur* to point out concepts which should be applied to all our prayers.

Concepts of Prayer

"He attends to the prayer of one who cries unto Him."
(Psalms 102:18)

R' Yitzchak interpreted this verse to apply to these generations, which have neither king nor prophet, neither Kohen nor Urim VeTumim (the parchment which conveyed God's response to questions posed by the High Priest). They have nothing but prayer. David said to God, "Master of the universe! Do not turn away their prayer."

(Vayikra Rabbah 30)

Tefillah - The Multimedia Communication

Many Hebrew words lose much of their meaning in translation. For example, the word *tzedakah* is usually translated as charity. A charitable transaction involves two individuals: the donor, who may feel magnanimous, and the recipient, who may feel broken in spirit due to his need for alms. *Tzedakkah*, however, is not charity. *Tzedakah* means "justice." For reasons known only to God, He made some people wealthy and others poor. He instructed the wealthy to share their wealth with the poor. It is only "just" that they do so. The donor does not have any right to think of himself as superior to the mendicant, nor should the latter feel shame. They are both engaged in an act of justice. Indeed, the Talmud says that what the recipient does for the donor exceeds what the donor does for the recipient (*Vayikra Rabbah* 34:10).

Another word that has fallen victim to inadequate translation is *tefillah*. For lack of a better word, *tefillah* is generally translated as "prayer." The connotation of "prayer" is supplication. We are asking God for something. A bit more broadly, "prayer" may be thought of as the glorification of God. *Tefillah* is all of these, but it is so much more.

One of the roots of *tefillah* is the word "to bond" (*Rashi, Genesis* 30:8). *Tefillah* is, therefore, a bonding between man and God. Bonding infers a relationship and is dependent upon communication, a bilateral communication. The Chassidic master, R' Moshe of Sambor said, "The Torah is what God gave to man. It is the God-given method whereby we can bond with Him. *Tefillah* is what man gives to God. It is the means whereby we can bind Him to us."

(In the Talmud, *tefillah* usually refers to the *Amidah*, the *Shemoneh Esrei* prayer. However, throughout the ages, *tefillah* has come to mean the entire prayer service.)

This concept of *tefillah* makes comprehensible a rather cryptic statement in the Talmud. "How do we know that God prays? Because the prophet quotes God as saying, 'I will bring them to My holy mountain and I will gladden them in the house of *My* prayer (*tefillasi*).' It is not 'the house of *their* prayer,' but of '*My* prayer.' Ergo, God prays" (*Berachos* 7a). In the usual sense of prayer, it is difficult to conceive of God praying. God does not have any needs nor would He glorify Himself. If, however, *tefillah* refers to a bonding and a relationship, then God's *tefillah* makes perfect sense. God relates to us and we relate to him. We bond with God and He bonds with us. God communicates with us and we communicate with Him. The bilateral character of this relationship is clearly stated: "You have distinguished Hashem today to be a God for you, and to walk in His ways, and to observe His decrees, His commandments and His statutes, and to hearken to His voice. And Hashem has distinguished you today, to be for Him a treasured people, as He spoke to you, and to observe all His commandments" (ibid. 26:17-18).

Communication can be effected in many different ways. The Torah says, "You are children unto God" (*Deuteronomy* 14:1). Parents and children relate in various ways.

Children ask their parents for many things. When these requests are appropriate, parents enjoy fulfilling them. When they are not, parents may deny the requests, often to the chagrin of the children. Children may not understand why their parents refuse them what they want. They may cry and complain. They may even be angry or resentful. When they receive what they want, they may be very grateful. Children may adore their parents and tell others how wonderful their parents are. Parents may have to discipline their children, and, when necessary, even punish them. Parents protect their children, sometimes in ways that the children cannot understand, as when they submit their infants to painful immunizations intended to protect them from dreaded diseases.

All the various means of communication that occur between parents and children can likewise occur between God and man. These are all ways of *tefillah,* of relating. And when we relate, we bond. We bond with God when we make a request or voice a complaint. We bond with Him when we thank Him or praise Him. God bonds with us when He grants us what we ask for or when He denies it. Denial of a request is no less a form of relationship than sanctioning it. God bonds with us when He protects us, but also when He disciplines or punishes us.

Communication can take the form of verbalization, by word, by song and by wordless melodies. We communicate by action and by body language. Inasmuch as God has access to our thoughts and feelings, we communicate with Him by thinking and feeling. And yes, silence, too, is a method of communication.

Understood in its broader sense, *tefillah* takes on new dimensions, much different than what we usually think of as "prayer." It confirms what one Chassidic master said: "You can be for God or you can be against God. You just cannot be without God." If, in the pages ahead, I resort to the word "prayer" for convenience, I beg the reader to think of it as *tefillah:* bonding, communicating and relating.

Bonding can vary anywhere from a loose bond to a tight bond. The most intimate bond can be of an intensity that may actually jeopardize one's existence. The Talmud states that the relationship of *tzaddikim* to God is similar to that of a candle in proximity to a torch (*Pesachim* 8a). The flicker of the candle is drawn to the much larger flame, and may actually leap over to meet it, causing the candle to be extinguished. The bond of the *neshamah* to God may be so fast and firm that it may not return to the body.

> *The Rebbe of Cherkassy said, "My father had a chassid, R' Yirmiyah, whose devotion in prayer was intense. One time I felt that his bonding in tefillah was so fervent that he was in danger of expiring, so I removed the tefillin from his head to sever the bond between his neshamah and God."*

> *R' Uri of Strelisk would bid farewell to his family before leaving for shul each morning. He felt that his bonding to God in prayer might well be irreversible.*

While we may not aspire to this intensity of bonding, neither should we resign ourselves to the all too frequent rote recitation of *tefillah*. True, we may find a degree of solace in the following anecdote.

> *R' Levi Yitzchok of Berditchev overheard a man rapidly mumbling the morning prayers. He went over to the man and mumbled some unintelligible sounds. "I don't understand what you are saying," the man said.*
>
> *"Then why are you mumbling unintelligible sounds in your prayer?" R' Levi Yitzchok asked.*
>
> *The man responded, "An infant may make sounds that are unintelligible to others. However, his parents understand which sounds indicate hunger, which thirst, and which a need to be changed. My mumbling may be unintelligible to you, but God is a parent, and He understands."*

This notwithstanding, our prayer often lacks the quality of sincere communication. I was made acutely aware of this when I was praying at the Western Wall, and I thought I was praying fervently. I then saw a blind man being led to the Wall. He ran his fingers over the ripples of the stones, as if feeling the 2,000 years of Jewish history embedded within them. He began speaking to God, telling

Him of various things that had recently transpired. He stopped abruptly, paused momentarily and said, "Oh! I already told You that yesterday," and then resumed his conversation with God. I realized how my prayer paled before his. I did not have as complete a certainty that everything I said had been heard.

Converting rote prayer to *tefillah* requires preparation. The Talmud states that the *tzaddikim* of yore would meditate for a full hour before beginning their prayer (*Berachos* 30b). This preparation served to remove the barriers that impair our communication with God.

Let us think of our communication with God as "wireless," much the same as our cell-phone communication. Not infrequently we find that we cannot hear nor can we be heard, because we are in an area where there is no satellite access. We have much to say, but in order to communicate it, we must position ourselves elsewhere. This is our "preparation" for wireless communication.

The vehicle for our communication with God may be defective. The fault may lie in our lack of *kavannah* (concentration, attention, intention, devotion). It may lie in our distraction and the wandering of our thoughts to extraneous matters. It may lie in our personal character defects. For example, Rambam states that speaking *lashon hara* creates a barrier between man and God. The Kabbalists state that various sins interrupt the conduits whereby God relates to us. Preparation for true *tefillah* requires positioning ourselves in a way that allows communication to occur. Therefore, *tzaddikim* of yore would spend a full hour in meditation to eradicate the character defects that constituted barriers in communication with God.

Perhaps because he realized that few people meditated adequately before praying, R' Elimelech of Lizhensk composed an introductory prayer. In this prayer we humble and efface ourselves before God in order to eliminate the cardinal defect of vanity, a trait which repels the Divine Presence. We confess our misdeeds and pledge ourselves to do *teshuvah*. We ask God to strengthen our resolve and to assist us to pray properly. And perhaps of greatest importance, we ask of God to help us overcome envy of others and rid us of feelings of hatred toward other people. In a most beautiful verse R' Elimelech says, "Enable us to see the virtues of other people, and not their faults."

R' Levi Yitzchok of Berditchev cited the verse, "He perceived no iniquity in Jacob and saw no perversity in Israel. Hashem his God is with him" (*Numbers* 23:21). R' Levi Yitzchok commented, "If a person sees no faults in another Jew, he can be certain that God is with him."

> *R' Levi Yitzchok once came across a person who was eating on Tishah B'Av. "My dear friend," he said, "you have certainly forgotten that today is Tishah B'Av."*
>
> *"No," the man said. "I know it is Tishah B'Av."*
>
> *"Ah!" R' Levi Yitzchok said, "then you are under doctor's orders not to fast."*

"I am perfectly healthy," the man said. "I am not under doctor's orders."

R' Levi Yitzchok lifted his eyes toward heaven. "Master of the Universe!" he said. "See how precious Your children are. I gave this man two opportunities to defend his actions, but he is steadfast in his insistence not to deviate from the truth!"

My father used to tell of a Chassidic rebbe who spent a Shabbos in Berlin. Prior to reciting the Kiddush he said, "In Berlin Kiddush is really necessary. Kiddush is a testimony that God created the world in six days and rested on the seventh day. Testimony is necessary only when something is not certain. Back in my shtetl everyone observes Shabbos, so there is no need for any testimony. Here in Berlin, where so many Jews violate Shabbos, one must testify."

He then tried to begin the Kiddush, but was unable to get the words out of his mouth. He set down the wine goblet and meditated for a while, then recited the Kiddush.

The Rebbe explained, "When I was unable to say the Kiddush, I realized that it was because I had spoken disparagingly of the Jews in Berlin. By doing so, I lost my contact with God. I meditated on this and resolved never again to speak disparagingly of any Jew. Then my contact with God was reestablished."

The Baal Shem Tov was asked, "How can I develop love for God?" He answered, "Develop love for your fellow man, and love for God will follow." In expressing our desire to establish a more respectful and loving relationship with people, we eliminate the barriers that interrupt our communication with God.

It should be noted that R' Elimelech's prayer is in itself a supplication. We are doing no less than asking God to help us rid ourselves of the barriers to a relationship with Him. This thought is expressed by King David, "The desire of the humble You have heard, O God. Guide their heart, let Your ear be attentive" (*Psalms* 10:17). Developing the proper attitude toward *tefillah* is something we cannot achieve on our own. We can do so only with God's assistance. This is in keeping with the Talmudic statement, "Every day a person's *yetzer* renews itself and tries to destroy him. If not for the help of God, a person could not withstand it" (*Kiddushin* 30b).

If all a person must do, then, is to have a desire for a proper attitude and God will do the rest, why is it necessary to devote so much time and effort to it? Why did the *tzaddikim* of yesteryear spend a full hour in preparatory meditation?

The answer was given by R' Mendel of Kotzk. The Midrash quotes God as saying, "Open for Me a portal of *teshuvah* as tiny as the point of a needle, and I will open for you portals wide enough to admit wagons" (*Shir HaShirim Rabbah* 5:3). R' Mendel said, "Yes, but the opening we provide must penetrate through and through." In other words, it is true that all we must do is initiate the process with our desire, but that desire must be absolutely sincere. It required a full hour for the *tzaddikim* to develop this desire.

A woman once remarked to me that when she passed the shul, she could see the *minyan* praying. "I paused to watch them and I began to cry. I felt so spiritually bereft. There they were, all praying to God. I wished I could pray to God, but I know nothing about prayer."

I could not help but feel rebuked. There I was, probably using my prayer to ask God for my personal needs, whereas this woman was in pain because she did not know how to draw closer to God. Her unspoken prayer was, "God, please help me find out how I can draw closer to You." I had to conclude that her attitude toward prayer was superior to mine.

> *Prior to Rosh Hashanah, the tzaddik of Sanz would relate the parable of a king who exiled his son to a distant land for behavior unbecoming a prince. Never having learned a trade, the prince had no way to support himself. He became a shepherd, since watching the flock did not require special skills. The other shepherds built themselves small huts to protect them from the sun. He tried to build a hut, but since he lacked both know-how and dexterity, the hut always collapsed. He continued to suffer from the torrid heat.*
>
> *One day he heard that the king was visiting the country and that there was going to be a huge parade. The custom was that people wrote their wishes on small pieces of paper and threw them at the royal coach. Whichever petitions landed in the coach were granted.*
>
> *The prince wrote his petition, "I want to have a thatched-roof hut to protect me from the sun." His petition landed in the royal coach. The king recognized his son's handwriting and broke into sobs. "What has happened to my son?" he cried. "He has completely forgotten that he is a prince. His request should have been to return to me and once again live the life of a prince in the palace. Instead, he has resigned himself to being a shepherd, and his aspirations are no greater than to merely have a little hut!"*

The tzaddik wept along with the king, "We should be asking God to bring us close to him, to return us to the holy Temple where we can be princes," he said. "Instead, all we ask for is our petty personal needs. Do we not bring suffering to God?"

There is a parable about a king who wished to reward several of his subjects. He told them that he would grant each of them one wish. After all of them made their respective requests, the last and wisest person said, "I wish to be taken into the presence of the king every day." The others then realized how foolish they had been. This person would have countless opportunities to present his requests to the king.

So it is with us. If we could draw ourselves closer to God, we would lack nothing.

True *tefillah* is a request to bond with God. This cannot occur when one rushes through the prayers and out of the synagogue in record time. Nor can there be even a semblance of *tefillah* when we engage in conversation during prayer. Think for a moment of how offended you would be if someone who was talking to you abruptly turned away to talk with someone else, clearly demonstrating that his relationship with you was rather unimportant. Talking during prayer should not be thought of as a sin, but rather as an insult, an affront to God with Whom we should be communicating.

The Talmud states that the proper attitude for *tefillah* is one of profound reverence (*Berachos* 30b). Elsewhere it states that *tefillah* should be approached with the feeling of "joy emanating from a mitzvah" (ibid. 31a). At first glance it may seem that profound reverence and joy are mutually exclusive. That these do not conflict is evident from the Psalmist's statement, "Rejoice with trembling" (*Psalms* 2:11). The question remains, however, how does one blend these two diverse attitudes?

A chassid presented R' Shneur Zalman (author of Tanya) with a petition wherein he enumerated all his problems and his many unmet needs. After studying the petition, R' Shneur Zalman said, "It appears that you have spent much time clarifying your various needs. Have you spent equal time clarifying why you are needed?"

The chassid trembled at the words of the Rebbe. Yet he was overcome by a feeling of joy. The Rebbe had told him that he was needed, and that he was a significant part of creation. He was important to God. True, he had been derelict in defining the purpose of his existence. While he trembled because of his dereliction, he rejoiced in the awareness that in this immense universe he was significant.

As we approach *tefillah*, we should be struck with awe that we are bonding with God. At the same time, we should be overwhelmed with joy that God wishes us to bond with Him.

If we give proper thought to *tefillah* by adequate preparation and *kavannah*, our communication and bonding with God is greatly enhanced. The principle of *middah keneged middah* (commensurate Divine response) assures us that God will bond firmly with us.

But let us not fall into despair if we find we cannot attain the proper *kavannah*. We may be comforted by the words that the Chafetz Chaim said to a person who was discouraged because he could not achieve the *kavannah* described by our sages.

"When farmers bring their harvest to the markets," the Chafetz Chaim said, "the grain merchants will examine the grain carefully, testing its quality and noting how much chaff is mixed in. However, in a year of famine when grain is very scarce, they quickly buy whatever is available without examining it.

"When most Jews were observant of Torah and prayed regularly," the Chafetz Chaim continued, "God was very meticulous about the quality of their prayers. In our time, when so many Jews have strayed and only a minority pray regularly, it is like a famine and God accepts all prayers, even if they are of a lesser quality."

Nevertheless, we should devote ourselves to developing the utmost *kavannah*. This is by no means a simple task. We are all aware how quickly our minds are distracted by a myriad of other thoughts. Let us see what we can do to avoid this distraction.

The word *tefillah* has yet another meaning which complements the concept of bonding. The root word of *tefillah* is פלל, which means "judgment" or "disputation." When Pinchas prayed to God to halt the epidemic (*Psalms* 106:30), the Talmud states that he entered into an argument with God (*Sanhedrin* 82b). When the Patriarch Abraham prayed to God to spare Sodom and Gomorrah, he said, "It would be sacrilege to You to do such a thing, to bring death upon the righteous along with the wicked" (*Genesis* 16:25). When Jacob prayed to be saved from Esau, he reminded God of His promise, "You said 'I will do good with you'" (ibid. 32:13). On several occasions, Moses' prayer for the Israelites has the flavor of an argument (*Exodus* 5:22-23; 32:11-13). When Moses prayed to be permitted to enter the Promised Land, he presented many arguments for his case.

This aspect of *tefillah* is limited to the great *tzaddikim*, who have the privilege of presenting arguments to God. The average person may not do this. But even here, the connotation of *tefillah* as judgment is valid.

The author of *Avodas HaLev* (Service of the Heart, found in the Introduction to Siddur *Otzar HaTefillos*) points out that פלל can mean "to clarify and to distinguish." The function of a judge is to analyze the facts brought before him, and by distinguishing truth from falsehood, he clarifies the issue that is disputed by the litigants. *Tefillah* is, therefore, a process whereby a person should distinguish among the slew of thoughts that fill his mind. *Tefillah* is a clarification and a resolution of the confusion and conflicts that reverberate in our minds.

This concept of *tefillah* sheds additional light on *kavannah*, which, as we have seen, is variously translated as intention, concentration, attention, or devotion. Indeed, *kavannah* can mean all of these.

Ideally, *kavannah* should begin even before prayer.

> *Once when the tzaddik of Sanz was on his way to shul, he abruptly stopped and returned home. He then promptly set out for shul again. To his bewildered followers, the tzaddik said, "I realized that when I left, I did not have in mind that I was setting out to do a mitzvah. I lacked the proper kavannah for going to shul. That is why I had to go back and leave for shul with the proper kavannah."*

Kavannah has yet an additional meaning. The word כִּיווּן means "direction." We are pulled in any number of directions by our urges, desires and ambitions. By divesting ourselves of extraneous thoughts through the clarifying aspect of *tefillah*, we can identify and single out the proper כִּיווּן (direction) we should be taking.

We can now understand why the pious people of yesteryear would spend a full hour in preparation for *tefillah*. Eliminating all extraneous thoughts that may divert a person's attention is a most difficult task. These thoughts have a way of intruding upon a person and distracting him from his concentration.

Is it possible for a person to totally focus his thoughts and avoid distraction? Of course. A tightrope walker thinks of nothing other than maintaining his delicate balance. At other times his mind may be diverted in a variety of directions. When he is walking a tightrope hundreds of feet in the air, he knows that any distraction may cause him to lose his balance and fall to his death. Because his very life is at stake, his thoughts are on nothing other than maintaining his balance.

It may seem too much to ask of a person, but if we understood our bonding with God to be vital, we could attain a singularity of attention and concentration similar to that of the tightrope walker.

> *A chassid asked the Maggid of Mezeritch for a berachah (blessing) that his mind should not wander during his prayers. The Maggid told him to consult R' Zev of Zhitomir for guidance how to achieve this.*
>
> *The chassid arrived in Zhitomir late at night, and knocked on the door of R' Zev's house. When there was no response to his persistent knocking, he knocked on the back door and on the window shutters, but to no avail. He then sat in the doorway and fell asleep.*
>
> *At dawn, R' Zev woke him and invited him into his home. He served him a hot drink and said, "Well, do you have the answer to your problem?" The man just sat in bewilderment.*

"Don't you see?" R' Zev said. "You tried desperately to get into my house last night, seeking entrance through both doors and windows. You could not get in because I am master of my house. If I do not wish to let anyone in, he does not get in.

"Various thoughts attempt to get into your mind during prayer. You can be master of your mind. You can refuse entrance to anything you do not wish to allow in."

Such mastery might seem to be within the capability of only great *tzaddikim*. In a lighter vein, a comment from one of my patients can bring this down to the capacity of the average person.

This patient said, "When I heard about people with a dual personality, I was envious of them. I didn't have a *dual* personality; I had about *twenty* different personalities in my mind, each telling me to do something else. I eventually realized that *I am chairman of the board*. I don't have to listen to any of them!"

The key to achieving a *kavannah* that is impervious to distraction is to realize the importance of bonding with God. In the Chassidic and *mussar* works this bonding is referred to as *deveikus*, which means cleaving to and adhering to God.

The commentaries on *tefillah* state that when reciting the *Shema*, a person should resolve that if he were put to the test of denying God or being put to death, he would accept martyrdom. We can attain this *mesiras nefesh* (willingness to sacrifice our lives) if we realize that life without God is not worth living. This same realization should make us realize that bonding with God is as vital to us as balance is to the tightrope walker. We can then be undistractable. This was, no doubt, the thought which dominated the meditation of the pious of yore.

It may be difficult to maintain proper *kavannah*, free of alien thoughts. We should remember that we are masters of our houses, and we are chairmen of the board.

A frequent mistake in trying to eliminate intrusive thoughts is attempting to push them away. This is much like compressing a coiled spring: The more you push down on it, the greater is the upward pressure. It is common experience that when you try to rid yourself of an alien thought it comes back with greater force. Trying to concentrate harder on the words of the prayer is somewhat better, but is still often unsuccessful.

The optimum way to achieve *kavannah* is to think *how vital bonding with God should be to you*. A drowning person who is thrown a lifeline will not be distracted by anything else. If a million dollars were within easy reach, he would not let go of the rope for a single second to get it. It would not even occur to him that perhaps he should try to reach for the money. When one's very life is at stake, nothing else has any importance. That is how we should value our bonding with God.

R' Shneur Zalman, author of *Tanya*, was once found to be crying out to God, "I am not interested in Your *Gan Eden* (Paradise). I am not interested in Your *Olam Haba* (Eternal World). I want only You!"

The concepts of *tefillah* as bonding and as finding direction enable us to understand a nuance which is often overlooked. The word we use for prayer is לְהִתְפַּלֵּל (*lehispallel*). This is a reflexive form of the verb. The non-reflexive form is וַיְפַלֵּל (*vayefallel*), "he prayed," as seen in Psalms 106:30. If *tefillah* is primarily a supplication, we should refer to praying as לְפַלֵּל (*lefallel*). The reflexive form indicates that the function of prayer is primarily *to bring about a change in the person who is praying.*

That some changes are necessary to allow proper bonding to occur is easily understood. Simply look at the directions on any package of bonding cement. The instructions are to first scrape away foreign material from the surfaces of the items to be bonded.

It is no different when we wish to bond with God. We must first "scrape away" any material that would interfere with the bonding. These are the negative character traits which constitute a barrier between man and God.

Tefillah as clarification and as finding direction has broad implications, far beyond prayer. Many people live in a state of confusion. They are so bombarded by the many stresses of everyday needs and activities that they lose sight of what their life is or should be all about. It is said that R' Levi Yitzchok of Berditchev climbed to the top of a building in the midst of the busy market of Berditchev, where people were buzzing about like bees in a hive, and cried out, "My brothers and sisters! Do not forget that there is a God!" The clarification of the primary goal in life as bonding with God leads to a lifestyle that will facilitate and enhance this relationship.

Allowing God to Enter

When the Patriarch Jacob met his beloved son Joseph for whom he had grieved for twenty-two years, he said, "I dared not accept the thought that I would ever again see your face" (*Genesis* 48:11). The word in the Hebrew text is פִּלָּלְתִּי. R' Samson R. Hirsch explains the etymology of this word, which conveys the idea, "I did not allow the thought to enter my mind." It is as though the thought that Joseph was still alive was before him, hovering, as it were, before his mind, but Jacob refused to allow it to enter his consciousness. Indeed, the Midrash states that Jacob's granddaughter, Serah, the daughter of Asher, sang hymns to her grieving grandfather, in which she said that Joseph was still alive. Much as he would have wished to believe this, Jacob could not risk a bitter disappointment.

Based on this philology, Hirsch says that the word *tefillah* means "to allow Godly thoughts to penetrate into one's mind."

This is a most interesting concept. It means that one does not have to generate Godly thoughts. They are there before us. We just have to allow them entry.

When R' Mendel of Kotzk was a young man, his master, R' Bunim of P'shis'che asked him,

"Young man, where is God?"

"God is everywhere," R' Mendel responded.

R' Bunim asked again, "Young man, where is God?"

R' Mendel quoted the verse from the prophets, "His glory fills the entire world" (Isaiah 6:3). When the master again repeated the question, R' Mendel said, "If my answers are not correct, then you tell me."

R' Bunim said, "God is present wherever He is permitted entry."

Yes, the Divine Presence is everywhere, but man may sometimes repel it, as when one is vain and arrogant. "I cannot be in the presence of a vain person," God is quoted as saying (*Arachin* 15b). "I reside with the humble" (*Isaiah* 57:15).

We find this concept as well in the *Shema*. "Let these words that I command you today be upon your heart" (*Deuteronomy* 5:6). Note that it does not say "*in* your heart." We begin by letting the Torah teachings be "upon our hearts," and we can then work to give them entry. In the service, the *Shema* is followed by the *Amidah*. The proper *kavannah* of the *Amidah* should break down the barriers and allow the Torah teachings to penetrate.

With this we can understand the Divine statement we noted previously, "Open for Me a portal of *teshuvah* as tiny as the point of a needle, and I will open for you portals wide enough to admit wagons." R' Mendel of Kotzk commented, "But the needle-point opening must penetrate through and through." The dynamics of this is simple. A dam can hold back an enormous amount of water, but just a tiny hole in the dam will allow all the water to flow through. A sincere desire to allow Godly thoughts to enter one's mind is all that is necessary, but as R' Mendel said, it must be sincere.

> *A disciple of the Chassidic master, R' Shlomo of Karlin, complained that he had not been able to reach the level of devotion he desired. "What can I do?" R' Shlomo said, "I have not been able to find the key to your heart."*
>
> *The student cried out in desperation, "A key?" Use an axe!"*
>
> *R' Shlomo said, "Never mind. Your heart has just been opened."*

I remember that as a child I resented having to learn with my tutor when my friends were playing outdoors. I said to my tutor, "I have no objection to learning. I just wish that there was a machine that could put all this knowledge in my head so that I would be free to play." Indeed, today there are some people who play tapes while they sleep in the hope that they will absorb the knowledge.

Neither Torah knowledge nor sincere devotion can be acquired without effort. God is indeed present everywhere, but it may take a great deal of effort to open our hearts to allow Him entry. As long as we are primarily involved with gratifying our physical desires rather than our spiritual needs, as long as we are totally absorbed with ourselves rather than sharing with others, as long as we have not effaced ourselves before God, we deny Him entry.

Before the *Amidah* we say, "O God! Open my lips, and let my mouth speak Your praise." Perhaps we would like God to open our lips with a key. Sincere desire is when we are ready to have our lips pried open with an axe.

The Finest Kavannah - Blessing God

"But as for me, may my prayer be to You, O God, for but one instant of favor; O God, [Who even while judging remains] in the abundance of Your loving-kindness, answer me with the truth of Your salvation" (Psalms 69:14).

We may not always be in a state of merit that warrants our prayers being answered. God is indeed a loving Father, but sometimes a child may behave in a way that so angers the father that he turns away and does not wish to listen to the child.

As the self-centered quality of our prayers decreases, their receptivity is enhanced. Even if the father is displeased with the child and may not wish to address his personal requests, he will listen when the child is not asking for himself but for others in the family. This is why our supplications in the *Amidah* are all in the plural: forgive *us*, heal *us*, bless *us*, etc. The Talmud gives great commendation to *tefillah b'tzibbur* (communal prayer). Citing the above verse, the Talmud says, "When is the time of favor? When the community prays together" (*Berachos* 8a). Communal prayer is superior to individual prayer. "Communal prayer is never turned away" (*Devarim Rabbah* 2).

Although we may think of communal prayer as that of a *minyan* (a quorum of ten), some commentaries point out that this is not the *tefillah b'tzibbur* that is especially effective. If each person is praying for his own needs, it is not really communal prayer, but the separate prayers of a number of individuals who happen to be in the same room. A person may be *saying* "bless us" but meaning "bless me." It is only when the prayer is truly communal, i.e., for the welfare of all, that it is *tefillah b'tzibbur*.

The Talmud says, "One who prays for mercy for another person when he is in need of mercy for himself, his prayer is answered first" (*Bava Kamma* 92a). Hillel said that the essence of Torah is "Love your neighbor as yourself" (*Shabbos* 31a). If a person can set aside his own needs in favor of another person's needs, that is a merit which warrants his prayers being answered.

There is a kind of *kavannah* which is superior to even that of communal prayer. When special prayers for rain were offered during a drought, the community leaders put ashes on their heads as a sign of mourning. Ashes were also placed on the Holy Ark to indicate that God shares in our suffering (*Taanis* 16a). "I am with him in distress" (*Psalms* 91:15).

Yes, God suffers when we are in distress.

> *A 7-year-old child underwent open-heart surgery. I was with the father when the child was taken to the treatment room to suction the secretions from the bronchial tree, which is a very uncomfortable procedure. I accompanied the child and suggested to the father that he wait outside the treatment room. The child began crying, "Daddy, help! They are hurting me!" The father could not restrain himself. He came into the treatment room and tearfully pleaded with the child not to resist the doctor. "Let them do this," he said. "You will be able to come home sooner." The father knew that the procedure was necessary, but the child was not capable of understanding that this painful procedure was for his own good.*

It was evident that the father was suffering along with the child, and his distress may have been even greater than that of the child. I understood then how God must suffer when we are in distress, and for reasons known only to Him, He must allow us to experience the pain.

If, when we are in distress, we realize that God is suffering along with us, and we pray not for our own relief but rather that God be relieved of His distress, that is *kavannah* at its finest. Such prayers are most propitious.

A father who must discipline a child suffers along with the child when he punishes him. The Talmud states that God grieves for the loss of the Temple which had to be destroyed because the Jews were not deserving of it. We should be sensitive to God's grief.

> *R' Michel of Zlotchow lived in abject poverty. Someone said to him, "You are a great tzaddik. Surely if you would ask God for relief from your poverty, He would not turn you down."*
>
> *R' Michel responded with a parable: A king once threw a lavish party to celebrate his daughter's marriage. The daughter died suddenly, and all the quests quickly dispersed, leaving the sumptuously laden tables behind. One vulgar man helped himself to the delicacies. Was it not gross of this*

person to partake of the wedding feast when the king was in profound grief?

"God is weeping over the loss of His Temple. Would it not be crass insensitivity if I asked him for prosperity?"

King David prayed, "Not for our sake, O God, not for our sake, but for Your Name's sake give glory ... Why should the nations say, 'Where is their God now?' " (*Psalms* 115:1-2). When God wished to annihilate the Israelites because of their worship of the Golden Calf, Moses prayed, "Why should the Egyptians say, 'With evil intent did He take them out, to kill them in the mountains'?" (*Exodus* 32:12). Moses and David prayed that Israel be spared so that the glory of God not be marred.

There is a parable about a person who was shabbily dressed and approached the palace, asking to be allowed to see the king. "Away with you, miserable wretch," the palace guard said. "The king has no interest in listening to your complaints."

"I am not coming with any request for myself," the man said. "I overheard someone plotting to harm the king, and I wish to give him this information for his own good."

This person is certain to be admitted to the king.

When we pray to be relieved of our distress so that God will not suffer, that prayer is certain to be accepted.

In the *Amidah* we ask for redemption "for You are a powerful Redeemer." We ask for healing "for You are the faithful and compassionate Healer." This is best understood with a parable of the Maggid of Dubnow.

The Maggid points out that when the Israelites worshiped the Golden Calf, God was angry with them, saying that they are "a stiff-necked people" (Exodus 32:9). After God revealed to Moses His traits of compassion, grace and forgiveness, Moses prayed, "Please, let God go among us, for they are a stiff-necked people" (ibid. 34:6-9). Why did Moses invoke the obstinacy of the Israelites in their defense when God had indicated that this was His reason for His anger toward them?

The Maggid gave a parable about a group of peddlers who assembled at the end of the day to share their experiences. One peddler complained that he had not made a single sale of his wooden cutlery. "Where were you peddling?" his friends asked. "Why, in the wealthiest section of town," he said.

"You fool!" his friends said. "Did you expect wealthy people to buy cheap wooden cutlery? They use utensils of silver and gold. They have no need for your cheap merchandise. You

should have peddled in the poor section of town. Those people can use your goods."

The Maggid explained, "When God revealed to Moses His attributes of compassion, grace and forgiveness, Moses said, 'Let God go among us, for we are a stiff-necked people. We can make use of Divine compassion, grace and forgiveness. If You remain in Heaven among the Heavenly angels, You will have no opportunity to manifest these attributes. Angels are not obstinate, and they do not sin. Come among us, a stubborn people, and You will have ample opportunity to put Your attributes to use.'"

Similarly, we pray, "Redeem us, for You are a powerful Redeemer ... Heal us, for You are the faithful and compassionate Healer." Like Moses, we are saying, "If You do not use Your great benevolent powers with us, where will You use them?"

Here, too, we are praying for God as much as for ourselves.

R' Zvi Elimelech interprets the verse of Psalms cited above along this line.

"But as for me, my prayer shall be *to You,* O God, for but one instant of favor; O God, Who even while judging remains in the abundance of Your lovingkindness, answer me with the truth of *Your salvation.* My prayer is not for me, but for You. If You answer my prayers, You will be relieved of the suffering You share with us, and it will be, as it were, *Your* salvation."

This gives us a new insight into the meaning of our *berachos.* What do we mean when we say, "*Baruch atoh Hashem,* Blessed are You, O God?" How can we bless God? Most commentaries interpret *Baruch atoh,* Blessed are You, to mean "You are the source of all blessings." However, we find a fascinating passage in the Talmud that relates that when the High Priest, R' Yishmael, entered the Holy of Holies on Yom Kippur, he heard God's voice saying, "My child Yishmael, bless Me." R' Yishmael said, "May Your mercies overcome Your wrath, and may You conduct Yourself with compassion toward Your children." God was pleased with R' Yishmael's blessing (*Berachos* 6a).

The Talmud says that God did this to teach us that one should value all blessings, even from someone far inferior to oneself. This is similar to the interpretation that God sought the counsel of the angels before He created man. God needs neither blessings nor advice. He wished to model for us that even the greatest should value the least.

But there is also another interpretation. R' Mendel of Kotzk says that the phrase "fear of God" means not only that we should fear God, but that we should have the same fear that God has.

God has divested Himself of controlling a person's moral and ethical behavior. God will not intervene to stop a person from committing a sin. But sin is destructive, and inasmuch as God will not intervene to prevent a sin, He has a fear that a person will harm himself, and He cannot stop him. It is much like a father seeing his small child running into the street. He cannot stop the child, and fears that the child may be hurt.

R' Mendel said that this is "the fear of God." We, too, should have a fear of harming ourselves. This would prevent us from committing sin.

God is infinite goodness, and wishes to bestow His kindness on all His creations. "God is good to all; His mercies are on all His works" (*Psalms* 145:9). But having limited Himself to operate within the confines of His law, *God cannot bestow His kindness on those who do not deserve it.*

The Kabbalists say, "The nature of the good is to do good." Although we cannot speak of the "nature" of God, the Kabbalists use this idea as an explanation for Creation. God wished to have recipients of His goodness. It pleases God to be good to His creations.

When we fulfill the Divine wish and merit reward, we provide God with the opportunity to exercise His infinite goodness and bestow His kindness upon us. This is, as it were, *a blessing for God. We are giving Him something which He needs — recipients who deserve the kindness He wishes to bestow.*

This idea may appear strange, but there are a number of Talmudic references to this concept. "Israel gives light to the One Who illuminates the entire universe" (*Bamidbar Rabbah* 15). "Israel adorns God with ten garments" (*Devarim Rabbah* 2:26). "Israel gives Me (God) *parnassah* (sustenance)" (*Shir HaShirim Zuta* 1:15).

When we do a mitzvah or praise God, we are earning His kindness. This is a blessing for God. It enables God to forgive our sins within His system of justice, and to be merciful toward us. This was the blessing God sought from the High Priest, R' Yishmael.

When we recite a *berachah*, when we say *Baruch atoh*, we, mere mortals, are blessing Almighty God.

Familiarity and Reverence

Many commentaries seek to explain the grammatical shift in the wording of the *berachos*. We begin by saying "Blessed are *You*," addressing God in the second person, and then continue, "Who has sanctified us with *His* commandments," referring to God in the third person.

The various commentaries are in essential agreement that the bonding between man and God must consist of closeness and intimacy, but must also be one of reverence, standing in awe of Infinite God. The modality of intimacy is expressed by addressing God directly as *You*, much as one would address a close friend. However, familiarity that is not tempered with reverence could result in a laxity of obedience. It is, therefore, necessary to stand back, as it were, and realize that intimacy notwithstanding, we are in the presence of the Sovereign of the universe.

As we shall see, the concept of God as Sovereign connotes His omnipotence. Whereas a child has a sense of security in the knowledge that his father loves him and cares for him, this feeling of insecurity is limited if the child does not think that the father has the wisdom to know what his needs are, the capacity to provide for them and the strength to protect him. We must, therefore, be aware of God's omniscience and omnipotence as well as of His love for us. This is expressed by the third-person statement, "King of the universe, Who has sanctified us."

An additional explanation of the grammatical shift is that the directness of addressing God in the second person relates to whatever He has revealed of Himself to us. Referring to God in the third person indicates that His essence is concealed from us and is unfathomable and unknowable to the human mind.

What we can know about God is only what He has revealed to us through the prophets and what we can gather from the greatness of His works. The essence of God is beyond the grasp of the human mind.

Prayer is based on faith. Faith begins at the point where human knowledge ends. Referring to God in the third person is an expression of our *faith* in God and in our realization that His essence is unknowable.

❧

Avinu Malkeinu (Our Father, Our King)

The bonding between man and God occurs in two modes: as a child to a father, and as a subject to a king. These two modalities are not mutually exclusive. They both exist at all times. We are always God's children, and we are always His subjects. In human experience, the father-child relationship is not dependent on behavior. A wayward son is a son nevertheless. At times when we are not deserving to be referred to as God's nation, we are nevertheless His children (*Hosea* 2:1). On the other hand, when our behavior is not in accordance with His will, we may lose the distinction of being *referred to* as God's children, but that does not sever the factual relationship.

There are times when one modality predominates. On Rosh Hashanah and Yom Kippur, when we are brought before God for judgment, we refer to Him as King. Yet, in the prayer following the sounding of the shofar, we ask for Divine compassion both as His children and as His subjects. When pleading for His mercy we address God as our Father, invoking the love and mercy that a father shows to even a disobedient child.

It is of interest that in the evening service prayer of *Hashkiveinu* (make us lie down to sleep), R' Yitzchok Luria (the Arizal) modified the wording of "God, our Lord, make us lie down" to "Our Father, make us lie down." The reason for this change is that if one feels himself to be in the king-subject modality, it is an audacity to lie down to sleep in the presence of the king. We, therefore, shift to the father-child modality. In the intimacy and familiarity of this modality, one can lie down in the presence of one's father.

Earlier we noted that in many prayers there is a shift from the second person to the third person. A notable exception to this is *Modeh Ani*, the prayer that is said immediately upon awakening, even before we sit up in bed. *Modeh Ani* is entirely in the second-person mode. Given the Ari's modification of *Hashkiveinu,* we can understand why this is so. A prayer that is recited while reclining in bed can be said comfortably only when we feel ourselves in the presence of a father rather than a monarch.

❧

Humility

The importance of humility is repeatedly emphasized in the Talmud and in the ethical writings. "Be exceedingly humble in spirit" (*Ethics of the Fathers* 4:4). In his letter to his son, Ramban states that humility is the finest of all human traits. Its efficacy in prayer is stated in *Psalms* (10:17) "You have heard the desires of the humble." In his prayer for forgiveness, David says, "The proper offering to God is a broken spirit. A broken and contrite heart You will not reject" (ibid. 51:19). This is interpreted as meaning that a humble spirit is dearer to God than all the sacrificial offerings. The Talmud adds that a person's prayer is not accepted unless he effaces himself (*Sotah* 5a).

Vanity, on the other hand, is considered so obnoxious a trait that God removes His presence from a vain person. Based on the verse in *Psalms* (101:5), the Talmud quotes God as saying, "A vain person and I cannot coexist in the same world" (*Arachin* 15b).

One can hardly expect to address God if his vanity has caused God to withdraw from him.

Pleasant Mood

The Talmud states that the mood for prayer should not be one of sadness, indolence, nor levity. Rather, the mood should be one of *simchah shel mitzvah* (the joy of performing a mitzvah) (*Berachos* 31a). The Divine Presence shuns dejection and welcomes joy.

It is of interest that the Talmud relates that R' Chanina did not pray on a day that he lost his temper! (*Eruvin* 65a). He felt that his attitude was not conducive to proper prayer. Of course, we cannot apply this to ourselves. R' Chanina's prayer was normally with such intense *kavannah* that he felt he would not be able to reach this *kavannah* if he had experienced anger. Inasmuch as we do not have even a shadow of R' Chanina's *kavannah*, and our prayers lack such an attitude even on days on which we have no anger, we cannot exempt ourselves from prayer for reasons such as this. But the point is nevertheless valid. We should conduct ourselves in a manner that will allow us to develop the best possible mood for prayer.

It is customary to give *tzedakah* before prayer. *Tzedakah* is a mitzvah of great merit regardless of the intent with which it is given. The knowledge that one has done a precious mitzvah should arouse a mood of *simchah*, which is conducive to proper prayer.

The Divine Appellations

The two Names referring to God which appear most often in our prayers are the Tetragrammaton, which is never pronounced as written but rather as A-do-noy (which we will henceforth refer to as *Hashem*), and Elo-him (which we will refer to as *Lord*). The first, which refers to God as Infinite, is generally associated with Divine compassion and mercy. The latter appellation is associated with the Divine manifestation of might and of absolute justice and firmness of judgment.

Inasmuch as we believe that God is absolute goodness, we must accept that what appears to us to be harsh judgment is actually good at the core. Our perception of happenings as being bad can be compared to the infant's perception of the painful immunization injection as bad. The infant cannot understand why his loving mother would collaborate with the white-clad villain who is about to stab him with a sharp needle. There is no way that the infantile mind can possibly grasp that this momentary pain will prevent him from having crippling and deadly diseases.

The gap between the human mind and the infinite wisdom of God is far greater than even that of the infant and the mother. We may bitterly resent God's inflicting pain or allowing suffering to occur. It requires a leap of faith to accept that what appears to us to be blatantly bad is for some ultimate good.

> *During the lifetime of R' Dov of Mezeritch, the Baal Shem Tov's successor, there were no harsh anti-Semitic decrees. When these recurred after R' Dov's death, his disciples wondered why the master, in the heavenly realm, was not protecting his people as he did in his lifetime. R' Dov appeared in a dream to one of his disciples and said, "When I was alive and with my human perception saw a decree as being harmful, I prayed for its abrogation. From my present vantage point I can see the ultimate good that will result. I cannot intercede to annul what is ultimately good. If you, with your human perception, see things as being bad, then you should pray for relief from them."*

The Book of Job is an exhaustive treatise on why bad things happen to good people. A variety of arguments are presented by Job's friends and are all refuted. God then says to Job, "Where were you when I created the world?" By this is meant that any single event can be understood only as part of a Divine master plan which stretches over eons of time and immeasurable space. The only one who can understand how any event fits into the master plan is one who has a comprehensive view of endless time and space. No human being can understand how "bad" happenings are part of the master plan which leads to an ultimate good. This is known only to God and requires an act of faith.

In the *Shema* we say, "Hear, O Israel! Hashem, our Lord, Hashem is one." We refer to God by both Appellations, but repeat "Hashem." Would it not have sufficed to say "Hashem, our Lord, is one?" Why is "Hashem" repeated? Furthermore, what is the significance of covering one's eyes when reciting the *Shema*?

The *Shema* is not only a testimony to the unity of God, but also that He is the source of everything. We do not ascribe any evil happenings to God. We believe that what appears to our human eyes as evil is actually for an ultimate good. The *Shema* is a refutation of the Zoroastrian belief in a duality of gods. They could not reconcile a good god doing bad things, and concluded that there are two gods, one benign and the other malevolent. They were unable to conceptualize that what we may see as bad is actually for an ultimate good.

We, therefore, say "Hear, O Israel! *Hashem* (referring to God as merciful and compassionate, *Elokeinu* (our Lord Who may manifest Himself to us in harsh judgments), *Hashem* is one. "There is but one God, and He is absolute goodness. Everything that God does is with mercy and compassion, even that which we see as being harsh. To symbolically demonstrate that our human perception is imperfect, we cover our eyes when reciting the *Shema*. This act is a statement, "Yes, we see, but our faith in the absolute goodness of God overrides our human vision."

The Effectiveness of Prayer

One of the problems that many theologians have grappled with is: "Why and how does prayer work?" If a sick person prays for recovery, he is assuming that God has allowed him to become sick. Is he to believe that his prayer can make God change His mind?

One of the answers given is that there is a constant outpouring of Divine benevolence to the world. Just as the sun radiates light, yet there are areas of darkness in enclosures where the sunlight does not reach, so does the Divine benevolence not reach where there are barriers that obstruct it. These barriers are a person's actions that are contrary to the will of God.

As we have seen, genuine, sincere prayer brings a person into a closer relationship with God. The barriers to the Divine benevolence are thereby removed or circumvented, and the person can then receive this benevolence. The blessing and improvement in the person's health is not the result of a change in God's will, but of a change in the status of the recipient.

This is similar to Rambam's explanation for the effectiveness of *teshuvah* (repentance). *Teshuvah* is not merely regretting a wrong that one has done. Rather, *teshuvah* consists of a person realizing how and why he came to commit a sin, and to advance himself spiritually so that it would be impossible for him to commit that sin if the same circumstances and temptation recurred. This amounts to a significant change in one's character. The person who has done proper *teshuvah* is now a new person. His personality has changed and he is not the same person who committed the sin. It is, therefore, justified that this newly emerged person not be held responsible for the actions of the previous person.

This also applies to the effectiveness of prayer. Genuine prayer brings about a transformation in a person. The newly emerging person can be receptive of the Divine benevolence to which the former person was impervious.

This may explain why a person's prayer in his own behalf is effective. But why is it effective when one person prays for another person? The Talmud says that if a member of the family is sick, "let him go to a Torah scholar and ask him to pray for him" (*Bava Basra* 116a). In this case, the sick person is not undergoing a character transformation that would make him a new person. How can the scholar's prayer cause God to change His mind?

The Torah relates that on several occasions Moses interceded with prayer on behalf of the Israelites. Following their worship of the Golden Calf, God wished to destroy them. Moses interceded and "God repented for the harshness He was going to do to His people" (*Exodus* 32:14). Here it would seem that Moses' prayer did cause God to change His mind, yet we know that any kind of change in God is an impossibility.

This can be explained by God's statement to Moses, "Now, *leave Me*, and My wrath will destroy them" (ibid.). The Talmud says that by the words "leave Me" God indicated that if Moses interceded for the Israelites, He would not destroy them. There was thus no change in God's will. God's will was: "I will destroy them if you do not pray for them. If you do pray for them, I will forgive them." To us it appeared that God had repented, but in fact, His will never changed.

We might ask: Why would God make forgiveness or recovery for one person dependent on another person's prayer. The answer to this can be found in the Talmudic statement, "The reign of Heaven is similar to the reign on earth." For reasons known only to Him, it is God's will that there be a heavenly tribunal that sits in judgment on a person. Just as in a court there are prosecuting attorneys and defense attorneys, so in the Heavenly tribunal there are prosecuting angels and defending angels. They present their arguments before God, and God issues a decree. His will never changed. As with Moses, the Divine will was, "If the person has adequate merits, I will forgive him." The Torah scholar who prays for a person has undertaken the role of a defense attorney.

But does God not know the degree of a person's merits? The scholar's prayer is not going to add anything to God's knowledge.

Here we invoke another Talmudic statement.

> *The Talmud relates a fascinating incident of a dispute between R' Eliezer and the sages. R' Eliezer refused to yield to the opinion of the majority, and said, "If I am right, let that tree demonstrate it." The tree was uprooted and moved. The sages were not impressed. "Trees do not enter into disputes of halachah." "Then let the stream prove I am right," R' Eliezer said. The flow of the stream reversed itself.*

"Streams do not determine halachah," the sages said. "Let the walls of the house of study prove that I am right," R' Eliezer said. The walls began to cave in. R' Joshua exclaimed, "What right do walls have to interfere in a dispute between Torah scholars?" The Talmud relates that in honor of R' Eliezer, the walls did not become upright, nor did they fall because of the honor of the sages. The walls, therefore, remained in an inclined position.

R' Eliezer then said, "Let Heaven prove that I am right." A voice emanated from Heaven, "Why do you dispute with R' Eliezer? The halachah is always like his opinion." The sages remained firm. "The Torah is not in Heaven. The Torah states that the halachah is the opinion of the majority (Exodus 23:2), and that is the way it shall be."

This episode tells us that God's will never changes. The will that He expressed in the Torah that the halachah is with the majority never underwent any change.

The commentaries state that this episode teaches us that the Divine will is that which follows Torah. Thus, when we kindle Chanukah candles we recite the *berachah* which states that God has instructed us to light the Chanukah candles. The Talmud asks, since the miracle of Chanukah occurred long after Sinai, how can we say that God instructed us to light the Chanukah candles? Inasmuch as the Torah states that we are to follow the instructions of Torah authorities (*Deuteronomy* 17:11), we are fulfilling the Divine will when we do so.

R' Zvi Elimelech (author of *Bnei Yisass'char)* applies this principle to *tefillah.* It was *always* God's will that if a person prays for himself or if someone else prays for him, the prayer will be accepted. God never has a "change of mind."

We can further understand why prayer may be effective even though God does not change His mind.

For reasons known only to God, Divine justice may decree that a particular person must undergo suffering. This person shares his pain with a friend, who is so moved by his friend's distress that he suffers along with him and prays for him. However, Divine justice never decreed that the second person suffer. Therefore, in order to relieve the friend from unwarranted suffering, Divine justice requires that the first person be relieved of his distress.

The concern for the friend's suffering must be sincere. This is why the Talmud says that if one prays on another person's behalf rather than pray for himself, his own prayers are answered quickly (*Bava Kamma* 92a).

R' Yechezkel Levenstein says that sometimes a person is given distress to stimulate him to pray. He bases this on the Midrash which states that the reason the Patriarchs were barren for so lengthy a time was because God desired their prayers.

God has no selfish motivation. The reason he wished the Patriarchs to pray is because prayer elevates a person spiritually.

The Talmud says that had we not been given the Torah, we would have been obligated to learn proper life habits from the observation of God's creatures. Perhaps we would have learned something about growth from the observation of lobsters.

A lobster is a soft animal that resides within a rigid, inflexible shell. As it grows, the shell becomes very confining. When it becomes oppressive, the lobster retreats to an underwater rock formation where it is safe from predatory fish, sheds its shell, and forms a larger, more spacious one. Eventually this new shell becomes oppressive as the lobster continues its growth, and the process is repeated several times until the lobster reaches its maximum size.

The stimulus for the lobster to throw off its restraining shell so that it may grow is *discomfort*. This may be true for human beings as well. If we are comfortable, we are unlikely to do anything to advance ourselves. The greater the discomfort, the greater is the stimulus for growth. The Patriarchs' desire for offspring was so intense that they were moved to profound prayer. It was this intensity of prayer that elevated them to such lofty spirituality.

This is further borne out by the Midrashic statement that after the ordeals of Esau, Laban and Dinah, the Patriarch Jacob wished to live in tranquility. God said, "Tranquility is reserved for the eternal world," and Jacob was subjected to the suffering of the loss of his beloved son, Joseph (*Rashi, Genesis* 37:2). It is not that God wishes to deny anyone tranquility, but that tranquility is not conducive to spiritual growth. The latter is catalyzed by distress.

R' Yechezkel explains that inasmuch as the purpose of distress is to stimulate a person to prayer, it is only logical that when this purpose is achieved, the distress disappears.

Prayer is effective, whether we pray for ourselves or for others.

Forms of Prayer

We are most familiar with the prayers in the *siddur.* These are the formal prayers which were formulated primarily by the Men of the Great Assembly some 2,000 years ago. We are encouraged to add prayers of our own. R' Nachman of Breslov is specifically reknowned for his many spontaneous prayers.

The Talmud states, "God desires the dedication of the heart" (*Sanhedrin* 106b). Some of the most effective prayers were spontaneous, charged with profound feeling.

> *One Rosh Hashanah, R' Levi Yitzchok of Berditchev delayed the sounding of the shofar. He explained, "There is a young man who was orphaned as a child, and did not have the opportunity of going to a cheder (Hebrew school). Consequently, he never learned how to read the siddur. When he saw people streaming into the shul today, his heart ached because he could not join them in prayer. He tearfully lifted his eyes to Heaven and said, 'Dear God! I don't know how to read the prayers like others do. All I know is the letters of the aleph-beis. I will recite them to You, and You please put them together to make up the prayers.'*
>
> *"We must delay the sounding of the shofar, because God is occupied putting together the letters of the aleph-beis for this young man."*

We know that God attends to multiple prayers simultaneously. R' Levi Yitzchok's message to his congregants was that they should develop as sincere a desire to communicate with God as this young man did.

There are many anecdotes about the effectiveness of sincere prayer.

On Yom Kippur, one of the Chassidic masters was concerned that the prayers were not being accepted favorably. He exhorted the worshipers to ever greater kavannah. As the intensity of the prayers increased, one woman was heard to exclaim, "Dear God! How can you not accept these prayers? I have seven children and I often do not have enough food to go around. When they cry to me, my heart is broken. I wish I could give them what they want. But You, God, You can give Your children everything they want. How can You listen to their crying and not respond?" The Rebbe exclaimed, "Our prayers have been accepted. This woman's heartfelt plea to God broke through all the barriers to Heaven!"

A similar story is that of a woman who was overheard saying to a friend at Ne'ilah (closing prayer on Yom Kippur), "I know we are going to have a good year."

"What makes you so sure?" her friend asked.

"Why even a highway robber with a heart of stone would yield to such intense pleas," the first woman said. "How could it be God will not?"

My father would tell about R' Levi Yitzchok of Berditchev, who one Yom Kippur eve expressed his concern that there were harsh decrees in Heaven, and urged the congregants to pray with greater fervor. Abruptly his demeanor changed to joy. He sent the shammes (beadle) to ask a particular woman to come to the shul.

When the woman came, R' Levi Yitzchok asked, "What did you do that reversed all the harsh decrees?"

"I did not do anything special," the woman said. "For several years after our marriage we had no children. I prayed for a child and this year God blessed me with a beautiful baby. I never left the baby unattended for a moment.

"This morning I thought, 'What will I do for Kol Nidrei? Everyone else will be in shul, and I will be unable to find someone to stay with the baby.' But I have never missed Kol Nidrei in my life. All day I was torn between staying with the child and going to shul.

"When evening approached, I decided I must go to shul. I fed the baby and tucked him in his crib. The shul is just a short distance from my home and I would only be away briefly.

"All during Kol Nidrei I was tormented. Why did I leave the baby? Perhaps he woke and cried so hard that he shook the crib and fell out. As soon as Kol Nidrei was over I ran home in a panic, expecting the worst. I found the baby safe in the crib, sleeping soundly. I was so grateful to God. I said, 'Dear God! You have been so kind to me. How can I ever repay You? All I can do is wish You that just as You have given me nachas in my child, You should have nachas in Your children.'"

R' Levi Yitzchok beamed. "It was this woman's fervent wish that turned the tables for us," he said.

A particularly heartrending story is related by Dr. Shmuel Feuerstein (Biblical and Talmudic Antecedents of Mediated Learning Experience Theory). It was told to him by a Holocaust survivor. As a youngster of 15 in the Bergen-Belsen concentration camp, he had hidden a piece of bread under his pillow for the next day. Suddenly he felt someone touching him, and he was afraid it was someone trying to steal his bread. Instead, it was one of his comrades who woke him up. He was holding the headpiece of the tefillin and said, "Quick! Touch it and say a berachah!" The youth went from one person to another, asking them to do the same thing. Even though he was warned that the Nazis would kill him for this, he went from barrack to barrack with his mission.

Technically, it is not permissible to say a *berachah* for touching *tefillin*. But can anyone put a value on this child's *mesiras nefesh*, trying to help his fellow Jews keep a conscious contact with God in the most despairing moments of the Holocaust?

These anecdotes emphasize the importance of sincerity in prayer. On the other hand, the Baal Shem Tov upon entering a synagogue said, "What a house full of prayer!" The congregants thought he was complimenting them until he explained, "The *Zohar* says that prayers without *kavannah* do not ascend to Heaven. Many of the prayers in this synagogue were recited out of rote. They never ascended to Heaven, so that this synagogue is full of these prayers."

My father would quote the Talmudic statement, "The ordinary conversation of Torah scholars deserves study" (*Avodah Zarah* 19b). He explained that man was intended to be in constant communication with God. When man sinned, he gave Satan entry and lost the ability to maintain this constant relationship. The Patriarch Abraham, therefore, established the *Shacharis* (morning) prayer. Certainly for a circumscribed period of time a person would be able to maintain contact. But Satan soon intervened, introducing extraneous thoughts during prayer to break the contact.

The Patriarch Isaac reasoned that perhaps a person could not concentrate for the lengthy morning service, so he formulated the *Minchah* (afternoon) service, which is brief. Certainly for so short a period of time a person could control his thoughts. But before long Satan interrupted the *Minchah* service as well.

The Patriarch Jacob then reasoned that because the *Shacharis* and *Minchah* services were obligatory, Satan sought to undermine them. He therefore designated *Maariv* as an optional service, which would not attract Satan's attention. But here, too, Satan interfered.

Throughout the ages various *tzaddikim* sought ways to strengthen *kavannah* in prayer to resist Satan's wiles. Finally, the Baal Shem Tov came up with the idea, which would work at least for Torah scholars. They were to speak what seemingly appeared to be ordinary conversation, but their intention with their speech was that it was to be a prayer. Inasmuch as Satan has no access to a person's inner thoughts, he would not recognize it as prayer. This is why the Talmud says that the ordinary conversation of Torah scholars deserves study. Their words may have much greater content than the manifest meaning.

There are a number of anecdotes that demonstrate this technique.

> *A woman came to beseech the Seer of Lublin to pray for her. Her newborn infant refused to take cow's milk, and she did not have enough milk to nurse the child. The Seer went into the kitchen and said to the kitchen help, "Why don't I get enough milk when I ask for it? Don't I deserve a bit more milk?" The kitchen help had no idea to what the Seer was referring. Furthermore, he had never complained about food. When they related this to the Seer's shammes, he understood that this was the Seer's way of praying for the woman in a way that would outwit Satan.*

Let me digress for a moment. In a somewhat related manner, R' Isaiah Horowitz (the "Shelah") sought to mitigate the condemnation of communities that chose a cantor for the High Holidays purely for his musical skills, overlooking the halachic requirement that the person who leads the services should be of impeccable character.

> *The Shelah gave a parable about an official who had aroused the envy of others of the king's court, and they conspired to have him imprisoned. They knew that if he were able to communicate with the king, he could prove his innocence. They, therefore, were very careful that he should not have any contact with anyone who could carry a message to the king.*
>
> *When the janitor came to remove the trash, the official slipped him a note with instructions to get it to the king. It never occurred to the guards that he might try to send his message via someone of such low status, and he succeeded in getting his message to the king.*
>
> *"Similarly," the Shelah said, "Satan tries to interfere with our prayers reaching God. The community, therefore, chose a cantor of questionable character. It does not occur to Satan that he would be the one who conveys the congregation's prayers to God. This is a clever ploy to outwit Satan."*

To return to our theme, we can practice *tefillah* in many ways. Anytime we do anything that brings us closer to God, we are engaging in *tefillah*.

It is noteworthy that R' Shlomo Luria (the Arizal) instructs us to preface the morning service with, "I accept upon myself to fulfill the mitzvah of 'loving one's neighbor as oneself.' " What is the relevance of this mitzvah to prayer? The Baal Shem Tov was asked how we can develop love for God, inasmuch as we cannot see Him or have any physical contact with Him. The Baal Shem Tov said, "The royal road to love of God is love of your fellow man. If you will eliminate the behaviors that obstruct love of your fellow man, you will come to love God."

It is common practice to give *tzedakah* before prayer. *Tzedakah* and acts of *chesed* bring us closer to others. This facilitates our bonding with God.

The sage Hillel told a proselyte that the essence of Torah is "Do not unto others as you would not have others do unto you." R' Akiva made a similar statement, "The all- encompassing rule of Torah is 'Love your neighbor as yourself'" (*Jerusalem Talmud* 9:4). The Talmud states that Moses conveyed the 613 mitzvos of the Torah to us. King David condensed them into eleven character traits enumerated in Psalm 15 (*Makkos* 24a). In keeping with the teaching of the Ari, some congregations recite Psalm 15 in the morning service prior to the Verses of Praise. Let us look at this psalm.

מִזְמוֹר לְדָוִד ה׳ מִי יָגוּר בְּאָהֳלֶךָ מִי יִשְׁכֹּן בְּהַר קָדְשֶׁךָ:
הוֹלֵךְ תָּמִים וּפֹעֵל צֶדֶק וְדֹבֵר אֱמֶת בִּלְבָבוֹ: לֹא רָגַל עַל לְשֹׁנוֹ
לֹא עָשָׂה לְרֵעֵהוּ רָעָה וְחֶרְפָּה לֹא נָשָׂא עַל קְרֹבוֹ: נִבְזֶה
בְּעֵינָיו נִמְאָס וְאֶת יִרְאֵי ה׳ יְכַבֵּד נִשְׁבַּע לְהָרַע וְלֹא יָמִר:
כַּסְפּוֹ לֹא נָתַן בְּנֶשֶׁךְ וְשֹׁחַד עַל נָקִי לֹא לָקָח
עֹשֵׂה אֵלֶּה לֹא יִמּוֹט לְעוֹלָם:

A psalm by David. Hashem, who may sojourn in Your Tent? Who may dwell on Your Holy Mountain? One who walks in perfect innocence, and does what is right, and speaks the truth from his heart; who has no slander on his tongue, who has done his fellow no evil, nor cast disgrace upon his close one; in whose eyes a contemptible person is repulsive, but who honors those who fear Hashem; who can swear to his detriment without retracting; who lends not his money on interest; nor takes a bribe against the innocent. The doer of these shall not falter forever.

King David was well aware of the importance of all the ritual mitzvos. However, observing these is not sufficient to establish a bond with God. As the Baal Shem Tov said, the path to love of God is the love of other people. One cannot love others if one is selfish and totally absorbed in oneself. Developing the eleven character traits of Psalm 15 eliminates the barriers to the love of others. Only then can a person "sojourn in God's tent and dwell in His Holy Mountain." Only by developing these traits can one aspire to a lasting bond with God. "Whoever does these shall not falter forever." This psalm is, therefore, a fitting preface to the Verses of Praise.

I Am a Prayer

"In return for my love, they despise me, and *I am a prayer*" (*Psalms* 109:4).

The term "I am a prayer" is rather strange. R' Bunim of P'shis'che explained it well.

"Suppose," R' Bunim said, "you respond to a knock on your door and you see a well-dressed person who appears to be in good health. You have no inkling why he has come to you. You must ask him what it is that he wants, and only when he tells you will you know.

"On the other hand, if the person is dressed in tattered clothes, and his lean, drawn face indicates that he has not eaten in days, you do not need to ask what he wants. His very appearance tells you he needs your help to get food and clothing.

"This it what David said. 'Master of the Universe! You see me as I really am. My outer appearances may impress others, but You know the truth. You can see how bereft I am of spirituality. My very appearance tells You my needs. I do not have to express my wants. You know what it is that I need. I, myself, constitute the prayer. I am my prayer.' "

In our ordinary walks of life, we present ourselves to other people in a variety of ways, depending on what the particular circumstances call for. Just as we dress differently for different occasions, so do we act differently in different situations. We may be authoritative and assertive in one situation, passive in another, flexible in a third, firm in a fourth, etc. The variety of attitudes we assume are our "outer garments," as it were. We may not even be fully aware of our own identity. "Who am I really?"

There is a charming anecdote about a person who was forever misplacing his clothes and could not locate them on arising. He decided to make a list before retiring, stating where each item was. In the morning he consulted his list. "Here is my shirt, here are my shoes, here are my socks, here are my trousers, here is my hat, here is my jacket." Then he paused and said, "All's well and good, but where am I?"

We may lose an awareness of the self in the myriad of attitudes we adopt.

We may also be confused about just what *is* our true self. For example, the narcotic addict says, "I want drugs. I must have drugs." When he recovers from his addiction, he realizes how destructive drugs are and that they could have destroyed him. No one wishes to be destroyed. When he said, "I want drugs," it was not the real "I" that craved drugs. Rather, it was the *body of the "I,"* the physical unit in which the "I" was housed that had been so affected that it wanted something that could destroy the "I." The real "I" is not the body. It is the essence of the person. The "I" is the *neshamah* (soul).

It is the body's desires that can detract from spirituality and interfere with the bonding between man and God. The body does not desire *tefillah.* It is the true "I" that wishes to bond with God. Hence, "I *am* the prayer."

> *R' Hillel of Paritsch saw a simple, unlearned person crying bitterly during prayer. When he inquired as to the cause of his crying, the man said, "This Divine neshamah is trapped within this earthly body. The neshamah wishes to be close to God and to unite with God, but all the body wants is to eat, drink and sleep. All the body's desires are antithetical to the neshamah. How the neshamah must be suffering in its entrapment within the body. I am crying out of compassion for the neshamah which is in such anguish." R' Hillel said that in spite of his erudition in Talmud and in Chassidic teachings, he had not achieved this feeling of spiritual desperation.*

This is why David exclaimed, "I *am* the prayer." He set aside all the attitudes he had to adopt when interacting with people. He divested himself of all earthly desires. He totally effaced his ego, revealing the true "I." As he said, "My soul thirsts for You, my flesh longs for You" (*Psalms* 63:2).

The great ethicists point out that effacement of the ego is not self-degradation. Humility is not a denial of one's character assets. To the contrary, only a person who is aware of his personality assets is sufficiently secure to efface one's ego.

The vain, ego-driven person prides himself on his accomplishments and feels that these make him superior to other people. A person who is aware of his personality assets may realize that precisely because he is gifted his responsibilities are commensurately greater. The truly humble person does not boast of his achievements. His accomplishments pale before his awareness of how much he must yet do. The father of the *mussar* movement, R' Yisrael of Salant, was one of the most humble people on earth. He said, "I know that my mind is equal to a thousand others. Precisely for that reason, my obligations are a thousandfold greater. I am remiss in not having properly discharged my duties commensurate with my capabilities. As we shall see in our discussion of the Patriarch Abraham's relationship with God, it was his utter self-effacement and humility that invited the Immanent Presence of God. When a person allows the true "I" to emerge from its physical bondage, he can achieve this humility. As he draws himself closer to God, God draws Himself closer to him. This allows the bonding of *tefillah* to occur.

Prayer - An Instrument for Change

In the account of creation, God brings everything into being: the earth, the sky, the waters, vegetation, all living creatures, super-galaxies. When it comes to creation of man, God says, "Let *us* make man" (*Genesis* 1:26). Why is God enlisting the participation of others in the creation of man, and whom is He addressing?

The Baal Shem Tov explained that God created everything in a state of completion. Angels do not grow or undergo change of any kind. All vegetation and all living things are created with a genetic structure that enables them to become what God wished them to be. Tiny seeds have within them the capacity to become giant trees. Tiny animals can grow into huge animals. No creature needs to do anything to transform itself into something other than what it was created to be. Even the caterpillar that becomes a beautiful butterfly does not do this as a volitional act. The transformation is coded into its genes. A caterpillar cannot stop the process of turning into a butterfly.

The sole exception is man. After creating everything else in the universe, all in a state of completion, God wished to create a totally different creature: a being that would be created with a potential, but that would be free to direct that potential in any direction. God wished that creature to achieve a state of completion, to be the spiritual being He desired, *but to achieve that completion by its own effort.* In contrast to all other living things, both angels and animals, God gave this unique creature free will. Man is to exercise this free will in order to bring himself to a state of spirituality. A ready-made spiritual being would simply have been another angel.

But God did not want another angel. He wanted *man.* His definition of man is a being that develops itself into the finished product He desired. God, therefore, needs the participation of man to bring about the unique spiritual being He desired. God was, therefore, addressing *man* when He said, " Let *us* make man. I will give you the potential, but you must develop it. I will give you a *neshamah*, but you must implement the *neshamah*. You must transform yourself into a spiritual being. If you fail to do so, you will be essentially like the myriad of other living things I created. You will not be *man*."

Man, at birth, is pure potential. As a person grows, one can mature and become spiritual, or one can grow only physically and intellectually and become a mere *homo sapiens,* nothing more than a hominoid with intellect.

It is of interest that the Talmud refers to a person who fulfills the Divine wish as "becoming a partner with God in the work of creation." A partner, indeed. God desired man's participation in his own creation.

The task of becoming spiritual is formidable. The physical body within which the *neshamah* abides has no spiritual strivings. It wants only to eat, sleep and gratify all the desires characteristic of its animal nature. The body's urges are powerful, and resisting or limiting them is a major challenge. Furthermore, the human intellect is inordinately sagacious. It can rationalize and delude a person into thinking that his bodily urges are indeed proper and should be gratified.

It appears that man was given an almost impossible task. The animal forces within him can be overpowering and prevent his becoming spiritual. God, therefore, said to man, "No need to fear. True, I have given You free will, but I will help you direct it properly *if you ask for My help. I will help you become spiritual.*"

God relied on man's intellect to make the right choice. Think of it in this way. Two young children receive Chanukah *gelt*. One races to the candy store and buys all kinds of sweets, then goes to the toy store and spends the rest of the money on toys. He ends up with a stomachache from indulging in candy, and several days later the toys are either broken or lie in a pile of other toys in which he has lost interest.

The second child gives the Chanukah *gelt* to his father, saying "Put it in the bank for me." Of course, the father does this for the child. The money collects interest, or is perhaps invested in a way that makes it grow in value.

Which child is the wiser? Both exercised their freedom of choice. The first child chose foolishly. The second child chose wisely.

In order to be like the wise child we must sacrifice. The candy appears luscious, and the toys seem to promise endless fun. True, these are illusions, but the juvenile mind may not understand this.

We can turn to God and say, "You gave me this enormous potential and the free will to use it as I see fit. But my intellect is so limited. I realize that I may think something is good when it may in fact be bad. Here, Father, *show me how to use this free will to my own betterment.*

This last statement is prayer. Prayer at its finest. *Prayer is not to get what we want, but to become what we should be.*

The force of our animal nature is not to be minimized. The Talmud says that "A person's *yetzer* (animalistic component) grows in strength and wishes to destroy him. Without the help of God man cannot triumph over it" (*Kiddushin* 31b). The *yetzer* wishes to destroy man as the unique being God desires.

It is our mission to change ourselves from the totally self-gratifying being we are at birth to the spiritual being which man was intended to be. Prayer enables us to make this change. We cannot do it alone.

We have noted the Talmudic statement that the *tzaddikim* of yore spent an hour in meditation before prayer. The Talmud says that they also spent an hour in meditation *after* prayer. What was the purpose of that? It was to see how they could apply what they had learned in prayer to the way they lived. In the letter to his son, Ramban instructs him to follow each period of Torah study with an analysis of how he can apply what he has learned to his behavior. The *tzaddikim* of yore did this with prayer. They were desirous of spiritual progress, and felt that unless their prayer had effected a change in them, it had not served its purpose.

Perhaps you may say, "I see no need for change. I think I am fine the way I am." This, too, is a rationalization. Everyone tries to better themselves socially and economically. You no doubt desire to be promoted at work, and want your next automobile to be an upgrade over your present one. Unless one is totally devoid of all spirituality, one does wish to improve spiritually.

Of course you want to improve yourself spiritually. Why would anyone who does not care about spirituality pick up a book about prayer?

But What if I Can't Pray?

At a "spirituality" Shabbaton for people in recovery from alcoholism and drug addiction, there were a number of people who said that they did not wish to attend services. It was, therefore, decided to hold a discussion, "Why I Am Not at Services."

I will try, to the best of my recollection, to convey the dialogue at that session, which was conducted by a rabbi. I attended as an observer.

> *"I can't pray," one of the group said. "I don't believe in God."*
>
> *"That's okay," the rabbi said. "God believes in you, and that's enough reason to pray."*
>
> *"That's a wisecrack, Rabbi. I don't believe God exists."*
>
> *"What is your concept of the God that others believe in?" the rabbi asked.*
>
> *"I grew up in an Orthodox home, and I was sent to Hebrew classes after school to prepare me for my Bar Mitzvah. I resented having to sit in a boring class while my friends were playing football. We were taught how to read Hebrew, but never what the words meant. After four years of this, I recited the Haftarah in the synagogue and parroted a speech I had spent many hours memorizing. We had a huge party, and I got a lot of gifts. That's the only part I liked. I was never taught anything in Hebrew school about God."*
>
> *"You have every right to resent being deprived of a proper education," the rabbi said, "but why should that result in not believing in God?"*

"We had a kosher home" he said, "and if my father found out that I had eaten something at the home of a friend who was not kosher, he screamed at me and said that God was going to punish me for eating tereifah. My friend's family seemed to be having a good life even though they were not kosher. In fact, they had a nicer home than we did. I didn't see where God was punishing them

"I went to shul with my father until my Bar Mitzvah. It was a big shul, half empty. All the prayers were in Hebrew, which I did not understand. People talked with each other during the services. The rabbi gave a speech in Yiddish, and I had no idea what he was talking about. After the service everybody went into the social hall for Kiddush. Some people drank to excess. I liked the Kiddush, because I could get all the wine I wanted. I could not believe that God was going to punish me for having a piece of cake or that He wanted people to get together once a week to recite prayers which many of them did not understand, and then celebrate it all with drinking."

The rabbi responded, "You are in good company. The God you don't believe in, I don't believe in either. Are you familiar with the use of a computer?"

"Sure," the man answered. "What's that got to do with God?"

"How proficient is your father with a computer?"

"He doesn't know the first thing about computers. He can't program a VCR or even his telephone. I have to do that for him."

"This reminds me of a story in the Midrash. Elijah the prophet came across a man who was tying ropes together to fashion a fishing net. 'Are you spending any time studying Torah?' Elijah asked.

"'No,' the man answered, 'I never was taught anything about Torah.'

"'How do you know how to make a fishing net?' Elijah asked. You were not born with that skill. Did anyone teach it to you?'

"'Not really,' the man answered, 'but I needed a livelihood and decided I would be a fisherman. I watched the other fishermen make nets, and that's how I learned to do it.'

"'Because earning a livelihood was important, you found a way to learn something you did not know. If you know that

Torah is important, you will find a way to learn Torah too,' Elijah said.

"In your case, you knew very little about God. Because your father did not teach you anything about God, you gave up on it. But your father didn't teach you anything about computers either. You were interested in learning about computers, so you sought information and are now quite adept at computers. If you would seek information about God as you did about computers, you could get to believe in Him," the rabbi said.

"Touché!" the man said. "How do I go about finding God?"

"By looking for Him," the rabbi said. "That's the way it all started. Our ancestor Abraham came to the conclusion that this marvelous world could not be an accident. There had to be an Intelligent Being that created it. He lived in a pagan environment, and knew that the inanimate idols could not possible be that Intelligent Being. He thought that perhaps the moon was God, or the sun, or the majestic mountains. Eventually he concluded that none of these could be God, but that there is a God somewhere. At that point God revealed Himself to Abraham and said, 'I am the One you are looking for.'

"The Torah says, 'If you will seek God, you will find him.' But it qualifies this, 'if you search for Him with all your heart and with all your soul'" (Deuteronomy 4:29).

"Are you saying that if I search for God with all my heart and soul, I will have a vision and God will reveal Himself to me like He did to Abraham?" the man asked.

"I didn't say that. The Torah says 'you will find Him.' That does not mean you will have a prophetic revelation like Abraham."

"Well, what do I have to do to find God?" the man asked.

"You won't have the difficulty that Abraham encountered. First of all, you live in a monotheistic culture where the overwhelming majority of people believe in one God. Second, we have a wealth of guidance in several thousand years of Torah writings that Abraham did not have. But there is one problem with this search that Abraham did not have.

"Abraham was willing to go in whatever direction the truth led. He was fully committed that when he found God, he would subordinate Himself to His will, regardless of what

impositions this would make on him. His sincerity was proven years later when he did not hesitate to sacrifice his beloved son Isaac, and was held back only by the hand of an angel.

"Some people today do not have that kind of dedication. They profess to believe in God, but are not willing to subordinate themselves to His will. When the Divine instructions, as conveyed in the Torah, cause them some inconveniences, they change the Torah laws to suit them.

"The Torah promised that you will find God if you seek Him, provided that you search for Him with all your heart and with all your soul. That's what Abraham did, and he found God. If you are looking for a God that will cater to your wishes, forget it. If you will look for the truth and follow it wherever it takes you, you will find God.

"This means that your search is not going to be easy. Many times along the way you will run into things that are contrary to your own desires. Your natural inclination may be to chuck it and say, 'I'd rather be comfortable. I don't want to give up some of the things I enjoy.' If you can overcome these hurdles and be persistent, you will find God."

At that point I asked for the floor and said, "It's not only a question of giving up some things one enjoys. There is a major ego problem that may be even more difficult to overcome than giving up some pleasurable activities.

"I attended an Alcoholics Anonymous meeting in Jerusalem. One person related his drinking history and recovery. He said, 'When I first came to AA and I heard that I had to "turn my life over to a higher power, God as I understood Him" I turned around and left. I am an atheist. I do not believe in God.

" 'My drinking got worse, and I realized I would die if I didn't stop drinking. I said to the group, "Look, I need this program. But I cannot pledge myself to something I don't believe. I'll follow everything you want except the part about God." The group said okay.

" 'After a few meetings, I was told to get a sponsor, which I did. One day my sponsor asked, "Do you pray every day?" I told him that I don't pray because I am an atheist. He said, "Okay, then don't pray to God. Just pray anyway."

" 'I said, "That's ridiculous. It doesn't make any sense to pray if there is no God."

"'My sponsor said, "Look here, you numbskull! Do you want to stay sober or do you want to get drunk? If you want to stay sober, then you'd better pray every day, and that's all there's to it."

"'I didn't want to go back to drinking, so I started to pray. I've been praying every day for over six years. I still don't believe in God. But when I pray, that reminds me that I'm not God.'

"One of the problems of the alcoholic is that he cannot accept that he has no control over alcohol and that his life has become unmanageable. This is nothing but a delusion of omnipotence. The alcoholic thinks he can control everything. In other words, he is his own God. It is only when he relinquishes this delusion that he can recover.

"As was just said, we live in a monotheistic culture. Ever since people rejected paganism with its plurality of gods, reasonable people know that there is only one God. The Ten Commandments spells this out clearly. 'I am the Lord, your God … You shall have no other gods before Me.'

"To believe in God one must surrender the idea of being one's own God. There cannot be two gods. As long as a person hangs on to the idea that he is in control of everything, he is being his own god and cannot accept belief in the true God.

"Giving up this delusion of omnipotence is not easy. A person may have a need for this grandiosity and will not give it up easily. Searching for God is bound to be futile as long as you think of yourself as being your own God. This ego need may be so strong that you will find a myriad of reasons why not to believe in God. It is not only giving up some enjoyable things that may cause resistance to believing in God. It is not seeing belief in God as a threat to our ego."

The discussion then switched to humility as a crucial ingredient in recovery. It soon became evident that the humility that is necessary for recovery is the same humility that can clear the way for finding God.

The next day, this man was at services. "I'm not convinced, but I'm willing to give it a try," he said.

"Wherever it will take you?" I asked.

The man took a deep breath. "Yeah, wherever it will take me."

Do We Know What to Pray for?

My attitude toward prayer was deeply affected by several comments my mother made. At a wedding ceremony, she would say, "For that young couple, this day is their Yom Kippur. This is a special moment for them, most propitious for acceptance of their prayers. But do they know what to pray for? They have no idea what awaits them in the years ahead. Are they praying for healthy children, and to be able to raise them without distress? Are they praying for their children to be decent, God-fearing people? Are they praying for a long, happy and peaceful life together? Are they praying for family love and unity, and to be spared from the strife that afflicts so many families?"

This has made me cognizant of the fact that we often fail to exploit propitious moments, perhaps squandering them on prayers for things of little value.

My mother also told me that when I took my first steps as an infant, a loud cheer went up. "*Dos kind geht!*" (The child is walking.) Everyone clapped their hands in glee at my achievement.

One of those present in the room was a rabbi who traveled from town to town soliciting funds. He remarked sadly, "When I took my first steps as an infant, I'm sure everyone was overjoyed and exclaimed '*Dos kind geht!*' But now, '*Ven men zeht mich gehn keiner is nisht zufrieden.*' (When people see me walking [toward them], no one is happy.) My lot in life is soliciting money, and when people see me coming, they are not pleased at all."

My mother would say, "When a child starts walking and the parents are happy, that is when they should pray that he grows up to be a person whose steps will always be welcomed. They should pray that he be loved and appreciated, and that others will be as happy with his presence as they are." Not only would this be a significant prayer, but it would also focus the attention of the parents on raising the child in a way that people will be happy with his company.

There are indeed many special moments such as these when we should pray. If the young couple under the *chuppah* (wedding canopy) would pray for the really important things in life, they might be more likely to act toward each other in a way that would contribute to the fulfillment of their prayers.

But even in our regular daily lives there are many times when we should pray. Unfortunately, we are often deluded by the thought that we are in control of our lives and that we can make things happen solely by our efforts. The following story contains an important teaching.

> *The Baal Shem Tov once expressed a desire for wine from Bessarabia. One disciple, R' Dovid of Mikalov, volunteered to carry out the master's wish. Toward the end of the summer, when it was grape-harvest season, R' Dovid made his way to a village in Bessarabia. Of course, it was essential that no one other than a strictly observant Jew come in contact with the wine, because otherwise it would not be permissible for use.*
>
> *Unfortunately, there were no pious Jews in this village, and R' Dovid did all the work himself. Once the grapes were crushed, he personally had to perform all the processes in the wine-making, and had to be on constant alert that no one dare touch the barrel.*
>
> *The time of year when wine is made is the month of Elul, when R' Dovid had always been in the company of his comrades, fellow disciples of the Baal Shem Tov. Now he had to say the Selichos services without a minyan. The wine was not yet ready for transport when the High Holidays arrived, and R' Dovid spent Rosh Hashanah, Yom Kippur and Succos in solitude. This was most distressing, but he was willing to sacrifice everything to provide the master with the wine. Many a night he remained awake to keep a watchful eye on the wine.*
>
> *Finally the day arrived when the wine could be transported. R' Dovid loaded the barrel onto the wagon himself, and remained with it on the long trip back to Mezhibozh. As they entered the town, R' Dovid was elated that he had fulfilled the master's wish. All the work, the sleepless nights, and the deprivation of a minyan for the weeks of Elul and Tishrei were worth it.*
>
> *Shortly after entering Mezhibozh, R' Dovid was confronted by a gendarme. "What are you carrying there?" he demanded.*
>
> *"Wine," R' Dovid answered.*
>
> *"You cannot deceive me so easily," the gendarme said. "You are smuggling in liquor, contraband." R' Dovid's protestations were of no avail. The gendarme pushed him aside, pried open*

the barrel, and dipped his finger into the wine. "It is wine indeed," he said, "and good wine at that." He smacked his lips. "You may go on," he said.

R' Dovid was crushed. All his efforts had been in vain. The long sleepless nights, the hard work, the solitude on the holidays, all for naught. The wine was no longer fit for use.

R' Dovid wept before the Baal Shem Tov. It was clear that he was not deserving of fulfilling the master's wish.

The Baal Shem Tov comforted him. "Everything that occurs to a person is a teaching, and the more important the teaching, the greater a price one must pay for its acquisition.

"You did everything with total devotion, R' Dovid," the Baal Shem Tov said. "You invested great effort in this project. You took it upon yourself to make sure that no one else come in contact with the wine. You made only one error. You forgot to pray that God bless your efforts with success and keep the wine safe from alien contact. You thought that by your diligence and your constant vigilance you could protect the wine without God's help.

" You have learned an important lesson, R' Dovid, and it is well worth the high price you paid for it. There is nothing we can succeed at without God's assistance, regardless of how assiduous we may be. We must always pray for Divine assistance in everything we do."

The Talmud says, "Make for yourself a teacher, and acquire a friend" (*Ethics of the Fathers* 1:6). Our judgment is so heavily influenced by our desires that we cannot know whether the judgments we are making are indeed proper. The cocaine addict's desire for the drug makes him think that its use and whatever he must do to obtain it is justified. The desire for profit has caused many people to justify some very dishonest acts. We can never be free of personal interest. The only way to avoid the pitfalls of distorted reasoning is to have a teacher who can guide us and a trusted friend in whom we can confide. These are the essentials for proper living. "But," said R' Yaakov Yitzchak of P'shis'che, "how often do we pray for a proper teacher and a trusted friend? This is a most vital prayer, and one that God will surely answer."

The Talmud says, "It would be good if a person would spend the entire day in prayer" (*Berachos* 21a). That would indeed be ideal. But inasmuch as that is impractical, we could at least pray a bit more often. We should not restrict prayer to the synagogue. We should pray under the *chuppah*, when a child begins walking, when working on a project, and on many similar occasions.

The Value of Prayer

It has been correctly said that sometimes you do not adequately value a thing until you lose it.

I have prayed since my childhood. It was the thing to do. But I never fully appreciated the privilege of prayer. That is, not until it was taken from me.

When my father died, it was the first time I had lost a close relative and was subject to the rules of *aninus*, the intense mourning period between death and burial. During this period, one is not permitted to pray or to recite a *berachah*.

I was unable to say a *berachah* for food. How was I going to eat? I had never put a morsel of food in my mouth without thanking God for it. I chose to avoid eating rather than to eat without a *berachah*. Only then did I realize how foolish I had been all these years to take *berachos* for granted.

The grief at the loss of my father was exceedingly painful. If only I could assuage the pain by saying *Tehillim* (Psalms). Yes, I could cry, but crying with the words of David would have been much more comforting. David expressed it so beautifully. "The pains of death encircled me; the confines of the grave have found me; anguish and sorrow I would find. Then I would invoke the Name of God. 'Please God, save my soul'... For You have delivered my soul from death, my eyes from tears" (*Psalms* 116:3-8). Yes, I could think these words, but I could not *say* them.

David gave voice to the most profound human emotions. Yes, we know that God never abandons us, but this intellectual knowledge may sometime be overridden by our emotions. Dare we complain to God and accuse Him of abandoning us? "My God, my God, why have You forsaken me? Why is my help so distant from the words of my cry? My God, I call by day but You do not answer, and at night, but there is no pacification for me? … Our fathers trusted in You and You did deliver them. They cried unto You and they were removed from harm; they trusted in You and they were not deceived" (ibid. 22:2-6).

All the prayers I had said for my father's recovery! The many prayers offered for him by the countless people whom he had helped, who loved him so. When he prayed for other people's recovery, You accepted His prayers. Why were the prayers for him not heeded? Was I permitted to think this way? David said it, so this was not blasphemous!

But David's cries of anguish are followed by the assurance of Divine salvation. "From the straits did I call upon God; God answered me with expansiveness" (ibid. 118:5). "Allow me to hear joy and gladness once more; the bones which You have deprived of strength shall have cause to rejoice again" (ibid. 51:10). "Yea, though I walk through the valley of the shadow of death, I will fear no evil, for You are with me. Your rod and Your staff, they comfort me" (ibid. 23:4).

These words would have been a balm to my wound, cool water to a parched throat. Why may I not say them? Why deprive me of the comfort of prayer when I need it the most?

Our sages were not inconsiderate. As a psychiatrist, I have seen many cases of depression due to unresolved grief. In Western civilization there is often a denial of death. Euphemisms are often used to avoid the very word "dead." Lavish coffins costing thousands of dollars may be provided "to give father or mother the best," as though they were still living and could enjoy the comfort of quilted satin and the beauty of polished bronze.

Our sages were wise. Death is an undeniable fact. It must be accepted, dealt with, and then put behind us so that we may go on with the important business of living. The period of *aninus* leaves one with nothing else to focus on than the reality of what has occurred. There are no distractions whatsoever.

But whatever the reason, the deprivation of prayer brought home to me its inestimable value. Now when I kiss a *siddur* before restoring it to its place, I do so with gratitude, appreciation and love.

Why Prayers Should Be Verbalized

The commentaries on *tefillah* ask: Inasmuch as God knows our innermost thoughts, why do we have to speak our prayers? Why is it not enough to just meditate on them?

Some answer that verbalizing prayers enhances the quality of *kavannah*. Even when we recite the prayers our thoughts tend to wander. This diversion would be much worse if we prayed only by meditation. In fact, with the exception of the *Amidah* which is said silently, some authorities say that we should pray aloud. Actually hearing the words we recite decreases the wandering of our thoughts and enhances concentration. Those of us who suffer from forgetfulness and cannot find something we put away have found it helpful to say aloud to ourselves several times, "The tickets are in the top drawer of the desk."

Another reason given for verbalizing prayers is that the unique feature that distinguishes human beings from other living things is the ability to communicate by speech. Onkelos translates the verse, "God formed the man of dust from the ground, and He blew into his nostrils the soul of life *and man became a living being*" as "*man became a spirit that can speak*" (*Genesis* 2:7). Inasmuch as the ability to verbalize characterizes our humanity, we should use this capacity in prayer to remind us of our mission on earth as humans.

As I mentioned in the previous chapter, when I was in *aninus* and was not permitted to pray, I could *think* the words of the psalms, but this did not give me the solace that reciting them with the traditional *niggun* (melody) would have done.

There is yet another advantage to verbalizing our prayers and hearing the words we say.

There appears to be an inner resistance to acknowledging gratitude. Already the first human being, Adam, was an ingrate

(*Rashi, Genesis* 3:12). Moses sharply rebuked the Israelites for being ingrates. This reluctance can be seen even in small children. Mother may say, "Now say 'thank you' to the nice man for the candy," and the child replies with a grunt that indicates he has no intention of doing so.

Tosafos (*Avodah Zarah* 5a) says that the reason the Israelites did not want to acknowledge their gratitude to God was because they did not want to feel beholden to Him. This is a profound psychological insight. When we have strong negative feelings about something, our minds may render us oblivious to it. Even small children may react this way.

It is even more difficult to feel obligated and beholden to another human being than to God. We may find it easier to express our gratitude to God. If we do so frequently, and accustom ourselves to pronounce the words "I thank you" to God, we may lower the resistance to saying them to another person. This is one advantage of verbalizing our prayers.

A second area where there is some resistance is the expression of love for another person. During courtship, a young man and a young woman may indeed say "I love you" or write these words on the card accompanying flowers. For some strange reason, marriage seems to curtail the expression of love. A couple may live together for fifty years without verbally expressing their love for each other. They may say, "Why do I have to say it? He/she knows I love him/her." True, but it is still very pleasant and reassuring to hear it.

When we declare our love to God in prayer, we realize that although we love God and God knows that we love Him, we express our feelings verbally anyway. That is a good precedent. We should apply it also to the people we love.

In *tefillah* we confess our sins. We express our regret for having done wrong and pledge not to repeat our sins. In human interaction, admitting one was wrong is met with great resistance. People may rationalize and justify their actions and may be obstinate in refusing to admit they were wrong. When we say to God, "I have sinned and I ask Your forgiveness," we may reduce the resistance to saying this to other people.

The phrases, "I thank you, I love you, and I'm sorry for what I did ... I was wrong," are like magic charms in any relationship. Many broken marriages might have been saved if the spouses had used these simple phrases more frequently.

It is not enough to meditate on gratitude, love and remorse. We must hear ourselves pronounce these words. If we apply our intelligence, we will use them more often.

שער השמים
פירוש על התפלה
אמשטרדם

Upon Arising

מוֹדֶה אֲנִי לְפָנֶיךָ, מֶלֶךְ חַי וְקַיָּם, שֶׁהֶחֱזַרְתָּ בִּי נִשְׁמָתִי בְּחֶמְלָה – רַבָּה אֱמוּנָתֶךָ.

אֱלֹקַי, נְשָׁמָה שֶׁנָּתַתָּ בִּי טְהוֹרָה הִיא. אַתָּה בְרָאתָהּ אַתָּה יְצַרְתָּהּ, אַתָּה נְפַחְתָּהּ בִּי, וְאַתָּה מְשַׁמְּרָהּ בְּקִרְבִּי, וְאַתָּה עָתִיד לִטְּלָהּ מִמֶּנִּי, וּלְהַחֲזִירָהּ בִּי לֶעָתִיד לָבֹא. כָּל זְמַן שֶׁהַנְּשָׁמָה בְקִרְבִּי, מוֹדֶה אֲנִי לְפָנֶיךָ, ה׳ אֱלֹקַי וֵאלֹקֵי אֲבוֹתַי, רִבּוֹן כָּל הַמַּעֲשִׂים, אֲדוֹן כָּל הַנְּשָׁמוֹת. בָּרוּךְ אַתָּה ה׳, הַמַּחֲזִיר נְשָׁמוֹת לִפְגָרִים מֵתִים.

I gratefully thank You, O living and eternal King, for You have returned my soul within me with compassion – abundant is Your faithfulness!

My God, the soul You placed within me is pure. You created it, You fashioned it, You breathed it into me, You safeguard it within me, and eventually You will take it from me, and restore it to me in Time to Come. As long as the soul is within me, I gratefully thank you, Hashem, my God and the God of my forefathers, Master of all works, Lord of all souls. Blessed are You, Hashem, Who restores souls to dead bodies.

It is only appropriate that we begin with the first prayer. Indeed, these are the very first words uttered when we return to a conscious awareness of the world upon awakening in the morning. The Talmud (*Berachos* 60b) states that we should recite the prayer *Elokai Neshamah* upon awakening. Inasmuch as this prayer mentions the Name of God, which should not be pronounced before one's hands have been washed, the prayer *Modeh Ani* was composed at a later date. This prayer expresses the idea of *Elokai Neshamah,* but omits the Divine Name. We therefore say *Modeh Ani* immediately upon awakening, and we say *Elokai Neshamah* after we say the *berachah* for washing our hands.

Our relationship to God is not just that of a child to a parent, but of an *infant* to a parent. An infant is totally dependent on his parents, and develops a trust in his parents knowing that his needs will be addressed and provided. One aspect of *tefillah* is that we become aware of our utter dependence on God not only for our needs, but for life itself, and that we develop a profound trust that He will provide these for us.

Immediately upon awakening we declare that we are fully aware of our dependence on God. During the night we are essentially in a state of suspended animation. Tradition has it that while we sleep, our *neshamah* ascends to heaven. It is cleansed and returned to us in a pure state. As we open our eyes in the morning we attest to our awareness that our *neshamah* has mercifully been returned to us. We acknowledge our dependence and our trust in God.

The Chafetz Chaim, who devoted his life to the eradication of *lashon hara,* said that we can learn *mussar* from technology. The telephone teaches that what we say in one place can go around the world. From the tape recorder we learn that every word we say may be recorded and saved, to be played back to us at a later date.

We may extend this to our understanding of *Modeh Ani.* The patient who undergoes a heart transplant has sufficient trust in his doctor that he allows him to essentially take his life by removing his heart, and "resurrect" him by inserting another heart in its place. That is the trust in God we should feel as we retire.

> *The Maggid of Chernobyl once asked a man to describe his daily routine. The man said that when he wakes up, he goes to his store to see that everything is prepared for the upcoming business day, then continues on to shul for davening (prayer).*
>
> *The Maggid told the man about a merchant who was returning home from the market with a large sum of money. He stopped at an inn for the night, but there were no personal safe-boxes as we have in modern hotels. The innkeeper told him he would put his money in a safe place, and the man had no choice but to give him the money. He gave the innkeeper the bag with the large sum, and also his coin purse.*
>
> *The merchant spent a restless night. How could he be sure that the innkeeper was honest? What would*

prevent the innkeeper from taking some large bills from the bundle? He had no proof of how much he had given him.

In the morning the innkeeper returned the bag of money and the coin purse. The man counted the money, and was greatly relieved to find that all the money was there. He then counted the few coins in his coin purse.

Was not the latter act foolish? If the innkeeper was proven trustworthy for thousands of dollars, what sense did it make to suspect him of taking a few pennies?

"You entrusted God with your neshamah, your very life, when you went to sleep at night," the tzaddik said. "When God demonstrates his trustworthiness by returning your neshamah in the morning, is it not foolish to check before davening whether everything in your business is intact? If you trust Him with your very life, do you suspect that He is not trustworthy of keeping your store intact?"

Modeh Ani also contains another important element of *tefillah*. We express our gratitude to God for His kindness in giving us another day of life. Acknowledging a kindness and expressing gratitude are pivotal in Judaism and are a recurrent theme in *tefillah*.

Feeling and expressing gratitude should not be taken lightly. There seems to be an inherent reluctance to do this. Mothers will tell you how reluctant youngsters may be to say "thank you." One of Moses' sharpest rebukes of the Israelites was for their ingratitude. *Tosafos* comments that their reluctance to acknowledge their gratitude to God was due to their discomfort at feeling beholden to their Benefactor (*Avodah Zarah* 5a).

The reluctance to acknowledge and express gratitude undoubtedly has its origin in feelings of low self-esteem. People who harbor inferiority feelings may interpret receiving a favor as being dependent on others. Just as a small child who feels dwarfed in a world of grownups will stand on a chair and declare, "Look how big I am!" so may people who feel inferior try to demonstrate their superiority. Indeed, the great ethicist Rabbeinu Yonah states that vanity is nothing but a desperate attempt to overcome feelings of unworthiness. "I am totally self-sufficient and do not need any help" is the equivalent of the child's attempt to show his height.

"It is indicative of God's great love for man that it was made known to him that he was created in God's image" (*Ethics of the Fathers* 3:18). This refers to the Divine gift of the *neshamah*, which is identified with God Himself. The awareness that we have a Divine *neshamah* within us should banish feelings of inferiority. We should, therefore, not have any difficulty in feeling and expressing gratitude.

"But," one may say, "how can I feel pride when I have so abused the Divine *neshamah* with my sinful behavior?" The prayer *Elokai Neshamah* removes this objection. "My God, the *neshamah* You placed within me is pure." While we were asleep, the *neshamah* was cleansed, and we awaken in the morning with a clean slate.

Can it be that all our sins have been forgiven while we slept, even though we may not have done adequate *teshuvah*? Again, technology comes to our rescue. As with the computer, our sins have been "deleted" rather than erased, and they are in a "recycle bin" where they are retrievable. Our screen is fresh and clean, and is not contaminated by the folly we wrote on it yesterday. Of course, if we retrieve our errant behavior from the recycle bin, we clutter up the screen once more. With *teshuvah* we empty the recycle bin. Yet, even then the material may be retrievable from the hard drive, and we must take additional steps to totally eliminate it. We can accomplish total eradication of our sins with a *teshuvah* that stems from our love for God.

But even prior to adequate *teshuvah* we begin the day with a "clean screen," a pure *neshamah*. This not only provides us with the self-esteem that enables us to acknowledge and express gratitude, but also empowers us to make this day a spiritual one, regardless of how we may have acted in the past. The awareness that we have a Divine *neshamah* should banish feelings of inferiority.

There is another reason why a person may actually feel himself cleansed of sins. The Midrash states that if a person experiences a miracle and expresses his gratitude to God, he may be assured that his sins are forgiven (*Midrash, Tehillim* 18:6). If a person realizes that he was without his *neshamah* during the night, understands that his awakening in the morning is indeed a miracle, and is sincere in his gratitude to God for this miracle, he is at a level of spirituality that merits forgiveness.

"Blessed are You, God, Who restores *neshamos* to dead bodies." Granted, we were in a suspended state while we slept, but we were not really dead, were we?

We may understand this with the Talmudic statement, "The wicked are considered dead even when they live" (*Berachos* 18b). The human being is a composite creature, composed of an essentially animal body and a Divine spirit. If one's actions are only to gratify the bodily needs and desires, then the body is indeed alive, but that is an animal existence. It is only when we exercise the Divine spirit that we differ from other forms of life and can pride ourselves in our humanity. A person can be physiologically alive but spiritually dead. A wicked person, who eschews spiritual behavior, is alive as an animal, but dead as a human.

"Blessed are You, God, Who restores *neshamos* to dead bodies." The human body without the *neshamah* is spiritually lifeless. The return of the *neshamah* in the morning is indeed giving human life to a body that would otherwise be physiologically alive but spiritually dead.

The *neshamah* comes from the most sublime of sources; the Torah tells us that when God created man, He Himself "blew a spirit of life" into man (*Genesis* 2:7). The *neshamah* craves to reunite with its source. We can implement this bonding with our *tefillah*.

בָּרוּךְ אַתָּה ה׳ אֱלֹקֵינוּ מֶלֶךְ הָעוֹלָם, אֲשֶׁר יָצַר אֶת הָאָדָם בְּחָכְמָה, וּבָרָא בוֹ נְקָבִים נְקָבִים, חֲלוּלִים חֲלוּלִים. גָּלוּי וְיָדוּעַ לִפְנֵי כִסֵּא כְבוֹדֶךָ, שֶׁאִם יִפָּתֵחַ אֶחָד מֵהֶם, אוֹ יִסָּתֵם אֶחָד מֵהֶם, אִי אֶפְשַׁר לְהִתְקַיֵּם וְלַעֲמוֹד לְפָנֶיךָ. בָּרוּךְ אַתָּה ה׳, רוֹפֵא כָל בָּשָׂר וּמַפְלִיא לַעֲשׂוֹת.

Blessed are You, Hashem, our God, King of the universe, Who fashioned man with wisdom and created within him many openings and many cavities. It is evident and known before Your Throne of Glory that if but one of them were to be ruptured or but one of them were to be blocked it would be impossible to survive and to stand before You. Blessed are You, Hashem, Who heals all flesh and acts wondrously.

In the secular world there is an attitude, "Give to God what is God's and to Caesar what is Caesar's." A person may be religious, but religion need not apply to things other than sacramental functions. Not only should there be a governmental division between "church and state," but there should also be clear boundaries between the secular and the religious in daily life.

Judaism categorically repudiates this attitude. Our Sages ask, "Which is a small verse upon which the entire Torah is dependent? 'Know God in all your ways' " (*Proverbs* 3:6). The *entire Torah* is dependent on this single verse. Torah observance is not limited to rituals. Every action a person does must be within the parameters of Torah. One's conversation, work, business dealings, eating, sleeping, recreation and interactions with people must all follow Torah principles. There is no dichotomy of sacred and secular. Rejecting this concept is tantamount to rejecting the entire Torah.

A person arises in the morning and performs his physiologic functions. A *berachah* is recited in appreciation of the marvelous function of the human body.

As a physician, this *berachah* is especially meaningful. It is regrettable that many people's appreciation of this is limited by lack of knowledge of the wondrous human body. The Vilna Gaon is alleged to have said that to the degree that one lacks an awareness of the wonders of nature, his lack of appreciation of Torah is tenfold. This *berachah* illustrates the Gaon's statement.

The Talmud says that when infant is born, "the closed passages open and the open passages close, otherwise the infant could not survive for even one hour" (*Niddah* 30b). It is obvious to everyone that if the airway passages were open *in utero*, the lungs would fill with fluid. If they did not open immediately at birth, the infant would be deprived of oxygen. What is less known is that there are openings and passages within the circulatory and respiratory systems that close upon birth. Failure of these to close may result in heart disease.

"Blessed are You, God, Who heals all flesh and acts wondrously." The Talmud interprets the verse, "Blessed is God, Who alone performs great wonders (*Psalms* 72:18), as meaning that most often the beneficiary of a miracle is not aware that a miracle occurred (*Niddah* 31a). When things happen in a regular manner, we may attribute them to "natural causes," forgetting that the Hand of God directs all things.

The wording of this *berachah* is significant: "It is evident and known before Your throne of Glory." This expression is not found frequently in the liturgy. That it is included in this *berachah* is to emphasize the belief in *hashgachah pratis* (Divine Providence).

> *My father told me that when he was at the Mayo Clinic in Rochester for surgery, he was approached by a man who was suffering from a difficult urologic condition. "Rabbi," the man said, "on Yom Kippur eve we put on the tallis and kittel and with great solemnity recite Kol Nidrei.*
>
> *"What is so special about Kol Nidrei that it warrants all this attention? It is only a declaration that we annul all the vows we may make during the coming year. Why is that so important as to require a tallis and kittel and encircling the chazzan (cantor) with Torah scrolls?*
>
> *"I suggest," the man said, "that when a person recites the asher yatzar blessing, in which he thanks God for the ability to perform his physiologic functions, that is also when we should put on the tallis and kittel — to help us realize the importance of this berachah. Life does not depend on vows,*

but it does depend on our ability to perform our physiologic functions. Yet we generally mumble this berachah without thinking of its importance."

My father would often quote this man's observation and point out how we may be remiss in our lack of appreciation of the many wondrous things God does for us. God takes an interest in the minutest detail of human function.

By reciting this prayer at the beginning of the morning services and giving serious thought to its meaning, we can develop a proper mindset for *tefillah.*

One Great Word

*A*men is one of the most frequently used words in prayer. It is said upon hearing a person say a blessing or when the Divine blessing is invoked.

Amen is related to *emunah* (belief, trust) and means "I believe this is true." It is also related to *imun* (to train or bring up). It can, therefore, be an expression of affirmation or of a wish to be fulfilled ("may it be so").

When one answers *amen* upon hearing another person recite a blessing, one is saying "I, too, believe this is so." Essentially one is condensing the blessing into a single word. The affirmation is equivalent to one's having said the blessing oneself.

The Talmud says that a person should recite at least 100 blessings each day. During the weekdays, this is rather easily accomplished. The *Amidah* is comprised of 19 blessings. Saying the *Amidah* three times daily totals 57 blessings. The remainder of the blessings are achieved by the various blessings one recites during the day.

On Shabbos, however, the *Amidah* contains only seven blessings. There is, therefore, a shortfall of 36 blessings to be made up. This can be accomplished by being alert to answer *amen*. Inasmuch as the affirmation of a blessing is equivalent to have recited it oneself, the total of 100 blessings can easily be reached.

The Talmud states that *amen* is a mnemonic for the Hebrew words *Keil Melech Ne'eman*, "God, the trustworthy King." It is, therefore, a reaffirmation of one's belief in God. Inasmuch as this is a fundamental mitzvah, every time one says *amen* and thinks of this meaning, one is fulfilling the mitzvah of believing in God.

I knew a man who would come to school and give children candy, saying, "Now say the *berachah*." He would answer *amen* with sincere devotion. Just think how many mitzvos this man accumulated!

The response of *amen* is more than equivalent to reciting a blessing. The Talmud says that the person who answers *amen* has an even *greater* mitzvah than the one who recited the blessing (*Berachos* 53b). Why is this so?

The reciting of a blessing is an expression of gratitude or praise. When recited over food, one is thanking God for it. When recited in the *Amidah,* one is extolling the greatness of God. When recited prior to doing a mitzvah, it is an expression of gratitude to God for sanctifying us with His mitzvos. In each case, there is a personal gain. One enjoys the food, one is privileged to praise God, and one adds a mitzvah to one's merits. These are very worthy benefits, but there is, nevertheless, an element of personal interest in the *berachah.*

However, when another person recites a *berachah* over food, *he* is the one enjoying it. When he praises God or performs a mitzvah, *he* is the one accruing the merits. When I answer *amen* to another person's *berachah,* it is without any conscious or subconscious intent of any personal gain. *Amen* is, therefore, the purest expression of devotion to God. This is why the Talmud (ibid.) says that answering *amen* is an even greater mitzvah than reciting the *berachah.*

The Wisdom of Hindsight

בָּרוּךְ אַתָּה ה׳ אֱלֹקֵינוּ מֶלֶךְ הָעוֹלָם, פּוֹקֵחַ עִוְרִים.
בָּרוּךְ אַתָּה ה׳ אֱלֹקֵינוּ מֶלֶךְ הָעוֹלָם, מַלְבִּישׁ עֲרֻמִּים.
בָּרוּךְ אַתָּה ה׳ אֱלֹקֵינוּ מֶלֶךְ הָעוֹלָם, מַתִּיר אֲסוּרִים.
בָּרוּךְ אַתָּה ה׳ אֱלֹקֵינוּ מֶלֶךְ הָעוֹלָם, זוֹקֵף כְּפוּפִים.
בָּרוּךְ אַתָּה ה׳ אֱלֹקֵינוּ מֶלֶךְ הָעוֹלָם, רוֹקַע הָאָרֶץ עַל הַמָּיִם.
בָּרוּךְ אַתָּה ה׳ אֱלֹקֵינוּ מֶלֶךְ הָעוֹלָם, שֶׁעָשָׂה לִי כָּל צָרְכִּי.
בָּרוּךְ אַתָּה ה׳ אֱלֹקֵינוּ מֶלֶךְ הָעוֹלָם, הַמֵּכִין מִצְעֲדֵי גָבֶר.
בָּרוּךְ אַתָּה ה׳ אֱלֹקֵינוּ מֶלֶךְ הָעוֹלָם, אוֹזֵר יִשְׂרָאֵל בִּגְבוּרָה.
בָּרוּךְ אַתָּה ה׳ אֱלֹקֵינוּ מֶלֶךְ הָעוֹלָם, עוֹטֵר יִשְׂרָאֵל בְּתִפְאָרָה.
בָּרוּךְ אַתָּה ה׳ אֱלֹקֵינוּ מֶלֶךְ הָעוֹלָם, הַנּוֹתֵן לַיָּעֵף כֹּחַ.

Blessed are You, Hashem, our God, King of the universe, Who gives sight to the blind.
... Who clothes the naked.
... Who releases the bound.
... Who straightens the bent.
... Who spreads out the earth upon the waters.
... Who has provided me my every need.
... Who firms man's footsteps.
... Who girds Israel with strength.
... Who crowns Israel with splendor.
... Who gives strength to the weary.

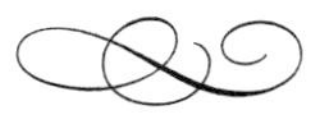

Our sages were not haphazard in their choice of words. It is, therefore, noteworthy that all the *berachos* of gratitude are in the present tense: "Blessed are You ... Who *gives* sight to the blind ... Who *clothes* the naked ... Who *releases* the bound ... Who *straightens* the bent ... Who *spreads out* the earth ... Who *firms* man's footsteps ... Who *girds* Israel with strength ... Who *crowns* Israel with splendor ... Who *gives* strength to the weary." The one notable exception is "Who *has provided* me my every need." Why the change in tenses?

> *We are simple humans. Few of us have achieved the spirituality of R' Zusia of Anipoli, who was sickly and lived in abject poverty. Someone who saw R' Zusia dressed in tattered clothes asked him, "How can you be sincere in saying the berachah 'Who has provided me with all my needs' when you are so woefully lacking?" R' Zusia responded, "God knows what I need more than I do. He must know that one of my needs is poverty."*

We are not R' Zusia. Nor are we R' Baruch of Mezhibozh.

> *One Friday night R' Baruch was reciting the prayer before Kiddush. When he came to the verse, "I gratefully thank You, my God and God of my forefathers, for all the kindness You have done with me, and which You will do with me...," he paused and reflected. "Why must I thank God now for future kindnesses? I can thank Him when they occur." He then concluded, "It is because I may not recognize some things as being kindness. To the contrary, I may see them as distress and perhaps I may be resentful rather than grateful. That is why I must thank Him in advance."*
>
> *R' Baruch then began crying. "How tragic it is that we can be so blind! God will be doing kindness with me, but I may not recognize it. I may actually resent His kindness rather than thank Him for it."*

R' Zusia saw everything as Divine kindness. R' Baruch was distressed that he might not see this. We are so far from their spirituality. When we suffer adversity, we are resentful and complain.

However, after time passes we may see that something which we had thought to be an adversity was actually a blessing, but it came down in disguise. Many things are much clearer when we look through the "retrospect scope."

Since we are not R' Zusia, we would be deceiving ourselves if we said the *berachah* in the present tense, thanking God "Who *provides* me with all my needs." Today I do not feel that all my needs have been provided. I can make a list of the things I need that I still lack. The sages did not want us to say a *berachah* if our heart is not in it.

However, as we reflect on the past we may better recognize the truth. "When I did not get the job I applied for, I was bitter. But later I found a much better job with far better pay. I was lucky I did not get that first job." Or, "When I lost my job, I thought my world had come to an end. But I went back to school and earned an advanced degree. If I hadn't lost that job I'd still be doing menial work."

We are much wiser in hindsight. We may see that in the past God did indeed provide for all our needs. What R' Zusia saw in the present, we can only see in the past.

That is why the sages formulated this *berachah* in the past tense. We may be able to say with full sincerity that God did indeed provide for our needs in the past, even though we were unable to recognize it then.

When we arise in the morning, we recite a number of *berachos*, thanking God for giving us the ability to do many things. We thank Him for giving us sight, for enabling us to sit up, to stand upright, to walk, to clothe ourselves, to gird ourselves, and to cover our heads. We thank Him for giving us energy.

Two *berachos* are conspicuous by their absence. We do not say a *berachah* for the ability to speak, nor for the ability to hear! This is all the more striking because the ability to speak and communicate verbally is the outstanding human feature. In his translation of the verse, "And He blew into his nostrils the soul of life, and man became a living being," Onkelos says, "man became a spirit that can *speak*" (*Genesis* 2:7). Inasmuch as our ability to speak constitutes our very identity, why do we omit it when we recite all the other abilities, some of which we share with animals?

One of the *berachos* we recite is an expression of gratitude, "that God did not make me a heathen." The commentaries ask why this *berachah* is worded in the negative. Why do we not express thanks "for making me a Jew"?

The answer given is that the Talmud relates a debate among the sages that extended for a two and a half years. The issue was: "Is it better for man that he was created, or would it have been better had he not been created?" The issue was decided "when they took a count," and they concluded that it would have been better had man not been created (*Eruvin* 13b).

Maharsha explains that the count referred to was not a show of hands. Rather, they counted the mitzvos of the Torah. There are 365 prohibitions, but only 248 positive commandments. Therefore, it is statistically more likely that a person will transgress a prohibition than fulfill a positive commandment.

Because man is closer to sin than to virtue, it would have been better had he not been created.

The Midrash states that before God created man, He took counsel with the angels. The Angel of Truth objected to the creation of man, because "man will be full of falsehood." God expelled the Angel of Truth and created man.

Unfortunately, man has abused his power of speech. People frequently speak falsehood, as the Angel of Truth predicted. What is perhaps worse is that they speak *lashon hara*, which the Talmud says is equivalent to the three cardinal sins: idolatry, illicit relations and murder. The Chafetz Chaim stresses that listening to *lashon hara* is equally grave. Given the widespread abuse of speech, man would have been better off if he could not speak. Just as we cannot thank God for "creating me a Jew" because creation of man is not to our advantage and we can only express our gratitude in the negative, "that He did not make me a heathen," so we cannot extol our ability to speak and hear. We have abused this wonderful privilege.

When we recite the morning *berachos*, we should note that the expression of gratitude for the most singular human trait is missing. It is missing because we have abused it. It is as though one was given a beautiful, delicate silk garment and wore it to collect and dispose of trash. If he were to appear before his benefactor with the silk garment soiled and torn and thank him for it, would that not be the worst insult? It is essentially saying, "I do not value your gift." It is far better that he remain silent.

The absence of the *berachos* for speech and hearing is the sharpest reprimand. It is a reminder that we should adopt the teachings of the Chafetz Chaim, and take great heed about what we say and hear.

Be on Guard Against Delusion

בָּרוּךְ אַתָּה ה׳ אֱלֹקֵינוּ מֶלֶךְ הָעוֹלָם, הַמַּעֲבִיר שֵׁנָה מֵעֵינָי וּתְנוּמָה מֵעַפְעַפָּי. וִיהִי רָצוֹן מִלְּפָנֶיךָ, ה׳ אֱלֹקֵינוּ וֵאלֹקֵי אֲבוֹתֵינוּ, שֶׁתַּרְגִּילֵנוּ בְּתוֹרָתֶךָ וְדַבְּקֵנוּ בְּמִצְוֹתֶיךָ, וְאַל תְּבִיאֵנוּ לֹא לִידֵי חֵטְא, וְלֹא לִידֵי עֲבֵרָה וְעָוֹן, וְלֹא לִידֵי נִסָּיוֹן, וְלֹא לִידֵי בִזָּיוֹן, וְאַל תַּשְׁלֶט בָּנוּ יֵצֶר הָרָע. וְהַרְחִיקֵנוּ מֵאָדָם רָע וּמֵחָבֵר רָע. וְדַבְּקֵנוּ בְּיֵצֶר הַטּוֹב וּבְמַעֲשִׂים טוֹבִים, וְכוֹף אֶת יִצְרֵנוּ לְהִשְׁתַּעְבֶּד לָךְ. וּתְנֵנוּ הַיּוֹם וּבְכָל יוֹם לְחֵן וּלְחֶסֶד וּלְרַחֲמִים בְּעֵינֶיךָ, וּבְעֵינֵי כָל רוֹאֵינוּ...

Blessed are You, Hashem, our God, King of the universe, Who removes sleep from my eyes and slumber from my eyelids.

And may it be Your will, Hashem, our God, and the God of our forefathers, that You accustom us to [study] Your Torah and attach us to Your commandments. Do not bring us into the power of error, nor into the power of transgression and sin, nor into the power of challenge, nor into the power of scorn. Let not the Evil Inclination dominate us. Distance us from an evil person and an evil companion. Attach us to the Good Inclination and to good deeds and compel our [Evil] Inclination to be subservient to You. Grant us today and every day grace, kindness and mercy in Your eyes and in the eyes of all who see us …

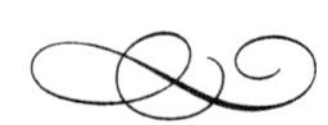

This prayer poses a problem. The Talmud states, "Everything is in the Hands of God except for the fear of God" (*Berachos* 33b). This means that God does not determine whether a person does good or evil, right or wrong. In matters of ethical and moral behavior, God does not intervene. If a person wishes to commit a sin, God will not stop him from doing so. Man has absolute freedom of choice in issues of right and wrong. How, then, can we ask God to compel our Evil Inclination to be subservient to Him? God will not interfere with the counsel of the Evil Inclination.

In his book on prayer, Rabbi Schwab addresses this problem. He points out that the prayer refers to *yitzreinu*, our impulse, and not to *yetzer hara*, the evil impulse. Therefore, Rabbi Schwab says, it may be referring to the *yetzer tov*, our Good Inclination.

Why would we need to ask that God compel the *yetzer tov* to obey Him? Because, Rabbi Schwab says, it is possible for the *yetzer tov* to go awry. He points out that the *yetzer tov* may wish to exceed halachah, and points to the incident of Nadab and Abihu, whose desire to come closer to God than they were permitted resulted in their death. Rabbi Schwab correctly points out that a zealot for Torah observance may sometimes humiliate a person who violates Torah, and this is forbidden by halachah.

Nonetheless, whatever the motivation may be, the *yetzer tov* would not urge a person to transgress halachah. Humiliating someone publicly is a sin, regardless of the motivation behind it. Such an act could not be the counsel of the *yetzer tov.*

We are left with the accepted interpretation that *yetzer*, in this prayer, indeed refers to the Evil Inclination. We are back with the question How can we ask God to compel the *yetzer hara* to obey him?

The Baal Shem Tov provides an explanation. God created Satan and his henchman, the *yetzer hara,* to entice people to commit sin. That is the assignment of the *yetzer hara*. Somewhere along the line, Satan usurped the power to delude people into thinking that wrong is actually right, and that a sin is a mitzvah. As in the example given by Rabbi Schwab, the *yetzer hara* might say, "That person is evil. He is a profligate sinner. It is a mitzvah to expose him and shame him publicly." Or the *yetzer hara* may say, "Giving *tzedakah* is the greatest of mitzvos. Therefore, it is a mitzvah to make money even by dishonest means in order to give *tzedakah.*" When the *yetzer hara* disguises a sin as a mitzvah, we are at a great disadvantage. We may wish to do only mitzvos, yet — under the delusion that a particular act is a mitzvah — we actually commit a sin.

But Satan was never authorized to delude people. His assignment was to inspire people to sin, but not to present sins as though they were mitzvos. Therefore, the Baal Shem Tov said, we ask God, "Compel the *yetzer hara* to obey You and to do the mission You wished him to do. If he tells us to sin, we can much more easily resist him. If he deludes us into thinking that a sin is a mitzvah, we are defenseless."

> *A Chassidic master wished to impress upon his followers that the yetzer hara can cloak itself with an attitude of piety, and*

delude one to think that the Torah wishes him to do an act which is in fact improper. One day the Rebbe ran into the beis midrash, and his followers looked on as he ran up and down the aisles, his arms outstretched as if he wished to grasp the object of his pursuit. Eventually the Rebbe fell against the bookcase containing many Torah writings. He then turned to his followers and said, "The yetzer hara was here, and I ran after it to seize it. But it ran and hid itself among the Torah writings in the bookcase. It is very difficult for me to extricate it from there."

The Rebbe's point was precisely that which we cited above. The *yetzer hara* has the cunning to hide itself in Torah writings and present a sin as a mitzvah. We must be forever on guard against such delusions.

The only method to avoid this pitfall of the *yetzer hara's* cunning is to accept the guidance of competent Torah authorities. Left to our own devices, we may be misled into thinking that wrong is right.

The teaching of this prayer, according to the Baal Shem Tov, is that we must always be on the alert for the wiles of the *yetzer hara*.

Blessings That Are Not in Disguise

. . . וְתִגְמְלֵנוּ חֲסָדִים טוֹבִים. בָּרוּךְ אַתָּה ה׳ גּוֹמֵל חֲסָדִים טוֹבִים לְעַמּוֹ יִשְׂרָאֵל.

And bestow beneficent kindnesses upon us. Blessed are You, Hashem, Who bestows beneficent kindnesses upon his people Israel.

The wording of this *berachah* appears redundant. "Beneficent kindnesses?" Is not all kindness beneficent? Is there such a thing as a kindness that is not beneficent?

The answer is that while all kindnesses are beneficent in their essence, that is not necessarily how they are viewed or experienced. As we have noted, the mother who has the doctor administer a painful injection to her infant to protect him from devastating and incurable illnesses is being kind to him. However, the infant has no way of understanding this. He feels the sharp needle thrust into his thigh as very painful, and he believes that the doctor is harming him. The infant cannot understand why his mother, who is always so loving and protective of him, would now collaborate with the villainous doctor to hurt him.

The gap between our mortal minds and the infinite wisdom of God is far greater than that between the infant and the mother. We cannot understand why God allows suffering to occur. We cannot understand why bad things happen to good people. It is only by the profound conviction of our faith that God is absolute benevolence that we can say, "Somehow, these terrible occurrences fit into the Divine plan for an ultimate good that is not achievable otherwise."

We therefore pray to God, "We know that everything You do is kindness. However, we are like an infant who cannot grasp that the pain is for a greater good. Medical science has not yet found a way to immunize against these diseases without pain. But You, God, are omnipotent. You can bring about the desired end in a painless way. We are such fragile mortals. When we experience suffering, our logical thinking may fail us. Instead of realizing that You never do anything injurious to us, we may err in our thinking and feel angry. We love You, God, and we do not wish to feel anger for even a fleeting moment. Therefore, we ask that You give us kindnesses that we are able to recognize as beneficent."

That is what is meant by "beneficent kindnesses."

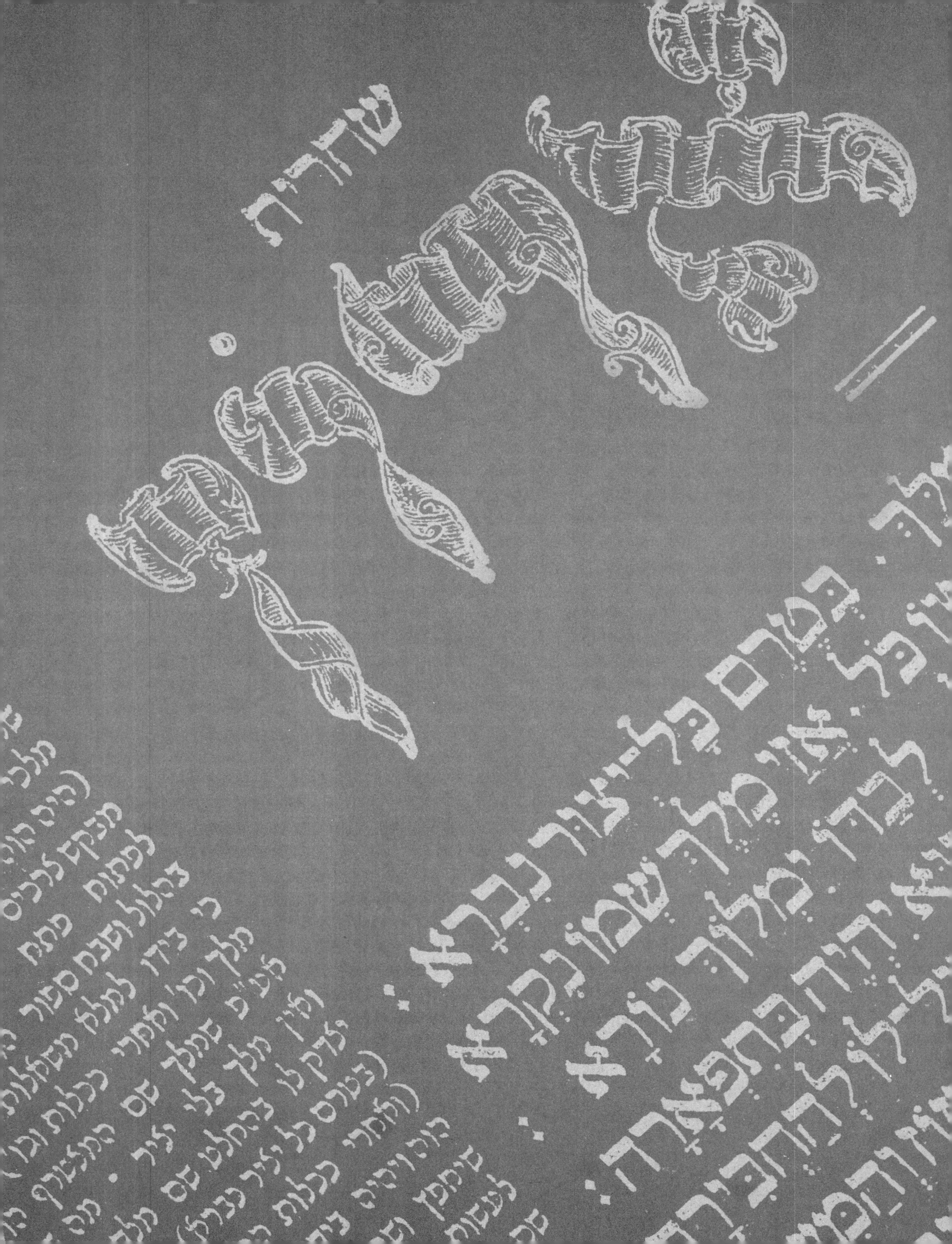
שחרית

Shacharis - The Morning Service

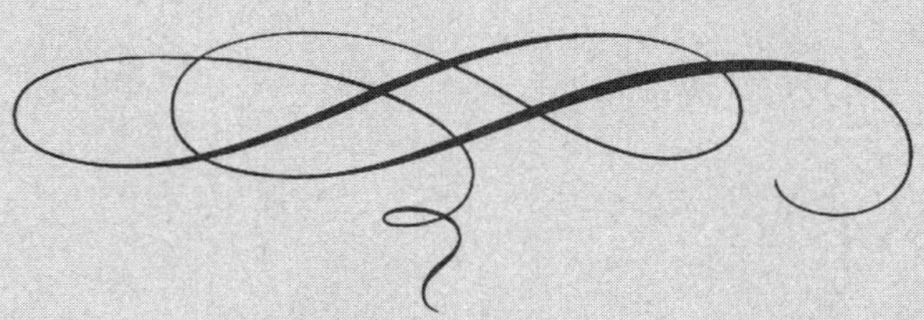

מַה טֹּבוּ אֹהָלֶיךָ יַעֲקֹב, מִשְׁכְּנֹתֶיךָ יִשְׂרָאֵל. וַאֲנִי בְּרֹב חַסְדְּךָ אָבוֹא בֵיתֶךָ, אֶשְׁתַּחֲוֶה אֶל הֵיכַל קָדְשְׁךָ בְּיִרְאָתֶךָ. יהוה אָהַבְתִּי מְעוֹן בֵּיתֶךָ, וּמְקוֹם מִשְׁכַּן כְּבוֹדֶךָ. וַאֲנִי אֶשְׁתַּחֲוֶה וְאֶכְרָעָה, אֶבְרְכָה לִפְנֵי יהוה עֹשִׂי. וַאֲנִי, תְפִלָּתִי לְךָ יהוה, עֵת רָצוֹן, אֱלֹהִים בְּרָב חַסְדֶּךָ, עֲנֵנִי בֶּאֱמֶת יִשְׁעֶךָ.

How goodly are your tents, O Jacob, your dwelling places, O Israel. As for me, through Your abundant kindness I will enter Your House; I will prostrate myself toward Your Holy Sanctuary in awe of You. O Hashem, I love the House where You dwell, and the place where Your glory resides. I shall prostrate myself and bow, I shall kneel before Hashem my Maker. As for me, may my prayer to You, Hashem, be at an opportune time; O God, in Your abundant kindness, answer me with the truth of Your salvation.

With this verse we begin the morning service. To understand why this verse was chosen to initiate our bonding with God, we must examine its context.

The Torah relates that the wicked sorcerer, Bilaam, was engaged by the king of Moab to cast an evil spell on Israel. Despite every effort, Bilaam's desire to curse was thwarted, and his words came out as blessings. Realizing that he was unable to pronounce a curse, Bilaam sought to invoke God's wrath on Israel by recalling the sin of the Golden Calf. However, when he saw that the Israelites had arranged their tents in a way that the openings of the tents did not face each other, he understood that the Israelites were mindful not to intrude on the privacy of others. He realized that this attitude of respect and consideration for others was so dear to God that even being reminded of the sin of the Golden Calf would not incite His anger (*Rashi, Numbers* 24:5).

This is indeed borne out by a Talmudic statement: "When Israel is united, God forgives even the sin of idolatry" (*Kallah* 8). Unity is brought about by mutual respect and consideration.

The importance of respect for others can be seen from a statement cited in *Reishis Chochmah* (*Yirah* 12). "When a person leaves this world, he is asked, 'Did you accept the sovereignty of God every morning and evening? Did you conduct yourself in a royal and pleasant manner toward your fellow man?'" Accepting the sovereignty of God and behaving with respect to other people are given equal status.

"Thus said God to Israel: 'My children, is there anything that I lack? What I ask of you is that you love one another and treat each other with respect" (*Tanna D'Vei Eliyahu Rabbah* 28).

The words of Bilaam indicate the overriding importance of respect of others. Inasmuch as this is equivalent to accepting the sovereignty of God, it is therefore an appropriate means for initiating our contact with God.

But human nature is such that love and respect of others may be difficult to sustain throughout the day. In business and social interactions we may find ourselves in disagreement with other people. This disagreement may sometimes lead to harsh words and resentments. When the day is over and we are ready to allow the *neshamah* to ascend to heaven, we recite the *Shema* to reaffirm our acceptance of Divine sovereignty. In order that this not be hampered by our failure to respect others and perhaps incurring their anger, we recite a brief prayer of forgiveness, הֲרֵינִי מוֹחֵל before the *Shema*. By sincerely forgiving others, we dedicate ourselves to the respect and consideration of others.

The first prayer of the day, therefore, paves the way for our bonding with God in the morning, and at night the last prayer of the day reinforces this bond.

אֲדוֹן עוֹלָם אֲשֶׁר מָלַךְ, בְּטֶרֶם כָּל־יְצִיר נִבְרָא. לְעֵת נַעֲשָׂה בְחֶפְצוֹ כֹּל, אֲזַי מֶלֶךְ שְׁמוֹ נִקְרָא. וְאַחֲרֵי כִּכְלוֹת הַכֹּל, לְבַדּוֹ יִמְלוֹךְ נוֹרָא. וְהוּא הָיָה וְהוּא הוֶֹה, וְהוּא יִהְיֶה בְּתִפְאָרָה. וְהוּא אֶחָד וְאֵין שֵׁנִי, לְהַמְשִׁיל לוֹ לְהַחְבִּירָה. בְּלִי רֵאשִׁית בְּלִי תַכְלִית, וְלוֹ הָעֹז וְהַמִּשְׂרָה. וְהוּא קֵלִי וְחַי גֹּאֲלִי, וְצוּר חֶבְלִי בְּעֵת צָרָה. וְהוּא נִסִּי וּמָנוֹס לִי, מְנָת כּוֹסִי בְּיוֹם אֶקְרָא. בְּיָדוֹ אַפְקִיד רוּחִי, בְּעֵת אִישַׁן וְאָעִירָה. וְעִם רוּחִי גְּוִיָּתִי, ה׳ לִי וְלֹא אִירָא.

Master of the universe, Who reigned before any form was created. At the time when His will brought all into being — then as "King" was His Name proclaimed. After all has ceased to be, He, the Awesome One, will reign alone. It is He Who was, He Who is, and He Who shall remain, in splendor. He is One — there is no second to compare to Him, to declare as His equal. Without beginning, without conclusion — His is the power and dominion. He is my God, my living Redeemer, Rock of my pain in time of distress. He is my banner, a refuge for me, the portion in my cup on the day I call. Into His hand I shall entrust my spirit when I go to sleep — and I shall awaken! With my spirit shall my body remain. Hashem is with me, I shall not fear.

Adon Olam

This beautiful prayer inaugurates the morning service. R' Yehudah HaChassid and Rav Sherira Gaon said that whoever says *Adon Olam* with proper *kavannah* is assured that his prayers will be accepted, and that no adversary will interfere with his prayer. His prayers on Rosh Hashanah and Yom Kippur will ascend without any obstacle, and even the *yetzer hara* may desist from him.

What is so special about this prayer that warrants such accolades?

The Vilna Gaon said that *Adon Olam* was chosen to initiate the morning service because this service was instituted by the Patriarch Abraham (*Berachos* 26b), and Abraham was the first person to refer to God as *"Adon"* (ibid. 7a). How can this be? Adam recognized God as the Creator of the world. Enosh, Methuselah and Noah were all great *tzaddikim*. Certainly they acknowledged God as Master of the world.

The Talmud is giving us insight into the concept of recognizing God as *"Adon."* The Patriarch is distinguished from earlier *tzaddikim* by his profound humility. When Abraham pleaded with God to spare the cities of Sodom and Gomorrah from destruction, he began his prayer with, "I desire to speak to my Master even though I am but dust and ashes" (*Genesis* 18:27).

The Patriarch Abraham is the first person cited in the Torah as praying. The second person noted for prayer is Moses, who repeatedly pleaded for Divine forgiveness when the Israelites sinned. The third person is King David, whose psalms comprise much of our liturgy. These three advocates of prayer are characterized by their profound humility. Abraham thought of himself as "dust and ashes." Moses said, "For what are we?" (*Exodus* 16:7), and David said, "I am but a worm and not a man" (*Psalms* 22:7). The Talmud states that humility is the key to prayer (*Sotah* 5a). [Incidentally, commentaries point out that the perfection of man lies in humility, and that the intended goal of the creation of Adam was achieved by the paragons of humility, **A**braham, **D**avid, and **M**oses, whose initials spell the Hebrew **ADM** (Adam).]

Inherent in the relationship of an *"adon"* (master) toward an *"eved"* (servant) is the fact that an *eved* has no will of his own. He sees his function as solely to serve his master, and the *eved* effaces himself totally before the *adon*. Whereas there were pious people before Abraham, none had achieved the utter self-effacement and humility of the Patriarch. The others indeed recognized God as the ruler of the universe, but not until Abraham was there a relationship between God and man as *Adon* to *eved,* Master to servant. Abraham was, therefore, the first person to relate to God as *Adon*.

We can now understand the promises of Rav Sherira Gaon for one who says *Adon Olam* with the proper *kavannah*. This requires a total self-effacement before God, surrendering one's will and having no desire other than to do the will of God.

Moses said, "I stood between God and you" (at Sinai, *Deuteronomy* 5:5). Chassidic writings interpret this as "it is the 'I,' the ego, that stands as a barrier between man and God." If we eliminate the ego barrier by being humble, we can then come close and bond with God in *tefillah*.

In the introductory prayer of R' Elimelech of Lizhensk, he says, "Elevate us from level to level that we may merit achieving the level of the

Patriarchs, Abraham, Isaac and Jacob." Is it not absurd to aspire to the spirituality of the Patriarchs?

While the greatness of the Patriarchs is unattainable, we can emulate them in achieving profound humility. Not long ago there walked among us a *tzaddik* and Torah giant, the Chafetz Chaim, whose self-effacement may have approached that of the Patriarchs. The Chafetz Chaim once arrived in a city where a throng of people who came to greet him so filled the train station that it was necessary for police to make a path for him. The Chafetz Chaim turned to R' Shmuel Greineman who was accompanying him and asked, "What happened here that there is such a crowd and a police escort?" R' Shmuel explained that the people had come to see him. In full sincerity, the Chafetz Chaim asked, "But why would they want to see me?" It simply did not occur to him that he was an outstanding personality.

The *neshamah* is pure and Divine and is free of ego. It is capable of achieving the passionate fervor of *kavannah*. It is the encumbrance of our body — along with its desires that are alien to the *neshamah* — that interferes with the *neshamah's* craving to bond with God. With self-effacement and humility we free the *neshamah* from this encumbrance.

> *A chassid complained to the Maggid of Mezeritch that he was unable to generate kavannah in prayer. The Maggid said, "If you wish to find hot coals, you must look among the ashes."*
>
> *If one thinks of himself as "dust and ashes," one can develop the fire of impassioned kavannah.*

If we truly dedicate ourselves to fulfilling the will of God and set aside our own will, we can identify with Abraham. We can then initiate the morning service with *Adon Olam* and bond with God.

In some congregations, *Adon Olam* is repeated at the end of the services. Why?

If you open a volume of the Talmud, you will note that the first page is numbered *beis* (two) rather than *aleph* (one). R' Levi Yitzchok of Berditchev said that this is to indicate that Torah is infinite, and infinity has no beginning. As much Torah as one may have learned, one has not yet even reached the *aleph*, i.e., one should think of oneself as not even having begun.

This may be the reason for repeating *Adon Olam* at the end of the service. After one has *davened* (prayed), one might feel, "I have fulfilled my prayer obligation." Repeating the *Adon Olam* with which one initiated the service is a way of reminding a person, "You have not exhausted your obligation of prayer. In fact, you've just barely begun."

The Teachings of the Akeidah

וַיָּבֹאוּ אֶל הַמָּקוֹם אֲשֶׁר אָמַר לוֹ הָאֱלֹקִים, וַיִּבֶן שָׁם אַבְרָהָם אֶת הַמִּזְבֵּחַ, וַיַּעֲרֹךְ אֶת הָעֵצִים, וַיַּעֲקֹד אֶת יִצְחָק בְּנוֹ, וַיָּשֶׂם אֹתוֹ עַל הַמִּזְבֵּחַ מִמַּעַל לָעֵצִים. וַיִּשְׁלַח אַבְרָהָם אֶת יָדוֹ, וַיִּקַּח אֶת הַמַּאֲכֶלֶת לִשְׁחֹט אֶת בְּנוֹ. וַיִּקְרָא אֵלָיו מַלְאַךְ ה׳ מִן הַשָּׁמַיִם, וַיֹּאמֶר, אַבְרָהָם, אַבְרָהָם, וַיֹּאמֶר, הִנֵּנִי. וַיֹּאמֶר, אַל תִּשְׁלַח יָדְךָ אֶל הַנַּעַר, וְאַל תַּעַשׂ לוֹ מְאוּמָה, כִּי עַתָּה יָדַעְתִּי כִּי יְרֵא אֱלֹקִים אַתָּה, וְלֹא חָשַׂכְתָּ אֶת בִּנְךָ אֶת יְחִידְךָ מִמֶּנִּי.

They arrived at the place which God indicated to him. Abraham built the altar there, and arranged the wood; he bound Isaac, his son, and he placed him on the altar atop the wood. Abraham stretched out his hand, and took the knife to slaughter his son. And an angel of Hashem called to him from heaven, and said, "Abraham! Abraham!" And he said, "Here I am." And he said, "Do not stretch out your hand against the lad nor do anything to him, for now I know that you are a God-fearing man, since you have not withheld your son, your only one, from Me."

As part of the morning service, we read the portion of the Torah that relates the supreme test of the Patriarch Abraham's loyalty to God. God commands Abraham to bring his beloved son, Isaac, as an offering. Abraham does not question the Divine command. An angel stays Abraham's hand just as he is about to sacrifice Isaac. Abraham's devotion to God is proven beyond any shadow of doubt.

We indeed invoke the merit of the Patriarch and the Divine promise to reward his children because of his virtue. But the episode of the A*keidah* has additional teachings. If *mesiras* *nefesh,* the willingness to surrender one's life or that of one's child, were the sole point of the *Akeidah,* there might be more reason to read the account of Hannah, the mother who during the time of the Chanukah miracle saw her seven sons executed before her eyes for refusal to deny their God.

There are at least two additional features of the *Akeidah* that are of note. One is the verse, "So Abraham woke up early in the morning" (to proceed to the site of the sacrifice, *Genesis* 22:3). This is often cited as a sign of the Patriarch's diligence to fulfill the Divine will. But there is something more striking. If Abraham awoke early in the morning, *he must have been asleep.* The knowledge that on the following day he was to sacrifice his beloved son did not disturb his sleep! This is the true indication of Abraham's total devotion to God's will, and of the fact that he indeed had made God's will his own. If it was God's will that he have a son, Abraham accepted that. If it was God's will that he surrender his son, he accepted that just as well. Whatever was God's will was accepted with equanimity.

A second point is a teaching of great practical value. The Midrash states that Abraham grew up in a pagan culture, and that he campaigned vociferously against paganism. In particular, Abraham denounced human sacrifice. He rebuked people for believing that God would desire that they sacrifice their children.

But now he received a Divine command to sacrifice his son. What would he say to all those people whom he had been chastising for decades? How would he be able to face the people whom he had told that God would never ask for human sacrifice and that they were in error? He would have to admit that he had been wrong all these years. Indeed, for all his life he had been wrong and they were right.

This was the greatness of the Patriarch. He was uncompromising on truth. He was ready to admit that he had been in error in rebuking people for their belief.

How many people are willing to admit that they were wrong at all? How many are willing to admit that everything they had embraced and believed was a mistake? When we see the enormous reluctance of people to admit that they may have been wrong, we can appreciate the quality of the Patriarch's character. This is something we would do well to remember every day.

History in Prayer

אַתָּה הוּא עַד שֶׁלֹּא נִבְרָא הָעוֹלָם, אַתָּה הוּא מִשֶּׁנִּבְרָא הָעוֹלָם, אַתָּה הוּא בָּעוֹלָם הַזֶּה, וְאַתָּה הוּא לָעוֹלָם הַבָּא. קַדֵּשׁ אֶת שִׁמְךָ עַל מַקְדִּישֵׁי שְׁמֶךָ, וְקַדֵּשׁ אֶת שִׁמְךָ בְּעוֹלָמֶךָ. וּבִישׁוּעָתְךָ תָּרִים וְתַגְבִּיהַּ קַרְנֵנוּ. בָּרוּךְ אַתָּה ה׳, מְקַדֵּשׁ אֶת שִׁמְךָ בָּרַבִּים.

It was You before the world was created, it is You since the world was created; it is You in This World, and it is You in the World to Come. Sanctify Your Name through those who sanctify Your name, and sanctify Your Name in Your universe. Through Your salvation may You exalt and raise our pride. Blessed are You, Hashem, Who sanctifies Your Name among the multitudes.

A careful study of prayer can be a lesson in Jewish history.

The above prayer, which is a tribute to the many faithful Jews who chose martyrdom rather than renounce their loyalty to God, appears to have been composed during one of the periods when the ruling power prohibited Jews to gather for prayer. The closing verse, "Who sanctifies Your Name among the multitudes," is a prayer that they may see the day when they will again be permitted to pray publicly.

Unfortunately, this is not an isolated incident in Jewish history. In the *Kedushah* of the Shabbos *Mussaf*, the *Shema* is recited. In the 5th century, Jews in Persia were forbidden to declare their belief in God by reciting the *Shema*, and government agents were placed in the synagogue to enforce this prohibition. When the agents, who followed the service, saw that the *Shema* had been deleted, they departed. The congregation then recited the *Shema* in the *Kedushah* when the government agents were no longer present. When the ban was lifted, the recitation of the *Shema* in the *Mussaf Kedushah* was retained as a remembrance of this episode.

We again find a similar incident on Purim. We read the *Megillah* (Book of Esther) at night, and recite the *berachah* of *shehecheyanu*, which we say the first time we perform a seasonal mitzvah. However, when we read the *Megillah* in the morning, we repeat the *shehecheyanu* blessing even though we have already read the *Megillah* the previous evening.

This is because the original time for reading the *Megillah* was on the day of Purim. When the ruling power forbade this, R' Yochanan ben Nuri clandestinely read the *Megillah* on the eve of Purim. The sages then instituted this as a regular practice, even after the ban was lifted. Inasmuch as the evening reading was the first reading of the day, the *shehecheyanu* was recited. However, since this *berachah* had originally accompanied the morning reading, that practice was not changed. This explains why the *shehecheyanu* is said twice for the same mitzvah.

Pesukei D'Zimrah

Baruch Sheamar

בָּרוּךְ שֶׁאָמַר וְהָיָה הָעוֹלָם, בָּרוּךְ הוּא. בָּרוּךְ עוֹשֶׂה בְרֵאשִׁית, בָּרוּךְ אוֹמֵר וְעוֹשֶׂה, בָּרוּךְ גּוֹזֵר וּמְקַיֵּם, בָּרוּךְ מְרַחֵם עַל הָאָרֶץ, בָּרוּךְ מְרַחֵם עַל הַבְּרִיּוֹת, בָּרוּךְ מְשַׁלֵּם שָׂכָר טוֹב לִירֵאָיו, בָּרוּךְ חַי לָעַד וְקַיָּם לָנֶצַח, בָּרוּךְ פּוֹדֶה וּמַצִּיל, בָּרוּךְ שְׁמוֹ. בָּרוּךְ אַתָּה ה׳ אֱלֹקֵינוּ מֶלֶךְ הָעוֹלָם, הָקֵל הָאָב הָרַחֲמָן הַמְּהֻלָּל בְּפֶה עַמּוֹ, מְשֻׁבָּח וּמְפֹאָר בִּלְשׁוֹן חֲסִידָיו וַעֲבָדָיו, וּבְשִׁירֵי דָוִד עַבְדֶּךָ. נְהַלֶּלְךָ ה׳ אֱלֹקֵינוּ, בִּשְׁבָחוֹת וּבִזְמִרוֹת. נְגַדֶּלְךָ וּנְשַׁבֵּחֲךָ וּנְפָאֶרְךָ וְנַזְכִּיר שִׁמְךָ וְנַמְלִיכְךָ, מַלְכֵּנוּ אֱלֹקֵינוּ. יָחִיד, חֵי הָעוֹלָמִים, מֶלֶךְ מְשֻׁבָּח וּמְפֹאָר עֲדֵי עַד שְׁמוֹ הַגָּדוֹל. בָּרוּךְ אַתָּה ה׳, מֶלֶךְ מְהֻלָּל בַּתִּשְׁבָּחוֹת.

Blessed is He Who spoke, and the world came into being — blessed is He. Blessed is He Who maintains Creation; blessed is He Who speaks and does; blessed is He Who decrees and fulfills; blessed is He Who has mercy on the earth; blessed is He Who has mercy on the creatures; blessed is He Who gives goodly reward to those who fear Him; blessed is He Who lives forever and endures to eternity; blessed is He Who redeems and rescues — blessed is His Name! Blessed are You, Hashem, our God, King of the universe, the God, the merciful Father, Who is lauded by the mouth of his people, praised and glorified by the tongue of His devout ones and His servants and through the psalms of David Your servant. We shall laud You, Hashem, our God, with praises and songs. We shall exalt You, praise You, glorify You, mention Your Name and proclaim Your reign, our King, our God. O Unique One, Life-giver of the worlds, King Whose great Name is eternally praised and glorified. Blessed are You, Hashem, the King Who is lauded with praises.

This prayer and *Yishtabach* (v. infra) comprise the opening and closing blessings which encompass the *Pesukei D'Zimrah,* the Verses of Praise.

We begin this segment of prayer by referring to God as the Creator of the world. However, at the revelation at Sinai, God referred to Himself as "I am your God, Who took you out of the enslavement of Egypt" rather than "Who created the universe." Why do we refer to God in *tefillah* as the Creator, whereas in giving the Torah He referred to Himself as the One Who delivered us from bondage?

In the Haggadah *From Bondage to Freedom,* I pointed out that Passover is much more than an Independence Day celebration. One can be as much a slave to the tyranny of one's animal body as to a cruel despot. Passover is a celebration of spiritual freedom, and the Haggadah is its text.

The Ten Commandments are instructions governing our behavior. These are indeed restrictive, restraining us from gratifying some of our impulses and drives. To anyone who asks why we must adhere to these commandments, God says, "I am the One Who pulled you out of the mire of slavery to give you freedom. I know what it is to be enslaved and I know what it is to be free. Without the dictates of Torah you will be as enslaved as you were by Pharaoh, but you will have the delusion that you are free. Observe My commandments, and you will be truly free."

Tefillah is not a set of instructions, but a way in which we bond with God. One might ask, "What is the purpose of bonding with God?" *Baruch She'amar* provides the answer.

Once the question of "what is the purpose" of anything in life is raised, the issue of ultimacy comes into play. There can be a multitude of intermediate purposes. The purpose of the ignition key is to start the automobile engine, whose purpose is to move the vehicle, whose purpose is to get people to a destination, in order that they may earn a livelihood, so that the family may function comfortably. But what is the function of the family? What is the purpose of human existence? Unless we are satisfied with intermediate purposes and avoid thinking about ultimacy, the question as to what is the purpose of existence demands an answer.

> *Two vagrants were brought before the judge. "What were you doing when the officer arrested you?" the judge asked one of*

them. "Nothing," the man responded. The judge turned to the second vagrant. "And what were you doing when you were arrested?" he asked. This man pointed to the other vagrant and said, "I was helping him."

It is readily apparent that if one is helping someone who is doing nothing, one is doing nothing.

We cannot begin to address the purpose of bonding with God unless we believe that the world has a purpose. A world that was not created but came into being as the result of a freak accident does not have a purpose. In order to think of *tefillah* as having the purpose of enabling us to bond with God, we must posit that the world was purposefully created. This is why *Baruch She'amar* is the opening blessing. "Blessed is He Who spoke and the world came into being."

We might ask, "What is the point of 'He Who spoke and the world came into being'? Why not just 'Blessed is the Creator of the world'?"

The words of our prayers were very carefully chosen.

The Chafetz Chaim dedicated his life to obliterating *lashon hara* (deragatory speech). He emphasized the far-reaching effects of *lashon hara* by citing the Midrash, "*Lashon hara* kills three people: the one who speaks, the one who listens, and the one about whom it is spoken" (*Devarim Rabbah* 8:10).

Some people minimize the gravity of *lashon hara*. There is a popular aphorism, "Sticks and stones may break my bones but words will never harm me." This is an outright mistake. Words are hurtful and can harm, and as the Midrash says, you can kill someone by speaking badly about him. The prophet says, "Their tongue is a sharp arrow" (*Jeremiah* 9:7). Words even pierce an armor capable of repelling an arrow.

The sages wanted to stress the power of the spoken word. The entire universe came into being by way of a spoken word. Just as a spoken word can create a world out of nothingness, it is also capable of destroying a world into nothingness.

"Blessed is He Who speaks and does. Blessed is He Who decrees and fulfills." Is this not redundant?

The Rebbe of Rimnitz was imprisoned on a false charge of treason. All his possessions were taken from him, and he had neither tallis nor tefillin. He was grateful that he was allowed to keep his yarmulka.

When he said the Baruch She'amar, he reflected on this apparent redundancy. Furthermore, why is it a praise of God that He keeps His word?

The Rebbe then concluded that the word "mekayeim" can also mean "he supports" as well as "he fulfills." This is the meaning that is intended. "God decrees and supports." I.e., when Divine justice metes out a harsh decree, God gives the recipient the strength to withstand the stress of the decree. The Rebbe then applied this to his own circumstances. He was reassured that God would give him the strength to survive the ordeal he was experiencing.

"Blessed is He Who gives goodly reward to those who revere Him." What is meant by "goodly reward?" Are there rewards that are not good?

There certainly are. A recent study revealed that a number of people who were suddenly enriched by winning a huge amount of money in the lottery experienced tragic consequences as a result of what they had thought was a bonanza.

Human intelligence is limited. We cannot be certain that what we think is good is in fact good. God's rewards are always good.

"Blessed are You, God, King Who is lauded with praises." This concludes the introductory *berachah* for the Verses of Praise.

One might ask: Does God really wish to hear all these praises? A human being with an insatiable ego may wish to be lauded, but this is certainly not true of God.

The answer is that, of course, God has no need for praise, but *we* have a need to praise God.

The Divine commandments were given to us for *our* betterment. We have a mission for which we were brought into the world, and the only way we can fulfill that mission is by observing the Divine commandments. Even if we understand this intellectually, there is an inordinate tendency to gratify our own desires and fulfill our own will rather than the will of God. The Talmud sums this up by saying, "Make God's will your will, and negate your will before His" (*Ethics of the Fathers* 2:4).

The purpose of praising God is to impress *us* with His sovereignty and majesty. We can overcome the resistance to surrendering our own will only if we realize that we are totally and utterly dependent upon God. We must realize that with the exception of freedom of choice regarding morals and ethics, everything is under God's control.

We can be obstinate in believing that we control our own destiny.

Listen to the words of Moses. "You should know today that it is not your children who did not know and who did not see the chastisement of God, His greatness, His strong hand and His outstretched arm; His wonders and His deeds that He performed in the midst of Egypt, to its horses and riders, over whom He swept the waters of the Sea of Reeds when they pursued you ... and what He did for you in the wilderness ... and what He did to Dathan and Abiram ... when the earth opened its mouth wide and swallowed them ... Rather, *it is your own eyes that saw all the great work that God did*" (*Deuteronomy* 11:2-7)

"It was not with our forefathers that God sealed this covenant, but with us — we who are here, all of us alive today. God spoke to you face to face on the mountain, from amid the fire" (ibid. 5:3-4).

How well Moses understood human psychology! "Take care lest you forget your God, by not observing His commandments ... Lest you eat and be satisfied, and you build houses and settle, and your cattle and sheep and goats increase, and you increase silver and gold for yourselves, and everything that you have will increase, *and your heart will become haughty and you will forget God*" (ibid. 8:11-14).

The generation of the Exodus, which witnessed the wondrous plagues in Egypt, the miraculous splitting of the Sea, the Revelation at Sinai, the Clouds of Glory that encircled the Israelites, the daily manna and the Well of Miriam that sustained them during forty years of sojourn in the desert, *this* generation had to be warned that when they inherit the Promised Land with all its riches, they should not say, "My strength and the might of my hand made me all this wealth" (ibid. 8:17). "It was not God Who gave this to me. It was by my own cunning and power that I achieved success."

One of the strongest human drives is for independence. This can be seen in young children, even tiny tots who wish to do things for themselves. The resistance to acknowledge one's dependency can be so fierce that the mind renders one oblivious to any evidence of dependence. We can deny something that is right before our eyes.

If the generation that were eyewitnesses to God's control of the world and who were the beneficiaries of His manifest might were capable of denying their dependence on God, how much greater is our vulnerability to be deluded and think of ourselves as independent and self-sufficient. Our mastery in harnessing many of the forces of nature, developing nuclear power, transplanting organs, reaching the moon and planets — and achieving the other marvelous advances of science and technology — has intensified our feelings of power, control and self-sufficiency. We are more than ever in need of constant reminders that we are totally dependent on God.

The Midrash cites the verse, "Let every *neshamah* (soul) praise God" (*Psalms* 150:6), and says that we can also read this verse as "Let us praise God for every *neshimah* (breath)." We should realize that we are dependent on God for every breath we take.

Moses warned the Israelites that if they forget their dependence on God, they will act in ways that will be self-destructive. We must recognize our vulnerability to this pitfall. By reciting the praises of God and listening to what we are saying, we can be reminded of our total dependence on Him and take great caution not to transgress His will.

God does not need to be reminded of His Majesty and Infinite Might. We do.

The Sin of Wastefulness

מִזְמוֹר לְתוֹדָה, הָרִיעוּ לַה׳ כָּל הָאָרֶץ. עִבְדוּ אֶת ה׳ בְּשִׂמְחָה, בֹּאוּ לְפָנָיו בִּרְנָנָה. דְּעוּ כִּי ה׳ הוּא אֱלֹקִים, הוּא עָשָׂנוּ, וְלוֹ אֲנַחְנוּ, עַמּוֹ וְצֹאן מַרְעִיתוֹ. בֹּאוּ שְׁעָרָיו בְּתוֹדָה, חֲצֵרֹתָיו בִּתְהִלָּה, הוֹדוּ לוֹ, בָּרְכוּ שְׁמוֹ. כִּי טוֹב ה׳, לְעוֹלָם חַסְדּוֹ, וְעַד דֹּר וָדֹר אֱמוּנָתוֹ.

A psalm of thanksgiving, call out to Hashem, everyone on earth. Serve Hashem with gladness, come before Him with joyous song. Know that Hashem, He is God, it is He Who made us and we are His, His people and the sheep of His pasture. Enter His gates with thanksgiving, His courts with praise, give thanks to Him, bless His Name. For Hashem is good, His kindness endures forever, and from generation to generation is His faithfulness.

We grew up hearing our mothers' refrain, "It's a sin to throw out good food."

Our mothers were right. It *is* a sin to throw out good food. Jewish folklore holds that this is one reason for the fact that many Jewish mothers are overweight. Due to their inability to commit a sin by throwing out good food, they eat it, all of it.

Where do we find the origin of the assertion that it is sinful to discard good food? In the above prayer.

Chapter 100 of *Psalms* is a prayer of gratitude. In the days of the Temple, when a person recovered from a serious illness or emerged safely from a precarious situation, he was required to bring a *korban todah,* thanksgiving offering. In absence of the Temple, we recite the psalm of gratitude during our weekday prayers.

Expressing gratitude is a given in Judaism. The very first words upon awakening in the morning are *Modeh Ani* (I thank

You). In the repetition of the *Amidah*, the congregation must be silent and listen to the reader. However, when he reaches the prayer of *Modim* (gratitude), the congregation must participate. Expressing thanks by proxy is not acceptable. As we have noted, Moses sharply rebuked the Israelites for their failure to be grateful.

As important as this prayer is, it is omitted on the day before Yom Kippur, the day before Passover and on the intermediate days of Passover. Why? Because a thanksgiving offering may be eaten only on the day it is brought and the ensuing night. The thanksgiving offering included ten loaves of bread. On the day before Yom Kippur, the consumption of this offering would be curtailed. On the day before Passover, we would be precluded from eating it beyond the time permissible to eat leavened bread. The uneaten portion would have to be discarded. It was, therefore, forbidden to bring a *korban todah* on a day when it was likely that some of it would go to waste. As our mothers said, "It is a sin to throw out good food."

This principle has broader applications. Whereas miserliness is despicable, wastefulness is equally condemned, and this is not limited to food. I am irritated when I see excessive floral arrangements at a wedding. Of course there may be a judicious display of flowers to brighten the wedding hall and add color to the festive occasion. But when tens of thousands of dollars are squandered on flowers that will soon end up in the trash bin, that is unconscionable. There are families who cannot afford adequate food, and there are educational institutions that are months in arrears in paying their teachers their rather meager salaries. A much better gift to the young couple would be the merits of giving the money to the needy.

When we recite the prayer of gratitude, we should be aware that it is omitted on those days when a thanksgiving offering was not brought in the Temple. We should be mindful of our mothers' admonition that it is a sin to be wasteful.

רַבּוֹת מַחֲשָׁבוֹת בְּלֶב אִישׁ, וַעֲצַת ה׳ הִיא תָקוּם. עֲצַת ה׳ לְעוֹלָם
תַּעֲמֹד, מַחְשְׁבוֹת לִבּוֹ לְדֹר וָדֹר.

Many designs are in man's heart, but the counsel of Hashem — only it will prevail. The counsel of Hashem will endure forever, the designs of His heart throughout the generations.

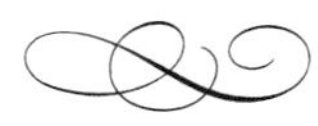

How foolish it is for a person to think that he can thwart God's will!

R' Simchah Zissel cites a commentary on the Scriptural episode of Joseph's brothers selling him into slavery. God said, "You are trying to thwart My plan (to make Joseph into a monarch as was prophesied in his dreams) by selling him into slavery. I will not disrupt your actions, because that would be interfering with your free will. However, you will see that the very stratagem you are using to thwart My plan will result in its realization." Indeed, it was Joseph's sale into slavery that ultimately propelled him into becoming viceroy of Egypt (*Genesis* 39-41). Whatever God wishes will come to be.

R' Simchah Zissel cites the verse, "God *shall* rejoice in His works" (*Psalms* 28:9). He points out that it does not say God *rejoices* in His works, but s*hall rejoice.* At the moment, the realization of God's design may be delayed by acts of man's free will, but ultimately, He will rejoice in His works, because they will come to be.

R' Simchah Zissel expands upon this theme. The Joseph epic is evidence of how God may transform acts that are opposed to His will into becoming the very vehicles of realizing His will. Inasmuch as man was created "in the image of God," man, too, has this ability. But in which capacity? It cannot be where if someone sustains a loss of money, that loss is not reversed when he gains money. If he had not had the loss, he would have even more after the gain.

The only place where a negative can be transformed into a positive is in the spiritual realm. If a person who has sinned develops a profound love for God, and consequently sincerely regrets that he disobeyed God, this intense *teshuvah* will transform his sin into merits (*Yoma* 86b).

> *R' Levi Yitzchok of Berditchev once met a sinner and said to him, "How I envy you for your reward in Paradise."*
>
> *"Surely you jest, Rabbi," the man said.*
>
> *"No, no," R' Levi Yitzchok said. "I do not jest at all. You have a holy neshamah which longs for God. Unfortunately, you have fallen victim to the seduction of the yetzer hara. But one day your neshamah will prevail, and you will feel an intense love for God. You will then do profound and sincere teshuvah out of your love for God. All your sins will then be converted into merits. You will have far more merits than I can ever accumulate."*

Just as God's intention will prevail, it is also possible for the *neshamah* to prevail. When that occurs, the negatives will be transformed into positives.

The ancient alchemists spent their lifetime trying to transform lead into gold. Who would be so foolish as to not utilize a method of converting one's sins into merits? Of course, inasmuch as our days are numbered, we must take advantage of this unique Divine ability while we can.

As we recite the verse, "... but the counsel of God — only it will prevail," we should think of R' Simchah Zissel's comments and be inspired to achieve a love of God that will enable us to transform spiritual base metals into spiritual gold.

סוֹמֵךְ ה׳ לְכָל הַנֹּפְלִים, וְזוֹקֵף לְכָל הַכְּפוּפִים.

Hashem supports all the fallen ones and straightens all the bent.

The Talmud states that whoever recites Psalm 145 (*Ashrei*) three times each day is assured of a portion in the Eternal World (*Berachos* 4b). Of course, the Talmud is referring to profoundly meditating on the contents of the psalm rather than just reading it. Even so, what is it that gives this particular psalm such great importance?

The Talmud gives two reasons for the significance of this psalm. (1) It contains the verse, "You open Your hand and satisfy the desire of every living thing," and (2) the verses are in the order of the *aleph-beis*.

The first reason is clearly valid. The awareness that God provides for all man's needs is fundamental. "Blessed is the person who trusts in God, for God will be his security" (*Jeremiah* 17:7). This psalm also expresses the concept of Divine benevolence. "God is good to all; His mercies are on all His works." A person who reinforces his trust in God three times daily is indeed deserving of a portion in the Eternal World.

However, what is so special about the verses being in alphabetical order? Granted, this may facilitate memorizing the psalm, but reciting verses that are arranged alphabetically hardly seems sufficient reason to warrant so great a reward. The alphabetical order seems to contribute little to one's spirituality.

The alphabetical arrangement of the psalm gives rise to a nuance of which the Talmud takes note. There is no verse for the letter *nun*. The Psalmist proceeds from the letter *mem* to the letter *samech*. The Talmud explains that this is because the letter *nun* may represent the word *nophel*, to fall, and David wished to avoid a reference to the ominous verse "If Israel falls, it may not arise again" (*Amos* 5:2).

However, in the verse that follows beginning with *samech*, David says, "God supports all *the fallen* and sets upright those who are bent." David does introduce the *nun* and the term *nophel*, but only after he states that God supports the fallen. A fall is disastrous only when there is no support. Once one is assured of Divine support, a fall is no longer ominous.

In Torah writings there is a concept of "descent in the interest of ascent." It is possible that a fall may be constructive, a necessary prelude to growth. The prophet says, "Do not rejoice over me, my enemy, for after I have fallen I have arisen" (*Micah* 7:8). The Midrash comments, "Had I not fallen I would not have arisen." Some spiritual heights may not be attainable without a regression. The Talmud says that the spiritual level attained by a person who has erred and done *teshuvah* may surpass that of someone who has always been a perfect *tzaddik* (*Berachos* 34b). And again, "A person may not have a full grasp of a halachah until he makes an error in judgment" (*Gittin* 43a). While one wishes to avoid a fall, the awareness that not only is there a "safety net" but that a fall may at times be essential in order to advance can eliminate much anxiety.

This extremely important concept, that God supports those who fall and that a regression may be a necessary precursor to spiritual growth, would not have been conveyed had the psalm not been arranged in alphabetical order. It is only the latter that calls our attention to the obvious omission of the *nun* and its restoration after the *samech*.

If we assert our belief three times a day that God will provide for all our needs and reinforce our faith that even adversity may be for our spiritual betterment, we are indeed deserving of Divine reward.

אֲהַלְלָה ה׳ בְּחַיָּי, אֲזַמְּרָה לֵאלֹקַי בְּעוֹדִי.

I will praise God when I live, I will sing to my God when I exist.

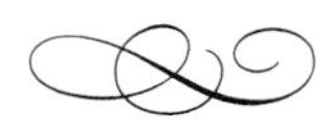

The theme of self-esteem is one that is woven into every book that I have written. In *Angels Do Not Leave Footprints* I elaborated on the pivotal role of self-esteem in having a healthy life style. Feelings of unworthiness can result in a person's failure to enjoy life and the inability to do mitzvos properly. The *yetzer hara* may discourage a person from the pursuit of spirituality. "You are not capable of being spiritual," the *yetzer hara* may say. "You are too much of a sinner to pray. It would be chutzpah for you to approach God."

My grandfather explained the above verse as meaning that we are always capable of praying, and that God hears our prayers regardless of what level of spirituality we have or lack. "When I live" refers to when we live an active and productive life. But there may be times when we are not active and productive, and when we feel that we merely exist. Even then, the Psalmist says, We are not absolved of the obligation to pray. "I will praise God when I live, and I will sing to my God even when I feel I am no more than existing."

We are prone to accepting secular values. We may think that people of wealth or those in powerful positions are indeed important, but that our humble station in life makes us insignificant. The Psalmist points out that these qualities are ephemeral at best. "Do not rely on nobles ... When his spirit departs he returns to the earth." Death is a great equalizer, and we should not determine a person's value by the brief time he spends on earth. Before God, every person is important, and He cares for all. "He gives bread to the hungry, releases the bound, gives sight to the blind, straightens the bent."

The Talmud relates that R' Yochanan greeted every person he met, without discrimination regarding the person's status. "If God considers him worthy of existence, I must accord him proper respect" (*Kiddushin* 33a). At moments of self-doubt and when we may be gripped by self-abasement, we should apply this attitude toward ourselves. "Even if I only exist, I must praise God."

> *A psychiatrist told me that he had a patient who was in a deep depression. His negative attitude was all pervasive. "I am no good to my family. I fail at everything I do. There is no purpose in my living. I am of no use to anyone," he said.*
>
> *"Of course you can be of use," the psychiatrist quipped. "You can be the tenth person for a minyan."*

The Talmud says that when ten Jews gather together, the Divine presence joins them. Nine *tzaddikim* do not constitute a *minyan*, but ten simple people do.

"I will sing to my God when I exist." My very existence gives me value.

Avoiding Dejection

הָרוֹפֵא לִשְׁבוּרֵי לֵב, וּמְחַבֵּשׁ לְעַצְּבוֹתָם.

He is the Healer of the brokenhearted, and the One Who binds up their sorrows.

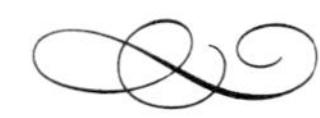

Close analysis of our prayers can provide important psychological insights.

One of the commentaries notes that David says, "The proper offering to God is a broken spirit; a broken and contrite heart, O God, You will not reject" (*Psalms* 51:19). This seems to indicate that having a "broken heart" is salutary. Why, then, would God heal the brokenhearted and deprive a person of a constructive emotion?

Herein lies an important distinction. There may be only a subtle, hairsbreadth difference between "brokenheartedness" and "sadness," but this difference is crucial.

Our ethical writings stress the virtue of humility. Regardless of how far a person has advanced spiritually, one should always feel that he has not done enough and that there is so much more that one must do.

One of the Baal Shem Tov's disciples complained that he was frustrated in his efforts to develop a close relationship with God. "Many times I have felt that I am coming closer to God, but then I suddenly find myself more distant than ever."

The Baal Shem Tov said, "That is exactly the way things should be."

"Imagine this scene," the Baal Shem Tov said. "A father has an infant son whom he wishes to teach to walk. The child is able to stand upright, but is fearful of taking the first step lest he fall. The father places himself close to the child and

extends his hands to just inches from the child, beckoning him to come closer. Seeing his father's hands near enough to catch him if he were to fall, the child has the courage to take the first step. The father then moves back a bit, again beckoning to the child. Having taken a step without falling and seeing the father still close enough, the child ventures a second step. The father then retreats a bit further, and this pattern repeats itself, with the child continuing to walk.

"If you put yourself in the child's mind, he must be thinking, 'What is going on here? The more effort I make to reach my father, the further away he goes!'

"What the child cannot understand is that he and the father have different goals. The child's desire is to reach the father, but the father's desire is to teach the child how to ambulate independently. The moment the father allows the child to reach him, the lesson is over and the progress comes to a halt.

"Your desire is to reach God," the Baal Shem Tov said. "God's desire is to teach you to grow spiritually, and that can occur only as long as you search for him. If He were to allow you to reach Him, your spiritual growth would come to a halt."

The Baal Shem Tov's parable helps us understand the verse, "The heart of those who seek God rejoices" (ibid. 105:3). It is the search for God that is important, and one should rejoice in the search.

The meritorious trait of "brokenheartedness" to which the Psalmist refers is the feeling described by the Baal Shem Tov's disciple. It is the feeling that the goal is constantly receding. This could give rise to a feeling of frustration and futility, resulting in resigning oneself to failure to achieve progress. The Baal Shem Tov's teaching is that while there may be a feeling of frustration, we should realize that this is in fact a stimulus to further progress. The awareness that we are growing spiritually and that we can advance ourselves should encourage us to greater effort. Indeed, we should "rejoice in the search for God."

Inasmuch as there is danger that the ever receding goal of reaching God may result in a feeling of futility and resignation, God protects us from this. He does not remove the "brokenheartedness" which is the stimulus for growth, but He prevents it from developing into destructive dejection.

This is the teaching of the verse cited above. "God heals the brokenhearted." How? "By soothing their sadness," i.e., by encouraging them to continue to seek to reach Him. With the sadness of despair removed, the brokenheartedness can lead to spiritual growth.

So precious a lesson in psychology in just a few words!

Testimony of Nature

הַלְלוּקָהּ, הַלְלוּ אֶת ה׳ מִן הַשָּׁמַיִם, הַלְלוּהוּ בַּמְּרוֹמִים. הַלְלוּהוּ כָל מַלְאָכָיו, הַלְלוּהוּ כָּל צְבָאָיו. הַלְלוּהוּ שֶׁמֶשׁ וְיָרֵחַ, הַלְלוּהוּ כָּל כּוֹכְבֵי אוֹר. הַלְלוּהוּ שְׁמֵי הַשָּׁמָיִם, וְהַמַּיִם אֲשֶׁר מֵעַל הַשָּׁמָיִם. יְהַלְלוּ אֶת שֵׁם ה׳, כִּי הוּא צִוָּה וְנִבְרָאוּ. וַיַּעֲמִידֵם לָעַד לְעוֹלָם, חָק נָתַן וְלֹא יַעֲבוֹר. הַלְלוּ אֶת ה׳ מִן הָאָרֶץ, תַּנִּינִים וְכָל תְּהֹמוֹת. אֵשׁ וּבָרָד, שֶׁלֶג וְקִיטוֹר, רוּחַ סְעָרָה עֹשָׂה דְבָרוֹ. הֶהָרִים וְכָל גְּבָעוֹת, עֵץ פְּרִי וְכָל אֲרָזִים. הַחַיָּה וְכָל בְּהֵמָה, רֶמֶשׂ וְצִפּוֹר כָּנָף. מַלְכֵי אֶרֶץ וְכָל לְאֻמִּים, שָׂרִים וְכָל שֹׁפְטֵי אָרֶץ. בַּחוּרִים וְגַם בְּתוּלוֹת, זְקֵנִים עִם נְעָרִים. יְהַלְלוּ אֶת שֵׁם ה׳, כִּי נִשְׂגָּב שְׁמוֹ לְבַדּוֹ, הוֹדוֹ עַל אֶרֶץ וְשָׁמָיִם. וַיָּרֶם קֶרֶן לְעַמּוֹ, תְּהִלָּה לְכָל חֲסִידָיו, לִבְנֵי יִשְׂרָאֵל עַם קְרֹבוֹ, הַלְלוּקָהּ.

Halleluyah! Praise Hashem from the heavens; praise Him in the heights. Praise Him, all His angels; praise Him, all His legions. Praise Him, sun and moon; praise Him, all bright stars. Praise Him, the most exalted of the heavens and the waters that are above the heavens. Let them praise the Name of Hashem, for He commanded and they were created. And He established them forever and ever, He issued a decree that will not change. Praise Hashem from the earth, sea giants and all watery depths. Fire and hail, snow and vapor, stormy wind fulfilling His word. Mountains and all hills, fruitful trees and all cedars. Beasts and all cattle, crawling things and winged fowl. Kings of the earth and all governments, princes and all judges on earth. Young men and also maidens, old men together with youths. Let them praise the Name of Hashem, for His Name alone will have been exalted; His glory is above earth and heaven. And He will have exalted the pride of His people, causing praise for all His devout ones, for the Children of Israel, His intimate people. Halleluyah!

The more one is aware of everything in nature, from super galaxies to subatomic particles, the greater is one's sense of the majesty of God. It is nothing but folly to think that the perfection of the universe, macrocosm and microcosm, occurred by chance.

הַשָּׁמַיִם מְסַפְּרִים כְּבוֹד קֵל וּמַעֲשֵׂה יָדָיו מַגִּיד הָרָקִיעַ

"The heavens declare the glory of God, and the expanse of the sky tells of His handiwork" (Psalms 19:2*).*

We often hear the question: Why did God reveal Himself to the prophets of earlier days. Why does He not reveal Himself to us now? Perhaps it is because in ancient times there were no powerful telescopes and microscopes. People's knowledge of nature was so rudimentary that they could naively assume that the world was not created by a Supreme Intelligence. Our knowledge of the intricacy, complexity, and perfection of nature is the greatest of all revelations. If one only keeps an open mind, one will come to the obvious conclusion stated by the Psalmist in the above verse.

Psalm 104 is an enchanting ode to nature. After describing the beauty of nature, the Psalmist declares, "May the glory of God endure forever!" (ibid. 104:31). Psalm 148 develops this theme.

In *Duties of the Heart*, Rabbeinu Bachya goes to great lengths in descrbing how one can come to a belief in God and admiration of God through observation of the marvels of nature (*Shaar HaBechinah*). This theme is repeatedly emphasized by many Torah commentaries and ethicists. It is of interest that Rabbeinu Bachya cites six steps of appreciation of God through nature as a prerequisite to an understanding of the Torah (ibid. Ch. 4). This enables us to understand the rather abrupt transition in this chapter from the appreciation of nature to praise of the Torah.

There is a beautiful ballad, *Perek Shirah* (The Chapter of Song). Its authorship is unknown, but it is evidently of the pre-Talmudic era. *Perek Shirah* can be found in the more comprehensive *siddurim*, and is introduced as follows:

"Whoever recites *Perek Shirah* in this world will merit success in the study of Torah and will retain it. He will be free of the *yetzer hara* and will be spared the harsh judgment of Gehinnom. He will merit the days of Mashiach and eternal life."

The Midrash states that when King David completed composing Psalms, his spirits were elevated and he said, "Master of the Universe! Is there any other being You created in Your world that sings more songs and praises than me?" At that point a frog appeared and said, "David! Do not be so vain. I sing more and better praises to God than you do."

The message is clear: Even the lowly frog is a superb testimony to the majesty of God. We need only study the intricate physiology of the frog, the complexity of each cell and the incredible way all its systems work in unison to see the marvelous work of God.

Of course, the human body is so much more intricate. We are hardly aware that each time we make even the lightest movement many thousands of messages are transmitted to multiple centers in the brain. Indeed, if all the super computers in the world were connected, the combined system would be like a Tinkertoy in comparison to the human brain.

A physician said to me, "I was peering through the microscope at a fertilized ovum, and I realized that from this point on nothing would be added to this minute single cell other than water, oxygen, and certain elements. Out of these, this tiny cell would produce a human being! At that point I realized that there was a God." How true the Scriptural statement, "I see God from my flesh" (*Job* 19:26).

All that is required to arrive at an awareness of God through nature is evident from the following anecdote.

> *A businessman whose life was in shambles due to his drinking was admitted to our facility for treatment. He refused to attend a meeting of Alcoholics Anonymous because, "They talk too much about God." He said, "I'm an atheist. That program is not for me." There was no point in coercing him, and he retired to his room.*
>
> *About halfway through the meeting he entered. "I thought you did not want to be involved with this program because it focused too much on God," I said.*
>
> *"Well," he said, "it's like this. I was sitting in my room, looking out the window, and I saw all the beautiful, tall trees. I began thinking, 'Who takes care of those trees to keep them so strong and straight? Well, whoever it is, he is doing a much better job on the trees than I am doing on myself. My life is a mess. Maybe if I let him take care of my life, I could be like those trees.' So I came down."*

From the rich rewards promised those who study Perek Shirah, we can see the great value our sages accorded the appreciation of God through nature.

R' Yaakov Emden states that the various verses assigned to different creations are the particular praises which people should sing to God when observing these phenomena. R' Yaakov states that there are also esoteric, kabbalistic concepts that make these particular verses relevant. While we may not be privy to these, we can appreciate the beauty of Perek Shirah in its manifest meaning. Let me cite several verses.

> *The heavens say, "The heavens declare the glory of God, and the expanse of the sky tells of His handiwork" (Psalms 19:2).*
>
> *The earth says, "The earth is to God, and its fullness, the inhabited land and those who dwell in it" (ibid. 24:1).*
>
> *The seas say, "More than the roar of many waters, mightier than the waves of the sea — You are mighty on high, O God" (ibid. 93:4).*
>
> *The rivers say, "Rivers will clap hands, mountains will exult together" (ibid. 98:8).*
>
> *The stars say, "It is You alone, O God, You have made the heaven, the most exalted heaven and all their legions, the earth and everything upon it, the seas and everything in them and You give them all life; the heavenly legions bow to You (Nehemiah 9:6).*
>
> *The dew says, "I will be like the dew to Israel, blossoming like a rose, and striking its roots like Lebanon" (Hosea 14:6).*
>
> *The trees of the field say, "Then the trees of the forest will sing with joy before God for He will have arrived to judge the earth" (I Chronicles 16:33).*

In all, there are ninety-three verses which relate how everything in the world, both animate and inanimate, is a testimony to the Majesty of God.

It is regrettable that *Perek Shirah* is rarely recited. Regular reading of this beautiful ode to God can greatly enhance one's spirituality.

יְהַלְלוּ שְׁמוֹ בְמָחוֹל, בְּתֹף וְכִנּוֹר יְזַמְּרוּ לוֹ. כִּי רוֹצֶה ה׳ בְּעַמּוֹ, יְפָאֵר עֲנָוִים בִּישׁוּעָה. יַעְלְזוּ חֲסִידִים בְּכָבוֹד, יְרַנְּנוּ עַל מִשְׁכְּבוֹתָם.

Let them praise His Name with dancing, with drums and harp let them make music to Him. For Hashem favors His people, He adorns the humble with salvation. Let the devout exult in glory, let them sing joyously upon their beds.

On several occasions dancing is utilized as an expression of Divine service. On Simchas Torah it is customary to dance. It is related that when the great Kabbalist R' Yitzchak Luria (Arizal) would finish dancing following the *Hakafos* (procession with the Torah) on Simchas Torah, he would go to other shuls and join in their dancing.

The Talmud states that it is a mitzvah to dance before a *kallah* (bride) to increase her joy. One of the Talmudic sages would juggle myrtle branches when dancing before a *kallah*. The Talmud relates that when this sage died, his bier was encircled by a heavenly fire in the shape of a myrtle branch, a sign that God had been pleased with his dancing before the *kallah*.

Chassidim placed great emphasis on dancing as an expression of joy in being fortunate to serve God. One of the Chassidic masters said that the reason dancing can be a Divine service is because when you dance, you break contact with the ground and elevate yourself a few inches toward heaven. Dancing should be understood as being symbolic of distancing ourselves from our earthly desires and reaching upward toward spiritual goals.

There are several Hebrew words for dance. The word for dance in the above verse is מָחוֹל, which refers to a circular dance. In any other formation, there can be a distinction of position. One dancer may be in a more prominent position than another, and there may be inequality. In a circular dance one's position makes no difference. Everyone is equidistant from the center of the circle. Any position that was occupied by one person is immediately occupied by another.

The most virtuous human trait is *anivus* (humility). The most abhorrent trait is *gaavah*. Dancing as a service to God should be with *anivus*, with a feeling that regardless of one's achievements, one should not think of oneself as superior to another person. The Divine praise is, therefore, בְּמָחוֹל, with a circular dance.

There is dancing and there is dancing. Dance as an expression of joy should not be affected. The physical expression should occur when the joy is of such magnitude that it cannot be contained.

I had the privilege of observing my father on Simchas Torah. He would embrace the Torah and sing along with others, standing still and swaying almost imperceptibly. Then suddenly he would erupt in a dance. It was clear that his joy with the Torah had reached an intensity that could no longer be contained, and it burst into dance.

"Let Israel exult in its Creator, let the Children of Zion rejoice in their King." It is when the joy and exultation overwhelm a person that "they praise His Name with dancing."

וַיְבָרֶךְ דָּוִיד אֶת ה׳ לְעֵינֵי כָּל הַקָּהָל, וַיֹּאמֶר דָּוִיד: בָּרוּךְ אַתָּה
ה׳, אֱלֹקֵי יִשְׂרָאֵל אָבִינוּ, מֵעוֹלָם וְעַד עוֹלָם. לְךָ ה׳
הַגְּדֻלָּה וְהַגְּבוּרָה וְהַתִּפְאֶרֶת וְהַנֵּצַח וְהַהוֹד, כִּי כֹל בַּשָּׁמַיִם
וּבָאָרֶץ; לְךָ ה׳ הַמַּמְלָכָה וְהַמִּתְנַשֵּׂא לְכֹל לְרֹאשׁ. וְהָעֹשֶׁר
וְהַכָּבוֹד מִלְּפָנֶיךָ, וְאַתָּה מוֹשֵׁל בַּכֹּל, וּבְיָדְךָ כֹּחַ וּגְבוּרָה, וּבְיָדְךָ
לְגַדֵּל וּלְחַזֵּק לַכֹּל. וְעַתָּה אֱלֹקֵינוּ מוֹדִים אֲנַחְנוּ לָךְ, וּמְהַלְלִים
לְשֵׁם תִּפְאַרְתֶּךָ.

And David blessed Hashem in the presence of the entire congregation. David said, "Blessed are You, Hashem, the God of Israel, our forefather, from This World to the World to Come. Yours, Hashem, is the greatness, the strength, the splendor, the triumph, and the glory, even everything in heaven and earth; Yours, Hashem, is the kingdom, and the sovereignty over every leader. Wealth and honor come from You and You rule everything — in your hand is the power and strength and it is in Your hand to make anyone great or strong. So now, our God, we thank You and praise Your splendrous Name."

The above prayer was said by King David after he had assembled the gold and silver for the Temple which God said that his son, Solomon, would build.

Rashi explains that although David had acquired the gold and silver as a result of his triumphs, he did not attribute the credit for these to his own cunning and skills. Rather, he recognized that every aspect of his greatness, his strength in battle, the splendor of his riches, his triumph against his enemies, and the glory of his king-

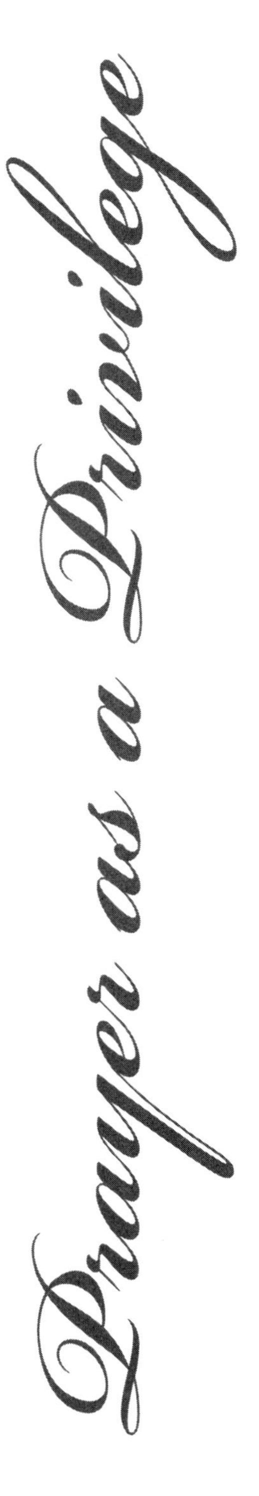

ship were all gifts from God. The Temple in which the Divine service would take place was made possible by God. When man serves God, it is because God has made it possible for him to do so.

The Midrash quotes God as saying, "Who is it that has preceded Me that can claim he deserves reward? He could put a *mezuzah* on his house only because I enabled him to have a house. He could circumcise his son only because I gave him a son" (*Vayikra Rabbah* 27:2). So it is with all the mitzvos. We can do them only because God has given us the wherewithal to do them. Nor could we pray if God had not given us the power of speech.

When we pray or do mitzvos, we might think that God is indebted to us for fulfilling His wishes. But God owes us nothing. His kindness and reward are gifts, and we should appreciate them as such.

As we near the completion of the *Pesukei D'Zimrah* (Verses of Praise), we recite the expression of gratitude of David. We should recognize that the ability to pray is a Divine privilege.

Raising the "Rock Bottom"

וַתֵּרֶא אֶת עֳנִי אֲבֹתֵינוּ בְּמִצְרָיִם.

You observed the suffering of our forefathers in Egypt.

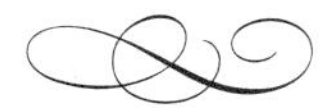

In the book *Rabbi Schwab on Prayer,* the Rav suggests that the translation "You saw the suffering of our forefathers in Egypt" is inaccurate. A more accurate translation is "You saw the *poverty* of our forefathers in Egypt." He states that this refers to the spiritual poverty of the Israelites. The sorry state of spirituality of the Israelites in Egypt is borne out by the Midrash that states that the heavenly angels asked God why He is saving the Israelites. "They are no better than the Egyptians. Both are equally idolatrous." The Arizal states that the Israelites had descended to so low a spiritual nadir, that had they remained any longer in Egypt they would have been beyond redemption.

The concept that redemption occurs at the point of crisis is explicitly stated in the Midrash. "Israel said, 'Master of the Universe! When will You redeem us?' God responded, 'When you sink to the lowest level, at that time I will redeem you' " (*Yalkut Shimoni, Hosea* 533).

This is a very depressing thought. But it need not be so.

> *In the treatment of alcoholism there is a truism, "An alcoholic does not recover until he hits rock-bottom." However, "rock bottom" is a relative concept. One alcoholic entered*

treatment and recovered because his wife indicated she would leave him if he did not stop drinking. Another alcoholic was separated from his wife and three children but continued to drink. He was fired from an important executive position because of his drinking, but this did not phase him. He drank away his savings, his home, his car and eventually his welfare check, but nothing stopped him from drinking. He sold his blood to get money for alcohol. One day, he checked into the hospital. "I give up," he said.

Curious, I asked, "What finally made you decide you have to quit drinking?"

The man answered, "When I had that top position in the company, I was the leader of the United Way charity drive. This past week I have been panhandling quarters. I can't live like that."

Compare the two cases. In the first case, the possibility that his wife would leave him was a "rock bottom." In the second case, neither the loss of the entire family, job, home and car constituted a "rock bottom." Nor did selling his blood for alcohol constitute a crisis. But begging for money was intolerable for this man.

It is evident that what may be a rock bottom for one person will not be so for another person. One of our tasks in treatment of alcoholism is to make the person realize that where he is now should be his rock bottom. There is no need to descend further. Or as one alcoholic put it, "Alcoholism is a descending elevator. You can get off at any floor you choose."

God will redeem us when we are at our lowest level, but we can determine what constitutes a "lowest level." If we can understand to what spiritual heights we are capable of rising, then we can feel that our lack of spirituality is our lowest level. If we understand the level of perfection of character we can attain, then falling short of this can be our lowest level.

When God sent Moses to liberate the Israelites, He said, "I am Hashem, your God, Who takes you out from under the burdens (סִבְלֹות) of Egypt" (*Exodus* 6:7). R' Yitzchak Meir of Ger pointed out that the word סִבְלֹות can also mean "tolerance." The problem was that the Israelites had been accustomed to being slaves and had become tolerant of their degraded state. It was Moses' challenge to convince them that they could be free, dignified human beings.

"The Children of Israel groaned because of the work and they cried out. Their outcry because of the work went up to God. God heard their moaning ... God saw the Children of Israel; and God knew" (ibid. 2:23-25). Knew what? He knew that they were no longer tolerant of being slaves. They had reached their "rock bottom" and were ready for redemption.

At any point in our lives we may be satisfied or dissatisfied with our level of spirituality. Our *neshamah* craves greater spirituality, but we may have accommodated to our less-than-adequate status. Many people have come to a crisis later in life, and become aware of their lack of spirituality. How wonderful it would be to avoid crises! If we only reflected on, "I am content with where I am now, but should I be?" Most people would like to improve their economic status and are not content with where they are. We should feel similarly about our spiritual status.

We need not be depressed by the thought that salvation occurs only at one's lowest point. If we aspire to spiritual heights, then where we are now can be our lowest.

The Song of Triumph

וַיּוֹשַׁע ה׳ בַּיּוֹם הַהוּא אֶת יִשְׂרָאֵל מִיַּד מִצְרָיִם, וַיַּרְא יִשְׂרָאֵל אֶת מִצְרַיִם מֵת עַל שְׂפַת הַיָּם: וַיַּרְא יִשְׂרָאֵל אֶת הַיָּד הַגְּדֹלָה אֲשֶׁר עָשָׂה ה׳ בְּמִצְרַיִם, וַיִּירְאוּ הָעָם אֶת ה׳, וַיַּאֲמִינוּ בַּה׳ וּבְמֹשֶׁה עַבְדּוֹ:

Hashem saved — on that day — Israel from the hand of Egypt, and Israel saw the Egyptians dead on the seashore. Israel saw the great hand that Hashem inflicted upon Egypt and the people feared Hashem, and they had faith in Hashem and in Moses, His servant.

Whoever recites the "Song of the Sea" every day with proper kavannah will merit saying it in the World to Come (Zohar, Beshalach 54).

While saying this song has great merit, there appears to be some reservation. The Talmud states that when the Egyptian army was destroyed, the heavenly angels wished to sing praises to God, but were silenced. "The works of My hands are drowning in the sea, and you wish to sing My praise?" (*Megillah* 10b). It is apparent that although God rejoiced in the salvation of the Israelites, He was nonetheless saddened that this came at the cost of human lives, albeit these were the bitter enemies of the Israelites. All human life is dear to God. The Baal Shem Tov said, "I wish I had the love for the greatest *tzaddik* that God has for the worst *rasha* (wicked person)." Why, then, is Moses' Song of Triumph given such high regard? Why does God welcome the praise of the Israelites when He rejected that of the angels?

The verse in the Torah immediately preceding the Song of the Sea is, "Israel saw the great hand (might) that God inflicted upon Egypt and the people feared God, and they had faith in God and in Moses, His servant." Even after all the miracles that Moses had wrought in Egypt, the Israelites' faith in God was not absolute. The revelation that accompanied the miraculous parting of the waters solidified the Israelites' faith in God and in Moses. This revelation was so impressive that the Midrash states that even the simplest of the Israelites had a prophetic vision that surpassed the vision of the prophet Ezekiel (*Mechilta*).

The faith resulting from the miracle of the parting of the waters was far-reaching. The Israelites were trapped between the sea and the oncoming Egyptian army. They cried out to God to rescue them, but no one could guess how the salvation could occur. The Israelites had indeed witnessed the judgments that God had inflicted upon Egypt in the Ten Plagues. Perhaps He would bring down a storm of hail and lightning that would frighten off the Egyptian army. Or perhaps they would be stricken as they were in the plague of the firstborn. No one dreamed that the sea would split asunder and that the Israelites would traverse the sea on dry land.

The salvation occurred in a manner that no one could possibly have expected. It was then that the Israelites recognized that *Divine help may occur in a way that no one can expect.*

> *A chassid complained to his rebbe that he was in desperate need of money. He had been very wealthy and suddenly lost everything. He was now deeply in debt and could not face his many creditors. He asked the Rebbe for a berachah. The Rebbe told him to buy a ticket in the sweepstakes and gave him a berachah that he would win.*
>
> *When the chassid's ticket failed to win the prize, the Rebbe complained to his mentor, "My berachos are worthless!" His mentor said, "Your berachos can be very effective. You should have just given this man a berachah that God will help him. Your mistake was in telling him in what way his help would come, i.e., by telling him to buy a ticket in the sweepstakes. You were instructing God how to help him. God does not need your advice."*

We pray to God for help, but we cannot know in what form His help will come. *The great teaching of the miracles of the Splitting of the Sea was that God's help may come in a way that one might never have considered.*

It was their attainment of this type of faith in God that the Israelites celebrated by the Song of Triumph. "They came to believe in God and in Moses, His servant." Az *yashir*, *then* Moses and the Children of Israel *sang* this song to God. It was not so much a song of gratitude for their salvation as it was a song of praise for their spiritual elevation to an unwavering trust in God.

The faith of the heavenly angels was not enhanced by the miracle of the parting of the waters. In contradistinction to humans who are subject to bouts of weakness in faith, the heavenly angels are never in doubt. They are always in the Immanent and Manifest Presence of God. The miracle did not result in any spiritual elevation for the angels. They could praise God only for the destruction of the Egyptians, and this God rejected. The praise by the Israelites was an expression of their having achieved a greater awareness of God's majesty, and this type of praise was welcome.

Reciting the Song of the Sea should strengthen our faith and trust in God. Whatever it is that we ask for, we should be confident that God will respond in a way that is to our ultimate advantage. We may not have any idea just how His help will manifest itself, but we should be secure in the knowledge that it will surely come.

The Psalmist says, "I raise my eyes to the mountains; whence will come my help? My help is from God, Maker of heaven and earth" (*Psalms* 121:1-2). Just as God created heaven and earth out of nothingness, so His salvation may come "out of nothingness," in ways we may not anticipate.

The reinforcement of our faith in God requires that we recite the Song of the Sea with proper *kavannah*. We should meditate and imagine ourselves in the position of the Israelites. We are standing at the shore of the sea, with the mighty Egyptian army advancing toward us. We should feel the terror of our ancestors, and the awesome and startling astonishment at seeing the mighty sea divide before our eyes, forming towering walls of water, with a dry path for our passage.

It is related that when the Chassidic master, R' Shmelke of Nikolsburg, read the Song of the Sea on Passover, the listeners were so moved by his reading that they lifted the hems of their caftans as if they were about to walk into the sea. If we can identify with the experience of our ancestors and acquire a spiritual elevation when we recite the Song of the Sea, we indeed merit the promise of the *Zohar* that we will merit singing it in the World to Come.

"Israel saw the great hand (might) that God inflicted upon Egypt and the people feared God, and they had faith in God and in Moses, His servant." The faith of the Israelites was reinforced by the punishment meted out to the Egyptians. One might ask: Is it really fair to punish someone in order to strengthen another's faith?

The Maggid of Lublin answered this question with a parable. A young mother died after giving birth to a child, and a wet nurse was engaged to nurse the infant. After a bit of time, the infant became quite sick. A doctor examined the infant and prescribed a number of medications. The father was appalled. "There is no way we can get all those medications into the baby," he said.

"Don't fret," the doctor said. "The baby does not have to take these medications. The wet nurse will take them, and they will be transmitted to the baby when he nurses."

When the wet nurse heard of this, she protested. "I don't want to take those bitter-tasting medications. I'm not the child's mother. It's not my responsibility to enable the child to recover. If that is what is expected of me, I quit! Get yourself another wet nurse," she said.

"You're wrong," the doctor said. "You see, the child's illness is due to germs which you transmitted to him. You behaved in a dissolute manner which caused you to become infected, and you passed on the disease to the infant. Inasmuch as you caused the disease, it is very much your responsibility to be the vehicle for the cure."

So it was with the Israelites and the Egyptians, the *Maggid* said. When Jacob and his descendants came to Egypt, their faith in God was firm. Over the succeeding two hundred years, associating with the pagan Egyptians caused the erosion of the Israelites' faith. Inasmuch as the Egyptians were responsible for the deterioration of the faith, it was their responsibility to be the vehicle for its restoration.

Beautifying the Mitzvos

זֶה קֵלִי וְאַנְוֵהוּ, אֱלֹקֵי אָבִי וַאֲרֹמְמֶנְהוּ.

This is my God, and I will build Him a Sanctuary; the God of my father, and I will exalt Him.

The Talmud explains this verse to mean that we should perform the mitzvos in a beautiful manner; i.e., by having beautiful *tefillin*, a decorated *succah*, a crown for the *Sefer Torah*, a beautiful *esrog* and an attractive container for it, etc. (*Shabbos* 133b). One of my favorite pastimes is to visit museums of Judaica and see the variety of adornments for mitzvos. I love to see the intricate filigree and engravings of the Chanukah menorahs, *Megillah* cases, *Havdalah* spice boxes, and crowns and various other accouterments for Torah scrolls. I marvel at the artistry that went into the pre-printing press *siddurim* and *machzorim*. These reflect the love and devotion that Jews have had for mitzvos throughout our history.

All this notwithstanding, I must cite a comment by the Chafetz Chaim. One of his students, the son of a wealthy merchant, proudly showed the sage a new pair of *tefillin* he had acquired. The parchments were written by an expert *sofer* (scribe) and the *battim* (the leather containers that house the parchments) were constructed in the finest fashion. The *tefillin* were indeed exceptionally beautiful.

> *"How much did these tefillin cost?" the Chafetz Chaim asked.*

"Eighteen rubles," the student answered.

"Eighteen rubles!" the Chafetz Chaim exclaimed. "That is a small fortune. One can acquire a set of kosher tefillin for one ruble."

"Yes," the student responded, "but I wished to have the most beautiful tefillin available, in keeping with 'This is my God and I will beautify Him.'"

The Chafetz Chaim nodded and said, "Yes, yes, my dear child. It is indeed important to beautify the mitzvos. But one must be careful that the eighteen rubles were also obtained by beautifying the mitzvos. There are many mitzvos involved in earning money. We must be scrupulously honest. We may not overcharge or deceive a customer. We may not charge interest. We must give honest weight and use honest measures. We should not demean the merchandise of others.

"When a person earns money by observing all the mitzvos that govern commerce and uses that money to beautify the mitzvos, that is indeed a way of adorning and honoring God. But if one is negligent in conducting business according to the Torah regulations and uses his earnings to beautify mitzvos, that is hardly pleasing to God.

"A kosher pair of tefillin bought or an honestly earned ruble is dearer to God than a superb pair that were bought for money that was not earned by strict observance of Torah laws."

We have no knowledge of what prompted the Chafetz Chaim to make this comment to this student. Perhaps he was concerned that the father's wealth was acquired by business practices that are considered legitimate in commerce but fail to meet Torah standards. However, the message is important. We should beautify mitzvos in a manner that is pleasing to God as well as attractive to the observer.

אלהינו מלך העולם יוצר
אור ובורא חושך עושה שלום
את הכל
המאיר לארץ ולדרים
ובטובו מחדש בכל יום
מעשה בראשית
מה רבו מעשיך
מלאה הארץ קנינך
המשבח והמפואר
אלהי עולם
רחם עלינו
אדון

The Shema and Its Blessings

Prior to the Shema

בָּרוּךְ אַתָּה ה׳ אֱלֹקֵינוּ מֶלֶךְ הָעוֹלָם, יוֹצֵר אוֹר וּבוֹרֵא חֹשֶׁךְ,
עֹשֶׂה שָׁלוֹם וּבוֹרֵא אֶת הַכֹּל.

Blessed are You, Hashem, our God, King of the universe, Who forms light and creates darkness, makes peace and creates all.

The *Shema* is probably the most moving of all prayers. *Hear, O Israel, Hashem is our God, Hashem, the One and Only.* These few words are undoubtedly the most familiar phrase of our liturgy. The declaration of faith in the one true God is not only the fundamental statement of Judaism, but also constitutes *kabbalas ol malchus Shamayim,* acceptance of servitude to God. The *Shema* is also the phrase with which countless martyrs returned their *neshamos* to the Creator.

Our sages saw fit to compose two prefatory *berachos* to the *Shema*. The first praises God for His creation of light and darkness. "Blessed are You, Hashem, our God, King of the Universe, Who forms light and creates darkness, makes peace, and creates all." Earlier (*The Testimony of Nature*) we noted that the awareness of the grandeur of nature leads to an appreciation of the majesty of God. Yet, in what way is this particular aspect of Creation relevant to the *Shema*?

We read that on the first day of Creation "God separated between light and darkness"(*Genesis* 1:4). Rashi comments that prior to the separation, light and darkness functioned in a "jumble." This is hardly understandable. To the best of our knowledge, light and darkness cannot coexist. Darkness is the absence of light. How could they possibly function together?

In the beginning of *Genesis,* Rashi points out that if the Torah were purely an instruction book, it should have begun with the first mitzvah. Furthermore, Ramban comments that the true meaning of the account of Creation is beyond our ability to understand. We can only conclude that although the account of Creation is not an actual mitzvah, it does provide valuable teaching and guidance for proper living.

If we cannot understand how light and darkness can coexist in a literal sense, we can understand that symbolic "light and darkness" can coexist. Light represents truth, whereby one can perceive reality. Darkness represents falsehood, which obscures perception of reality. Truth and falsehood can indeed coexist in a person's mind. When this occurs, a person's thinking may be chaotic.

R' Chaim Shmulevitz gives several examples of coexistence of "light and darkness" in a person's thoughts. He cites the Midrashic account that Esau sent his son Eliphaz to kill Jacob. Having been raised by the Patriarch Isaac, Eliphaz could not bring himself to kill Jacob. However, he asked, "What can I do to fulfil my father's wishes?" R' Chaim points out that although he pursued Jacob without the intent of killing him, he nevertheless felt morally obligated to fulfill his father's wish. This is an example of how morality and immorality can coexist.

R' Chaim cites the incident of the two women who came before Solomon, each claiming to be the mother of the living child and stating that the dead child was the other woman's. When Solomon ordered that the child be cut in half, the true mother said, "No! Give her the child!" while the lying woman said, "Yes! Cut the child in two. Neither she nor I shall have him." R' Chaim points out that even though the woman who had exchanged her dead child for the living child was motivated to do so by the maternal instinct to care for a child, nevertheless she agreed to have the child killed. Compassion and cruelty, light and darkness, coexisted within her (*Sichos Mussar* 5733:7).

As noted, light represents truth, a true perception of reality. Darkness or obscure thinking is the result of personal interests that prevent a person from seeing what he does not wish to see. In psychology, we refer to obscure thinking as *denial.* Denial can occur even in the most intelligent person who may be extremely wise in other matters. However, an intense emotion may blind this wise person from having an accurate perception of reality. "A bribe will blind the eyes of the wise" (*Deuteronomy* 16:19). Our personal interest may constitute a bribe that distorts our thinking.

Creativity requires clarity of thought. A befuddled mind in which light and darkness are raging cannot be creative. It is only when one can distinguish between mental light and darkness, separating truth from falsehood and recognizing each for what it is that one can eliminate the obfuscation resulting from the conflict of these coexisting opposites. Only then can one be creative. Such separation brings about a "peace of mind," not in the sense of being relaxed and at ease, but rather in the sense of freedom from conflict and confusion.

To teach us this, the Torah tells us that Creation did not proceed until light and darkness were separated. By distinguishing between the two, God eliminated the conflict and made "peace." The first prefatory *berachah* to the *Shema* relates this phenomenon of Creation. God made peace between the two conflicting forces by separating them, and only then "created all." We, too, must eliminate the obfuscation of our thinking if we wish to be creative.

The relevance of this *berachah* to the *Shema* is that it is a prerequisite for the refutation of paganism and for *kabbalas ol malchus Shamayim*, accepting God's absolute sovereignty.

Some people who do not accept the rule of Torah may present a variety of philosophical arguments questioning the authenticity of Torah. One freethinker did just this in a discussion with R' Chaim of Brisk. R' Chaim said to him, "Your arguments are not valid reasons. Rather, they are logical-sounding excuses. You find the restrictions of Torah inconvenient. You have, therefore, conjured up a number of objections to Torah to justify your behavior and assuage your conscience."

The Scriptural history of the Jews reveals their propensity to idol worship. It is difficult to envision Jews being so foolish as to believe that a hand-sculptured image is a god. The Talmud states, "The Jews knew full well that idols were of no substance at all. They ascribed to idolatry only because they desired a sanction for relationships which the Torah forbids" (*Sanhedrin* 63b). Idol worship was nothing other than a rationalization. It is the nature of rationalization that one comes to believe one's own lies.

The obscurity of thinking, the darkness which may occur even in the presence of the light of wisdom, is due to the distortion of thought arising from our earthly desires. Solomon stated this succinctly: "All the ways of a person are right in his own eyes" (*Proverbs* 21:2).

Acceptance of the Divine rule is facilitated if we realize that the mitzvos of the Torah were given for the benefit of man. The juvenile mind cannot understand why the sweets one craves may be detrimental to growth. The distorted thinking of the narcotic addict cannot perceive that the drug he craves to provide him with a pleasurable sensation may be lethal. The mature mind understands, "Now, O, Israel, what does your God ask of you? Only ... to go in all His ways ... to observe His commandments and His decrees *for your benefit*" (*Deuteronomy* 10:12-13).

To arrive at this truth and be guided by its unadulterated light we must be objective. We must eliminate the factors that may distort our thinking. We can then recite the *Shema* and accept the Divine rules for living.

The Berachos of the Shema

הַמֵּאִיר לָאָרֶץ וְלַדָּרִים עָלֶיהָ בְּרַחֲמִים, וּבְטוּבוֹ מְחַדֵּשׁ בְּכָל יוֹם תָּמִיד מַעֲשֵׂה בְרֵאשִׁית. מָה רַבּוּ מַעֲשֶׂיךָ ה׳, כֻּלָּם בְּחָכְמָה עָשִׂיתָ, מָלְאָה הָאָרֶץ קִנְיָנֶךָ.

תִּתְבָּרַךְ צוּרֵנוּ מַלְכֵּנוּ וְגֹאֲלֵנוּ, בּוֹרֵא קְדוֹשִׁים. יִשְׁתַּבַּח שִׁמְךָ לָעַד מַלְכֵּנוּ, יוֹצֵר מְשָׁרְתִים, וַאֲשֶׁר מְשָׁרְתָיו כֻּלָּם עוֹמְדִים בְּרוּם עוֹלָם, וּמַשְׁמִיעִים בְּיִרְאָה יַחַד בְּקוֹל דִּבְרֵי אֱלֹקִים חַיִּים וּמֶלֶךְ עוֹלָם. כֻּלָּם אֲהוּבִים, כֻּלָּם בְּרוּרִים, כֻּלָּם גִּבּוֹרִים, וְכֻלָּם עֹשִׂים בְּאֵימָה וּבְיִרְאָה רְצוֹן קוֹנָם. וְכֻלָּם פּוֹתְחִים אֶת פִּיהֶם בִּקְדֻשָּׁה וּבְטָהֳרָה, בְּשִׁירָה וּבְזִמְרָה, וּמְבָרְכִים וּמְשַׁבְּחִים וּמְפָאֲרִים וּמַעֲרִיצִים וּמַקְדִּישִׁים וּמַמְלִיכִים —

He Who illuminates the earth and those who dwell upon "it, with compassion; and in His goodness renews daily, perpetually, the work of Creation. How great are Your works, Hashem, You make them all with wisdom, the world is full of Your possessions .... May You be blessed, our Rock, our King and our Redeemer, Creator of holy ones; may Your Name be praised forever, our King, O Fashioner of ministering angels; all of Whose ministering angels stand at the summit of the universe and proclaim — with awe, together, loudly — the words of the living God and King of the universe. They are all beloved; they are all flawless; they are all mighty; they all do the will of their Maker with dread and reverence. Chazzan — And they all open their mouth in holiness and purity, in song and hymn — and bless, praise, glorify, revere, sanctify and declare the kingship of...

The first *berachah* of the *Shema* begins with the praise of God for the wonders of Creation and continues with an account of the praises the heavenly angels sing to God. The

Midrash states that God does not accept the praises of the angels until He first hears those of Israel. Why are human prayers superior to those of angels?

Angels are indeed holy because they were created holy. Angels do nothing to acquire *kedushah* (holiness) They are in a pure state of "light." No earthly desires characteristic of humans obscure their perception of truth. A human *kabbalas ol malchus Shamayim* requires effort and sacrifice. We may never reach the state of spirituality of angels, but to the degree that we achieve spirituality by our own efforts, we are superior to angels. This is why our praises are dearer to God than those of the heavenly angels.

The first prefatory *berachah* to the *Shema* impresses upon us the need for clarity of thought, of distinguishing between the light of truth and the darkness resulting from the obstruction of vision by our earthly desires. By achieving true perception, our acceptance of Divine rule elevates us to a position superior to even that of the heavenly angels.

Ahavah Rabbah

אַהֲבָה רַבָּה אֲהַבְתָּנוּ ה׳ אֱלֹקֵינוּ, חֶמְלָה גְדוֹלָה וִיתֵרָה חָמַלְתָּ עָלֵינוּ... אָבִינוּ הָאָב הָרַחֲמָן הַמְּרַחֵם, רַחֵם עָלֵינוּ... וְהָאֵר עֵינֵינוּ בְּתוֹרָתֶךָ, וְדַבֵּק לִבֵּנוּ בְּמִצְוֹתֶיךָ, וְיַחֵד לְבָבֵנוּ לְאַהֲבָה וּלְיִרְאָה אֶת שְׁמֶךָ ... בָּרוּךְ אַתָּה ה׳, הַבּוֹחֵר בְּעַמּוֹ יִשְׂרָאֵל בְּאַהֲבָה.

With an abundant love have You loved us, Hashem, our God; with exceedingly great pity have You pitied us ... Our Father, the merciful Father, Who acts mercifully, have mercy upon us ... Enlighten our eyes in Your Torah, attach our hearts to Your commandments, and unify our hearts to love and fear Your Name ... Blessed are You, Hashem, Who chooses His people Israel with love.

The second prefatory *berachah* tells of the love of God for Israel and contains a prayer for enlightenment in Torah. The sequence of the grandeur of Creation followed by the value of the wisdom of Torah is reminiscent of Psalm 19. There, too, David begins with "The heavens declare the glory of God." The extolling of the courses of the heavenly bodies is abruptly followed by "The Torah of God is perfect." The psalm then concludes with the verse, "May the expressions of my mouth and the thoughts of my heart find favor before You, God, my Rock and my Redeemer." This verse is said at the end of the *Amidah*, and is essentially a summation of the prayer. Its appearance in this psalm indicates that both the awareness of the grandeur of nature and the appreciation of the value of Torah are necessary for proper *tefillah.*

Rambam states that the way a person can develop love for God is by observing the greatness and wondrous nature of His works. A true understanding of these will result in so profound an appreciation of the Divine wisdom that it will lead to an intense admiration and love of God (*Yesodei HaTorah* 2).

> *Anyone who has attended a performance by a world famous symphony orchestra can understand this. Many years ago, I was privileged to hear a performance of Beethoven's Fifth Symphony by the Boston Symphony Orchestra conducted by Serge Koussevitsky. It was an unforgettable experience. As the masterful performance continued, the audience was spellbound, and one could feel the electricity in the air. When the last note of the symphony was played, the pent-up admiration exploded in deafening applause, and the audience simply refused to stop applauding. Even when Koussevitsky mounted the podium to conduct an encore, he could not begin playing because the applause continued. If it had been possible, people would have loved to have personally told Koussevitsky how moved they were by his performance.*

This appreciation would pale into insignificance in comparison to the wondrous works of God. If we truly appreciated these, we could hardly restrain ourselves from applauding His marvelous performance. We are fortunate in that we do have the privilege of personally expressing our appreciation to God.

It has been pointed out that the Hebrew word for *shema*, שְׁמַע, is the mnemonic for שְׂאוּ מָרוֹם עֵינֵיכֶם, "Raise your eyes on high." This verse continues. "and see Who created these: He brings forth their legions by number; He calls to each of them by name; because of His abundant might and powerful strength, there is not missing even one" (*Isaiah* 40:26).

Accepting the Yoke

שְׁמַע ׀ יִשְׂרָאֵל, ה׳ ׀ אֱלֹקֵינוּ, ה׳ ׀ אֶחָד:
בָּרוּךְ שֵׁם כְּבוֹד מַלְכוּתוֹ לְעוֹלָם וָעֶד.
וְאָהַבְתָּ אֵת ׀ ה׳ ׀ אֱלֹקֶיךָ, בְּכָל־לְבָבְךָ, וּבְכָל־נַפְשְׁךָ,
וּבְכָל מְאֹדֶךָ: וְהָיוּ הַדְּבָרִים הָאֵלֶּה, אֲשֶׁר ׀ אָנֹכִי
מְצַוְּךָ הַיּוֹם, עַל־לְבָבֶךָ: וְשִׁנַּנְתָּם לְבָנֶיךָ, וְדִבַּרְתָּ בָּם, בְּשִׁבְתְּךָ
בְּבֵיתֶךָ, וּבְלֶכְתְּךָ בַדֶּרֶךְ, וּבְשָׁכְבְּךָ וּבְקוּמֶךָ: וּקְשַׁרְתָּם לְאוֹת ׀
עַל־יָדֶךָ, וְהָיוּ לְטֹטָפֹת בֵּין ׀ עֵינֶיךָ: וּכְתַבְתָּם ׀ עַל־מְזֻזוֹת בֵּיתֶךָ,
וּבִשְׁעָרֶיךָ:

Hear, O Israel: Hashem is our God, Hashem, the One and Only.

You shall love Hashem, your God, with all your heart, with all your soul and with all your resources. Let these matters that I command you today be upon your heart. Teach them thoroughly to your children and speak of them while you sit in your home, while you walk on the way, when you retire and when you arise. Bind them as a sign upon your arm and let them be tefillin between your eyes. And write them on the doorposts of your house and upon your gates.

We have referred to the concept of *kabbalas ol malchus Shamayim*, as "accepting God's absolute sovereignty." The Hebrew word *ol* means "yoke." The literal meaning of the phrase is "accepting the *yoke* of heaven." This term was deliberately chosen.

The *Shema* is found in Deuteronomy 5:4, *Hear, O Israel, Hashem is our God, Hashem, the One and Only.* The term *shema* is found a bit earlier (ibid. 4:1) where Moses says, "Now, hear, O Israel, the decrees (*chukim*) and ordinances which I teach you." It is not coincidental that the term *shema* is used in both verses.

The Talmud states that the order of the *Shema* is that the paragraph of *kabbalas ol malchus Shamayim* be recited first, followed by the paragraph instructing the observance of mitzvos. But just what is *kabbolas ol malchus Shamayim* if not the observance of mitzvos?

The word *chukim* (decrees) refers to those Divine commandments which are beyond our understanding. We can understand the reason for refraining from work on Shabbos, or for commemorating the Exodus by eating matzah. We can understand why we may not lie and why we must do acts of *chesed*. But there is no logical explanation for the prohibition to wear a garment of mixed linen and wool. The latter and various other laws are *chukim*, decrees which we are to observe without the faintest idea of the rationale behind them.

Many of the mitzvos of the Torah might conceivably be observed for hygienic, humanitarian or nationalistic reasons. It is precisely the observance of laws which we cannot understand that indicates our servitude to God.

> *R' Avraham Grodzinski (Toras Avraham 29) cites an interesting passage in the Talmud. Antoninus asked R' Yehudah HaNasi, "At what point does the yetzer hara (evil impulse) enter? From the moment of the embryo's formation or at birth?" R' Yehudah HaNasi responded, "From formation."*
>
> *"That cannot be," Antoninus said, "for if so, the fetus would kick its way out of the womb. The yetzer hara does not enter until birth." R' Yehudah HaNasi conceded (Sanhedrin 91b).*

R' Grodzinski asks, inasmuch as we assume that the nature of the *yetzer hara* is to seek pleasure via gratification of physical desires, what could be the motivation for driving the fetus out of its mother's womb? The fetus is in an idyllic state, with all its needs being provided by its mother. What pleasurable gratification could there be in leaving the womb?

R' Grodzinski answers that we err in thinking that the primary drive of the *yetzer hara* is gratification of desires. *The primary drive of the yetzer hara is to be free and unfettered.* Indeed, it wishes to be free to indulge in pleasurable activities, but that is just one of the ways in which it wishes to be unrestricted. However, even in absence of actual pleasure, the *yetzer hara* seeks to be its own master.

The idyllic intrauterine existence of the fetus is offset by its confinement within the womb. If the *yetzer hara* were present in the fetus, it would incite it to kick its way out of the womb, even to perish rather than be confined.

R' Grodzinski has provided us with an important psychological insight. People may be driven to self-destructive acts by the impulse to be free and unfettered. Rebellion against authority is innate and not a product of the intellect. Parenthetically, this may explain why the most frequent psychiatric diagnosis of adolescence is "Oppositional Defiant Disorder." The modern-day release of social restraints has allowed the *yetzer hara* to achieve its primary drive.

The essence of Judaism, expressed in the *Shema*, is *kabbalas ol malchus Shamayim*, "accepting the *yoke* of heaven." This goes beyond servitude. It means total and unquestioning submission to God, accepting the restraints imposed by His will just as the ox is restrained by the yoke. "Oppositional Defiant Disorder" should be as impossible a phenomenon as an ox casting off the yoke.

Acceptance of the yoke of heaven can be taught only be modeling. Perhaps the reason that adolescents are so often rebellious is because they have never seen *kabbalas ol* in action. Even if they were raised in an ostensibly Torah observant home, there may have been a lack of *kabbalas ol*.

The two verses introduced by the word *shema* have in common acceptance of the yoke of Divine rule. "Now, hear, O Israel, the decrees (*chukim*) and ordinances which I teach you." Unquestioning observance of Torah laws, *especially those that we do not understand*, is as fundamental to Judaism as *Hear, O Israel, Hashem is our God, Hashem, the One and Only*.

R' Grodzinski's insight provides an answer to a question posed by the Chafetz Chaim.

The Chafetz Chaim points out a difficulty in the second paragraph. Moses tells the Israelites to observe the mitzvos and to serve God "with all their hearts and with all their souls." He then warns them not to deviate toward idolatry. Isn't that a bit strange? We can see a father of a Torah observant family sending off his son to school. He may tell him to remember to put on *tefillin* every day and to avoid doing anything on Shabbos that is not permissible. Knowing that partying and drug use is rampant among young people, he may say, "Don't allow yourself to join the partying and drug use. These can ruin your education and cause you serious health problems." However, it is rather unlikely that he will say, "Be careful that you don't eat *chazir* on Yom Kippur." That would appear to be an absurd statement. Why, then, does Moses tell the Israelites to be meticulously observant of all the mitzvos, and in the next breath warn them not to worship idols?

As we noted earlier, the Talmud says, "The Jews never thought that there is any validity in idolatry. The only reason they were idolatrous is because they wished to sanction the relationships that the Torah forbids" (*Sanhedrin* 63b). This is an extremely important insight. The Jews knew very well that the God of Abraham, Isaac and Jacob was the true God. However, accepting God's Torah would put too many restrictions upon them and deny them the pleasures they sought. It would be too brazen to identify oneself as Torah observant and be publicly defiant of Torah. Their way out was to say, "I now believe in this god, who says that these things are permissible."

The Talmud tells us that idolatry is nothing other than seeking approval to gratify all one's desires. Young people who use drugs and say, "There is nothing wrong with smoking marijuana," and then go on to justify this by quoting "authorities" who sanction marijuana are not any different than those who said, “This god says that what I want to do is okay.” One does not have to adopt another faith to be idolatrous. One who seeks official approval for giving in to all one’s desires is essentially idolatrous. R’ Grodzinski’s analysis is thus borne out. Idolatry is the elimination of restraint.

Moses’ warning to the Israelites is essentially no different than the warning of a father who tells his son to keep the mitzvos and avoid drugs and revelry. Moses exposes idolatry for what it really is: nothing other than seeking official approval for indulging their urges.

This message is as valid today as it was thousands of years ago. Those who claim to have official sanction for doing whatever they wish should carefully read and analyze the *Shema*.

Teaching by Modeling

וְלִמַּדְתֶּם | אֹתָם | אֶת־בְּנֵיכֶם, לְדַבֵּר בָּם, בְּשִׁבְתְּךָ בְּבֵיתֶךָ,
וּבְלֶכְתְּךָ בַדֶּרֶךְ, וּבְשָׁכְבְּךָ וּבְקוּמֶךָ: וּכְתַבְתָּם | עַל־מְזוּזוֹת
בֵּיתֶךָ, וּבִשְׁעָרֶיךָ:

Teach them to your children, to discuss them, while you sit in your home, while you walk on the way, when you retire and when you arise. And write them on the doorposts of your house and upon your gates.

As was noted in the introduction, there is much that is taught in *tefillah.* Let us pay close attention to the words in the second chapter of the *Shema.*

"Teach them to your children, to discuss them, while you sit in your home, while you walk on the way, when you retire and when you arise. And write them on the doorposts of your house and upon your gates."

In the first chapter of the *Shema* we find a similar verse, "Teach them to your children, and *you* should speak of them while you sit in your home, etc." However, in the second chapter, when it says "Teach them *to your children, to discuss them,*" it obviously means that you should teach your children to discuss and observe Torah at all times. It does not mean that your children should discuss Torah while *you* sit in your home or are on the way. The text, therefore, should read, "while *they* sit in *their* home, while *they* walk on the way, when *they* retire and when *they* arise. And *they* should write them on the doorposts of *their* houses."

The words of the Torah are very precise. What the second chapter is telling us is that we cannot accomplish much if we teach by lecturing. If we wish our children to adopt the ways of Torah, we must show them how it is done. If we behave according to Torah teachings while *we* are at home or are out in the business world, when *we* arise and when *we* retire, then we can expect them to emulate us. If we affix *mezuzos* to our doorposts, our children are likely to follow suit. If we teach them by didactics but do not model Torah ways for them, we are not likely to accomplish much.

Just a slight nuance means so much. That is why it is so important to study *tefillah* carefully.

אֲנִי | ה׳ | אֱלֹקֵיכֶם: אֱמֶת.

I am Hashem your God — it is true.

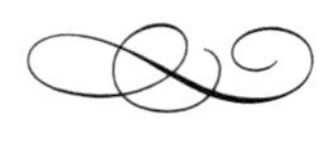

The concluding words of the third paragraph of the *Shema* are, "I am Hashem your God." The sages added the word *emes* (it is true) so that we should declare as did the prophet *Jeremiah* (10:10), "Hashem, your God, is true."

The completion, as it were, of the verse from *Numbers* with that in *Jeremiah* indicates the continuity of Torah. The prophets are as integral a part of Torah as are the Five Books of Moses.

The continuity of Torah is further symbolized by the word *emes,* אֱמֶת. The first word God spoke at Sinai was אָנֹכִי, "I am Hashem your God," beginning with the letter *aleph.* The first word of the Mishnah is מֵאֵימָתַי, "When is the time for reading the *Shema* in the evening," beginning with the letter *mem.* The first word of the *gemara* is תָּנָא, "What is the author of the Mishnah referring to?" beginning with letter *taf.* These three letters in sequence make up the word *emes.* This verse, therefore, represents a linkage of the Five Books of Moses with the Prophets and the Oral Law.

This principle is included in the *Shema*, which is the essential statement of the Jewish faith, to indicate that acceptance of the Scriptures and the Oral Law is fundamental to Judaism. At one time, the Ten Commandments were recited in the morning service. This was discontinued when the Sadducees used this as a support for their contention that only the Ten Commandments were of Divine origin. By completing the *Shema* with *emes* we assert our belief in the Divine nature of all of Torah.

Achieving Truth

"Hashem, your God, is true."
"The signet of God is truth" (Shabbos 55a).

We are to emulate the Divine attributes. But is truth within human reach? R' Dessler points out that every human interest is initiated by a desire or will for something. We make myriad judgments every day. Except for those judgments that are of a technical nature, where the decision is only *how* to achieve a particular goal, substantive judgments on whether or not to pursue a goal are subject to distortion by personal interest.

Whenever we are faced with a question, "Should I or I should I not do this?" there is always either an advantage or disadvantage in whether or not we do it. It is our nature to seek comfort and pleasure and avoid discomfort and distress. Consequently, there is a personal interest involved in every substantive decision.

The Torah states that a judge who takes a bribe cannot possibly be objective. Even the slightest personal interest "blinds the eyes of the wise and distorts the words of the just" (*Deuteronomy* 16:19). The wisest and most honest person cannot be objective if he has taken a bribe.

As we have previously noted, we are "bribed" by our natural desires. There is no way we can maintain objectivity in making a judgment which will affect our comfort. How, then, can we possibly achieve truth?

R' Dessler states that to the degree that we refine our *middos*, to that degree we lessen the degree of distortion. The more spiritual a person is and the less he seeks to gratify personal desires, the less is the impact of the latter on his decision-making processes. Perhaps we can lessen the degree of distortion by becoming more spiritual, but we cannot eliminate it totally.

Truth can only be achieved as a gift from God. Only God can prevent our judgment from being affected by our personal interests. "You grant truth to Jacob" (*Micah* 7:30). Truth is a grant, a Divine gift.

> *As a young man, R' Mendel of Kotzk was seen to be pleading before the open ark, "Please show me just a hairsbreadth of truth!" His pursuit of truth was uncompromising, and his teachings reveal a fierce devotion to truth.*
>
> *R' Mendel said, "Refraining from lying is not yet truth. The absence of falsehood is a negative. Truth is a positive.*
>
> *"When the spies sent by Moses returned with their account of what they saw in Canaan, they were not lying. They related what they saw. However, although it was not a lie, it was not yet the truth. Truth is what God says is true. Inasmuch as God had said that the Israelites were to conquer Canaan, a truthful report would have been, 'We saw the land, and we will conquer it as God has said.'"*

Our senses are vulnerable to illusion. Our reasoning is subject to distortion. The only truth is the word of God. We can achieve truth only by praying for it.

ꕥ

The Divine Benevolence

ה׳ אֱלֹקֵיכֶם אֱמֶת.

וְיַצִּיב וְנָכוֹן וְקַיָּם וְיָשָׁר וְנֶאֱמָן וְאָהוּב וְחָבִיב וְנֶחְמָד וְנָעִים וְנוֹרָא וְאַדִּיר וּמְתֻקָּן וּמְקֻבָּל וְטוֹב וְיָפֶה הַדָּבָר הַזֶּה עָלֵינוּ לְעוֹלָם וָעֶד. אֱמֶת אֱלֹקֵי עוֹלָם מַלְכֵּנוּ צוּר יַעֲקֹב, מָגֵן יִשְׁעֵנוּ, לְדֹר וָדֹר הוּא קַיָּם, וּשְׁמוֹ קַיָּם, וְכִסְאוֹ נָכוֹן, וּמַלְכוּתוֹ וֶאֱמוּנָתוֹ לָעַד קַיֶּמֶת. וּדְבָרָיו חָיִים וְקַיָּמִים, נֶאֱמָנִים וְנֶחֱמָדִים לָעַד וּלְעוֹלְמֵי עוֹלָמִים. עַל אֲבוֹתֵינוּ וְעָלֵינוּ, עַל בָּנֵינוּ וְעַל דּוֹרוֹתֵינוּ, וְעַל כָּל דּוֹרוֹת זֶרַע יִשְׂרָאֵל עֲבָדֶיךָ.

Hashem, your God, is true. And certain, established and enduring, fair and faithful, beloved and cherished, delightful and pleasant, awesome and powerful, correct and accepted, good and beautiful is this affirmation to us forever and ever. True — the God of the universe is our King; the Rock of Jacob is the Shield of our salvation. From generation to generation He endures and His Name endures and His throne is well established; His sovereignty and faithfulness endure forever. His words are living and enduring, faithful and delightful forever for our forefathers and for us, for our children and for our generations, and for all the generations of Your servant Israel's offspring.

"God is true. And certain, established and enduring, fair and faithful, beloved and cherished, delightful and pleasant, awesome and powerful, correct and accepted, good and beautiful is this affirmation to us forever and ever."

We use fifteen different expressions of affirmation of the *Shema*. Why fifteen? One of the commentaries states that these fifteen expressions of affirmation correspond to the fifteen favors enumerated in the

Dayeinu hymn of the Passover Haggadah. In the Haggadah *From Bondage to Freedom* it was noted that some of the verses of the hymn do not stand to reason. For example, "Had He given us their wealth, but not split the sea for us, it would have sufficed us." Of what possible value would the wealth have been if the sea would not have parted for the Israelites? Inasmuch as they were trapped between the oncoming Egyptian army and the sea, they were doomed to annihilation unless there were an escape route through the sea. There are similar problems with some of the other favors where the phrase "it would have sufficed us" appears incomprehensible.

We pointed out in that Haggadah that we must learn to be grateful for everything we receive, even if at the moment we cannot see its ultimate good. The refrain "it would have sufficed us" means that every incident in the many events of the Exodus was sufficient to elicit prompt gratitude from us, even though the eventual benefit might not have been immediately apparent.

Earlier we noted that the use of the two Divine appellations, *Hashem* and *Elokim,* in the *Shema* is to teach us that everything God does is out of compassion. Even the adversities we experience are for our ultimate good, although we may be unable to understand how this can be. We cover our eyes when we recite the *Shema* as a symbolic statement of faith. We accept that our human vision is limited, and that what we see as a harsh and painful judgment is in fact beneficial.

The fifteen expressions of affirmation of the *Shema* are, therefore, equivalent to the fifteen favors of the *Dayeinu* hymn. In both we assert our belief in the ultimate goodness of everything that God does, even though we may experience it as anything but good.

Linking the Exodus With the Amidah

צוּר יִשְׂרָאֵל, קוּמָה בְּעֶזְרַת יִשְׂרָאֵל, וּפְדֵה כִנְאֻמֶךָ יְהוּדָה וְיִשְׂרָאֵל. גֹּאֲלֵנוּ ה׳ צְבָאוֹת שְׁמוֹ, קְדוֹשׁ יִשְׂרָאֵל. בָּרוּךְ אַתָּה ה׳, גָּאַל יִשְׂרָאֵל.

Rock of Israel, arise to the aid of Israel and liberate, as You pledged, Judah and Israel. Our Redeemer — Hashem, Master of Legions, is His Name — the Holy One of Israel. Blessed are You, Hashem, Who redeemed Israel.

According to halachah, we may not interrupt in any way between the close of the verse describing the redemption of the Exodus and the beginning of the *Amidah*.

In the Haggadah *From Bondage to Freedom* I pointed out that Passover is much more than an Independence Day celebration. A human being can be fully independent in a political and social sense, yet be very much a slave. Animals are not truly free because they are totally dominated by their physical bodies. An animal cannot defy a bodily drive. If it is hungry, it cannot decide to fast. Animals are incapable of making conscious, ethical choices. The ability to choose and to defy a bodily urge is uniquely human.

When God liberated us from the enslavement of Egypt, He gave us the Torah, binding us to Him as His servants. "For the Children of Israel are servants to Me, they are My servants, whom I have taken out of the land of Egypt — I am the Lord, your God" (*Leviticus* 25:55). Abiding by the laws of the Torah enables one to become master of his body rather than its slave. Torah gives us the gift that is unique to man: freedom of choice.

But are we not servants to God, compelled to observe His will? Where, then, is our freedom?

Our freedom lies in our conscious choice of this servitude. As was noted in our discussion of the *Shema*, the reading of the

Shema constitutes *kabbalas ol malchus Shamayim,* acceptance of servitude to God. It is a servitude which we accept anew each day. We are not servants of God out of habit but out of free choice. Indeed, in the second paragraph of the *Shema* we say, "It will be that if you hearken to My commandments that I command you *today*" (*Deuteronomy* 11:13), which Rashi explains as meaning that the Torah should be as fresh and new as if we heard it for the first time today. In Egypt our servitude was because we had been enslaved initially and this status persisted. The enslavement to one's bodily urges is a matter of ongoing habit. But we are servants to God because we accepted His sovereignty *today* rather than because we were in servitude to Him yesterday.

The reciting of the Exodus is an extension of the *kabbalas ol malchus Shamayim* of the *Shema.* It is with this attitude that we approach the zenith of our prayers, the *Amidah.* No interruption is permitted. The concept of our unique freedom of choice as humans, of our being masters of our body rather than its pawns, and of voluntarily accepting the sovereignty of God must flow uninterruptedly into the *Amidah.*

ומצמיח ישועה
ונאמן אתה להחיות מתים
ברוך אתה ה' מחיה המתים :
כשם שמקדישים
ככתוב על יד נביאך
וקרא זה אל זה ואמר
את שמך בעולם
אותו בשמי מרום
קדוש קדוש קדוש
צבאות מלא כל הארץ כבודו :
לעמתם

The Amidah

Shemoneh Esrei Prayer

Penetrating the Barriers

The Talmud says that pious people of yore spend one full hour in preparation before beginning the *Amidah.* It is indeed unfortunate that today we often hurry through the *tefillah*, so that the entire prayer service may be completed in thirty minutes. Proper *kavannah* requires meditation.

Before beginning the *Amidah*, it is customary to take three steps forward. The source for this practice is R' Eliezer, Baal HaRokeach, who states that this represents the three layers on Sinai through which Moses had to pass to reach the *Shechinah* (Divine presence): "darkness, cloud and thick fog" (*Deuteronomy* 4:11). To make this practice effective, we should reflect on this when we take the three steps.

The Chassidic master, R' Mendel of Rimanov, was walking with his disciples when he found a child crying. When he inquired as to the reason for the crying, the child said, "I was playing hide-and-seek with my friends; I hid myself, but no one came to look for me." R' Mendel turned to his students and said, "Can you imagine the anguish of God, Who has concealed Himself in the world, but no one looks for Him."

The failure to look for God may be due to darkness; i.e., there is no awareness whatever that He is present. Just as in total darkness one is not aware of the presence of anything, so there can be a total lack of awareness of God's presence.

There are people who have an awareness that there is a God and that He is present in the world, but they cannot find Him because their thinking lacks the necessary clarity. Their thinking is, as it were, in a cloud. In contrast to the utter darkness, they may grope for God, but are without direction.

The third barrier to finding God is the most difficult to navigate. In a thick fog, one can detect that there are objects, but can easily mistake them for being something other than what they are. This corresponds to a view of the world where one observes things happening, but sees them as being due to "natural" or accidental causes. One fails to recognize the handiwork of God in everything. One sees things and can think fairly clearly, but his thinking leads to the wrong conclusions. Moses cautioned the Israelites not to be misled into thinking that their success is due to their own strength and cunning (*Deuteronomy* 8:12-18). Even after being eyewitnesses to the extraordinary miracles of the Exodus and the forty years in the wilderness, the Israelites were still vulnerable to the delusion that it was they, rather than God, who wrought their success.

Proper *kavannah* for the *Amidah* requires a conviction that God is present and is in constant control of the world. The three steps we take should not be mechanical but should stimulate our thinking. God has concealed Himself in the world and longs for us to find Him.

The Permission to Pray

ה׳ שְׂפָתַי תִּפְתָּח, וּפִי יַגִּיד תְּהִלָּתֶךָ.

My Lord, open my lips, that my mouth may declare Your praise

This introductory verse to the *Amidah* is taken from Psalm 51, the psalm of *teshuvah*. This is the psalm composed by David when the prophet Nathan reprimanded him for the incident with Bathsheba. This psalm is a heart-rending plea for forgiveness, in which David asks to be accepted again in the graces of God, and to be permitted the joy of having the prophetic spirit return to him once again. In the phrase cited above David expresses his awareness that prayer is a Divine gift and reveals how precious it is to him. He feels unworthy of praying to God, saying, "My Lord, open my lips, that my mouth may declare Your praise." Please, God, help me pray to You.

David felt that his misdeed had weakened if not ruptured his bonding with God. "Cleanse me from my sin … create for me a pure heart, and renew in me a true spirit … Do not cast me away from You, and do not take Your holy spirit from me … Restore to me the joy of Your salvation" (*Psalms* 51:4-14). He knew that the path to restoring the bond with God was through prayer, and he pleaded to be permitted to pray.

We care for things that we value highly. We protect our fine crystal from damage, we polish our silver to maximize its beauty and we take great caution that our diamonds not be stolen. That is how we should value our prayer. The words of the *Amidah* are precious jewels, and we should treat them as such.

It is unfortunate that in our haste to engage in our earthly pursuits we often rush through the *Amidah*, fracturing its words and allowing our *kavannah* to be stolen.

How does a person feel if in his folly he offended someone he loved, resulting in a break in the relationship? He may feel awkward in approaching the person to ask for forgiveness. He may feel that he lacks the proper words to convey his feelings of remorse and his longing to reestablish the relationship. He may begin by saying, "I'm sorry for what happened. Please try to understand what I am about to say." He has no assurance that his apology will be accepted and that the relationship will be restored.

David goes one step further. He not only asks to be understood, but asks of God to help him apologize, to give him the proper words to say. "Allow my tongue to sing joyously of Your righteousness" (ibid. v. 16). He is confident that His pleas will be accepted because "You, God, will not turn away a contrite heart" (ibid. v. 19).

This prefatory verse should also heighten our awareness of the need to purify our speech. "Let my mouth declare your praise." We are going to present God with beautiful words of prayer. Think of how you would feel if the finest delicacies were served to you on a soiled plate. Would you not be repelled by it? How, then, can we deliver words of praise to God with a mouth that has spoken *lashon hara*, untruths and indecent words?

The awareness that it is our mouth that will praise God should make us preserve the highest degree of cleanliness in our speech.

It is with these thoughts that we can approach the *Amidah*.

בָּרוּךְ אַתָּה ה׳ אֱלֹקֵינוּ וֵאלֹקֵי אֲבוֹתֵינוּ...

Blessed are You, Hashem, our God and the God of our forefathers …

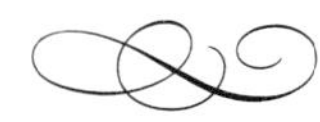

With this we begin the A*midah.*

"Ask your father and he will tell you, your elders and they will say it to you" (*Deuteronomy* 32:7).

These were among the last words spoken by Moses, and were meant to strengthen the faith of Israel in God.

It is only natural for our minds to reflect upon the mystery of eternity. We are baffled by the concept of an Eternal Being that always was, is, and will be. Some have allowed this inability to grasp the eternity of God to cause them to deny God. It is as though anything that they cannot understand or demonstrate in the scientific laboratory does not exist. They fail to realize that positing the eternity of matter does not solve the problem. One eternity is as unfathomable as another eternity. It is simply beyond the scope of human reasoning, and we must make the supra-rational leap of faith.

When problems of this nature would come to my mind, I would realize that my father was far wiser than I am. Certainly he had thought of these questions, and concluded that belief in God was valid. My father would tell us of his grandfather, the *zeide* R' Motele, who was a saintly scholar of enormous wisdom and knowledge. The *zeide* R' Motele held his grandfather in even higher esteem, and so on upward in generations. These intellectual giants had certainly thought of all the issues that bothered me. How foolish it would be of me to question their conclusion!

The genius of the Vilna Gaon is legendary. Anyone studying the works of the Gaon must stand in utter awe of his greatness. When someone suggested to the Gaon that he was as great as Rambam (*Maimonides*), he trembled. How dare anyone compare him with Rambam? Rambam was one of the foremost philosophers in history. And Rambam totally effaced himself before the sages of the Talmud. In comparison to the enormous intelligence of these early sages, my intellect is no greater than that of an ant. With my miniscule understanding, I can hardly challenge their conclusions.

In order that we pray the A*midah* with firm conviction of faith, we refer to God as the God in Whom our ancestors believed and Whom they served.

We also have an unbroken tradition of the revelation at Sinai, where some three million people heard the voice of God. Three million people transmitted an identical account of this revelation to their children and eventually to us.

How is it possible, then, for anyone to reject this tradition and/or deviate from our belief in God because he fails to understand God? I can answer this from my clinical experience. There is a psychological maneuver, *denial*, which enables a person to deny a reality that stares him in the face. Denial occurs when the acknowledgment of reality is undesirable. Denial allows a person to delude himself. I have observed this phenomenon countless times.

The Talmud states that the 613 mitzvos of the Torah can be condensed into the single statement of the prophet Habakkuk, "The righteous person shall live by his faith" (2:4). A sincere conviction of faith in God and the consequent recognition that one was created for a purpose will eliminate all the obstacles that obstruct a person's acceptance of the entire Torah.

We assert that we pray to "our God, the God of our forefathers." We do so by the certainty of our recognition of their superior intellect and our tradition that their God is our God.

The Virtues of the Patriarchs

וְזוֹכֵר חַסְדֵי אָבוֹת.

Who recalls the kindnesses of the Patriarchs.

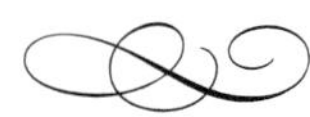

We begin the *Amidah* by citing the Patriarchs, Abraham, Isaac and Jacob: "Who recalls the kindnesses of the Patriarchs and brings a Redeemer to their children's children." It is by the merit of the Patriarchs that God pledged to help Israel throughout history.

I must preface the following discussion with a statement: **First, we must realize that we cannot gauge the actions of Torah personages by our own standards. They were of a completely different dimension. "If the earlier** (tzaddikim) **were like angels, then we are, by comparison, like humans"** (Shabbos 112b). **The standard to which they were held was far stricter and more exacting than that to which lesser people were held. Many facts about the great personages in the Torah are presented simply, and it takes the teachings of the Talmud and Midrash to understand what transpired.**

This notwithstanding, there are lessons that must be learned from the way the events are described in the Scripture, even though the full picture emerges only when one studies the events as they are presented in Talmud and Midrash.

The merits of Abraham and Isaac are clearly evident. Abraham was the first to recognize the true God. His defiance of the prevailing paganism resulted in his being cast into a fiery furnace from which he was miraculously saved. He was tested by ten trials and proved his unwavering loyalty to God.

Isaac, too, demonstrated his absolute devotion to God. At the age of 37 he willingly submitted to offer his life as a sacrifice to God. He said to Abraham, "Bind me tight to the altar, lest I panic at the last moment."

But what is there about Jacob that indicates the devotion of Abraham and Isaac? Furthermore, Jacob is referred to as "the choicest of the Patriarchs" (*Bereishis Rabbah* 76:1). The Midrash states that the image of Jacob is inscribed on the throne of God (*Targum Yonasan, Genesis* 28:12). Indeed, we refer to ourselves as the "Children of Israel (Jacob)."

Where do we find the greatness of Jacob? The Patriarchs Abraham and Isaac were extraordinarily great, superhumanly great.

The Torah account of Jacob is that he was *humanly* great.

Jacob prayed for God's protection and for his personal needs (*Genesis* 28:21-22). Jacob loved Rachel (ibid. 29:18). Jacob expressed his disappointment when he was denied Rachel (ibid. v. 25). "Jacob became angered and he disputed with Laban" (ibid. 31:36). Jacob was afraid of Esau (ibid. 32:8). Jacob feared the reprisal of the Canaanites (ibid. 34:30). After surviving these ordeals, Jacob hoped for tranquility, but instead suffered twenty-two years of grief and anguish over the disappearance of his beloved son, Joseph whom he feared was dead. Jacob sensed that God had somehow turned away from him (*Bereishis Rabbah* 91:13). Jacob summarized his life to Pharaoh, "The days of the years of my sojourn have been a hundred and thirty years. The days of the years of my life have been few and bad" (*Genesis* 47:9).

Of the three Patriarchs, Jacob is the only one with whose human emotions we can identify. But it was Jacob who in the last days of his life said, "*God Who shepherds me from my inception until this day*" (ibid. 48:15). Jacob deliberately chose the term "shepherds." A shepherd cares for his flock, sees that they have adequate food and water, and protects them from predators. In spite of the severe distress he experienced — as he described his life to Pharaoh — Jacob asserted his belief that God had cared for him, even in the years of his grieving for Joseph. "God Who shepherds me from my inception until this day." He affirmed his faith that God had never abandoned him. Whatever distress he had suffered was under the protection of a loving Shepherd.

We may not be put to the extreme tests of Abraham and Isaac, but we are subject to the emotions of Jacob: fear, love, grief, anger, disappointment and disillusionment. What the Patriarch taught us is that throughout all of this, we must remember that God is our Shepherd, and that He never abandons us.

Abraham and Isaac were our superhuman ancestors. Jacob was our human ancestor. As such, he was "the choicest of the Patriarchs." And we are the "Children of Israel."

R' Menachem of Amshinov solicited a wealthy man to help one of the latter's needy relatives. The man gave the rabbi a small sum. R' Menachem explained to him that his relative has a large family and is destitute. He requested a much larger donation.

"I don't feel obligated to give him that much money," the man said. "He is a very distant cousin."

"Did you pray this morning?" R' Menachem asked.

The man was taken aback. "Surely the Rabbi does not accuse me of not praying," he said.

"Then you asked for Divine help by virtue of the merits of our ancestors, Abraham, Isaac and Jacob," R' Menachem said. "They are much further removed from you than this cousin. If you request help because of your kinship to them, you should certainly provide help to a relative who is much closer."

R' Menachem's argument was irrefutable, and he received the desired sum.

As we invoke the memories of our distant ancestors and ask for redemption by virtue of their merits, let us remember that we have the responsibility to come to the aid of even the most far-removed of our kin, as the prophet says, "And from your own flesh do not turn away" (*Isaiah* 58:7).

The Indestructible Spark

בָּרוּךְ אַתָּה יהוה, מָגֵן אַבְרָהָם.

Blessed are You, Hashem, Shield of Abraham.

We should note that all the other eighteen blessings of the *Amidah* close with a reference to the Divine benevolence in the present; i.e., "the *Giver* of wisdom, Who *desires* repentance, Who *pardons* abundantly, etc." God gives us wisdom *now*, desires our repentance *now*, and forgives us *now*. The Divine act of protecting the Patriarch Abraham apparently refers to God's miraculously saving Abraham when he was thrown into the fiery furnace for denying paganism and asserting his belief in the true God. This is an historic event. Why does this blessing deviate from the pattern of the *Amidah* by referring to the past?

R' Yitzchok Meir of Ger explained that this blessing, too, refers to the present. R' Shneur Zalman in *Tanya* states that during the Inquisition, many simple, unlearned Jews who were coerced to accept Christianity under threat of being killed, chose to die rather than to deny their God. People who had not been regularly observant of mitzvos went to the stake crying out *Shema Yisrael*. Inasmuch as they had not been observant of Torah, why did they willingly forfeit their lives?

R' Shneur Zalman explains that every Jew, whether a biological descendant of the Patriarch Abraham or a child of Abraham by choice, has a spark within his *neshamah* which is indestructible. This spark of devotion to God was bequeathed by Abraham to all Jewish *neshamos* through eternity. It is because of this spark that Jews feel, even if only subconsciously, that they cannot separate from God.

The mitzvos are the vehicles which strengthen our bond with God. Some people may not understand this. They may not realize that by transgressing the laws of the Torah they are weakening their bond with God and distancing themselves from Him. However, when it is evident to them that they may lose this bond, they choose to sacrifice their lives rather than be separated from God. Although they may not realize that their failure to observe Shabbos distances them from God, they know that by accepting another faith they sever this bond. They feel that a life without being bonded to God is not worth living.

This is not an intellectual awareness. This phenomenon was noted in people who were hardly versed in Jewish theology. This feeling is due to the spark of the *neshamah* which is never extinguished. The Talmud says, "Regardless of how sinful a Jew may have been, he is always a Jew" (*Sanhedrin* 44a).

God promised Abraham, "I will be your shield" (*Genesis* 15:1). God has protected this bequest to Abraham throughout history. Regardless of what circumstances Jews have suffered, regardless of how much a person may have deviated from Torah observance, this spark of Abraham remains alive.

> *The Midrash relates that when the Romans sacked Jerusalem, they were afraid to provoke the wrath of God by entering the Temple. "Let a Jew go in first," they said. They told a Jew, Yosef Meshisa, to go into the Temple and take whatever he wished for himself. When he emerged with the Menorah, they said, "That is not suitable for secular use. Go in and take something else." Yosef replied, "I have angered my God once. I will not do it again!" The Romans then began torturing him, and Yosef repeatedly cried, "Woe unto me! I have angered my God" (Bereishis Rabbah 65:22).*

Just reflect for a moment. Yosef was so alienated from Jewishness that he dared to enter and plunder the Temple, something which even the Romans feared doing. Yet, he was suddenly overcome by an awareness of the awesomeness of his act, and his repentance was so sincere that as he tolerated inhuman torture, he did not cry in pain but in remorse. This was due to the spark of Godliness within his *neshamah,* which ignited his spirit to the height of martyrdom.

Early in our recitation of the *Amidah* we are reminded of this spark of Abraham which God sustains within each of us. If there is ever a time when our spirits are so low that we do not feel we can address God, we should remember that there is within us an inextinguishable spark of Godliness which God Himself has protected. Even if we feel that we have drifted away from closeness with God and that our *neshamah* is dormant, we should remember that with this spark we can always approach God and rekindle the flame of the *neshamah*.

The Essence of Teshuvah

הֲשִׁיבֵנוּ אָבִינוּ לְתוֹרָתֶךָ, וְקָרְבֵנוּ מַלְכֵּנוּ לַעֲבוֹדָתֶךָ,
וְהַחֲזִירֵנוּ בִּתְשׁוּבָה שְׁלֵמָה לְפָנֶיךָ. בָּרוּךְ אַתָּה ה׳,
הָרוֹצֶה בִּתְשׁוּבָה.

Bring us back, our Father, to Your Torah, and bring us near, our King, to Your Service, and influence us to return in perfect repentance before You. Blessed are You, Hashem, Who desires repentance.

Teshuvah (repentance) is more than remorse. Rambam states that *teshuvah* requires sincere regret for having done the act, and determination not to repeat the act that is so firm that "*the Searcher of all hearts will testify that the person will not return to that sin again*" (*Laws of Teshuvah* 2:2).

The obvious question raised by the commentaries is: Inasmuch as a person always has free will and God does not intervene in a person's moral and ethical behavior, how can it be said that God will testify that the person will not commit the sin again? A person is a free agent at any time to do right or wrong. The Talmud states that the High Priest Yochanan deviated from Torah after serving faithfully in his position for seventy years! Even with the most sincere remorse, a person is free to repeat a sinful act.

We may also ask: Why does Rambam choose to refer to God as "the Searcher of all hearts"? This is an appellation he rarely employs elsewhere.

The answer requires an understanding of behavior. A person's standards of morals and ethics are not etched in stone. A person may be very devout at one time, and may be less sincere in his belief at another time.

Human actions do not occur in a vacuum. If a person commits a sin, it is because at that particular time his spiritual level was at a point that allowed him to behave in that manner.

For example, a person who is meticulously observant with regard to *kashrus* will never consider eating in a non-kosher restaurant, regardless of how hungry he may be. His level of commitment to observance of *kashrus* is such that eating *tereifah* is simply not an option. If his commitment to *kashrus* weakens, it is conceivable that he would now eat something that was unthinkable at an earlier time.

This person, at the height of his commitment to *kashrus*, may happen to speak *lashon hara* (gossip) about someone. He may subsequently chastise himself for having done so. He may have sincere remorse and determine that henceforth he will be more careful about his speech.

That is only a partial *teshuvah*. For a true and complete *teshuvah* he must reflect, "How is it that I was able to do something which the Torah forbids? The same Torah that forbids eating a cheeseburger forbids *lashon hara*. Yet, the former is unthinkable to me, whereas I am obviously vulnerable to the latter. I lack the degree of internal resistance to *lashon hara* that I have to eating *tereifah*. I must do something to advance my spirituality so that speaking *lashon hara* will be as unthinkable as eating *tereifah*."

If this person, by whatever means, advances himself spiritually so that speaking *lashon hara* is no more an option than eating *tereifah*, his *teshuvah* will be complete. Rambam says that at this point, God, Who is the Searcher of all hearts and knows that the person is now at a higher spiritual level, can testify that the person has achieved a status at which it is no longer possible for him to speak *lashon hara*. Of course, it is possible that he may not maintain that level of spirituality. If he regresses spiritually, he may again speak *lashon hara*.

Rambam goes on to say that by doing a complete *teshuvah,* the person undergoes a character change. He has essentially transformed himself into a different person. This new person is not capable of committing the sin that the old person did. If one regresses and goes back to being the "old person," the sin may be repeated.

I once heard a recovering alcoholic with over twenty years of sobriety say, "The man I once was drank, and the man I once was will drink again. At one time in my life, I was sober, but my character was such that I drank. If I ever go back to having that character, I will drink again." *Teshuvah* from sin is very much like recovery from alcoholism. It requires a character transformation. Remorse alone is not enough.

We pray that God will assist us with *teshuvah*. Although God does not determine a person's moral behavior, He will help us if we make a beginning. "Open for Me a portal of *teshuvah* as tiny as the point of a needle, and I will open for you portals wide enough to admit wagons" (*Shir HaShirim Rabbah* 5:3). We must initiate the process.

How do we do this? The answer was given by R' Yisrael of Rizhin who was asked how to do teshuvah. R' Yisrael said, "How come you did not need instructions on how to sin?"

"I did not know it was a sin until after I did it," the man said.

"Then don't sin and you will know how to do teshuvah," R' Yisrael said.

This was not just a clever retort, but a psychological insight. As we noted, true *teshuvah* means eliminating the desire for the sinful act.

The Ibn Ezra asks: How is it possible for the Torah to command, "Do not covet your neighbor's belongings"? A person's emotions are not under voluntary control. One cannot turn off a desire for something.

Ibn Ezra explains that it is human nature not to desire something which is absolutely impossible to attain. The most avaricious person, if told that there were mountains of diamonds and gold on a star, which is 28,200,000,000,000 miles away, free for the taking, would not give it a second thought. One does not crave something totally beyond reach. Therefore, Ibn Ezra says, if a person were totally committed to the other commandments — You shall not murder, You shall not steal, You shall not commit adultery — he would never crave his neighbor's belongings because they would be as unattainable as the riches on a distant star.

The obstacle in the way of true *teshuvah* is that one's commitment never, but never, to repeat the sinful act is not absolute. A firm resolution that would make such an act unthinkable is essential for *teshuvah*. This requires the transformation of character we discussed earlier.

This is what R' Yisrael meant. Make a firm commitment never to repeat the sin, and *teshuvah* will follow.

Abundant in Forgiveness

סְלַח לָנוּ אָבִינוּ כִּי חָטָאנוּ, מְחַל לָנוּ מַלְכֵּנוּ כִּי פָשָׁעְנוּ, כִּי מוֹחֵל וְסוֹלֵחַ אָתָּה. בָּרוּךְ אַתָּה ה׳, חַנּוּן הַמַּרְבֶּה לִסְלוֹחַ.

Forgive us, our Father, for we have erred; pardon us, our King, for we have willingly sinned; for You pardon and forgive. Blessed are You, Hashem, the gracious One Who pardons abundantly.

God does not just forgive. He is *abundant* in forgiveness.

The prayer for forgiveness is proceeded by that for *teshuvah*. However, once we have done proper *teshuvah*, we must be able to accept forgiveness.

Failure to accept forgiveness can leave a person with baggage from the past that may prove extremely burdensome. We may continue to hold ourselves guilty for things we have done, and these negative feelings may depress our spirits, making a positive self-evaluation virtually impossible.

God has assured us through his prophet, "I have erased your sins like a fog, and your transgressions like a cloud. Return to Me, for I have redeemed you" (*Isaiah* (44:22). When a fog clears, no trace of it remains. The metaphor is very clear. Proper *teshuvah* totally eliminates all traces of a sin. Rambam (*Laws of Teshuvah* 7:6) says that a person who had been alienated from God because of his sins becomes very close and dear to God with *teshuvah*. Why can we not accept God's assurance?

While we should not make excuses to justify our behavior, we should realize that we have made mistakes because of our limited knowledge at the time we erred or because of other circumstances which influenced our actions. For example, parents may do things that they feel are in their child's best interest, only to later discover that they were wrong. Let's face it. We do not have children at age 70 when we are at our maximum wisdom and sobered by life's experiences. We have and raise our children when we are the least experienced. Sometimes the advice we receive is not the best. What shall we do when we discover that we made mistakes in parenting? Eat our hearts out?

Some parents who feel they made mistakes in parenting may continue to hold themselves responsible for problems their children may have as adults. They may try to compensate for their mistakes, but by doing so, *they may be relieving their children of the responsibility for taking control of their own lives.* Their reaction to this guilt may actually be harmful to their children. Residuals of guilt for sins can be equally destructive.

It is possible that the difficulty in accepting forgiveness is because we lack experience in forgiving. If we have been unable to completely forgive others for offending us, we may have no way of understanding that there is such a thing as complete forgiveness.

We are, of course, at risk of deceiving ourselves and believing we have done adequate *teshuvah.* The only way to avoid this pitfall is to have a mentor, a sensitive, knowledgeable person who is capable of helping us through *teshuvah* and making an objective judgment about the quality of our *teshuvah.*

The *mussar* writings emphasize the importance of periodically making a *cheshbon hanefesh* (a spiritual accounting). Many people think they may have done so by reflecting on their actions. However, if we have to do an accounting of the status of our business, we do not simply reflect on it. Rather, we use pen and paper and record the income and expenses. We may engage a professional accountant to help us. A *cheshbon hanefesh* should be no different. With pen and paper we should write down the things we have done and review them. Have we corrected the errors we made, and how have we done this? Have we capitalized and expanded on the good things we have done? Could we have done better?

> *When I became involved in the treatment of alcoholism, I wanted to understand the recovery process. I found that one of the required steps was to make a "fearless moral inventory" and share it with one's sponsor (mentor). To get the feel of it, I enlisted someone to be my sponsor, and proceeded to write a "moral inventory." Over a four-month period I laboriously wrote down every important thing I remembered doing. I submitted my compendium to my sponsor who returned it with the comment, "It's a good beginning. Work at it some more."*
>
> *Several months later I resubmitted my writing to him. This time his comment was, "You've only listed the mistakes you've made in your life. I'm sure you've done many good*

> *things. A business inventory requires looking at both the assets and liabilities. I want you to write down your character strengths as well as your weaknesses."*
>
> *I was surprised to find that it was more difficult for me to describe my character strengths than my weaknesses. However, I finally got the job done.*
>
> *My sponsor reviewed my inventory with me. He pointed to something I had written as a negative act. "Would you do that again if the circumstances repeated themselves?"*
>
> *"Of course not," I said.*
>
> *"Well then," he said, "that was a learning experience. A learning experience is a positive. Let's erase that from the negative column and put in the positive column where it belongs."*
>
> *By the time we finished, there were many more things in the positive column than the negative column, and I felt much better about myself.*

This exercise took about two years. I believe that a thorough *cheshbon hanefesh* requires at least that much time. Just as with a business *cheshbon* we often enlist the help of an expert, we should also enlist the help of a spiritual mentor with the *cheshbon hanefesh.*

Properly done, *teshuvah* can help us feel redeemed, as the prophet says.

Do We Mean What We Say?

תְּקַע בְּשׁוֹפָר גָּדוֹל לְחֵרוּתֵנוּ, וְשָׂא נֵס לְקַבֵּץ גָּלֻיּוֹתֵינוּ, וְקַבְּצֵנוּ יַחַד מֵאַרְבַּע כַּנְפוֹת הָאָרֶץ. בָּרוּךְ אַתָּה ה׳, מְקַבֵּץ נִדְחֵי עַמּוֹ יִשְׂרָאֵל.

Sound the great shofar for our freedom, raise the banner to gather our exiles and gather us together from the four corners of the earth. Blessed are You, Hashem, Who gathers in the dispersed of His people Israel.

Three times daily we pray for the ultimate Redemption, for God to gather the Jews who are dispersed all over the world and bring us all together in the Holy Land.

But what would happen if we suddenly heard the sound of the great shofar, and the prophet Elijah appeared with the long-awaited pronouncement that Mashiach was here? The thousands of years of exile have come to an end, and we are about to embark on the return to the Promised Land!

Surely we will all rush to follow Mashiach to the Holy Land. But is it possible that some might be hesitant to make this journey into the unknown? What will it be like? Will I have the comforts of my spacious, air-conditioned home? When a *chamsin* (heat wave) hits Israel, the heat can be intolerable. My modern home is fully computerized. Will I have these conveniences there? I really do not like apartment living. And what about my car? Many of the streets in Israel cannot accommodate a wide luxury car.

> *On one of his travels, the Maggid of Chernobyl lodged at an inn, and at midnight arose to recite the lamentations. He wept bitterly over the destruction of the Holy Temple and the anguish God feels over the fact that He had to drive His*

children into exile. His loud crying awoke the proprietor, who came to see what was wrong. Was the Rabbi perhaps feeling ill?

"No," the Maggid said. "I am well, but I am brokenhearted that we have lost our Holy Temple and that we are in exile. What is worse is that just as a father is hurt when he must chastise a child, so God suffers when he chastises His children. I am crying in prayer for God to forgive our sins and return us all to Jerusalem. This will happen when Mashiach will come. I am praying for the Redemption. If we all pray for the Redemption, we can hasten it. You, Chaim, must pray for the Redemption, too."

Chaim appeared bewildered. "I didn't know about any of this. What will happen with me if I go to Eretz Yisrael? I have no trade. Here I have this inn and a bit of a farm. What will I do there?"

"You have no need to worry, Chaim," the Maggid said. "When Mashiach comes, all our needs will be taken care of. We will be free to study Torah all day."

Chaim was unimpressed. "I don't know anything about Torah," he said. "This doesn't sound so good to me. I must ask my wife what she thinks about this."

A bit later Chaim returned. "My wife said she does not want to leave the inn and the farm with our two cows and the chickens. She does not think that Mashiach is good for us."

"But Chaim," the Maggid said, "here we are in exile, at the mercy of the bands of Tartars that repeatedly make pogroms. They attack us, plundering and killing us. What good are all our possessions if we are insecure with them and even with our very lives. Mashiach will redeem us from all of this. You must pray for Mashiach. The prayer of every Jew is important."

The memory of the last pogrom was still fresh in Chaim's mind. "Yes, I see," he said. "We must be free of attacks from the Tartars. But I must discuss this with my wife."

A few moments later, Chaim returned. "My wife has an excellent idea. When Mashiach comes, let him take all the Tartars to Israel and leave us here. We will then be free and can keep the inn and the farm."

We would be wise to do a bit of soul-searching. Our ancestors were liberated from the brutal enslavement of Egypt and indeed followed Moses into the desert. Yet, when faced with the challenges of the wilderness, some of them opted for return to Egypt. If they preferred the known hardship of slavery to the unknowns of freedom, may we not be even more reluctant to relinquish the comforts to which we are accustomed for the promise of spiritual liberty? Are we perhaps like Chaim and his wife?

There is a folk saying that every joke has a kernel of truth. The above story is amusing, but it has a tragic counterpart.

The historic work, *Seder HaDoros,* relates the horrible calamities that befell the Jewish community of Worms, which we commemorate in the Lamentations on Tishah B'Av. Following the destruction of the First Temple, some of the exiled Jews journeyed far north and settled in Worms, establishing a thriving Torah community there. When the Jews returned to Eretz Yisrael from Babylon seventy years later, the rabbis of Jerusalem sent a message to the leaders of the Jewish community of Worms, stating that they should leave the Diaspora and return to the Holy Land where they would be able to make the pilgrimage to Jerusalem on the three festivals. The Worms community responded, "You may live in the greater Jerusalem, but we prefer to remain in the small Jerusalem of Worms." The tragedies they suffered, says the *Seder HaDoros,* resulted because they refused to join their brethren in their return to Jerusalem and the Second Temple.

How welcome will the sound of the great shofar really be to everyone?

The Ultimate Blessing

. . . בָּרְכֵנוּ אָבִינוּ, כֻּלָּנוּ כְּאֶחָד בְּאוֹר פָּנֶיךָ, כִּי בְאוֹר פָּנֶיךָ נָתַתָּ לָּנוּ, ה׳ אֱלֹקֵינוּ, תּוֹרַת חַיִּים . . .

Bless us, our Father, all of us as one, with the light of Your countenance, for with the light of Your countenance You gave us, Hashem, our God, the Torah of life …

The *berachah* for peace follows the priestly blessings, recited either by the *Kohanim* or by the *chazzan*. The Talmud says, "God found no receptacle for His blessings other than peace" (*Uktzin* 3:12). Following the Divine blessing for prosperity, the Torah continues, "I will provide peace in the land" (*Leviticus* 26:6), upon which Rashi comments that without peace all the blessings for prosperity are worthless.

There seems to be a "Catch 22" here. We ask God to bless us with peace, yet we cannot receive this blessing nor any other unless we provide a receptacle to receive and contain the Divine blessing. That receptacle is peace. How, then, can we ask to be blessed with peace if we must first achieve peace ourselves?

The answer lies in the *berachah* recited by the *Kohanim* prior to their pronouncing the blessing, "He has sanctified us with the holiness of Aharon." The Talmud states that the High Priest Aharon was one "who pursued peace." If Aharon became aware that there was strife between two people, he would approach one of the two and say, "I met the person who had words with you. He regrets having offended you, and is truly remorseful. He wants to apologize, but he is afraid to approach you because you may be angry at him and will reject him." Aharon then went to the other party and repeated his words. Both felt that the other was remorseful but hesitant to apologize. When the two met again, each assumed that the other wished to apologize, and they approached each other with forgiveness in their hearts.

Peace between the two adversaries was not actually restored until they met and embraced. What Aharon did was lay the groundwork so that peace could ensue. This is what we must do. We, ourselves, cannot bring about peace, because peace requires a mutual desire by others. However, like Aharon, we can pursue peace and "lay the groundwork" to provide a receptacle for peace, which can then receive the Divine blessing of peace.

"Bless us, our Father, all of us as one, with the light of Your countenance, for with the light of Your countenance You gave us ... the Torah of life." This refers to the revelation at Sinai, where "Face to face did God speak with you on the mountain" (*Deuteronomy* 5:4). The Israelites merited this revelation because of the absolute unity that they had achieved at Sinai (*Rashi, Exodus* 19:2).

The perfect unity at Sinai was made possible by the phenomenon of the manna, the food which God provided daily in an amount just sufficient for each person's needs. If someone gathered an excessive amount of manna, it rotted. If one gathered less, the container would miraculously fill. The message was clear. God will provide for each person's needs daily. There was no point in taking what belonged to another, and there was no point in competing for manna. The fundamental cause of envy and divisiveness was eliminated. It was not until the worship of the Golden Calf and the ensuing decline in spirituality that the unity of Israel was shattered.

Someone asked a rabbi, "Are our prayers really heard?" The rabbi responded, "Do *you* listen?" Of course God hears our prayers. It is not as certain that we do.

If we have prayed and recited the *Amidah* sincerely, the elements that stand in the way of unity should have disappeared. True gratitude for what God has given us is dependent on our being satisfied with what we have. Giving and receiving forgiveness, and praying for others as well as for ourselves brings us closer together. If we have listened to our own prayers, we have laid the groundwork for peace, and we can then receive the ultimate Divine blessing.

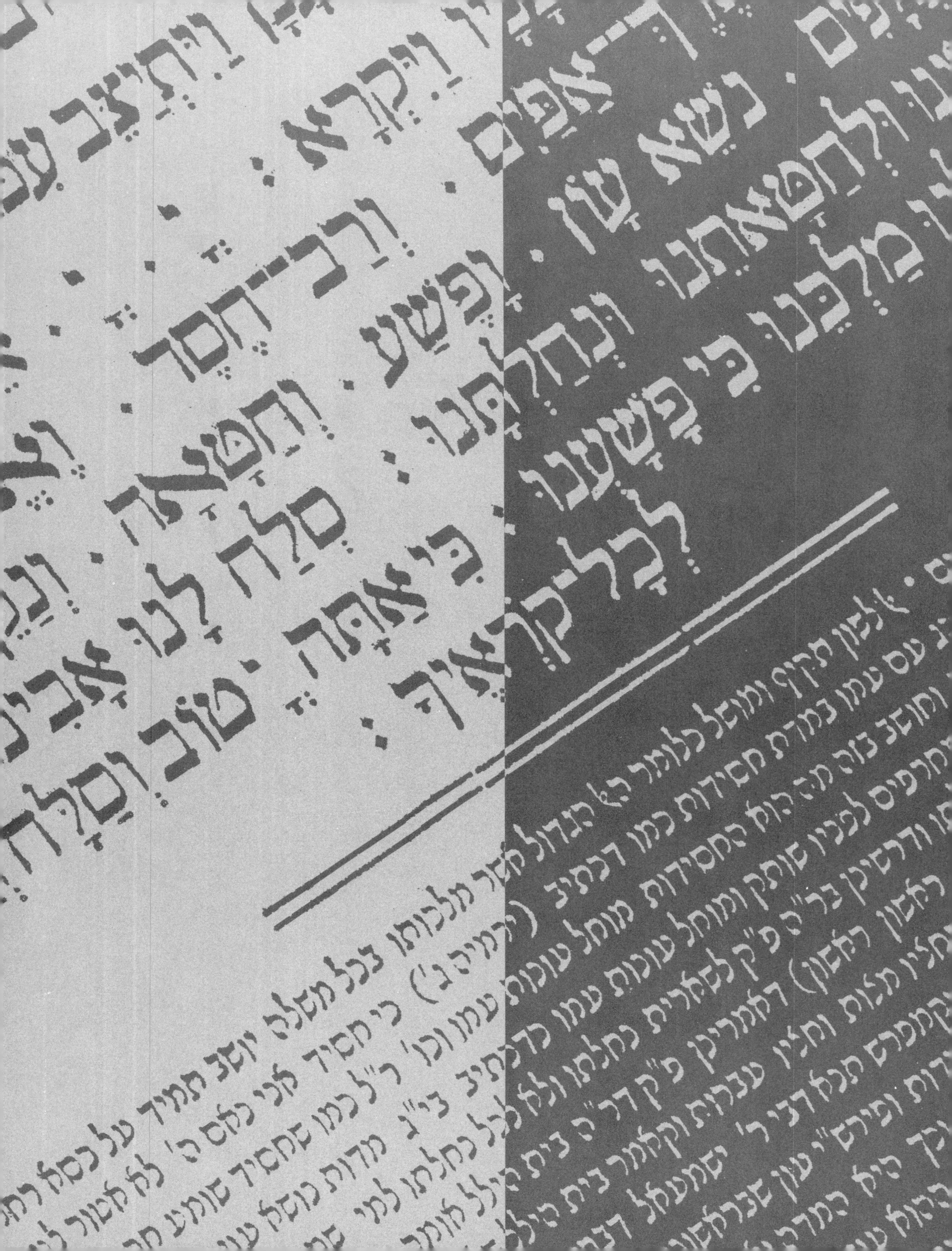

וַיִּקְרָא
וְרַב־חֶסֶד
וָפֶשַׁע וְחַטָּאָה
סְלַח לָנוּ אָבִינוּ
כִּי אַתָּה טוֹב וְסַלָּח
נֹשֵׂא עָוֺן
וּלְחַטָּאתֵנוּ וּנְחַלְתָּנוּ
מַלְכֵּנוּ כִּי פָשָׁעְנוּ
לְכָל־קֹרְאֶיךָ

Tachanun - The Prayer for Divine Compassion

אֱלֹקֵינוּ וֵאלֹקֵי אֲבוֹתֵינוּ, תָּבֹא לְפָנֶיךָ תְּפִלָּתֵנוּ, וְאַל תִּתְעַלַּם מִתְּחִנָּתֵנוּ, שֶׁאֵין אָנוּ עַזֵּי פָנִים וּקְשֵׁי עֹרֶף, לוֹמַר לְפָנֶיךָ ה׳ אֱלֹקֵינוּ וֵאלֹקֵי אֲבוֹתֵינוּ, צַדִּיקִים אֲנַחְנוּ וְלֹא חָטָאנוּ, אֲבָל אֲנַחְנוּ וַאֲבוֹתֵינוּ חָטָאנוּ.

אָשַׁמְנוּ, בָּגַדְנוּ, גָּזַלְנוּ, דִּבַּרְנוּ דֹפִי. הֶעֱוִינוּ, וְהִרְשַׁעְנוּ, זַדְנוּ, חָמַסְנוּ, טָפַלְנוּ שֶׁקֶר. יָעַצְנוּ רָע, כִּזַּבְנוּ, לַצְנוּ, מָרַדְנוּ, נִאַצְנוּ, סָרַרְנוּ, עָוִינוּ, פָּשַׁעְנוּ, צָרַרְנוּ, קִשִּׁינוּ עֹרֶף. רָשַׁעְנוּ, שִׁחַתְנוּ, תִּעַבְנוּ, תָּעִינוּ, תִּעְתָּעְנוּ.

Our God and the God of our forefathers, may our prayer come before You, and do not ignore our supplication for we are not so brazen and obstinate as to say before You, Hashem, our God, and the God of our forefathers, that we are righteous and have not sinned — rather, we and our forefathers have sinned.

*We have become guilty, we have betrayed, we have robbed, we have spoken slander. We have caused perversion, we have caused wickedness, we have sinned willfully, we have extorted, we have accused falsely. We have given evil counsel, we have been deceitful, we have scorned, we have rebelled, we have provoked, we have turned away, we have been perverse, we have acted wantonly, we have persecuted, we have been obstinate. We have been wicked, we have corrupted, we have been abominable, we have strayed, You have let us go astray.**

A Fault or a Virtue?

When the Israelites committed the sin of the Golden Calf, God said to Moses, "I have seen this people, and behold! it is a stiff-necked people" (*Exodus* 32:9). When Moses pleaded that God should not abandon the Israelites, he said, "Let God go among us, for it is a stiff-necked people, and You shall forgive our iniquity" (ibid. 34:9). The very trait that God cited in his rebuke of Israel is the one Moses used in their defense. Is obstinacy a fault or a virtue?

Of course, God was right. During their enslavement in Egypt, the Israelites had come under the sway of idolatry (*Yalkut Reuveini, Beshalach*). However, under the tutelage of Moses, having witnessed the extraordinary miracles that God wrought for them in Egypt and with the splitting of the Red Sea, and having witnessed the revelation at Sinai, one would think that every remnant of idolatry had been extirpated from them. But just a few short weeks following Sinai, in the absence of Moses, they relapsed into the idolatry of Egypt. "Let Me destroy this stiff-necked people," God said. "There is no hope that they can become spiritual."

But Moses argued well. True, their obstinacy caused them to regress. But they are only briefly removed from their Egyptian ordeal. Once they absorb the Torah and are bound to God, it is their stiff-neckedness that will sustain their faith and loyalty to God.

And Moses was right. We are an obstinate, stiff-necked people, and that is why we have survived.

Just look at world history. The once powerful Hittite empire, where is it? It exists only in traces of archaeological findings. And the mighty empires of Assyria, Babylon, and Alexander the Great, where are they all? They exist only in history books.

Rome once ruled the world. When Rome overran Israel, a mighty empire had crushed a tiny nation. Any reasonable person would have predicted that Rome would last forever, while Israel would disappear from the world scene.

> *Soon after the Yom Kippur war, I visited Israel. The tiny nation had suffered heavy losses, and morale was low. On my return, I stopped in Rome, and walked in the Forum among the ruins of the once mighty empire. I saw the Arch of Titus, with the inscription "Judea Capta" and a bas relief of Roman soldiers carrying away the Menorah from the Temple in Jerusalem. Underneath this scene was a chalk graffiti, "Am Yisrael Chai (The Jewish nation lives)." Yes, any reasonable person would have predicted that the Roman empire would live forever rather than Israel. Why did Israel survive? Because God chose a stiff-necked people.*

Jews have survived exile after exile, persecution after persecution. Here and there they may have had a few decades of safety, but the undying hatred toward them eventually results in their expulsion. We have been ravaged and massacred by the Crusades, the Inquisition, the pogroms, and the horrendous Holocaust. But Israel lives on. Many Jewish communities and institutions were built by the survivors of Auschwitz, survivors who bore tattooed numbers on their forearms.

The mighty empires in world history were not subject to the devastation that Jews have suffered, yet they withered away. *Israel has survived because we are a stiff-necked people.* Granted, we were foolish in our young days after emerging from Egypt, but once we pledged ourselves to God, we have never as a nation relapsed nor reneged. No other nation would have withstood the tortures we have suffered because of our stubborn devotion to the God of Abraham, Isaac and Jacob.

As we confess our sins, we admit that we are stiff-necked. But as Moses pleaded for us, that is also why we should be forgiven.

* In most congregations which *daven Nusach Ashkenaz, Vidui* is not said. However, there are some congregations where it is said every day, and others where it is said only on Monday and Thursday.

Tachanun - The Prayer for Divine Compassion

וַיֹּאמֶר דָּוִד אֶל גָּד, צַר לִי מְאֹד, נִפְּלָה נָּא בְיַד ה', כִּי רַבִּים רַחֲמָיו, וּבְיַד אָדָם אַל אֶפֹּלָה.

And David said to Gad, "I am exceedingly distressed. Let us fall into Hashem's hand for His mercies are abundant, but let me not fall into human hands."

David's statement to Gad and the episode leading to it provide some insight into a complex philosophical-theological problem.

Toward the end of his reign, David ordered that a census be taken in Israel. The Scripture says that David sinned by doing this. The commentaries are divided on the nature of the sin. Some refer to the Divine warning that a direct counting of heads is forbidden (*Exodus* 30:12). Rather, each person was to donate a half-*shekel* coin, and the coins were then counted. Others say that David's sin was that he had referred to God with lack of proper reverence (*Berachos* 62b). Some say that the people of Israel had sinned in joining Absalom's rebellion against David. Others say that they sinned in their failure to request the building of the Temple.

The prophet Gad told David that his sin and that of Israel must be expiated, and that he could choose one of three punishments: (1) seven years of famine, (2) three months of pursuit by enemies, or (3) three days of plague. David's response was that in famine there is discrimination between the wealthy and the poor, the strong and the weak; and in pursuit by enemies one is at the mercy of humans. Therefore, David chose the plague, stating that this punishment would be by the direct Hand of God, Whose mercy is abundant.

The Psalmist says, "Do not rely on nobles, nor on a human being, for he holds no salvation" (*Psalms* 146:3). And again, "It is better to take refuge in God than to rely on man" (ibid. 118:8). But there is some controversy on a more specific point: Does God intervene to protect a person from being harmed by another human being? The problem is that inasmuch as God does not interfere with a person's freedom of choice in moral and ethical behavior, will He stop an assailant from harming an innocent person?

R' Chaim ben Attar (*Ohr HaChaim*) comments on the episode where Reuben saved Joseph from being killed by his brothers by saying, "Shed no blood! Throw him into this pit in the wilderness, but lay no hand on him" (*Genesis* 37:22). Inasmuch as the Talmud says that there were scorpions and poisonous snakes in the pit, why does the Torah credit Reuben with saving Joseph?

Ohr HaChaim explains that Reuben knew that Joseph was a *tzaddik*, and that God would intervene and save him from death by scorpions and poisonous snakes. However, if the brothers wished to kill him, God would not intervene to save him because that would be interfering with the brothers' freedom in a moral and ethical act.

On the other hand, David repeatedly prays that God save him from his enemies (*Psalms* 2:7; 40:14; 59:3; 70:2; 144:11). "A lawless person lies in wait for the righteous man and seeks to slay him. But God will not leave him in his hand (ibid. 37:32-33)."

One possible resolution to this conflict is that although God would not intervene to stop an assailant from shooting the arrow, He may save an innocent victim by causing the arrow to miss its target.

It is evident from the *Tachanun* prayer that to surrender to the direct Hand of God is far wiser than to anticipate salvation when one is at the mercy of humans.

The Torah Reading

וְזֹאת הַתּוֹרָה אֲשֶׁר שָׂם מֹשֶׁה לִפְנֵי בְּנֵי יִשְׂרָאֵל.

This is the Torah that Moses placed before the Children of Israel (Deuteronomy 4:44).

The above verse is recited after the Torah has been read, when the Torah scroll is raised and displayed to the congregation. The verse is indeed appropriate and self-explanatory. However, one might say it is superfluous. The interpretation given by the Chafetz Chaim eliminates this objection.

To get its full meaning, the verse must be taken in context. God had instructed Moses to designate three cities in Transjordan, populated by the tribes Reuben, Gad and Menasheh, as safe havens for people who accidentally killed someone, to protect them from the vengeance of the victim's relatives. Three additional cities of safe haven were to be designated in Eretz Yisrael, which Moses was not permitted to enter.

All six cities became functional at the same time. In other words, the three designated cities in Transjordan did not become operative until Canaan was conquered and settled and its three safe haven cities designated and prepared for use. There was really little point, therefore, in Moses designating the Transjordanian cities, because they would not become operative until years after his death.

But Moses seized the opportunity to do a mitzvah. He could easily and with good reason have delegated the designation of all six cities to his successor, Joshua. He knew that he would not live to see the completion and fruition of this mitzvah, but fulfilling the Divine wish was so dear to him that he did whatever was within his ability.

At a scientific meeting, it was revealed that some important research was being neglected because the issue to be investigated required the study of several upcoming generations. The findings of this research would not become evident for at least 100 years. In other words, anyone initiating this research would not live to see its results. Few people were interested in investing their efforts in a project whose findings they would not see, and funding sources were reluctant to underwrite a project whose results would not be known until all the members of the funding body had long since died. There is a natural human desire to see the fruits of one's labor.

Moses rose above this. He did whatever he could, even though he would not see its implementation. It is after this account that the above verse follows. The full understanding of this is a precious teaching. When the Torah scroll is displayed and we say, "This is the Torah that Moses placed before the Children of Israel," we should think of the message it delivers. "Seize every opportunity to do a mitzvah. Do not delay for any reason." That was Moses' directive to the Children of Israel.

יהא שמה רבא מברך
לעלם ולעלמי עלמיא
ישראל בעגלא

The Kaddish

❧

The Six Remembrances

❧

The Thirteen Principles of Faith

The Kaddish

יִתְגַּדַּל וְיִתְקַדַּשׁ שְׁמֵהּ רַבָּא.

May the Name of God be exalted and sanctified.

Although this prayer is recited a number of times in the services, it is best known as the prayer which mourners say for a departed relative. As such, we would expect to find in the *Kaddish* words appropriate for a memorial prayer. However, such words are conspicuously absent.

Solomon says , "It is better to go to a house of mourning than to a house of festivity" (*Ecclesiastes* 7:2). This is because we can learn very little from merrymaking. However, when a human life has come to an end, this can serve as a valuable teaching.

Even though our lives are not replete with merrymaking, we are often so preoccupied with the business of living that we may fail to give much if any thought to what our purpose and goal in life is. We are indeed the beneficiaries of great achievements of science and technology, but these can enhance only the "how" of living, not the "why." Technology can give us better tools, but does not tell us what we should make with them. Science cannot tell us what it is that we must accomplish with our lives.

However, when a human life has come to an end, it is inevitable that we reflect, if only momentarily, on what life is all about. A person lived and acted on this earth. What did he accomplish with his life? In what way did he contribute to mankind? And if he did not make any evident contribution to the world, is it not tragic that he did not do so? This may stimulate one to ask, "And just what am I contributing to the world? What is my mission in life?"

Torah philosophy teaches us that it is our mission to bring Godliness into the world, to proclaim the sovereignty of God. The Midrash tells us that the Patriarch Abraham provided food and drink for wayfarers. After they ate he would say, "Now you must express your gratitude for the food you ate," and they would thank him heartily. Abraham would then say, "It is not me whom you should thank. The food is not mine. It belongs to God, as does everything else in the world. When we partake of anything in the world we must realize that it comes from God, and we must thank Him." This gave Abraham the opportunity to disseminate the belief in the true God to the pagan world.

As descendants of Abraham, we inherit his mission. Because we lack the great spirituality of the Patriarch, we cannot rely on our own resources to fulfill this mission. This is why God gave us the Torah, so that we should be "a kingdom of priests and a holy nation" (*Exodus* 19:6), and "a beacon of light to the nations of the world."

"May the Name of God be exalted and sanctified." The contemplation of the significance of life that occurs when a life is over should make one think, "What am I doing to exalt and sanctify the Name of God?"

"In a world that He created according to His will and established His kingdom." Everything in the world should be a testimony to the Divine will and to the fact that humans have accepted His sovereignty.

We pray that speedily, indeed in our lifetime, there should be universal recognition and acceptance of the sovereignty of God.

Rambam closes his great work with the hope for fulfillment of the prophecy that all mankind will come to have knowledge of God, "as thoroughly as water covers the seabed."

One of the Chassidic masters said that every Jew is a soldier in the army of God. Everyone has the potential to contribute to the ultimate triumph of truth over falsehood, resulting in all mankind coming to know the truth of Divine sovereignty. When a Jew dies, whether he actually contributed much or little to this goal, a soldier in the army has fallen. This is why the living must rededicate themselves to the achievement of this goal.

Another commentary voiced this opinion in similar terms. Every *neshamah* is, as it were, a particle of Godliness. When a person dies and his *neshamah* departs the earth, something of Godliness is now missing. "May the Name of God be exalted and sanctified" is a prayer that the element of Godliness that left the earth with the person's death be replenished.

Unfortunately, there are people whose life is anything but a manifestation of Godliness. Is it not absurd to speak of replenishing the lost element of Godliness upon the death of a person whose life was the very antithesis of Godliness? This can be clarified by two stories.

The first story is about R' Shalom Dov of Lubavitch, who demonstrated great love for simple, unlearned people. One chassid was bold enough to ask the Rebbe, "Just what is it that you see in these ignorant people that makes you esteem them so highly?"

This chassid happened to be a diamond merchant. R' Shalom Dov asked him, "Do you happen to have any of your wares with you?" The chassid said that he did, and took out a packet which he unfolded before the Rebbe, revealing a number of diamonds.

R' Shalom Dov pointed to a large diamond and said, "Ah! That is indeed a very beautiful jewel."

The chassid smiled. "I'm sorry, Rebbe," he said, "but you are mistaken. It is indeed a large stone, but it is full of flaws and is of relatively little value. Let me show you a truly beautiful stone," the chassid continued, pointing to a small diamond. "Now that is a valuable stone. It has a blue-white color and is free of any flaws."

"I don't think it is more valuable than the other stone," the Rebbe said. "The larger stone is more impressive."

The chassid said, "Rebbe, to know the value of diamonds one must have the expertise and be a mayven on diamonds."

"Exactly my point," R' Shalom Dov said. "To know the value of a Jew one must have the expertise and be a mayven. You are a mayven on diamonds, and I am a mayven on Jews."

This story demonstrates that simple, unlearned people may have great value, but what can one say about a person who was a scoundrel and anything but Godly? For that I must tell you a story from my personal experience.

In 1994 I began a small rehabilitation program in Israel for ex-prisoners whose drug use led them to a life of crime. In meeting with a group of ex-convicts, I pointed out that they all knew that the drugs they were using were harmful to them. I told them that if a person has a shiny, new luxury automobile, he takes great care that it not be damaged in any way. We have an inherent trait to protect things that are beautiful and valuable from being damaged. I told these men that if they would think of themselves as being beautiful and valuable people, they would be far less likely to relapse in the use of drugs.

One of the men, Avi, said, "What you are saying makes no sense to me. I am 34 years old. Sixteen of these years have been spent in jail. I have been imprisoned eight times. When I am released, no one will give me a job. When the social worker calls my family to inform them of my pending release, they become very upset. They do not want me out of jail. I am an embarrassment and a burden to them. They would prefer if I were dead. How do you expect me to see myself as beautiful and valuable when everyone, including my family, sees me as ugly and worthless?"

I recoiled from Avi's challenge, then said, "Avi, have you ever passed by a jewelry store which had a display of diamonds in the window?"

"Yes," Avi said.

"Those beautiful diamonds may be worth millions of dollars. But do you know what they looked like when they were extracted from the diamond mine? Just like chunks of rock covered with dirt. If one did not know any better, one would promptly throw these ugly rocks into the trash to avoid getting one's hands soiled.

"However, there is a mayven who examines the ore brought up from the mine. He discards the worthless rocks, but may abruptly emit an exclamation of excitement, 'Just look at this! This one has a priceless gem!'

"An onlooker will say, 'What is all the excitement about? That is just a dirty piece of rock. Throw it into the trash.'

"'No, no,' the mayven will say. 'Just wait until this rock is processed.'

"After the 'dirty piece of rock' goes through the processing plant, it comes out as a stunning, scintillating multi-carat diamond, worth millions of dollars.

"Avi," I said. "There is no way that anyone can put priceless beauty into a worthless rock. The beautiful gem was within the rock, but its beauty was concealed by the many layers of substance that covered it. The processing plant removed these layers of material and polished the gem that was within, revealing its extraordinary beauty and great value.

"Avi," I continued, "I am a mayven on people. You have a neshamah, a priceless spark of Godliness within you. Unfortunately, it has been covered by layers of very

objectionable behavior for so many years. But we will remove these layers and expose the beauty within you."

Avi underwent months of treatment, following which he was able to get a job and a small apartment.

A year or so later, Annette, the administrator of the treatment center, received a call from a family. Their elderly mother had died, leaving a completely furnished apartment for which they had no use. Having heard that the treatment center was being remodeled, they wished to donate the furniture. Annette thanked them, then called Avi, explaining that she had no way of transporting the furniture and could he help. Avi said he would take care of it.

Two days later Avi called Annette. He was at the apartment with a truck, but there was no point in bringing the furniture because it was old and dilapidated. Annette told him to bring it anyway because she did not want to refuse the family's offer.

The treatment center is on the second floor of a building, and Avi had to drag the furniture up the stairs. As he was dragging an old sofa, an envelope fell from the pillows. It contained 5,000 shekels. In his drug-using days, Avi would steal purses or break into homes for 10 shekels. Here he had 5,000 shekels of whose existence no one knew. He could easily have invoked the "finders-keepers" principle, which many upright, honest people might have done. But Avi called Annette and reported his find. Annette told him to report it to the family, who thanked him and requested that he give the money to the treatment center as a donation in their mother's memory.

Months later, I attended the housewarming celebration for the renovated center. This was when Annette told me the episode of Avi and the 5,000 shekels.

I said to Avi, "Do you remember when I told you that we would expose the diamond within you? Many 'honest' people would simply have pocketed the money. Your reporting the money is an expression of the neshamah-diamond within you."

Just to complete this story I must tell you that Avi had a brass plate engraved with the words "Mifal L' litush Yahalomim," or "Diamond Polishing Center." This plate is now affixed to the door of the center.

Anyone who knew Avi during his years as a drug addict and criminal would hardly have considered him a diamond. Yet, that is exactly what Avi is. For years the diamond had been concealed by very objectionable behavior.

These stories justify the assertion that every Jew has a precious, Godly *neshamah*, although it is not apparent to any observer. When any person dies, regardless of his lifestyle, an element of Godliness has left the earth. This justifies the restorative *Kaddish* prayer, "May the Name of God be exalted and sanctified."

Our Torah writings state that every Jew is represented by a letter in the Torah (*Sema* 186). If a single letter in a Torah scroll is missing, that scroll is considered defective and may not be used for the Torah reading. It makes little difference whether the missing letter is in the Ten Commandments or in the words spoken by the wicked Laban the Aramite. Similarly, when a Jew is missing, there is a defect in *klal Yisrael*, the body of the Jewish people. This is true even if the missing Jew was not devoted to Judaism.

When we hear the *Kaddish* being recited and think of it in this way, it should remind us that perhaps the nucleus of Godliness within ourselves may not be fully manifest. Perhaps there is much that we could be doing to reveal the infinite beauty of the *neshamah* we possess. While the *Kaddish* is an exaltation of God, it is also an exaltation of every single Jew. As we say in the *An'im Zemiros* hymn, "His splendor is upon me and my splendor is upon Him." The exaltation of God and Israel are interdependent.

Solomon was right. Such thoughts are not likely to occur at a house of festivity. One may gain more wisdom by visiting the house of a mourner and listening to the *Kaddish*. While the *Kaddish* is recited for the *neshamah* of the one who died, it is also a statement of the inestimable worth of those who are living.

The Lessons of the Past

לְמַעַן תִּזְכֹּר אֶת יוֹם צֵאתְךָ מֵאֶרֶץ מִצְרַיִם כֹּל יְמֵי חַיֶּיךָ.

רַק הִשָּׁמֶר לְךָ וּשְׁמֹר נַפְשְׁךָ מְאֹד, פֶּן תִּשְׁכַּח אֶת הַדְּבָרִים אֲשֶׁר רָאוּ עֵינֶיךָ, וּפֶן יָסוּרוּ מִלְּבָבְךָ כֹּל יְמֵי חַיֶּיךָ, וְהוֹדַעְתָּם לְבָנֶיךָ וְלִבְנֵי בָנֶיךָ. יוֹם אֲשֶׁר עָמַדְתָּ לִפְנֵי ה׳ אֱלֹקֶיךָ בְּחֹרֵב.

זָכוֹר אֵת אֲשֶׁר עָשָׂה לְךָ עֲמָלֵק, בַּדֶּרֶךְ בְּצֵאתְכֶם מִמִּצְרָיִם. אֲשֶׁר קָרְךָ בַּדֶּרֶךְ, וַיְזַנֵּב בְּךָ כָּל הַנֶּחֱשָׁלִים אַחֲרֶיךָ, וְאַתָּה עָיֵף וְיָגֵעַ, וְלֹא יָרֵא אֱלֹקִים. וְהָיָה בְּהָנִיחַ ה׳ אֱלֹקֶיךָ לְךָ מִכָּל אֹיְבֶיךָ מִסָּבִיב, בָּאָרֶץ אֲשֶׁר ה׳ אֱלֹקֶיךָ נֹתֵן לְךָ נַחֲלָה לְרִשְׁתָּהּ, תִּמְחֶה אֶת זֵכֶר עֲמָלֵק מִתַּחַת הַשָּׁמָיִם, לֹא תִּשְׁכָּח.

זְכֹר, אַל תִּשְׁכַּח, אֵת אֲשֶׁר הִקְצַפְתָּ אֶת ה׳ אֱלֹקֶיךָ, בַּמִּדְבָּר.

זָכוֹר אֵת אֲשֶׁר עָשָׂה ה׳ אֱלֹקֶיךָ לְמִרְיָם, בַּדֶּרֶךְ בְּצֵאתְכֶם מִמִּצְרָיִם.

זָכוֹר אֶת יוֹם הַשַּׁבָּת לְקַדְּשׁוֹ.

That you may remember the day of your departure from the land of Egypt all the days of your life.

Only beware and guard yourself carefully, lest you forget the things your eyes have seen and lest they stray from your heart all the days of your life. And you are to make them known to your children and to your children's children — the day you stood before Hashem, your God, at Sinai.

Remember what Amalek did to you on the way, as you departed from Egypt. How he encountered you on the way and cut down the weaklings trailing behind you, while you were faint and exhausted, and he did not fear God. It shall be that when Hashem, your God, lets you rest from all your surrounding enemies, in the land that Hashem, your God, gives you as a heritage to bequeath; you are to erase the memory of Amalek from beneath the heaven. Do not forget.

Remember, do not forget, how you angered Hashem, your God, in the Wilderness.

Remember what Hashem, your God, did to Miriam, on the way when you departed from Egypt.

Remember the Sabbath day to hallow it.

There is a popular aphorism that "Experience is a hard teacher, but fools will learn no other way." This is a gross error. Fools are those who do not learn from experience. It is only the wise who do so.

In my working with alcoholics I regularly observe the folly, if not insanity, of people who do not learn from past experience. It is characteristic of an alcoholic who has repeatedly gotten into serious trouble every time he drank to think, "But this time it will be different." This is not unique to alcoholism. Anyone who has a strong desire to do something may think that past adverse results will not occur this time.

In the hope that *tefillah* gives us a better quality of judgment, it is recommended that we recite the six remembrances after the morning service.

Remembering the holiness of Shabbos has an important impact on the workweek. Shabbos is a testimony to Creation. The universe is not the result of a haphazard accident, but was purposefully created by God. In this purposeful world every person has a mission to accomplish. A thorough appreciation of Shabbos enables a person to make life goal-directed. Everything we do during the workweek can become goal-directed and sanctified.

As we shall see in our discussion of the *Kiddush*, when Shabbos arrives, one should be able to bring closure to the past week. Carrying the worries of the workweek into Shabbos detracts from its holiness. Our activities during the workweek should be such that will enable us to totally dedicate ourselves to the spirituality of Shabbos. This requires that we remember the holiness of Shabbos during the workweek.

The goal in our lives must be the fulfillment of the Divine will as prescribed in the Torah. The Torah is not a man-made constitution nor a social contract which is subject to change. No legislature can legitimize immoral behavior or the taking of a life. Torah values derive from God, and were given to us at Sinai. Over two million people witnessed the revelation at Sinai and transmitted it to us. We must remember that the Torah is of Divine origin and hence is immutable.

The remembrance of Amalek is painful, but necessary. After suffering decades of brutal enslavement, the Israelites were liberated and were en route to the Promised Land. They had never offended the Amalekites and posed no threat whatever to them. Yet, the Amalekites attacked them in a most cowardly manner for no reason other than groundless hatred.

Centuries later, Haman, a descendant of Amalek, sought to achieve "the final solution" by eradicating all Jews. Throughout history, Jews have been the victims of unprovoked hatred.

In many countries where Jews settled they enjoyed periods of tranquility and even prosperity. Time after time there was exile, confiscation of property and massacres.

It is only natural to believe what we would like to be the truth. We may feel secure in a country which promises to protect all its citizens. Let us not forget our history. The only security we have is God, and the only true friends we have are each other. We cannot afford divisiveness.

After receiving the Torah, a small faction of Israelites reverted to the paganism and idolatry of Egypt. Rejecting the true God Whose laws were restrictive, they adopted an idol which would allow them to follow any impulse they had. The tendency to eliminate Torah laws because some of them may be inconvenient has recurred throughout our history. We should remember how we angered God by rejecting His Torah.

Of all sins, one of the gravest and most frequently committed is *lashon hara*. People who would not dream of ever physically harming another person do not think that words can be as destructive as bullets.

Miriam, Moses' sister, who was totally devoted to him, spoke negatively about him to their brother, Aaron. There was no malicious intent in her words, yet she was severely punished for this. The Talmud says that the spies sent by Moses should have learned from her experience that negative talk is destructive. Their negative report about Canaan resulted in a calamity from which we suffer and which we mourn to this very day.

Ramban in the letter to his son instructs him to give thought to what he is about to say before saying it. Remembering what transpired with Miriam should remind us to watch our words.

The aphorism states, "Those who do not learn from the past are condemned to repeat it." The six remembrances can help us avoid this pitfall.

The Prayer to Believe

אֲנִי מַאֲמִין בֶּאֱמוּנָה שְׁלֵמָה, שֶׁהַבּוֹרֵא יִתְבָּרַךְ שְׁמוֹ הוּא בּוֹרֵא וּמַנְהִיג לְכָל הַבְּרוּאִים, וְהוּא לְבַדּוֹ עָשָׂה וְעוֹשֶׂה וְיַעֲשֶׂה לְכָל הַמַּעֲשִׂים.

אֲנִי מַאֲמִין בֶּאֱמוּנָה שְׁלֵמָה, שֶׁהַבּוֹרֵא יִתְבָּרַךְ שְׁמוֹ הוּא יָחִיד וְאֵין יְחִידוּת כָּמוֹהוּ בְּשׁוּם פָּנִים, וְהוּא לְבַדּוֹ אֱלֹקֵינוּ, הָיָה הֹוֶה וְיִהְיֶה.

אֲנִי מַאֲמִין בֶּאֱמוּנָה שְׁלֵמָה, שֶׁהַבּוֹרֵא יִתְבָּרַךְ שְׁמוֹ אֵינוֹ גוּף, וְלֹא יַשִּׂיגוּהוּ מַשִּׂיגֵי הַגּוּף, וְאֵין לוֹ שׁוּם דִּמְיוֹן כְּלָל.

אֲנִי מַאֲמִין בֶּאֱמוּנָה שְׁלֵמָה, שֶׁהַבּוֹרֵא יִתְבָּרַךְ שְׁמוֹ הוּא רִאשׁוֹן וְהוּא אַחֲרוֹן.

אֲנִי מַאֲמִין בֶּאֱמוּנָה שְׁלֵמָה, שֶׁהַבּוֹרֵא יִתְבָּרַךְ שְׁמוֹ לוֹ לְבַדּוֹ רָאוּי לְהִתְפַּלֵּל, וְאֵין לְזוּלָתוֹ רָאוּי לְהִתְפַּלֵּל.

אֲנִי מַאֲמִין בֶּאֱמוּנָה שְׁלֵמָה, שֶׁכָּל דִּבְרֵי נְבִיאִים אֱמֶת.

אֲנִי מַאֲמִין בֶּאֱמוּנָה שְׁלֵמָה, שֶׁנְּבוּאַת מֹשֶׁה רַבֵּנוּ עָלָיו הַשָּׁלוֹם הָיְתָה אֲמִתִּית, וְשֶׁהוּא הָיָה אָב לַנְּבִיאִים, לַקּוֹדְמִים לְפָנָיו וְלַבָּאִים אַחֲרָיו.

אֲנִי מַאֲמִין בֶּאֱמוּנָה שְׁלֵמָה, שֶׁכָּל הַתּוֹרָה הַמְּצוּיָה עַתָּה בְיָדֵינוּ הִיא הַנְּתוּנָה לְמֹשֶׁה רַבֵּנוּ עָלָיו הַשָּׁלוֹם.

אֲנִי מַאֲמִין בֶּאֱמוּנָה שְׁלֵמָה, שֶׁזֹּאת הַתּוֹרָה לֹא תְהֵא מֻחְלֶפֶת וְלֹא תְהֵא תּוֹרָה אַחֶרֶת מֵאֵת הַבּוֹרֵא יִתְבָּרַךְ שְׁמוֹ.

אֲנִי מַאֲמִין בֶּאֱמוּנָה שְׁלֵמָה, שֶׁהַבּוֹרֵא יִתְבָּרַךְ שְׁמוֹ יוֹדֵעַ כָּל מַעֲשֵׂה בְנֵי אָדָם וְכָל מַחְשְׁבוֹתָם, שֶׁנֶּאֱמַר: הַיֹּצֵר יַחַד לִבָּם, הַמֵּבִין אֶל כָּל מַעֲשֵׂיהֶם.

אֲנִי מַאֲמִין בֶּאֱמוּנָה שְׁלֵמָה, שֶׁהַבּוֹרֵא יִתְבָּרַךְ שְׁמוֹ גּוֹמֵל טוֹב לְשׁוֹמְרֵי מִצְוֹתָיו וּמַעֲנִישׁ לְעוֹבְרֵי מִצְוֹתָיו.

אֲנִי מַאֲמִין בֶּאֱמוּנָה שְׁלֵמָה, בְּבִיאַת הַמָּשִׁיחַ, וְאַף עַל פִּי שֶׁיִּתְמַהְמֵהַּ, עִם כָּל זֶה אֲחַכֶּה לוֹ בְּכָל יוֹם שֶׁיָּבוֹא.

אֲנִי מַאֲמִין בֶּאֱמוּנָה שְׁלֵמָה, שֶׁתִּהְיֶה תְּחִיַּת הַמֵּתִים בְּעֵת שֶׁיַּעֲלֶה רָצוֹן מֵאֵת הַבּוֹרֵא יִתְבָּרַךְ שְׁמוֹ וְיִתְעַלֶּה זִכְרוֹ לָעַד וּלְנֵצַח נְצָחִים.

I believe with complete faith that the Creator, Blessed is His Name, creates and guides all creatures, and that He alone made, makes, and will make everything.

I believe with complete faith that the Creator, Blessed is His Name, is unique, and there is no uniqueness like His in any way, and that He alone is our God, Who was, Who is, and Who always will be.

I believe with complete faith that the Creator, Blessed is His Name, is not physical and is not affected by physical phenomena, and that there is no comparison whatsoever to Him.

I believe with complete faith that the Creator, Blessed is His Name, is the very first and the very last.

I believe with complete faith that the Creator, Blessed is His Name — to Him alone is it proper to pray and it is not proper to pray to any other.

I believe with complete faith that all the words of the prophets are true.

I believe with complete faith that the prophecy of Moses our teacher, peace upon him, was true, and that he was the father of the prophets — both those who preceded him and those who followed him.

I believe with complete faith that the entire Torah now in our hand is the same one that was given to Moses, our teacher, peace be upon him.

I believe with complete faith that this Torah will not be exchanged nor will there be another Torah from the Creator, Blessed is His Name.

I believe with complete faith that the Creator, Blessed is His Name, knows all the deeds of human beings and their thoughts, as it is said, "He fashions their hearts all together, He comprehends all their deeds."

I believe with complete faith that the Creator, Blessed is His Name, rewards with good those who observe His commandments, and punishes those who violate His commandments.

I believe with complete faith in the coming of the Messiah, and even though he may delay, nevertheless I anticipate every day that he will come.

I believe with complete faith that there will be a resuscitation of the dead whenever the wish emanates from the Creator, Blessed is His Name and exalted is His mention, forever and for all eternity.

We recite the Thirteen Principles of Faith to reinforce our belief in them.

The tzaddik of Sanz would begin saying Ani Maamin (I believe) and pause. "Chaim," he would say to himself, "how do you have the chutzpah to lie to God and say you believe, and yet 'with complete faith,' when you know this is not true?" Then he would repeat the Ani Maamin and say, "You are saying it, Chaim, but you still don't believe." And so it went until he felt he had achieved true belief.

We assert that we believe in Mashiach, but do we really? R' Moshe Teitelbaum of Uheli (Yismach Moshe) would keep his tallis, tefillin and cane at his bedside. If he heard any rumbling outdoors he would grab his tallis, tefillin and cane and run to the window to see if Mashiach had arrived. Shortly before he died, R' Moshe wept, saying, "Master of the Universe? Was it fair to deceive me? Had I known that Mashiach would not come during my lifetime, I could not have survived."

The Chafetz Chaim always took his Shabbos clothes along wherever he traveled, to be dressed appropriately to greet Mashiach.

If we are expecting delivery of an important item which we need immediately, we may look out the window frequently to see if the delivery van is there. Each time the doorbell rings, we are certain it is the delivery of the item.

We are not the Chafetz Chaim, nor the *tzaddik* of Sanz, nor R' Moshe Teitelbaum. Although we say we expect the coming of Mashiach every day, we hardly run to the window to see if he has indeed come. How then can we recite the *Ani Maamin*?

We can think of *Ani Maamin* as a prayer. We can recite it with the thought, "I *wish* to believe. Help me believe."

We certainly wish to embrace the Thirteen Principles of Faith. Many factors affect the level of our belief. We can pray for Divine help to overcome them.

The Belief in Reward

I believe with complete faith that the Creator, Blessed is His Name, rewards with good those who observe His commandments.

R' Levi Yitzchok of Berditchev is known for his unrelenting advocacy in pleading for compassion for his people before God. He would seize every opportunity to point out the merits of the Jews.

One time he met a young man who wore his hair long in the then prevalent style of non-Jewish men. "My child," R' Levi Yitzchok said, "A Jew should have an appearance of being Jewish. Why do you dress and wear your hair like the gentiles?"

The young man answered, "I am an apprentice in the service of a poritz (feudal lord). I do errands that bring me among the poritzim. This is the way I must dress."

R' Levi Yitzchok said, "I will give you a gulden if you will cut your hair short."

The young man politely refused. R' Levi Yitzchok took out a five-gulden coin, which was a respectable sum. "Here you have five gulden if you cut your hair." Again the young man declined, as he did when R' Levi Yitzchok offered him ten, then twenty gulden.

R' Levi Yitzchok then said, "If you cut your hair and dress like a Jew, I promise and guarantee you a place in Gan Eden (Paradise)." Without any hesitancy, the young man shook R' Levi Yitzchok's hand, saying, "I will do so this very day."

R' Levi Yitzchok lifted his eyes in prayer. "Master of the universe!" he said. "Look at the faith Your children have in You. I put twenty gulden in front of this young man to change his appearance. How much hard work he must do to earn twenty gulden! But this did not swerve him in the least. But when I promised him Gan Eden, something which neither he nor any living human being has ever seen, he promptly consented. Even the least observant of Your children have such strong faith in You. Do they not deserve to be treated with greater compassion?"

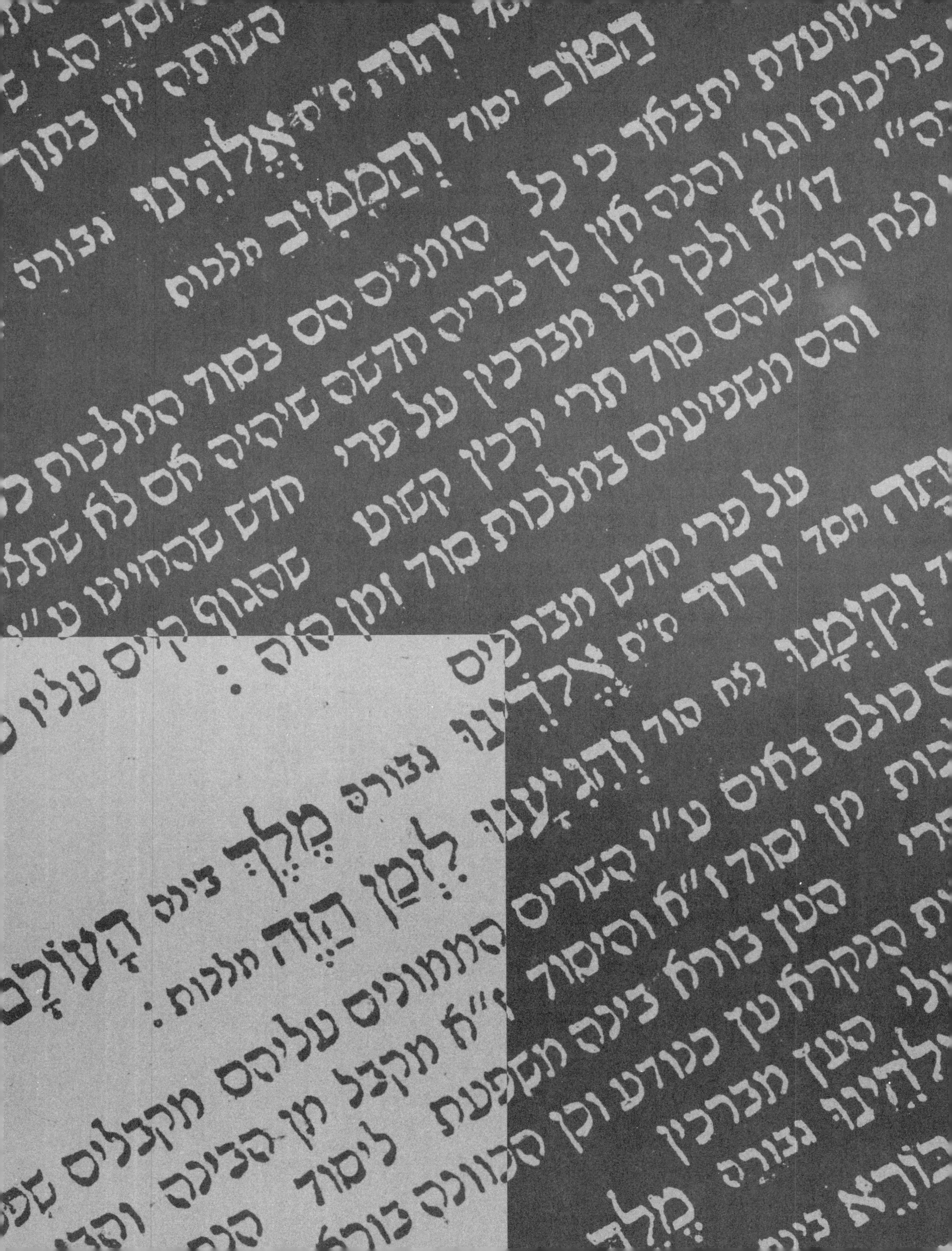

הטוב יסוד והמטיב מלכות
מלך העולם
לזמן הזה מלכות
וקימנו
והגיענו

Berachos — Blessings

Accepting Divine Kindness

We are accustomed to hear people complain when they suffer adverse circumstances, "Why did God do this to me?" It appears to be a natural reaction to question why God has allowed such distress to occur, and we can understand why people may have difficulty in accepting adversity. But why are there some people who cannot accept the good that happens?

One young woman was distraught with anxiety. She had a beautiful infant, but was unable to enjoy her baby. "Every morning I just dread going to her crib," she said. "I'm afraid I'm going to find her a crib death."

I said, "Why do you anticipate something so terrible?" I asked.

"Because," she said, "I don't think I deserve having such a beautiful child. I am afraid God is going to take her away from me."

Such fears are not uncommon. While this case may appear a bit extreme, I know of more than just a few incidents where people failed because they precipitated the failure. They may have had no awareness that this is what they were doing, and they would insist that they did their utmost to avoid failure. However, a careful study leaves no doubt that they were motivated, perhaps subconsciously, to fail. While they consciously certainly did not want to fail, something in their subconscious drove them to subvert their ventures. In many of these cases they anticipated failure because they felt undeserving of success. They had a conviction that their success would be short-lived and would be taken from them. The tension as to when this expected failure was going to occur resulted in such severe anxiety that they did something to bring about the failure. As unpleasant as failure was, it was easier to bear than the suspense and tension of when it was going to happen.

God is absolute kindness. When adversity occurs, we should remember the words of Moses, "God chastises you just as a father chastises his child" (*Deuteronomy* 8:5). True, many times we cannot understand why innocent people suffer. Even Moses was disturbed by this, and when he asked God to reveal to him why He allows the righteous to suffer, God told Moses that because he was a mortal he could not understand this (*Berachos* 7a). The Talmud says that Moses wrote the Book of Job (*Bava Basra* 14b), in which many arguments are presented to explain why the innocent may suffer. All these arguments are refuted, and we must accept adversity with faith in the infinite goodness of God.

While we cannot understand why an infinitely good God should allow bad things to happen, we should have no difficulty whatever in understanding why He makes *good* things happen. Even if we should feel that we are undeserving of good things, we should realize that God's kindness can override many considerations. In the Rosh Hashanah prayers we say that "He is good and does good to both the wicked and the righteous."

The above *berachah* expresses this concept. When a person emerges safely from a perilous state, he recites this *berachah* of gratitude. He gratefully acknowledges that God grants kindness even to those who may not deserve it. This *berachah* should be said in the presence of other people, who respond, "He Who has granted you goodness will continue to grant you good forever." This should be a reassurance, and should eliminate the anxiety of those who fear that they will lose the good they have received.

The psychological wisdom of our sages who formulated the *berachos* was indeed profound.

God Provides for All

בָּרוּךְ אַתָּה ה׳ אֱלֹקֵינוּ מֶלֶךְ הָעוֹלָם, הַזָּן אֶת הָעוֹלָם כֻּלּוֹ, בְּטוּבוֹ, בְּחֵן בְּחֶסֶד וּבְרַחֲמִים, הוּא נֹתֵן לֶחֶם לְכָל בָּשָׂר, כִּי לְעוֹלָם חַסְדּוֹ. וּבְטוּבוֹ הַגָּדוֹל, תָּמִיד לֹא חָסַר לָנוּ, וְאַל יֶחְסַר לָנוּ מָזוֹן לְעוֹלָם וָעֶד. בַּעֲבוּר שְׁמוֹ הַגָּדוֹל, כִּי הוּא קֵל זָן וּמְפַרְנֵס לַכֹּל, וּמֵטִיב לַכֹּל, וּמֵכִין מָזוֹן לְכָל בְּרִיּוֹתָיו אֲשֶׁר בָּרָא. בָּרוּךְ אַתָּה ה׳, הַזָּן אֶת הַכֹּל.

Blessed are You, Hashem, our God, King of the universe, Who nourishes the entire world, in His goodness — with grace, with kindness, and with mercy. He gives nourishment to all flesh, for His kindness is eternal. And through His great goodness, we have never lacked, and may we never lack, nourishment, for all eternity. For the sake of His Great Name, because He is God Who nourishes and sustains all, and benefits all, and He prepares food for all of His creatures which He has created. Blessed are You, Hashem, Who nourishes all.

Had our forefather Adam not sinned, we would have all our needs met without exertion on our part. As a result of Adam's sin, mankind was punished, "By the sweat of your brow shall you eat your bread" (*Genesis* 3:19). But although we must do something for a livelihood, we should not think that what we achieve is solely due to our effort. God said, "I will bless all the works of your hands that you do." Indeed, the Talmud says that how much one will earn that year is decreed on Rosh Hashanah.

It is unfortunate that some people may grossly neglect their spiritual lives and their families in an unrelenting pursuit to earn more money. They would be wise to spend more time with their family, in prayer, studying Torah and doing mitzvos.

The idea that greater exertion will bring them greater earnings is erroneous.

The Maggid of Dubnow stressed this point with a parable. In one town there were two people who were polar opposites in character. One was charitable and generous. His home was always open for the needy to have a meal. Just down the street lived a miser who would never part with a cent.

One day a man came to town seeking employment. He said he was hungry and would work for a meal. He happened upon the miser, who engaged him to weed his garden, cut the grass, and clean out the basement. When he finished, the miser said, "Now for your meal, go down to the house at the end of the block and you will be served," directing him to the home of the charitable person.

The man met others who were eating there, and in his conversation with them he told them how hard he had worked to earn this meal. When they heard this they said, "You fool! You didn't have to break your back to get this meal. This food is free. That miser took advantage of you. You actually worked for nothing!"

So it is with us, the Maggid said. Perhaps our food is not completely free, because we are required to do something to earn it. But it is foolish to think we will have more if we exert ourselves. Our earnings will not suffer if we spend our time wisely, with our families, in prayer, Torah study and performance of mitzvos.

To those who felt that unless they exerted themselves they could not earn enough, the Elder of Navarodok would tell the following story.

There was a blacksmith who worked from dawn to dusk in almost intolerable heat, inhaling soot and fumes. One of his acquaintances said to him, "You are very dexterous. You could have become a goldsmith and you would have had a much easier life. Why did you choose so difficult a trade?"

The blacksmith laughed. "It is my good fortune that I did not become a goldsmith. I would have died of hunger. In all my years, not a single person has brought me a golden object to repair. Some people come in to order tools made of iron. No one has ever ordered a gold ring from me."

"You fool!" the friend said. "No one is going to order a gold ring from a blacksmith. But if you had a clean,

attractive shop and advertised yourself as a goldsmith, they would indeed have ordered gold rings and brought you gold objects to repair. You could have earned your allotment with much less exertion and a cleaner environment."

So it is with the person who thinks that he earned only because he exerted himself. Of course, if that is the way he chooses, then God leaves him to his own resources and he must indeed devote all his time and expend his energies to earn a living. If he had chosen to work a bit less and be more reliant on God, he could have earned his allotment with much less work.

A man once consulted R' Yosef Dov Soloveitchik of Brisk. In the course of the discussion, R' Yosef Dov asked him, "What do you do?"

"I am a textile merchant," the man said. "I buy from the factories and sell to stores."

"And what is it that you do?" R' Yosef Dov asked.

Assuming that the Rabbi had not heard him, the man repeated his answer a bit louder. Again R' Yosef Dov asked, "And what is it that you do?"

"Pardon me, Rabbi. I have told you quite clearly what I do. I cannot understand what you want."

R' Yosef Dov said, "You have told me how you earn a living. That is something that God does for you. He provides you with the ideas and effort to earn a living. What I want to know is what it is that you do. God does not intervene to make a person more spiritual. That is something a person must do on his own. I kept on asking what it is that you do, and you kept on telling me the things that God does."

Our spiritual lives are totally dependent on our efforts. God provides for our physical welfare. We must take care of our spiritual welfare on our own.

A Partnership With God

רַחֵם ה׳ אֱלֹקֵינוּ עַל יִשְׂרָאֵל עַמֶּךָ, וְעַל יְרוּשָׁלַיִם עִירֶךָ, וְעַל צִיּוֹן מִשְׁכַּן כְּבוֹדֶךָ, וְעַל מַלְכוּת בֵּית דָּוִד מְשִׁיחֶךָ, וְעַל הַבַּיִת הַגָּדוֹל וְהַקָּדוֹשׁ שֶׁנִּקְרָא שִׁמְךָ עָלָיו. אֱלֹקֵינוּ אָבִינוּ רְעֵנוּ זוּנֵנוּ פַּרְנְסֵנוּ וְכַלְכְּלֵנוּ וְהַרְוִיחֵנוּ, וְהַרְוַח לָנוּ ה׳ אֱלֹקֵינוּ מְהֵרָה מִכָּל צָרוֹתֵינוּ. וְנָא אַל תַּצְרִיכֵנוּ ה׳ אֱלֹקֵינוּ, לֹא לִידֵי מַתְּנַת בָּשָׂר וָדָם, וְלֹא לִידֵי הַלְוָאָתָם, כִּי אִם לְיָדְךָ הַמְּלֵאָה הַפְּתוּחָה הַקְּדוֹשָׁה וְהָרְחָבָה, שֶׁלֹּא נֵבוֹשׁ וְלֹא נִכָּלֵם לְעוֹלָם וָעֶד.

Have mercy, Hashem, our God, on Israel Your people; on Jerusalem, Your city; on Zion, the resting place of Your Glory; on the monarchy of the house of David, Your anointed; and on the great and holy House upon which Your Name is called. Our God, our Father — tend us, nourish us, sustain us, support us, relieve us; Hashem, our God, grant us speedy relief from all our troubles. Please, make us not needful — Hashem, our God — of the gifts of human hands nor of their loans, but only of Your Hand that is full, open, holy, and generous, that we not feel inner shame nor be humiliated for ever and ever.

The Chassidic master of Apt heard that in a nearby village there was a proprietor of a small store who performed miracles. If he gave a berachah to a sick individual, even one who was critically ill, the person recovered. If he gave someone a berachah for success, the person prospered. Inasmuch as the storekeeper appeared to be an average person, no one understood where his wondrous powers came from.

The tzaddik of Apt was very curious, and went to observe this person. He watched him carefully for several days, and saw nothing special in the man's conduct to explain the potency of his blessings. Finally the tzaddik said to him, "I am the Rabbi of Apt. You must tell me how you acquired your special powers."

The man was stunned that the great tzaddik of Apt had come to see him. "I really do not have much to tell you, other than that I have great trust in God. Whenever I am in distress, I distribute whatever I have to the poor. One time I was serving a meal to the poor, when a messenger from the local magistrate came with a summons that I come to him immediately. I reasoned that inasmuch as God has commanded us to feed the poor, I was obeying orders from a higher authority and I did not have the right to leave them to respond to the magistrate's wishes.

"One time my circumstances were so bad that I had to sell all my possessions to feed my family. My wife insisted that we move elsewhere. Perhaps my mazal would improve. 'Go find yourself a partner with whom you can go into business. Two heads are better than one,' she said. I felt that God could help me just as well here as elsewhere, but I finally yielded and journeyed towards another town to find a partner and a business opportunity.

"On the way, I was distressed because I felt that I had compromised my trust in God. I began to cry, and I said, 'Master of the universe! You know that I am in dire straits. My wife insisted that I look for a partner and go into business with him. Why do I have to find a mortal partner? I cannot have full trust in another person the way I trust You. What if my partner dies? It is only You Whom I trust, and because You are eternal, I never have to worry that something will happen to You. I want You as my partner. I will divide my earnings with You: half to my family and half to tzedakah.'

"I then turned around and went home. I told my wife I had found a partner. I was able to borrow money to open this store, and I am earning a good living. I have two cash boxes. Whatever I earn I immediately divide, so that half goes to my 'partner' by way of tzedakah."

When the tzaddik of Apt heard this account he said, "Little wonder that all his blessings are fulfilled. The halachah states that if one partner in a business makes a commitment, the other partner must live up to it. Inasmuch as he has entered into a partnership with God, God must fulfill any commitments he makes."

This man's trust in God was simple and sincere. He did not want his livelihood to come from anyone other than God. When he said, "Make us not needful of the gifts of human hands," it was not lip-service, but a prayer from the depths of his heart.

The Divine Service of Eating

בָּרוּךְ אַתָּה ה׳ אֱלֹקֵינוּ מֶלֶךְ הָעוֹלָם, אֲשֶׁר קִדְּשָׁנוּ בְּמִצְוֹתָיו,
וְצִוָּנוּ עַל נְטִילַת יָדָיִם.

Blessed are You, Hashem, our God, King of the universe, Who has sanctified us with His commandments, and commanded us regarding washing the hands.

The above *berachah* is recited upon the ritual washing of the hands prior to a meal. Some people assume that the halachic requirement to wash our hands prior to eating is purely for hygienic reasons. The fallacy is that halachah requires that the hands be clean *prior* to the ritual washing. If the ritual washing was done when the hands were soiled, it must be repeated after the hands are cleansed.

The ritual washing is symbolic of the purification of the hands of the *Kohanim* (priests) before they ate the *terumah* (sanctified tithes). It also represents the ritual hand-washing of the *Kohanim* before they brought the offerings on the Altar in the Temple. The message for us is that we can elevate our eating to the status of a Divine service.

Animals eat because they are hungry. Man can go beyond that. We should eat with the conscious intent to obtain the necessary nourishment so that our bodies can be in optimal health. One's *neshamah* resides within the physical body and can achieve its nourishment, which consists of the performance of mitzvos, only via the vehicle of the body. Therefore, maintaining the body in optimal condition is likewise a mitzvah. The ritual washing of the hands should remind us that we can transform the physiologic act of eating into a spiritual experience.

Eating can further become a mitzvah when we share our food with the needy. This act of *gemillas chasadim* (kindness to others) is of unparalleled merit. The Patriarch Abraham is cited primarily for the virtue of providing food for hungry wayfarers.

R' Eliyahu Mani, Rav of Hebron, felt the need for sharing his food with others so intensely that he refused to eat unless he had a needy person at his table. On more than one occasion he chose to fast rather than to eat alone. We can well understand why the Talmud says that in the absence of the Temple, a person's table is compared to an altar.

It is customary to precede the above *berachah* with the Scriptural verse, "Lift your hands in holiness and give praise to God" (*Psalms* 134:2). This emphasizes that the washing of the hands is in preparation for a spiritual act.

We may ask, inasmuch as the institution of the ritual washing is a rabbinical rather than a Scriptural ordinance, why do the words of the *berachah* indicate that God commanded us to wash our hands? This is not stated in the Torah.

One answer is that we are commanded, "You shall be holy" (*Leviticus* 19:2). Ramban explains this to mean that over and above observance of all the Torah prohibitions, we should dedicate *all* our actions to the Divine service, as it is written, "Know God in all your ways" (*Proverbs* 3:6). Eating non-kosher food is, of course, forbidden. But eating kosher food should not simply be a means of satisfying one's hunger; one should eat with the intention of being in optimal condition to perform the mitzvos. Ramban states that there is nothing to prevent a person from being gluttonous with kosher food. It is possible to behave animal-like while eating only food that bears the most scrupulous *hechsher* (kosher supervision). The ritual washing of the hands is thus a fulfillment of the Divine command to seek holiness in everything we do.

Just as we prepare ourselves prior to eating with a ritual that emphasizes this uniquely human concept of food consumption, we reinforce this concept with the blessing following the meal. After declaring our awareness that God provides us with our food, we recite the prayer: "We thank You, our God, ... for Your Torah which You taught us and for Your statutes which You made known to us." The relevance of this prayer to the blessing after meals is that we should recognize that we eat not only to satiate our hunger, but to have the energy to fulfill the Divine commandments. When we are hungry, we wash our hands ritually, an act which says to us,"Take care that your appetite does not dominate you." After we have finished eating we recite the above prayer, which says to us, "Now use the energy derived from the food to fulfill your mission on earth."

There Is Holiness in Everything

בָּרוּךְ אַתָּה ה׳ אֱלֹקֵינוּ מֶלֶךְ הָעוֹלָם, הַמּוֹצִיא לֶחֶם מִן הָאָרֶץ.

Blessed are You, Hashem, our God, King of the universe, Who brings forth bread from the earth.

The painter working in our home in Israel took his lunch break. He washed his hands ritually and recited the *Hamotzi berachah.* He then touched the bread and kissed his fingers just as one does when kissing the *mezuzah* or the Torah. This was something new to me, and I asked him the reason for it. He looked at me with bewilderment, as though I were completely bereft of any Jewish knowledge. "Don't you understand?" he said. "This bread is *kodesh* (holy). I just said *'Hamotzi lechem min haaretz.'* G–d Himself brought this bread from the earth. It is something which God Himself is giving to me. That makes it holy."

I was deeply embarrassed. For years I had been reciting the *berachos* for bread, fruits and vegetables as an expression of gratitude to God, but this thought had never occurred to me. Some people who have an item that was in the possession of a *tzaddik* consider it to have been imbued with the holiness of a *tzaddik.* If an object that was touched by a *tzaddik* is thought of as holy, how much more so something that was touched by God!

It is important to note that these *berachos* are in the present tense. God *brings* forth bread from the earth; He *creates* the fruit of the earth; He *creates* the fruit of the tree. R'

Shneur Zalman in *Tanya* states that the Ten Utterances of Creation did not cease after they brought things into existence. Rather, the Divine Utterances continue to maintain Creation, which is an ongoing process rather than something that occurred in the past.

R' Shneur Zalman points out that nothing could be in existence if it did not have a nucleus of the Divine Utterances to maintain it. God's Utterances did not simply bring things into existence which now propagate independently of Him. The bread, fruits, and vegetables we eat are the current handiwork of God. They are indeed holy.

The Talmud states that if one eats something without reciting a *berachah*, that is equivalent to theft. If we borrow something for a specific purpose and then use it for something else against the owner's wish, this unauthorized use is equivalent to theft.

In our discussion of the *berachah* for the ritual washing of the hands, we noted how everything can be directed toward the Divine service. As we have seen, the goods of the world were indeed given for us to enjoy. However, we should enjoy them in the process of fulfilling the Divine will. By reciting these *berachos*, we acknowledge that the foods we eat are direct gifts from God.

After holding the *esrog* and *lulav* on Succos, some people kiss the *esrog* to show that an item used for a mitzvah is dear to them. As the painter said to me, foods, too, should be thought of as holy. The *berachos* should remind us to keep them holy.

Appreciating the World

The Jerusalem Talmud states that among the questions a person will be asked on his Judgment Day is, "Did you enjoy My world?" As the various blessings indicate, God provided man with abundant ways to enjoy the world. It is evident from the Jerusalem Talmud that a person is derelict if he fails to enjoy the world.

But a person must enjoy the world properly, as befits a dignified, intelligent human being. Animals do not think about how they satisfy their desires. They follow their instincts even when these may have destructive consequences. Man should be different.

The Midrash states that God created the Garden of Eden with everything that a person's heart could desire. He led Adam around the Garden and said, "I put everything here for you. Take care that You do not ruin My world."

Proper use of the world to achieve God's purpose for Creation permits enjoying the world. Enjoying the world in an abusive manner is destructive and defeats the purpose of Creation.

As wise as Adam was, his human intellect was unable to determine what might be ruinous to the world. This was why God commanded him to refrain from the Tree of Knowledge.

Although knowledge can be good, it can be destructive if it is wielded by people who are ignorant or who are malicious. On his first day in the world, Adam was not yet ready to use knowledge wisely and safely. Indeed, the Kabbalistic writings state that the prohibition of eating from the Tree of Knowledge would have been rescinded on Shabbos. It was necessary for Adam to experience the spirituality and holiness of Shabbos before he could be entrusted with knowledge. Unfortunately, his premature venture into knowledge brought ruin to the world. "Enjoy My world," God said, "but do not do so destructively."

A child who sees brightly colored pills thinks they are candy. A sharp-edged instrument may appear to him to be a toy. He wishes to enjoy these things, but his immature mind cannot understand that these may be lethal for him. His parents, with their superior wisdom, must protect him from harming himself. So it is with us. We may wish to enjoy things, but we may not realize they are harmful. We must heed the superior wisdom of God to avoid harm.

When we see a tree in beautiful blossom or a beautiful person, we recite a *berachah* declaring that God has given us many splendid things to enjoy. We must obey His commandments in order that our enjoyment not be harmful to us.

בָּרוּךְ אַתָּה ה׳ אֱלֹקֵינוּ מֶלֶךְ הָעוֹלָם, שֶׁהֶחֱיָנוּ וְקִיְּמָנוּ וְהִגִּיעָנוּ לַזְּמַן הַזֶּה.

בָּרוּךְ אַתָּה ה׳ אֱלֹקֵינוּ מֶלֶךְ הָעוֹלָם, דַּיַּן הָאֱמֶת.

Blessed are You, Hashem, our God, King of the universe, Who has kept us alive, sustained us, and brought us to this season.
Blessed are You, Hashem, our God, King of the universe, the true Judge.

One of the important concepts in psychology is "repression." Repression occurs when some idea or feeling is so reprehensible or anxiety provoking that a person cannot accept that he is capable of harboring it. The human mind is so adept at protecting itself that it banishes this idea or feeling. In fact, the person may not be aware that he had this idea or feeling even for a moment. The psychological defense system of the mind does not permit the objectionable idea or feeling to surface into awareness or consciousness. It is pushed into the subconscious portion of the mind. When the idea or feeling is blocked from one's awareness and is relegated to the subconscious mind, we say that it is "repressed."

The problem with repression is that the idea or feeling that was pushed into the subconscious mind does not lie there dormant. Rather, it tries to emerge into awareness, and a person must use psychic energy to keep it buried in the subconscious. Sometimes the idea or feeling emerges in a disguised form, which may constitute a neurotic symptom.

If a person could deal with unacceptable thoughts and feelings in some way other than repression, he would have more psychic energy to devote to other things and he might be free of neurotic symptoms. How can this be done? A person should recognize that a human being is a composite creature, consisting of a body that is animal in nature and a spirit that is uniquely human. A person cannot avoid having animalistic impulses. These are the expressions of the body. However, because one is a human being rather than an animal, one must be master over one's behavior and not be a slave to one's animalistic drives.

It is important that a person have confidence in his ability to be in control of his behavior, for otherwise the objectionable thoughts or feelings will provoke great anxiety. A person should realize, "Yes, I may have such thoughts and feelings. This does not make me a bad person. However, I am a human being, not an animal. I will act only in a way that is proper and dignified. *But there is no reason for me to disown any thoughts and feelings.*" This attitude may make a person much less anxious and much more productive.

The above two *berachos* are polar opposites. The *shehecheyanu berachah* is said on special, happy occasions. It is said on the festivals, when one buys a house or a new garment, or when one eats a new fruit that has been out of season. *Shehecheyanu* is an expression of gratitude to God "that He has brought me to this time."

Dayan ha'emes, on the other hand, is said when one has suffered serious adversity, such as when, God forbid, a close relative dies, or one has lost his fortune. *Dayan ha'emes* is an expression of accepting the Divine decree with serenity. Even though one is grieving the loss, one expresses his faith in God that His judgment is true, even though it may defy our understanding.

What happens when a person's father dies and leaves a huge inheritance? The son grieves over his father's death, but there is no way of denying that he has come into wealth. Dare one be happy over becoming very wealthy when it has come as a result of a father's death? Would it not be crass for a son to rejoice over being heir to a fortune at such a great loss? If the son were to feel any joy at becoming wealthy, he would berate himself, "How dare I feel this way! Only a son who is totally without a conscience could feel joy at a moment when he should be in grief." The feeling of joy would be so reprehensible that his mind would promptly reject this feeling and banish it from awareness. It would bury it in the subconscious. As we have seen, this feeling would try to surface into awareness. As it did so, the mind would continually have to force it back, and this would consume much psychic energy. To further convince himself that he could not possibly harbor any feeling of joy, the son might exhibit excessive mourning, far beyond what is the norm. This may affect his ability to function.

Our sages were very wise. Their message to the son is, "There is no need to disown any feelings. There is simply no denying that when a person acquires wealth, he is happy about it. It is possible for a person to sincerely grieve the loss of his father, and yet be happy that he has become wealthy. There is no need for the latter feeling to be driven out of awareness and buried in the subconscious. You are justified in having a feeling of joy *at the very moment that you are in grief.*"

Halachah states that a son who inherits wealth upon the death of his father must say two *berachos*. He must first say the *dayan ha'emes*, accepting with faith the Divine judgment on the death of his father which has caused him to grieve. He must then say the *shehecheyanu*, expressing his thanks to God that he has now inherited great wealth.

Our sages recognized that life is full of conflicts. Some conflicts result in repression, which, as we have seen, can be a costly defense maneuver. By prescribing these two *berachos*, the sages have enabled a mourner to adjust to a painful situation and resume a normal life. They have eliminated the need to repress and develop symptomatic defenses.

The Perfection in the World

בָּרוּךְ אַתָּה ה׳ אֱלֹקֵינוּ מֶלֶךְ הָעוֹלָם, בּוֹרֵא נְפָשׁוֹת רַבּוֹת וְחֶסְרוֹנָן, עַל כָּל מַה שֶּׁבָּרָא(תָ) לְהַחֲיוֹת בָּהֶם נֶפֶשׁ כָּל חָי. בָּרוּךְ חֵי הָעוֹלָמִים.

Blessed are You, Hashem, our God, King of the universe, Who creates numerous living things with their deficiencies; for all that You have created with which to maintain the life of every being. Blessed is He, the Life of the worlds.

The accepted interpretation of the above *berachah* is that God created those things necessary to satisfy the deficiencies of all living beings. Thus "deficiencies" refers to things that living beings lack and which they must have in order to survive, i.e., air, food, water, etc.

A recent article suggested an additional interpretation of "deficiencies." This was a speech given by a father whose son was a student at *Chush*, a school for special children with any of a variety of learning disabilities.

> *The father began by admitting that he had much difficulty in accepting that all that God did was perfection. "Where is the perfection in my child?" he asked. "He cannot do many of the things children his age do effortlessly."*
>
> *"One day," the father said, "I was walking with my son and we passed a playground where some children were playing baseball. My son recognized some of them. 'Do you think they will let me play with them?' he asked. Prepared to accept a painful rejection, I said, 'Let's ask them.'*

"The youngster we asked looked at the other youths, and getting no response he said, 'Sure. Shaye can be on our team.' The rationale for this decision was probably that they were losing by a score of nine to three in the eighth inning. Having despaired of winning, Shaye's participation could not hurt them. Shaye was given a glove and put into deep right field, where he was unlikely to have to do any fielding.

"But in the ninth inning, Shaye's team scored several runs. The score was now nine to seven, with two men on base and two outs. It was Shaye's turn to bat. Would they let Shaye bat to make the third out and forego any chance of winning?

"Shaye was given a bat, which he did not even know how to hold properly. The pitcher took a few steps forward and softly lobbed in the ball, at which Shaye waved the bat. Another teammate helped Shaye hold the bat, and when the pitcher lobbed in the ball, they swung together, hitting a slow ground ball to the pitcher. 'Run to first, Shaye!' the children shouted. Shaye had never run to first, so the boys directed him toward first base. The pitcher could have easily thrown the ball to the first baseman for the third out, but instead he threw it over the first baseman's head, deep into right field. 'Run to second, Shaye,' the children yelled, showing him the direction as the two men on base headed toward home plate. The right fielder got the message and threw the ball way over the third baseman's head. Shaye was directed to third, and then all his teammates ran with him. 'Run to home, Shaye!' they screamed. 'You'll win the game for us!' When Shaye triumphantly crossed home plate, both teams joined to carry him on their shoulders. 'Shaye hit a grand slam and won the game!' they shouted jubilantly.

"My question had been answered. Shaye was not a perfect creation, but God's perfection was in those seventeen youngsters who gladdened a child's heart and gave him an unforgettable experience."

When I heard this father's story, I thought that perhaps the above *berachah* might also mean that God created beings *with their deficiencies*, in order to give life to other living beings. Shaye's deficiencies were the opportunity for these children to earn merits, to enable them to reach their perfection.

בָּרוּךְ אַתָּה ה׳ אֱלֹקֵינוּ מֶלֶךְ הָעוֹלָם, שֶׁהַכֹּל בָּרָא לִכְבוֹדוֹ.

בָּרוּךְ אַתָּה ה׳ אֱלֹקֵינוּ מֶלֶךְ הָעוֹלָם, אֲשֶׁר יָצַר אֶת הָאָדָם בְּצַלְמוֹ,בְּצֶלֶם דְּמוּת תַּבְנִיתוֹ, וְהִתְקִין לוֹ מִמֶּנּוּ בִּנְיַן עֲדֵי עַד. בָּרוּךְ אַתָּה ה׳, יוֹצֵר הָאָדָם.

Blessed are You, Hashem, our God, King of the universe, Who has created everything for His glory. Blessed are You, Hashem, our God, King of the universe, Who fashioned the Man in His image, in the image of his likeness, and prepared for him — from himself — a building for eternity. Blessed are You, Hashem, Who fashioned the Man.

We have attended many weddings. We heard the rabbi chant the above *berachos*. These are indeed fine *berachos*, but just what is their relevance to marriage? The fact that God created everything for His glory and that He fashioned man in His image is indeed an important concept of Judaism, but it does not seem to have anything to do with marriage. Why did our sages assign these *berachos* for the wedding ceremony?

We live in an age where the permanence of marriages is precarious. Dissolution of marriages is frequent, and a divorce rate of 40 percent is alarming. What is going wrong? A young man and woman who seem to be very much in love lose interest in each other. Why?

It is important that we understand what real love is. R' Mendel of Kotzk once saw a young man who was heartily enjoying a dish of fish. "Why are you eating the fish?" R' Mendel asked.

The young man looked at him quizzically. "Because I love fish, that's why," he said.

"So," R' Mendel said, "because you love the fish, that is why you took it out of the water where it lived, killed it, and cooked it! That is a strange way to demonstrate your love for the fish! Young man," R' Mendel said, "you do not love the fish at all. You love yourself, and because the taste of fish pleases you, you killed it to gratify your appetite."

What Western civilization calls love is something akin to this. A young man and young woman become acquainted. He feels that she can provide for his emotional and psychological needs, and she feels that he is someone who can satisfy her emotional and psychological needs. But note! Each one is primarily concerned with their *own* needs being fulfilled. To put it bluntly, the other person is loved for selfish reasons. If, with the passage of time, one finds someone else who they feel can better satisfy their needs, then the relationship is over. Inasmuch as it was based on one's personal needs being satisfied, what reason is there to continue the relationship when this purpose can no longer be optimally fulfilled? I prefer to call this kind of love "fish love." A durable marriage cannot be based on "fish love." The two partners do not have a common goal as the foundation of the marriage.

There is no denying that having one's emotional needs satisfied is important, but it should not be the basis of the relationship. If a young man and a young woman marry because they wish to raise a family that will live in a way that will bring greater glory to God, then they have a common goal. If, at any time, they feel some frustration in their own needs not being met, the basis for the marriage has not been eroded. Any problems in the relationship can more easily be resolved.

Our sages, in their great wisdom, arranged that the very first *berachah* pronounced after the couple has been joined in wedlock by the giving of the ring is, "Blessed is God, Who has created everything for His glory." This is a message to the young couple. If this will be the basis of the marriage, then they will have a common goal. Any challenges to the relationship will not undermine its foundation, and the marriage can endure.

The *berachos* about man being created by God in His image are also a guide for a happy marriage. The noted ethicist, R' Yeruchem Levovitz says, "One who respects man, who was created in the image of God, is giving respect to God Himself" (*Daas Chochmah U'Mussar* 2:13). Similarly, "If one insults a person, it is an offense against God, because it shows that he does not believe in the sanctity of man who was created in God's image" (*Yalkut Me'am Loez, Ethics of the Fathers* 133).

The Torah requirement to respect every person does not allow for any exceptions. Husband and wife are, therefore, required by Torah law to respect one another. As newlyweds, they may not yet appreciate the mutual respect that a couple should have. A husband may not yet implement the Talmudic requirement that "a husband should love his wife as much as he loves himself, and respect her even more than he respects himself" (*Yevamos* 62b). Therefore, aside from the respect that they should accord each other as husband and wife, they must avoid offending each other simply on the basis that it is forbidden to offend another person. This is emphasized by the *berachah* that "God has fashioned man in His image."

If we would only heed the messages in these *berachos*, to have a common, unselfish goal in marriage and to respect one another, marriages would be much happier and more durable.

Our Responsibility to Future Generations

בָּרוּךְ אַתָּה ה׳ אֱלֹקֵינוּ מֶלֶךְ הָעוֹלָם, אֲשֶׁר קִדְּשָׁנוּ בְּמִצְוֹתָיו, וְצִוָּנוּ לְהַכְנִיסוֹ בִּבְרִיתוֹ שֶׁל אַבְרָהָם אָבִינוּ.

Blessed are You, Hashem, our God, King of the universe, Who has sanctified us with His commandments, and has commanded us to bring him into the covenant of Abraham, our forefather.

The above *berachah* is recited by the father at a *bris* (circumcision). It is a declaration that the *bris* marks the formal entrance of the newborn into the people of Israel as a descendant of the Patriarch Abraham. Important as the *bris* is as a mitzvah, it is even more important in preserving the Jewish identity.

R' Aryeh Levin was accustomed to go to the synagogue early on Friday evening to recite Shir HaShirim (Song of Songs). He once sat near his teacher, R' Chaim Berlin, and they recited the verses together. When they came to the verse, "You are lovely, my beloved, you are lovely; your eyes are like those of turtledoves" (Song of Songs 4:1), R' Chaim's eyes welled up with tears. R' Aryeh was bewildered. Inasmuch as the verse describes God's love for Israel, why did it cause R' Chaim to be sad?

R' Chaim explained, "When I was a rabbi in Moscow, a man asked to meet with me secretly. He then told me that his wife had just borne a son, and he wished me to do the circumcision. I told him that I would be pleased to do so, but what was the reason for the secrecy?

"The man explained that he was well-to-do, and that selling church appurtenances and religious items was how he made his living. If it were discovered that he was a Jew, that would be the end of his livelihood. That was why he wished to make a clandestine bris. He asked for my advice how to best do this.

"I suggested to him that he give all his household help a day off. I then performed the bris privately with only the two of us present.

"Several days later the man wished to pay me for my services. I told him that I would not accept payment for doing a mitzvah. I then said to him, 'I saw that your house was barren of anything Jewish. Inasmuch as you have become totally assimilated, what caused you to risk exposure by having a bris performed?'

"The man answered, 'I know that I have drifted away from Judaism, and I doubt that I can ever return. But who knows? I know I am Jewish, and if circumstances permit, I have the option of returning. But what if my son somehow discovers his Jewish ancestry when he grows up? If he is not circumcised, I have taken away his option of ever being a practicing Jew. I don't have the right to deprive my son of that option. That's why I wanted him circumcised.' "

R' Chaim continued, "When I came to the verse 'You are lovely, my beloved, you are lovely; your eyes are like those of turtledoves,' I remembered the Talmud's question, 'Why does the verse say "You are lovely" twice?' The Talmud answers that God is saying to Israel, 'You are lovely before you sin, and you are lovely even after you have sinned. Why? Because you are compared to the eyes of a turtledove. The turtledove will not fly beyond a distance from which it can see its nest. Similarly, even if Israel sins, it does not stray beyond a distance from which it can see its source, and it can always return.'

"Whenever I come to this verse in Shir HaShirim, I am reminded of the man who strayed so far from Judaism, yet he tried to keep some contact with his source, if only that his son have the opportunity to return to the faith of his fathers.

"My tears are both of pain and of joy. I am saddened that a Jew can stray so far, but I am happy that the contact with his God and his people is never irreparably broken."

The Journey of Life

יְהִי רָצוֹן מִלְּפָנֶיךָ ה׳ אֱלֹקֵינוּ וֵאלֹקֵי אֲבוֹתֵינוּ שֶׁתּוֹלִיכֵנוּ לְשָׁלוֹם, וְתַצְעִידֵנוּ לְשָׁלוֹם, וְתַדְרִיכֵנוּ לְשָׁלוֹם. וְתַגִּיעֵנוּ לִמְחוֹז חֶפְצֵנוּ לְחַיִּים וּלְשִׂמְחָה וּלְשָׁלוֹם, [וְתַחֲזִירֵנוּ לְבֵיתֵנוּ לְשָׁלוֹם,] וְתַצִּילֵנוּ מִכַּף כָּל אוֹיֵב וְאוֹרֵב (וְלִסְטִים וְחַיּוֹת רָעוֹת) בַּדֶּרֶךְ, וּמִכָּל מִינֵי פֻּרְעָנֻיּוֹת הַמִּתְרַגְּשׁוֹת לָבוֹא לָעוֹלָם, וְתִשְׁלַח בְּרָכָה בְּ(כָל) מַעֲשֵׂה יָדֵינוּ, וְתִתְּנֵנוּ לְחֵן וּלְחֶסֶד וּלְרַחֲמִים בְּעֵינֶיךָ וּבְעֵינֵי כָל רוֹאֵינוּ, וְתִשְׁמַע קוֹל תַּחֲנוּנֵינוּ, כִּי קֵל שׁוֹמֵעַ תְּפִלָּה וְתַחֲנוּן אָתָּה. בָּרוּךְ אַתָּה ה׳, שׁוֹמֵעַ תְּפִלָּה.

May it be Your will, Hashem, our God and the God of our forefathers, that You lead us toward peace, emplace our footsteps toward peace, guide us toward peace, and make us reach our desired destination for life, gladness, and peace [and return us to our homes in peace]. May you rescue us from the hand of every foe, ambush, (bandits, and evil animals) along the way, and from all manner of punishments that assemble to come to earth. May You send blessing in our (every) handiwork, and grant us grace, kindness, and mercy in Your eyes and in the eyes of all who see us. May You hear the sound of our supplication, because You are God Who hears prayer and supplication. Blessed are You, Hashem, Who hears prayer.

One might wonder about the propriety of the terms in this prayer in regard to modern travel. We are concerned about the possibility of accidents, but as a rule, we do not fear ambush, bandits, or wild animals.

R' Eizik of Vitebsk was a follower of R' Shneur Zalman, author of Tanya, and accompanied the master on a trip. After R' Shneur Zalman recited the Wayfarer's Prayer, he suggested to R' Eizik that it would be appropriate to say this prayer every day. After all, what is our earthly life other than a journey? He also said that a person should never worry, being secure that God watches over him.

R' Eizik said the Wayfarer's Prayer every day, and lived to be 97. Whenever something occurred that might cause him worry, he would say, "The Rebbe said there is no cause for worry," and his mood promptly became upbeat.

Some chassidim attributed R' Eizik's longevity to his freedom from anxiety. Others said that his daily recitation of the Wayfarer's Prayer kept the Angel of Death at a distance.

If we indeed think of life as a journey, the words of this prayer are appropriate even today. I tell my recovering alcoholic patients that they must be aware of the danger that lurks, because alcohol lies in ambush for them. For those who are not alcoholic, there are a myriad of dangers in life to which we may not be alert. As it were, they lie in ambush for us, and we would do well to pray for Divine protection from them.

Yes, there are bandits in modern life. Anyone who has a television has taken a bandit into the home, one that may rob him of precious, irreplaceable time. This bandit is especially dangerous to our children. And the violent behavior to which we, and especially our children, are exposed is every bit as perilous as the wild animals of earlier days. In the earlier days, the danger was that one might become a victim of a wild animal. Today's graphic violence has caused some young people to behave like wild animals.

We would be wise to give serious thought to R' Shneur Zalman's words. We might live our lives much differently if we think of life as a journey.

Minchah - The Afternoon Service

The term *minchah,* which means "a gift," is used in the Torah to refer to a meal-offering brought on the Altar (*Leviticus* 2:1). Sometimes the meal-offering was brought on its own; other times it accompanied other offerings. The verse in the Torah reads, "When a person (*nefesh*) offers a meal-offering to God, his offering shall be of fine flour." Rashi notes that this is the only time the word *nefesh* (soul) is used to mean "person" in all the votive offerings. This is because the meal-offering was generally brought by a person who could not afford anything more elaborate than a bit of flour. God said, "When a poor person brings as an offering whatever meager amount he can afford, I consider it as though he had offered his very soul to Me." A meager gift from a poor person is a greater sacrifice than an elaborate gift from a wealthy person.

My father used to tell the explanation given by our great-uncle, the tzaddik of Tolna, to an enigmatic statement in the Talmud, "Poverty stalks the poor" (Bava Kamma 92a). The Talmud states that when the wealthy brought the offerings of the first-ripened fruits in gold and silver trays, the fruit was accepted and the trays returned. However, when the poor brought their fruit in baskets woven out of reeds, both the fruit and the baskets were kept in the Temple. "Where is the justice in that?" asked the tzaddik of Tolna.

The tzaddik answered, "I travel to various towns and villages to raise money for the needy. When I inform a community that I plan to visit them, there are two opposite reactions. A poor chassid comes home with the joyous tidings, 'The Rebbe is going to be here soon!' Then his demeanor changes to one of sadness. 'Why are you so sad?' his wife asks. The man answers, 'I would like to give the Rebbe something for his tzedakah fund, but I just do not have any money.'

"The wife says, 'Don't let that worry you. I will do some extra baking and sell the pastries. I will earn a ruble for you to give the Rebbe.' Promptly the man's mood reverts to joy.

"The same day," the tzaddik continued, "the town's wealthy citizen returned home with a downcast appearance. 'What happened?' his wife asked. 'Did anything go wrong?'

" 'Not really,' the man answered. 'It's just that we were told the Rebbe is coming to town.'

" 'Why should that cause you to be sad?' the wife asked.

" 'Because the Rebbe will expect me to donate to his tzedakah fund. There goes 50 rubles down the drain.'

The tzaddik continued, "To me, the single ruble that is given with love and devotion is much dearer than the 50 rubles that are given grudgingly"

"It is possible that something similar occurred with the first-ripened fruit offerings," the tzaddik said. "There was a poor person who had a few fruit trees in his yard. One day he bursts into the house with the happy tidings, 'We have some fruits that are ripening! We can take them to the Temple in Jerusalem.' But abruptly his mood changes. 'What happened to you?' his wife asks. 'A moment ago you were so elated.'

" 'Yes,' the husband responds. 'I'm thrilled to take the fruit offering to the Temple. But in what shall I bring it? We don't own anything that can serve as a tray.'

" 'Don't let that worry you,' the wife says. 'Our daughter will help me and we will weave a reed basket that will be a piece of art.'

"That night," the tzaddik continued, "mother and daughter deftly wove a basket of reeds, with the purest of thoughts. They were fashioning something to bring to God in the Temple."

"On the other hand," the tzaddik said, "there was a wealthy man who owned many orchards. One day a worker came in from the orchards, saying, 'I thought I should tell you. Some of the fruits have begun to ripen.'

" 'So?' the wealthy man remarked. 'What of it?'

"'Don't you have to take them to Jerusalem?' the worker asked.

"'Oh, for heaven's sake!' the wealthy man said. 'I can't afford to take time off for a trip to Jerusalem. I've got some business transactions that I can't delay. But I guess it can't be avoided.' He paused a few moments, then said, 'But if I have to do it, I'm going to do it right. Last year some of the people flaunted their wealth by bringing the fruit on silver trays. I'm going to show them who's who. I'll bring my fruits on a gold tray. Let them eat their hearts out.'

"When the poor person brought his few fruits in a basket that had been woven with love and devotion, the basket was kept in the Temple. It, too, was holy. However, the gold basket that was brought to spite others and 'to make them eat their hearts out' was rejected and returned. Such gifts were not welcomed by God."

This explanation by the *tzaddik* of Tolna also explains why the meal-offering is so dear to God, and why the person who brings it is referred to as *nefesh*. It is given with one's soul. This offering is considered a *minchah*. It is indeed a gift to God.

The morning and evening prayers are more substantial. Furthermore, in the morning one prays for all one's needs of the day. In the evening, one entrusts his soul to God, and hopes it will be returned to him for another day of life. These are indeed important prayers, but they do have a modicum of self-interest. The afternoon prayer lacks the self-interest of the other two and is relatively meager in content. It is, therefore, a heartfelt expression of gratitude. It is a *minchah*, a gift.

This reason for the term *minchah* is further supported by the Talmudic statement that the *Minchah* service was formulated by the Patriarch Isaac. God had instructed Abraham to sacrifice Isaac as an *olah*-offering. However, the *olah*-offering must be accompanied by a *minchah*. Isaac assumed that he was going to be sacrificed, and inasmuch as an actual *minchah*-offering was lacking, Isaac compensated for it by designating an additional, midday prayer. This is, therefore, appropriately called the *Minchah* service. And Isaac's *minchah* was indeed the ultimate offering of one's *nefesh*.

A Blazed Path

Although *Minchah* is a brief service, consisting primarily of Psalm 145 and the *Amidah* (in many congregations the chapters of the offerings in the Temple are also recited), it is given special significance by the Talmud. "A person should be especially diligent with regard to *Minchah*, because the prophet Elijah was answered at *Minchah* (*Berachos* 6b). This refers to the episode in *I Kings* Chapter 18, where Elijah's prayer for a miracle was answered.

Granted that Elijah was answered at *Minchah*, how does that prove that the time of *Minchah* is propitious? Had Elijah prayed at any other time, his prayer would have been answered then.

My late brother, R' Shlomo, provided an answer. The Midrash states that Moses' mother, Yocheved, bore him when she was 137 years old. Isaac's birth when Sarah was age 90 is reported in the Torah as a miraculous happening, but nothing is mentioned of Moses' birth, although his mother was even older.

> *We may understand this with an anecdote about the Baal Shem Tov. One of his disciples was stymied by a very difficult Tosafos (commentary on the Talmud). He agonized over this Tosafos for days, researching all the later commentaries and praying fervently that he be enlightened. Ultimately, he resolved the thorny problem. A few days later, he came into shul and encountered two men, who were not profound Talmudic scholars, studying the portion of the Talmud and the difficult Tosafos, and they explained the Tosafos with the solution that had come to him so laboriously. He complained to the Baal Shem Tov, "Am I so*

dull that I had to agonize for days over something that was so obvious to these men?"

The Baal Shem Tov responded, "Assume there is an object on a high branch of a tree, beyond anyone's reach. An expert climber scales the tree and brings the object down. Anyone can now reach it, but only an expert climber could have brought it down.

"There are portions of Torah that have not yet been revealed to us. Only a great Torah scholar can ascend to the spiritual heights to bring them down to earth. Once they have been brought down, they are within anyone's reach. The men who easily understood the Tosafos were able to do so because you had brought the explanation to earth."

The principle of "breakthrough" applies to the spiritual as well as the physical world. It may take a mighty force to breach a fortress. Once an opening has been made, even weak people can walk through it.

The Matriarch Sarah "broke through" the laws of nature and bore a child in her old age. Sarah was the mighty force. Moses' mother "walked through" the breach that Sarah had made.

Certainly Elijah's prayers would have been answered at any other time. The fact is that it occurred at *Minchah*. This constituted a "breakthrough," and *Minchah* became a more propitious time for prayers to be answered because Elijah had blazed the trail.

Minchah is a brief service, and therefore it may not receive the same attention as the more lengthy morning service. Let us be aware that *Minchah* is indeed a propitious time for prayer.

Maariv -
The Evening Service

ברוּךְ ה׳ לְעוֹלָם, אָמֵן וְאָמֵן. בָּרוּךְ ה׳ מִצִּיּוֹן, שֹׁכֵן יְרוּשָׁלָיִם, הַלְלוּקָהּ.

Blessed is Hashem, forever, Amen and Amen. Blessed is Hashem from Zion, Who dwells in Jerusalem, Halleluyah!

Consideration of Others in Prayer

The above prayer was composed at a time when the people gathered in the fields for prayers and it was dangerous to be there alone. This additional prayer was inserted to be said just prior to the *Maariv Avidah*. It served to extend the service so that people who came late and could not finish the *Amidah* together with others would not be left alone and be exposed to danger (*Tosafos, Berachos* 2a).

While the Talmud is exceedingly harsh with someone who leaves another person alone in the synagogue, it heaps abundant blessings on those who will stay behind so that their comrade can pray in safety.

The mitzvos can be divided into those that are primarily between man and God and those that are between man and his fellow man. It is a gross error to think that one can be Torah observant by meticulously fulfilling ritual mitzvos while being derelict in relating properly to others. Failure to be considerate of others may invalidate the ritual mitzvos.

Prayer is a mitzvah between man and God. The Talmud states that if two people enter a synagogue to pray, and one leaves the synagogue while his comrade is still praying, "his prayer is torn up before his face" (*Berachos* 5b). God has no use for the prayers of a person who is inconsiderate of others.

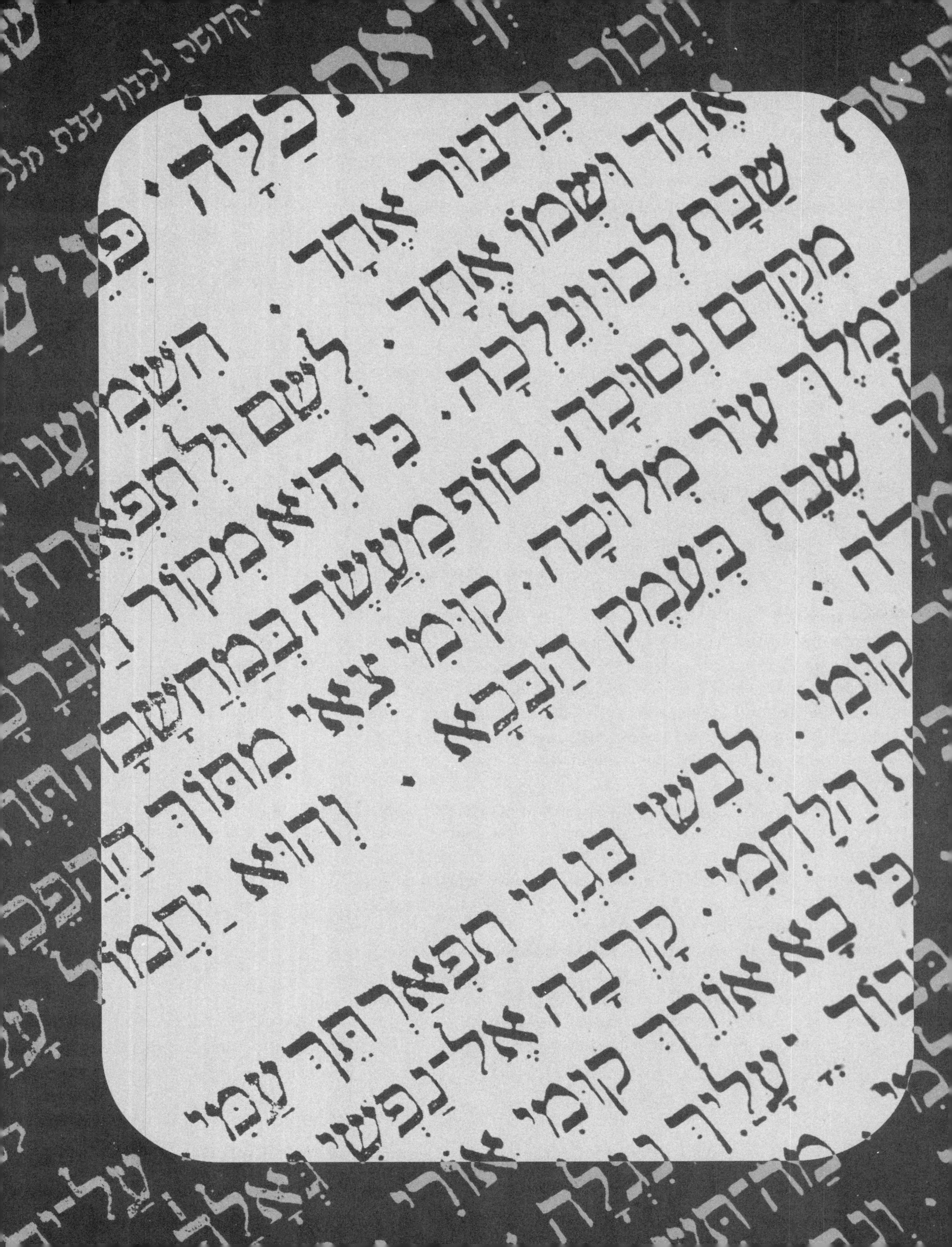

Shabbos -
The Sabbath

The Message of the Metaphor

Torah literature frequently uses the loving husband-wife relationship as a metaphor for the relationship of God to Israel. God is the husband, and Israel is the wife.

The Midrash considers the covenant of Sinai as equivalent to the marriage contract. This metaphor is again used in regard to Shabbos, but in this instance Shabbos is the bride, while Israel is the bridegroom.

It is traditional to recite Song of Songs *(Shir HaShirim)* on Friday afternoon as a prelude to welcoming the Shabbos. In this ballad Solomon portrays the exile of Israel and their distance from the Immanent Presence of God to a husband who left his wife because she strayed from him. So Israel, when it turned to foreign gods, strayed from God. However, God has not abandoned Israel. Both Israel and God long passionately for the restoration of their intimate relationship. Regrettably, such restoration is not possible as long as Israel deviates from the Divine will.

On Shabbos, this longed-for intimacy can be restored. "If one observes Shabbos properly, even if he had been as idolatrous as the generation of Enosh, he will be forgiven" (*Koheles Rabbah* 4). Shabbos observance can remove the barriers between Israel and God. As we begin the Shabbos, we are reunited with our Beloved God.

It is generally assumed that the purpose of the metaphor is to help us better grasp the relationship between God and Israel. Inasmuch as the concept of God is abstract, describing the relationship between us and God as that of a loving husband and wife facilitates our understanding of the relationship.

But the converse may also be true. The relationship between God and Israel may serve as a paradigm for what the husband-wife relationship should be.

The modern concept of conjugal love is fatally flawed. We live in a culture that is awash with the emphasis on love, yet an alarming 40 percent of marriages end in divorce. Both spouses and certainly the children suffer from the instability and rupture of the relationship, but the pattern continues. A young man and young woman appear to be deeply in love, but the fantasy of eternal wedded bliss is too often shattered.

The fundamental error in the Western civilization concept of love is that it is primarily the love of oneself rather than love of another. One loves the other person because one feels the relationship will be personally gratifying. The primary intent is not a readiness to sacrifice for the other's happiness, but just the reverse. The other person is expected to provide for one's own happiness.

As with all other human desires, gratification may terminate this desire. A person who is very hungry may be intensely desirous of food. He would just "love" to have something to eat. Satisfaction of the hunger eliminates it, and he may no longer have the slightest desire for food. That this can be true of a love relationship is stated in the Scriptures, where the passion of Amnon for Tamar turned into a bitter hatred once the passion dissipated (*II Samuel* 13:16).

A true love relationship is based on giving rather than receiving, on providing for the other's emotional needs rather than seeking personal gratification. This is a love of devotion, characterized by a willingness to sacrifice personal gratification to please another. True love is not threatened by personal frustration.

In a brilliant essay, R' Eliyahu Dessler states that the popular concept that "one gives to whom one loves" is erroneous. Just the opposite is true. *One loves someone to whom one gives.* Giving of oneself to another person creates and maintains love (*Michtav MeEliyahu* vol.1, *Chesed U'Nesinah*).

R' Dessler's analysis sheds light on a Talmudic statement. In the poetic ode on the miracles following the Exodus, there is a cryptic statement: אֶת וָהֵב בְּסוּפָה. This is translated as "The gift of the Sea of Reeds " (*Numbers* 21:14). Rashi translates the word וָהֵב as "gave," referring to the gifts of miracles God "gave" the Israelites. The Talmud (*Kiddushin* 30b) translates the word הַב to mean "love." We can now see that these two translations are not divergent. To give means to love.

God and Israel give to each other. God is desirous of our prayers. The *Zohar* states that when Israel sings the praises of God, He calls the heavenly angels and says, "See the praises that My children give Me" (*Zohar, Raya Mehemna, Bo* 40b). And certainly, God's gifts to Israel are beyond measure. Historically Israel has many times sacrificed itself for God. And there is a metaphor that God sacrifices for Israel. On the verse, "I have carried you on the wings of eagles," (*Exodus* 19:4) Rashi comments that when in flight an eagle carries its young above its wings to protect them from the arrows of hunters. "Let the arrow enter me rather than my young." For Israel there is no other God, and for God there is no nation that He considers His other than Israel.

The mutual giving, sacrifice, and exclusiveness that characterize the relationship between God and Israel should be the paradigm for the relationship between husband and wife.

Lighting the Candles

בָּרוּךְ אַתָּה ה׳ אֱלֹקֵינוּ מֶלֶךְ הָעוֹלָם, אֲשֶׁר קִדְּשָׁנוּ בְּמִצְוֹתָיו, וְצִוָּנוּ לְהַדְלִיק נֵר שֶׁל שַׁבָּת.

יְהִי רָצוֹן לְפָנֶיךָ, ה׳ אֱלֹקַי וֵאלֹקֵי אֲבוֹתַי, שֶׁתְּחוֹנֵן אוֹתִי [וְאֶת אִישִׁי, וְאֶת בָּנַי, וְאֶת בְּנוֹתַי, וְאֶת אָבִי, וְאֶת אִמִּי] וְאֶת כָּל קְרוֹבַי; וְתִתֶּן לָנוּ וּלְכָל יִשְׂרָאֵל חַיִּים טוֹבִים וַאֲרוּכִים; וְתִזְכְּרֵנוּ בְּזִכְרוֹן טוֹבָה וּבְרָכָה; וְתִפְקְדֵנוּ בִּפְקֻדַּת יְשׁוּעָה וְרַחֲמִים; וּתְבָרְכֵנוּ בְּרָכוֹת גְּדוֹלוֹת; וְתַשְׁלִים בָּתֵּינוּ; וְתַשְׁכֵּן שְׁכִינָתְךָ בֵּינֵינוּ. וְזַכֵּנִי לְגַדֵּל בָּנִים וּבְנֵי בָנִים חֲכָמִים וּנְבוֹנִים, אוֹהֲבֵי ה׳, יִרְאֵי אֱלֹקִים, אַנְשֵׁי אֱמֶת, זֶרַע קֹדֶשׁ, בַּה׳ דְּבֵקִים, וּמְאִירִים אֶת הָעוֹלָם בַּתּוֹרָה וּבְמַעֲשִׂים טוֹבִים, וּבְכָל מְלֶאכֶת עֲבוֹדַת הַבּוֹרֵא. אָנָּא שְׁמַע אֶת תְּחִנָּתִי בָּעֵת הַזֹּאת, בִּזְכוּת שָׂרָה וְרִבְקָה וְרָחֵל וְלֵאָה אִמּוֹתֵינוּ, וְהָאֵר נֵרֵנוּ שֶׁלֹּא יִכְבֶּה לְעוֹלָם וָעֶד, וְהָאֵר פָּנֶיךָ וְנִוָּשֵׁעָה. אָמֵן.

Blessed are You, Hashem, our God, King of the universe, Who has sanctified us with His commandments, and has commanded us to kindle the light of the Sabbath.

May it be Your will, Hashem, my God and God of my forefathers, that You show favor to me [my husband, my sons, my daughters, my father, my mother] and all my relatives; and that You grant us and all Israel a good and long life; that You remember us with a beneficent memory and blessing; that You consider us with a consideration of salvation and compassion; that You bless us with great blessings; that You make our households complete; that You cause Your Presence to dwell among us. Privilege me to raise children and grandchildren who are wise and understanding, who love Hashem and fear God; people of truth, holy offspring, attached to Hashem, who illuminate the world with Torah and good deeds and with every labor in the service of the Creator. Please, hear my

supplication at this time, in the merit of Sarah, Rebecca, Rachel, and Leah, our mothers, and cause our light to illuminate that it not be extinguished forever, and let Your countenance shine so that we are saved. Amen.

This most eloquent prayer is said by the woman as she kindles the Shabbos candles, ushering in the holy Shabbos.

The mitzvah of lighting the Shabbos candles is rich in content. The Talmud refers to the Shabbos candles as "the candles of *shalom.*" Perhaps this is because light cannot be confined. If you make a light for yourself, others can benefit from it as well. If you make the light for others, you, too, can benefit from it. Light is, therefore, a symbol of mutuality and togetherness.

The woman prays for her family, and particularly that God bless her children to be wise, loving of God, people of truth, bonded to God, and illuminating the world with their Torah and good deeds. Our Torah writings tell us that the Divine blessing must have something upon which it can be bestowed. In other words, we must do our share to begin the process or goal which we wish God to bless.

There is a symbolism in the traditional lighting of two candles, which correspond to the two verses in which the mitzvah of Shabbos was bestowed. In Exodus 20:8 the Torah says, "Remember the Shabbos day to keep it holy." In Deuteronomy 5:12 the Torah says, "Safeguard the Shabbos day to keep it holy." The Talmud states that these two expressions indicate that Shabbos is a twofold mitzvah. There is a restrictive, passive component, prohibiting work, and an active mitzvah, sanctifying the Shabbos.

There is a conspicuous difference between Shabbos and a secular day of rest. The latter is essentially to renew one's energy, "charge up the battery," if you will, so that one can work more efficiently in the workweek. The day of rest is thus subordinate to the workweek.

Shabbos is different. In our daily prayers we begin the week on Sunday with a chapter of Psalms "for the first day toward Shabbos," and Monday with a chapter "for the second day toward Shabbos," etc. We must indeed work for a livelihood, but the workweek is directed to and is subordinate to Shabbos. We sanctify the Shabbos with special prayers, with the *Kiddush*, with the Shabbos songs, with discussing Torah thoughts at the Shabbos table, with using the day of rest for Torah study and more intensive prayer, for visiting with friends and strengthening our friendship bonds. The two candles represent the dual nature of Shabbos, and remind us that we must make it a day of holiness as well as a day of rest.

There is a tradition in many families that with the birth of each child, the mother lights an additional candle. What a thrill it was to discover that the house was brighter because I existed, and that this brightness did not vary with my grades at school!

It is customary to give *tzedakah* prior to lighting the candles. In addition to being the greatest of mitzvos, *tzedakah* enhances our joy of Shabbos with the knowledge that we are easing the burdens of life for others.

> *A chassid of R' Hirsch of Liska would bring the tzaddik something for the Shabbos table when he came to spend Shabbos with him. One time he came from elsewhere than home, and could not bring food. He. therefore, bought some candles for Shabbos.*
>
> *R' Hirsch was overjoyed. "That is exactly what I needed," he said. "I did not have any money to buy candles for Shabbos, and this caused me great distress."*
>
> *The chassid noted that there was a purse with money on the table, but said nothing. R' Hirsch understood the unspoken question and said, "The money that you see is not mine to spend. That is tzedakah, and I have no right to use it for my own needs."*

We are fortunate that we can afford candles, but we must remember that *tzedakah* can bring light to those in need.

The ceremony of lighting the candles is beautiful and the prayer is eloquent. For the blessings of the prayer to be realized, we must model for our children. We must live in a way that shows our love of God, our dedication to truth and the glow of good deeds.

שבת
יום ראשון

The Shabbos Evening Service

The Longing of the Soul

יְדִיד נֶפֶשׁ אָב הָרַחֲמָן, מְשׁוֹךְ עַבְדְּךָ אֶל רְצוֹנֶךָ, יָרוּץ עַבְדְּךָ כְּמוֹ אַיָּל, יִשְׁתַּחֲוֶה אֶל מוּל הֲדָרֶךָ, יֶעֱרַב לוֹ יְדִידוֹתֶיךָ, מִנֹּפֶת צוּף וְכָל טָעַם.

הָדוּר נָאֶה זִיו הָעוֹלָם, נַפְשִׁי חוֹלַת אַהֲבָתֶךָ, אָנָּא קֵל נָא רְפָא נָא לָהּ, בְּהַרְאוֹת לָהּ נֹעַם זִיוֶךָ, אָז תִּתְחַזֵּק וְתִתְרַפֵּא, וְהָיְתָה לָהּ שִׂמְחַת עוֹלָם.

וָתִיק יֶהֱמוּ נָא רַחֲמֶיךָ, וְחוּסָה נָּא עַל בֵּן אֲהוּבֶךָ, כִּי זֶה כַּמָּה נִכְסֹף נִכְסַפְתִּי, לִרְאוֹת מְהֵרָה בְּתִפְאֶרֶת עֻזֶּךָ, אֵלֶּה חָמְדָה לִבִּי, וְחוּסָה נָּא וְאַל תִּתְעַלָּם.

הִגָּלֵה נָּא וּפְרֹשׂ חֲבִיבִי עָלַי, אֶת סֻכַּת שְׁלוֹמֶךָ, תָּאִיר אֶרֶץ מִכְּבוֹדֶךָ, נָגִילָה וְנִשְׂמְחָה בָּךְ. מַהֵר אֱהֹב כִּי בָא מוֹעֵד, וְחָנֵּנוּ כִּימֵי עוֹלָם.

Beloved of the soul, Compassionate Father, draw Your servant to Your will. Then Your servant will hurry like a hart to bow before Your majesty. To him Your friendship will be sweeter than the dripping of the honeycomb and any taste.

Majestic, Beautiful, Radiance of the universe — my soul pines for Your love. Please, O God, heal her now by showing her the pleasantness of Your radiance. Then she will be strengthened and healed, and eternal gladness will be hers.

All-worthy one — may Your mercy be aroused and please take pity on the son of Your beloved, because it is so very long that I have yearned intensely to see the splendor of Your strength. Only these my heart desired, so please take pity and do not conceal Yourself.

Please be revealed and spread upon me, my Beloved, the shelter of Your peace. Illuminate the world with Your glory that we may rejoice and be glad with You. Hasten, show love, for the time has come, and show us grace as in days of old.

This incomparable hymn, which depicts the intense craving of the *neshamah* for God, was composed by R' Elazar Azkiri, one of the great Kabbalists and halachists of the halcyon days of Tzefas (Safed) in 16th-century Eretz Yisrael. Perhaps a word about the personality of R' Elazar, as it comes down in legend, may provide additional flavor to this beautiful hymn. It is written that when one studies Talmud, one should try to imagine that the author of the particular passage is standing nearby. This may be true of our prayers as well. If we could think of the composer of the prayer standing near us, perhaps our *kavannah* might be of loftier quality.

The Jewish community of Tzefas in the 16th century was home to several of the greatest luminaries of Jewish history. The halachists were led by scholars of the caliber of R' Joseph Karo, author of the Shulchan Aruch. The Kabbalists' leaders were R' Moshe Cordovero and R' Yitzchok Luria (the Arizal). The chazzan (cantor) was R' Shlomo Alkabetz, composer of Lechah Dodi. The preacher was R' Moshe Alshich, one of the foremost Torah commentaries. The shammes (beadle) of the shul was R' Elazar Azkiri.

Throughout Jewish history, the position of shammes was not one of great distinction. The job description involved not only tending to the needs of the worshipers, but also being the janitor of the shul. R' Elazar was not considered to be an illuminary.

On Lag B'Omer, the yahrzeit of R' Shimon bar Yochai, when the Tzefas community was commemorating his illustrious life, the Arizal was dancing with a very saintly appearing person. He then took R' Elazar to join the dance. The Ari's disciples later asked him why he had taken the shammes into the dance. Wasn't it beneath his dignity to dance with the shammes? The Ari responded, "R' Shimon did not consider it to be beneath his dignity to dance with him, so why should I think differently?" The disciples realized who the saintly looking man was, and also that the humble shammes was a tzaddik in concealment.

Skeptics may ask, "Is that story true?" It makes little difference. As my friend, Rabbi Berel Wein, says, "Even if all the stories told about the Chafetz Chaim are not true, they do reveal much about him. Stories like that are not told about you and me."

In *Nusach Sefard* it is customary to chant *Yedid Nefesh* before inaugurating the Shabbos. Along with *Shir HaShirim* and *Lechah Dodi*, it depicts the intense love that should characterize the relationship between man and God.

"Draw Your servant to Your will. Then Your servant will hurry like a hart to bow before Your majesty."

If a person has such a passionate longing to hurry toward God, why does he have to be drawn toward him?

This very question is posed on the verse, "Draw me, and I will hurry after You" (*Song of Songs* 1:4). "Draw me" implies that there is a resistance, whereas "I will hurry after you" implies an uncontrollable urge to be close to God.

This question was answered by the Maggid of Dubnow, who cited the phrase in the prayer of the morning service, "Compel my *yetzer* to be subservient to You." He posed the question, "How can we ask God to compel the *yetzer hara* to do His will? He then cited the above verse in Song of Songs, and raised our question — that there appears to be an internal contradiction in this verse. If Israel indeed wishes to rush to God, then it does not need to be drawn to Him. "Draw me to you" implies that Israel is resisting coming close to God, and is hardly rushing to Him.

The Maggid cited a halachah that if a person who has an obligation to bring an offering is reluctant to do so, *beis din* has the authority to coerce him to fulfill his obligation (*Rosh Hashanah* 6:1). However, inasmuch as the Torah says that offerings are accepted only if one brings them with good will (*Leviticus* 1:3), how can one be coerced to do so against one's will?

Rambam addressed this problem and resolved it. The innermost desire of every Jew is to fulfill God's will. History has demonstrated that even wanton sinners, when confronted with the challenge to repudiate their faith at the threat of death, accepted martyrdom rather than deny God. This is because the nucleus of the Jew is faithfulness to God. If a Jew commits a sin, it is because the temptation was overwhelmingly intense and one could not muster up the inner strength to resist it. However, if one is compelled to do God's will and consents under coercion, this consent is valid. It is his innermost desire coming to the fore when the resistance of the *yetzer hara* is subdued by the coercion.

The verse in Song of Songs is saying, "My innermost wish is to rush unto You, but my *yetzer hara* is restraining me. Therefore, draw me unto You, and once I am compelled, I will be free to exercise my innermost drive to rush unto You."

> *The Maggid supported this interpretation with a parable. A widower remarried, and his second wife behaved toward his son like the wicked stepmother of fairy-tale fame, much to the chagrin of the father. When the son matured, he said to his father, "This situation is obviously intolerable. It would be best for all of us if I left home and lived independently. I can then finish my schooling and establish myself. However, inasmuch as I am not yet earning, I will need a sum of money from which to live."*
>
> *The father agreed, but he knew that his wife would never permit him to give the son a large sum of money. He, therefore, said to his son, "When I married your mother, she brought with her a dowry. According to halachah, that money is your inheritance. I will give you a document indicating your right to inherit your mother's dowry, and you will be able to claim it."*
>
> *When the son presented the document, the stepmother flew into a rage. "You are a thief!" she shouted. "That document is a forgery. You have nothing coming to you!"*
>
> *The father then took the son aside and said, "We know that the document is valid. Take it to court and press your claim against me. When the court orders me to pay, my wife will be powerless to stop me from complying with the court order."*
>
> *The son exclaimed, "What! I should go to court to sue my own father? Never!"*
>
> *"Don't be foolish," the father said. "This is not a hostile action. I want you to have the money. It is just that we must find a way to circumvent your stepmother. It is my desire that you sue me so that I can give you the money."*
>
> *The Maggid said, "This is what the verse says. 'Draw me and I will hurry after You.' I want You to coerce me, because then I will be free to rush unto You."*

This is what we mean when we pray for God to compel the *yetzer hara* to do His will. We are saying, "Please coerce me. I wish to be compelled. That will free my innermost desire to do Your will."

This, too, is the explanation for the words expressed in *Yedid Nefesh*: My innermost being craves to be close to You. Please release it from the oppressive resistance of the *yetzer hara*. I will then hurry to be with You.

> *"My soul pines for Your love (lit. my soul is sick for Your love). Please, O God, heal her now by showing her the pleasantness of Your radiance."*

If we imagine the composer of this hymn, R' Elazar Azkiri, standing near us, we may find it difficult to recite these words of intense emotion. Are our hearts truly sick, pining for a closer relationship with God? Are our prayers truthful?

There were many *tzaddikim* who truly pined for God. It is related that after the Pesach and Succos festivals were over, R' Levi Yitzchok of Berditchev would sit up all night at the window, anxiously awaiting the first sign of day. For the eight days of the festival, he did not put on the *tefillin*. Dawn would allow him to fulfill this precious mitzvah which he had not been able to perform for eight days. He did pine for God.

> *One time, after the Yom Kippur fast was over, R' Levi Yitzchok said, "I am hungry." When they brought him food he said, "No, no! Not this! I am hungry." Other food was brought, with the same reaction. R' Levi Yitzchok then took the volume of the Talmud, Succah, and said, "I am hungry for Torah," and studied the Talmud until dawn.*

We are not like R' Levi Yitzchok. We do not stay awake all night awaiting the dawn to do a mitzvah. And when Yom Kippur is over, we are hungry for food. But we can develop our spirituality so that we do crave a closer relationship with God.

> *"May Your mercy be aroused and please take pity on the son of Your beloved (the Patriarch Abraham), because it is so very long that I have yearned intensely to see the splendor of Your strength ... so please take pity and do not conceal Yourself."*

The words are indeed heartrending. One is pleading for mercy as if one were pleading to have his life spared. But are our feelings consonant with the words? Do we feel the desperation of not being closer to God? Should we even say *Yedid Nefesh* when what we are saying is not really true?

There are varying customs regarding reciting the *Vidui* (Confession) every morning. In many congregations the practice is not to say it, because people are in a hurry to get to work, and they would not recite the *Vidui* with proper *kavannah*. Inasmuch as the *Vidui* is optional, the rationale is not to express regret for one's sins when one cannot concentrate adequately. Perhaps this should be applied to *Yedid Nefesh* as well. Why say "take pity and do not conceal Yourself" when we do not have profound feelings of deprivation?

The only justification for reciting the *Yedid Nefesh* is similar to that for saying the *Ani Maamin*. We say it as a prayer rather than as a statement of fact. We pray, "Help me feel that I need this closeness to You. Help me realize that when You are distant from me, I am missing an integral part of life itself." The *Yedid Nefesh* then represents a goal to which we should aspire.

לְכָה דוֹדִי לִקְרַאת כַּלָּה, פְּנֵי שַׁבָּת נְקַבְּלָה.

בּוֹאִי בְשָׁלוֹם עֲטֶרֶת בַּעְלָהּ, גַּם בְּשִׂמְחָה וּבְצָהֳלָה, תּוֹךְ אֱמוּנֵי עַם סְגֻלָּה, בּוֹאִי כַלָּה, בּוֹאִי כַלָּה.

Come, my Beloved, to greet the bride. Let us welcome the Shabbath.
Enter in peace, O crown of her husband,
Even in gladness and good cheer,
Among the faithful of the treasured nation
Enter O bride! Enter O bride!

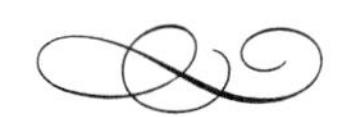

Lechah Dodi - The Shabbos Bride

This is indeed one of the most beautiful prayers in the *siddur*. In many congregations it is sung by all congregants. It is unfortunate that the depth of this prayer too often goes unrecognized.

"Come, my Beloved, to greet the bride. Let us welcome the Sabbath." *We* are inviting *God* to join us in greeting the Sabbath! We, infinitesimally small mortals, are inviting Infinite God to join us. Just this thought is enough to send chills up and down one's spine.

The reference to God as "my Beloved" is also found in Song of Songs, which is customarily read prior to the beginning of the Friday night service. In this ballad Solomon portrays the exile of Israel and their distance from the Immanent Presence of God. Regrettably, the restoration of the intimate relationship is not possible as long as Israel deviates from the Divine will.

On Shabbos, this longed-for intimacy is restored. "If one observes Shabbos properly, even if he had been as idolatrous as the generation of Enosh, he will be forgiven" (*Koheles Rabbah* 4).

Shabbos observance can remove the barriers between Israel and God. As we begin the Shabbos, we are reunited with our Beloved God.

Let us go on. Shabbos is always a bride. Shabbos never loses its charm and beauty. The Shabbos one observes after eighty years is still a young bride.

The inauguration of Shabbos is with the blessing *Mekadesh HaShabbos*, that God sanctified the Shabbos. This is the very term that bonds man and woman together in marriage: הֲרֵי אַתְּ מְקֻדֶּשֶׁת לִי, *You are hereby sanctified to me.* Like the Shabbos, one's wife should always be a bride. The love and the happiness of the wedding day should never fade.

God joins Israel in greeting the Shabbos bride, and God joins the couple when love and harmony prevail. "A man and his wife — the Divine presence is with them" (*Sotah* 17a).

In *Lechah Dodi* we refer to Shabbos as "the source of blessing." This is similar to what the Talmud says, "The source of blessing in the home is by the merit of the wife" (*Bava Metzia* 59a).

But even considering Shabbos a bride is not enough. When Shabbos comes to a close, we have a *seudah, Melaveh Malkah,* escorting the Sabbath Queen. We should bring this analogy home: The wife is not only a perennial bride, but also a queen.

On a visit to Tzefas I stood at the grave of R' Shlomo HaLevi Alkabetz, the composer of *Lechah Dodi*. I prayed that I would be able to say this beautiful prayer with even just a fragment of the devotion that its author invested in composing it.

Let us think of this as we sing *Lechah Dodi*. Let us bring home the spirit of Shabbos.

The first two stanzas are in praise of the Shabbos. The theme then abruptly changes to the plight of Israel since the destruction of the Temple, arousing the Jewish people to shake off the dust of the Diaspora and return to the splendor of yore. This can be achieved with the Redemption, and we can merit the Redemption by observing Shabbos properly. We are assured that our enemies will dissipate, and the Divine glory will once again shine upon us.

Lechah Dodi is an expression of yearning for reuniting with God. For *Klal Yisrael* (the Jewish people), this will occur with the Redemption. However, we can have our individual reunion by inviting the presence of God. The Talmud says that the Divine presence shuns sadness, but will come to rest (upon a person) only where there is *simchah shel mitzvah* (the joy associated with a mitzvah) (*Shabbos* 30b).

There is a cryptic statement in the Kabbalistic writings: "Shabbos is an appellation of God." Indeed, there were people who would refer to Shabbos in ordinary conversation as "the seventh day" but were cautious not to pronounce the word "Shabbos" except in prayer and Torah study because they considered it as subject to the prohibition of pronouncing God's Name in vain. Whatever the esoteric meaning is, it is clear that Shabbos is identified with God Himself. When we invite and welcome Shabbos, we are inviting and welcoming the Divine Presence.

"Enter in peace, O crown of her husband, even in gladness and good cheer, among the faithful of the treasured nation. Enter, O bride! Enter O bride!" (and in *Sefard siddurim,* "Enter, O Bride, the Shabbos Queen!"). If we see that peace, gladness and good cheer should prevail in the home, we not only greet and welcome Shabbos, but we also invite God into our home. We can then achieve the closeness and intimacy with God which we should be yearning.

The Song of Shabbos

מִזְמוֹר שִׁיר לְיוֹם הַשַּׁבָּת. טוֹב לְהֹדוֹת לַה׳, וּלְזַמֵּר לְשִׁמְךָ עֶלְיוֹן.

A psalm, a song for the Sabbath day. It is good to thank Hashem and sing praise to Your Name, O Exalted one.

We usher in the Shabbos by reciting the ninety-second psalm, dedicated to the day of Shabbos. It is noteworthy that nothing in the text of the psalm refers to Shabbos.

This psalm follows Psalm 91, composed by Moses, which is known as "the hymn that protects from all calamities." It relates God's watchfulness over Israel, and states that even when His infinite wisdom dictates that we must suffer, God suffers along with us.

There is an opinion that Psalm 92 was likewise composed by Moses, and continues this theme. The day of Shabbos protects us.

We are familiar with the term *shomer* Shabbos, observant of the Shabbos. The word *shomer* also means "watching over and protecting. " It has, therefore, been aptly said that even more than Israel was *shomer* Shabbos, observant of Shabbos, the Shabbos was *shomer* Israel, protective of Israel.

The workweek can present challenges to one's faith. We may see how corruption may enrich people, and we may join the prophet who said, "I will seek justice from God. Why do the wicked prosper?" (*Jeremiah* 12:1).

Jeremiah's challenge was also voiced by Moses, who wished to know why the righteous sometimes suffer while the wicked often prosper. Although Moses was privy to all of God's ways, this understanding was denied him (*Berachos* 7a). The Talmud says that Moses wrote the Book of Job, which seeks in vain to provide a logical response to this vexing question. After all proposed solutions are rejected, God says to Job, "And where were you when I laid the earth's foundation?" (*Job* 38:4). In other words, the reason for any one thing that occurs can be understood if one has a grasp of the entire expanse of the universe from its inception through eternity. Only God has this knowledge. He created the vast universe with a master plan, in which every event has its proper place.

Moses composed the ninety-second psalm, asserting our belief in God as the Creator. As we inaugurate the Shabbos as a testimony to Creation, we express our homage to God and our faith in His justice. True, we may not understand this. "How great are Your deeds, O God, how infinitely profound are Your thoughts." We are devoid of reason and cannot comprehend His ways. "I declare that God is just, my Rock, in Whom there is no wrong."

There is another theme in this psalm that gives it relevance to Shabbos. As a day of virtual total abstinence from our weekday activities, Shabbos serves as a model for a very important phase of life: our senior years. We are fortunate that medical science has prolonged our lifespan. However, many people fail to enjoy the retirement years, even if they are financially secure. In their younger years, their days were busy with work or caring for the family. With these activities gone, they find the days empty, long and boring

It need not be that way. The golden years can be enjoyable if we prepare for them. Shabbos is a prototype of the golden years, and helps us prepare for them. We do not work, cook, knit, do laundry, drive the car, or operate the computer. We pray longer, we study the Torah, and we have time to spend with family and friends.

Rambam states that the way to develop love for God is to see the wonders in Creation. In addition to Torah study, we can see the hand of God in Jewish survival throughout history, which we have time to study on Shabbos. If we read about the wonders of nature in order to better appreciate the majesty of God, we may do this on Shabbos. These are things we can do when we no longer go to the office or punch the time-clock.

The "Song of Shabbos" psalm says, "How great are Your deeds, O God ... a fool cannot understand this." We can gain wisdom into God's deeds in our golden years. Little wonder that the psalm concludes with, "They will still be fruitful in old age, vigorous and fresh they will be." Shabbos helps us preserve our youth in later life.

The Eternal Sign

וְשָׁמְרוּ בְנֵי יִשְׂרָאֵל אֶת הַשַּׁבָּת, לַעֲשׂוֹת אֶת הַשַּׁבָּת לְדֹרֹתָם
בְּרִית עוֹלָם. בֵּינִי וּבֵין בְּנֵי יִשְׂרָאֵל אוֹת הִיא לְעֹלָם,
כִּי שֵׁשֶׁת יָמִים עָשָׂה ה׳ אֶת הַשָּׁמַיִם וְאֶת הָאָרֶץ, וּבַיּוֹם הַשְּׁבִיעִי
שָׁבַת וַיִּנָּפַשׁ.

And the Children of Israel observed the Sabbath to make the Sabbath for their generations an eternal covenant. Between Me and the Children of Israel it is a sign forever, that in six days did Hashem make the heaven and the earth, and on the seventh day He rested and was refreshed.

The observance of Shabbos is without peer in Torah. The Talmud says that observance of Shabbos is equivalent to observance of the entire Torah (*Pesikta*). Indeed, if a person observes one Shabbos properly, it is as though he observed all the Shabbasos since Creation (*Mechilta, Ki Sisa*).

The Chafetz Chaim cited the above verse to explain the pivotal role of Shabbos. "It (Shabbos) is a sign forever." He gave the following parable.

> *A merchant was in such severe arrears that he had to close his business. He managed to pay off the debts, and reopened his store. This cycle repeated itself a number of times. People knew that the store closing was only temporary, because the sign with his name remained on the store. One time he closed the store and had the sign removed. This indicated that he no longer intended to reopen the store.*

"Shabbos is a sign," the Chafetz Chaim said. "If someone deviates from Torah observance but still has the Shabbos sign, there is hope that he will return to full Torah observance. If the sign is gone, there is little hope of return.

The Chafetz Chaim once pleaded with a wealthy merchant to close his store on Shabbos. The man said, "Rabbi, on Shabbos I do most of my business. I cannot afford to close the store on Shabbos."

The Chafetz Chaim said, "The Torah says 'You shall work six days and on the seventh day you shall rest.' If you rest on the seventh day, you will have six working days. If you do not rest on the seventh day, you will not have six working days."

The man replied in a derisive tone, "And a verse from the Torah will keep my store open?" The Chafetz Chaim said nothing.

During the Bolshevik revolution, the man's store and wealth were confiscated. He barely managed to save his life and escaped with only the clothes he was wearing. He later contacted the Chafetz Chaim and apologized. "You were right," he said. "A verse of the Torah could keep my store open."

The Shabbos Evening Meal

Welcoming the Angels

שָׁלוֹם עֲלֵיכֶם, מַלְאֲכֵי הַשָּׁרֵת, מַלְאֲכֵי עֶלְיוֹן,
מִמֶּלֶךְ מַלְכֵי הַמְּלָכִים הַקָּדוֹשׁ בָּרוּךְ הוּא.

Peace upon you, O ministering angels, angels of the Exalted one — from the King Who reigns over kings, the Holy one, Blessed is He.

The Talmud (*Shabbos* 119b) states that on Friday night, two angels accompany a person as he returns home from services. One angel is benevolent, the other malevolent. If they find the table set for Shabbos graced by the candles and challah, and the person is greeted happily by the family, the benevolent angel says, "May the coming Shabbos be like this." The malevolent angel has no choice but to concur and respond *amen*. If the house is not prepared for Shabbos, and the disharmony in the family casts a gloom over the home, the malevolent angel says, "May the coming Shabbos be like this," and the benevolent angel must respond *amen*.

As we chant the *Shalom Aleichem* greeting, let us think about the words we are saying. Imagine that you had a special emissary from the governor as your guest. What would be your mood, and how honored would you feel? Suppose that the special emissary was from the President, how much greater would your elation be? Suppose that this emissary brought you a personal greeting and an award from the President. Would you be able to contain your joy? Now you are welcoming the heavenly angels, emissaries of God, who are conveying His blessing to you. If we think about the words we say, it should require considerable restraint not to dance around the table.

Shalom Aleichem is more than just a greeting. It means "May peace be upon you." What is the point of wishing peace to the angels?

The Midrash states that prior to the creation of man, God took counsel with the angels. There was dissent among the angels; some were in favor of man's creation because he would be kind and charitable. Others opposed creation of man because it is man's nature to be quarrelsome and contentious.

When the angels visit the Jewish home Friday night and see the peace that prevails, they withdraw their objection to the creation of man. We, therefore, can restore peace among the heavenly angels.

The Baal Shem Tov told several of his disciples to accompany him to Apt, where he sent for Shabsi, the bookbinder. "Tell me about what happened this past Friday night," the Baal Shem Tov said.

Shabsi said, "My earnings are very meager. This past week I had not earned enough to provide for even the most austere Shabbos. I have never partaken of anything other than what I earned. I said to my wife, 'We shall not ask for help from anyone. If it pleases God that my Shabbos is without candles and food, then it must please us as well.' I then left to shul to recite the Tehillim (Psalms) until the evening service.

"When I returned home, I found the table beautifully set and the candles glowing. I concluded that my wife probably could not withstand the tribulations of a barren Shabbos, and must have asked the neighbors for tzedakah. My wife read the expression of disappointment on my face and said, 'God forbid! I would never go against your wishes. Not having anything to cook, I decided I would honor the Shabbos by making the house spic and span. As I cleaned a crevice in the wall, I found a silver button that must have been on my wedding dress. I sold it and was able to buy all the provisions for Shabbos.'

"I realized that this fortunate find was a direct blessing from God, and I was overjoyed that I would be able to celebrate Shabbos properly without recourse to human gifts. I was unable to contain my joy. I took my wife's hands in my own, and we danced around the Shabbos table."

At this point Shabsi's gaze dropped, and he asked the Baal Shem Tov, "Was my behavior improper?"

"Improper?" the Baal Shem Tov exclaimed. "Why, when you danced around the table, the heavenly angels danced along with you, and you caused great joy in heaven. You shall be amply rewarded. What is your wish?"

Shabsi said, "We are getting along in years, and we are childless."

"May God bless you with a son who will illuminate the world. I want him to bear my name, Yisrael."

One year later, Shabsi's wife gave birth to a son who became the great Chassidic luminary, R' Yisrael, the Maggid of Kozhnitz.

Kiddush - A Fresh Start

יוֹם הַשִּׁשִּׁי. וַיְכֻלּוּ הַשָּׁמַיִם וְהָאָרֶץ וְכָל צְבָאָם. וַיְכַל אֱלֹקִים בַּיּוֹם הַשְּׁבִיעִי מְלַאכְתּוֹ אֲשֶׁר עָשָׂה, וַיִּשְׁבֹּת בַּיּוֹם הַשְּׁבִיעִי מִכָּל מְלַאכְתּוֹ אֲשֶׁר עָשָׂה. וַיְבָרֶךְ אֱלֹקִים אֶת יוֹם הַשְּׁבִיעִי וַיְקַדֵּשׁ אֹתוֹ, כִּי בוֹ שָׁבַת מִכָּל מְלַאכְתּוֹ אֲשֶׁר בָּרָא אֱלֹקִים לַעֲשׂוֹת.

סַבְרִי מָרָנָן וְרַבָּנָן וְרַבּוֹתַי:

בָּרוּךְ אַתָּה ה׳ אֱלֹקֵינוּ מֶלֶךְ הָעוֹלָם, בּוֹרֵא פְּרִי הַגָּפֶן.

בָּרוּךְ אַתָּה ה׳ אֱלֹקֵינוּ מֶלֶךְ הָעוֹלָם, אֲשֶׁר קִדְּשָׁנוּ בְּמִצְוֹתָיו וְרָצָה בָנוּ, וְשַׁבַּת קָדְשׁוֹ בְּאַהֲבָה וּבְרָצוֹן הִנְחִילָנוּ, זִכָּרוֹן לְמַעֲשֵׂה בְרֵאשִׁית. כִּי הוּא יוֹם תְּחִלָּה לְמִקְרָאֵי קֹדֶשׁ, זֵכֶר לִיצִיאַת מִצְרָיִם. כִּי בָנוּ בָחַרְתָּ, וְאוֹתָנוּ קִדַּשְׁתָּ, מִכָּל הָעַמִּים. וְשַׁבַּת קָדְשְׁךָ בְּאַהֲבָה וּבְרָצוֹן הִנְחַלְתָּנוּ. בָּרוּךְ אַתָּה ה׳, מְקַדֵּשׁ הַשַּׁבָּת.

The sixth day. Thus the heaven and the earth were finished, and all their array. On the Seventh Day God completed His work which He had done, and He abstained on the Seventh Day from all His work which He had done. God blessed the Seventh Day and hallowed it, because on it He had abstained from all His work which God created to make.

By your leave, my masters, rabbis and teachers:

Blessed are You, Hashem, our God, King of the universe, Who creates the fruit of the vine.

Blessed are You, Hashem, our God, King of the universe, Who has sanctified us with His commandments, took pleasure in us, and with love and favor gave us His holy Sabbath as a heritage, a remembrance of Creation. For that day is the prologue to the holy convocations, a memorial of the Exodus from Egypt. For us did You choose and us did You sanctify from all the nations. And Your holy Sabbath, with love and favor, did You give us as a heritage. Blessed are You, Hashem, Who sanctifies the Sabbath.

We are told that we are to emulate God. Friday night is an excellent time to do so. At the close of the sixth day, God concluded the work of Creation. The universe was complete. This is how we should feel as the Shabbos approaches. The week that was is completed. There is nothing that remains. We enter the Shabbos as though everything we had to do was done. We do not think of any pending transactions, of any debts we owe or money owed us, or of any unfinished business. There is nothing unfinished.

On Shabbos we can put the past behind us, even our mistakes. Indeed, proper observance of Shabbos merits forgiveness of all one's sins (*Shabbos* 118b). Any differences that occurred between people should evaporate. It is related that in the household of R' Elimelech of Lizhensk the hours before Shabbos were like the eve of Yom Kippur. People asked one another for forgiveness and embraced in tears. The moment the candles were lit, the mood became one of ecstatic joy. All sins had been forgiven. Everyone had a clean slate, a new start in life.

There is a tradition in many families to serve *farfel* on Friday night. This custom is attributed to the Baal Shem Tov. The word *farfel*, which my mother served, symbolized that "Whatever happened until tonight is *farfallen* (bygone)." This delicious dish emphasized that Shabbos is to bring closure to the past and enable us to approach the future unencumbered by the burdens of the past.

The first part of *Kiddush* is a testimony to Creation. The second part is essentially a prayer of gratitude. It is out of His love for us that God gave us the precious gift of Shabbos, a day which He hallowed and whose observance enables us to become spiritual and holy. By casting off the enslavement to the workweek, Shabbos gives us a day of freedom. In this way it commemorates the Exodus.

Having welcomed the angels and liberated ourselves from both the burdens of the past and the subjugation to the workweek, we can partake of the Shabbos delicacies in spiritual joy.

כָּל מְקַדֵּשׁ שְׁבִיעִי כָּרָאוּי לוֹ, כָּל שׁוֹמֵר שַׁבָּת כַּדָּת מֵחַלְּלוֹ, שְׂכָרוֹ הַרְבֵּה מְאֹד עַל פִּי פָעֳלוֹ, אִישׁ עַל מַחֲנֵהוּ וְאִישׁ עַל דִּגְלוֹ.

Whoever hallows the Sabbath as befits it, whoever safeguards the Sabbath properly from desecration, his reward is exceedingly great in accordance with his deed — every man at his own camp, every man at his own banner.

Music has always held a prominent place in Judaism. It has been said that speech is the expression of the mind, whereas music is the expression of the heart. Inasmuch as *tefillah* is referred to as *avodah shebelev* (the service of the heart), it is little wonder that music often accompanied prayer.

Early references to the influence of music on the emotions can be found in the Scriptures. When King Saul was overcome by a mood of severe depression, "David would take his harp and play it with his hand; Saul would be relieved and feel better, and the evil mood would lift from him" (*I Samuel* 16:23). When the prophet Elisha was provoked to anger by King Jehoram, the Divine spirit left him. To regain his prophecy, he sent for a musician. "And it was when the musician played, the hand of God came upon him" (*II Kings* 3:15). In Psalms, David repeatedly mentions his use of the harp in singing his praises to God.

"If a person is overcome by sadness, he can relieve it by listening to music and song" (*Rambam, Eight Chapters* 5). A disciple of the Vilna Gaon quoted the Gaon's statement that without music one cannot properly understand much of Torah, and that Moses brought much music from Sinai (*Introduction to Pe'as Hashulchan*).

In David's time, even prior to the building of the Temple, there were 4,000 instrumentalists (*I Chronicles* 23:5). In the days of the Temple, the music of the Levites, both choral and instrumental, accompanied the offerings.

Music was employed both to enhance meditation and to stimulate cheer. Halachah requires that there be song at weddings (*Even HaEzer* 65).

In more recent times, the use of music in *tefillah* was revived by the Chassidic movement, with both devotional (*deveikus*) and spirited melodies. It is related that when R' Shneur Zalman was in Shklov, some scholars presented him with several thorny problems in understanding complex portions of the Talmud. R' Shneur Zalman said that he would address their questions, but he first wished to sing a *niggun* (melody). After he had sung a very moving, meditative tune, he said, "Now repeat your questions." The scholars realized that all their thorny problems had been resolved. The clarity of mind that was brought about by the meditative tune had allowed them to think more clearly, and eliminated their difficulties in comprehension.

Chassidic lore is replete with the efficacy of music. Many of the traditional tunes among chassidim can be traced to R' Yitzchak Eizik of Kalev (1751-1821). A few words regarding this fascinating individual are in order.

> *Chassidic lore relates that the tzaddik R' Leib, the son of Sarah, was inspired to find a holy neshamah in the Hungarian hills. He eventually made his way to the woods, where he found an 8-year-old boy guarding the sheep. He heard the child singing a heartrending lyric, "O God, O God, why are You so distant? O, why is our exile so long and protracted? If only we could exit the exile, we could come face to face with God." Profuse tears rolled down R' Leib's cheeks as the melody sung with the child's purity penetrated into his heart.*
>
> *"Where did you hear this lyric?" R' Leib asked.*
>
> *"It's something I heard the other shepherds sing," the child responded.*
>
> *"The shepherds sing it like that?" R' Leib asked.*
>
> *"Oh, no," the child answered. "They sing it as a love song, like this: 'O, Rosa, Rosa, how distant you are. O, forest, forest, how thick and huge you are. If only I could exit the thick forest, my Rosa and I could be together.' "*
>
> *"And you substituted your words?" R' Leib asked.*

"Yes," the child said. "Who is more beloved to us than God, and what separates us from Him as much as being in exile?"

R' Leib embraced the child. "Take me to your home," he said. "I wish to meet your parents."

"I don't have a father," the child said. "He died when I was a baby. But you can meet my mother."

R' Leib told the mother that she has a child with an exceptionally great and holy neshamah, and that he wished to take him to the yeshivah of R' Shmelke of Nikolsburg to learn Torah.

"But I am a widow," the mother said, "and my child is my sole support. He looks after the sheep and chickens."

"I will send you ample money every month for your support," R' Leib said, "if you will send the child with me."

"If this is God's will," the mother said, "then I am pleased to send my child with you."

The young Yitzchak Eizik became a disciple of R' Shmelke, and later became the renowned Rebbe of Kalev. He transformed many of the melodies he had heard from the shepherds into songs of praise and longing for closeness to God. The devotional character of these melodies are readily identifiable. "That must be a *niggun* of Kalev."

The later Chassidic masters added to the rich repository of liturgical music. Some were composers in their own right, such as the Rebbes of Modzhitz, Bobov, and Melitz. Others had composers in their court, as R' Abish Meir in the court of the *tzaddik* of Sanz.

One Friday, R' Abish Meir passed by a tavern and the melodies emanating from the tavern caught his ear. Being extraordinarily sensitive to music, the melody enchanted him and he went along humming it.

As he led the services Friday night, R' Abish Meir searched for a niggun with which to chant Lechah Dodi, and being that the melody he had heard earlier that day reverberated in his mind, he applied it to Lechah Dodi. Realizing that he had used a tune sung by drunkards for the prayer, he was horrified and expected a severe reprimand from the tzaddik. He quickly left after completion of the services to avoid the rebuke.

R' Abish Meir had never missed spending a Friday night at the tzaddik's tisch (Chassidic gathering with the Rebbe). He could not see himself missing tisch, yet feared the tzaddik's wrath for having profaned the service with a tavern melody. He decided that he would wait until all other chassidim had arrived, and then he would be able to enter without being noticed by the Rebbe.

No sooner did he enter than the tzaddik called out, "Abish Meir! Why are you so late? We have been waiting for you with the zemiros." Sheepishly, R' Abish Meir made his way to the head of the table. "Sing Kol Mekadesh!" the tzaddik said, "with the beautiful niggun you sang for Lechah Dodi."

R' Abish Meir breathed a sigh of relief, and sang the zemiros with the tavern melody. During the singing, the tzaddik was ecstatic, and later remarked, "When the Temple was destroyed and we were driven into exile, the Shechinah (Divine Presence) went into exile along with us. What happened to all the beautiful music of the Levites in the Temple? It, too, went into exile. The Levites' Temple melodies have been dispersed throughout the world. This melody, Abish Meir, was sung by the Levites in the holy Temple. Today you returned it to us and restored it into its kedushah (holiness)."

There are many Shabbos songs composed throughout the ages. A number of them have been widely accepted. They all follow the themes of the beauty of Shabbos, its testimony to Creation, the great merit for observing it, and the spiritual heights to which it elevates us. *Zemiros* are prayers which all can enjoy.

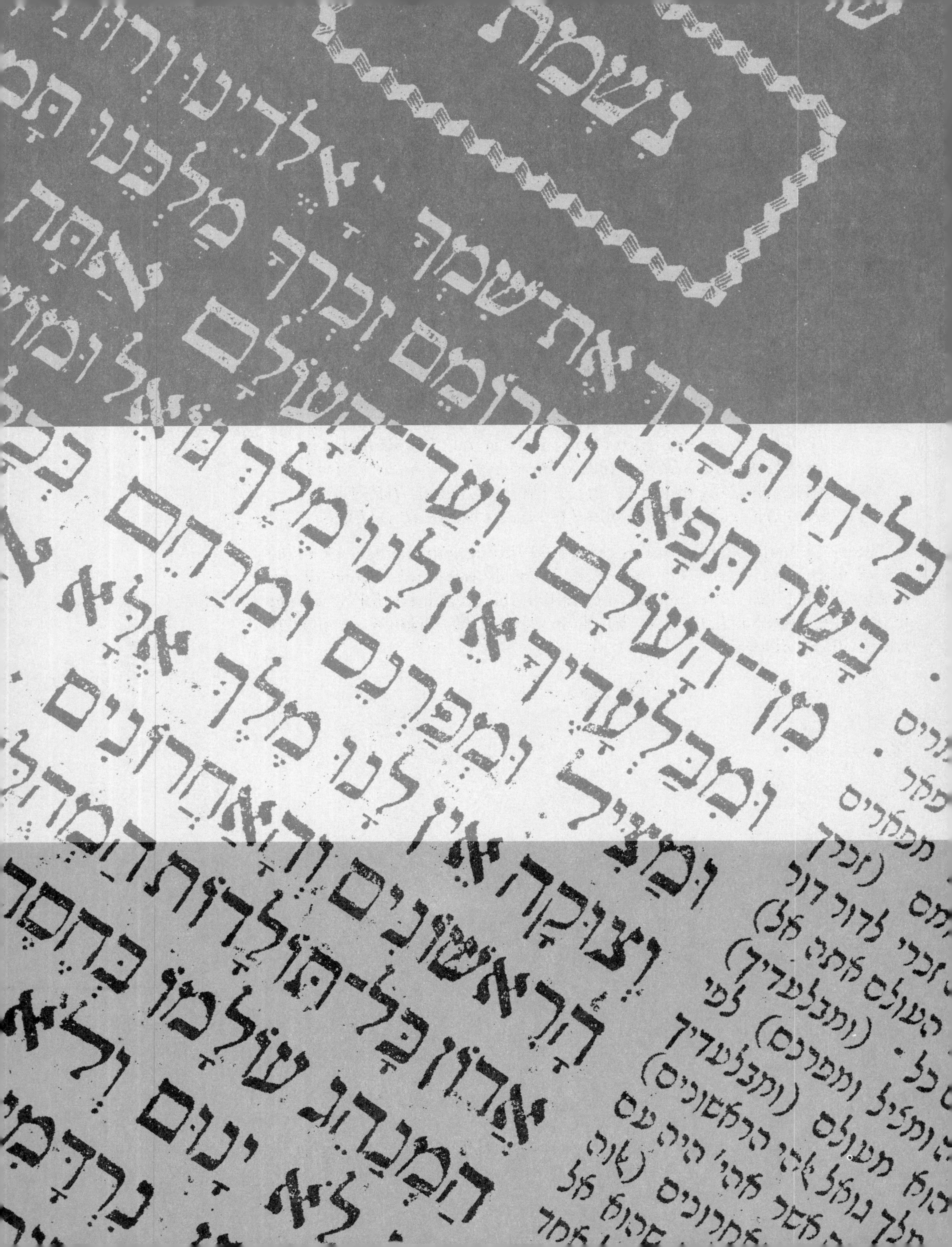

Shabbos Shacharis — Sabbath Morning Services

אִלּוּ פִינוּ מָלֵא שִׁירָה כַּיָּם, וּלְשׁוֹנֵנוּ רִנָּה כַּהֲמוֹן גַּלָּיו, וְשִׂפְתוֹתֵינוּ שֶׁבַח כְּמֶרְחֲבֵי רָקִיעַ, וְעֵינֵינוּ מְאִירוֹת כַּשֶּׁמֶשׁ וְכַיָּרֵחַ, וְיָדֵינוּ פְרוּשׂוֹת כְּנִשְׁרֵי שָׁמָיִם, וְרַגְלֵינוּ קַלּוֹת כָּאַיָּלוֹת, אֵין אֲנַחְנוּ מַסְפִּיקִים לְהוֹדוֹת לְךָ, ה׳ אֱלֹקֵינוּ וֵאלֹקֵי אֲבוֹתֵינוּ, וּלְבָרֵךְ אֶת שְׁמֶךָ עַל אַחַת מֵאָלֶף אֶלֶף אַלְפֵי אֲלָפִים וְרִבֵּי רְבָבוֹת פְּעָמִים הַטּוֹבוֹת שֶׁעָשִׂיתָ עִם אֲבוֹתֵינוּ וְעִמָּנוּ. מִמִּצְרַיִם גְּאַלְתָּנוּ ה׳ אֱלֹקֵינוּ, וּמִבֵּית עֲבָדִים פְּדִיתָנוּ. בְּרָעָב זַנְתָּנוּ, וּבְשָׂבָע כִּלְכַּלְתָּנוּ, מֵחֶרֶב הִצַּלְתָּנוּ, וּמִדֶּבֶר מִלַּטְתָּנוּ, וּמֵחֳלָיִם רָעִים וְנֶאֱמָנִים דִּלִּיתָנוּ. עַד הֵנָּה עֲזָרוּנוּ רַחֲמֶיךָ, וְלֹא עֲזָבוּנוּ חֲסָדֶיךָ. וְאַל תִּטְּשֵׁנוּ ה׳ אֱלֹקֵינוּ לָנֶצַח.

Were our mouth as full of song as the sea, and our tongue as full of joyous song as its multitude of waves, and our lips as full of praise as the breadth of the heavens, and our eyes as brilliant as the sun and the moon, and our hands as outspread as eagles of the sky and our feet as swift as hinds — we still could not thank You sufficiently, Hashem, our God and God of our forefathers, and to bless Your Name for even one of the thousand thousand, thousands of thousands and myriad myriads of favors that You performed for our ancestors and for us. You redeemed us from Egypt, Hashem, our God, and liberated us from the house of bondage. In famine You nourished us and in plenty You sustained us. From sword You saved us; from plague You let us escape; and from severe and enduring diseases You spared us. Until now Your mercy has helped us, and Your kindness has not forsaken us. Do not abandon us, Hashem, our God, forever.

Nishmas may be considered "the prayer of prayers," because it contains every element of prayer: praise of God, gratitude to God, our dependence on God, and our faith and trust in God.

Nishmas contains the answer to an often asked question: How can a mere mortal sing praises to the Infinite God? Is it not presumptuous of us to do so? Suppose a peasant would approach the palace and request entry to the throne room saying, "I wish to express my gratitude and praise for the king." The palace guards would surely deny him entry. Yet we do precisely this!

One of the commentaries cites an apparent contradiction in *Nishmas.* On the one hand we say, "Were our mouth as full of song as the sea, and our tongue as full of joyous song as its multitude of waves, and our lips as full of praise as the breadth of the heavens, and our eyes as brilliant as the sun and the moon, and our hands as outspread as eagles of the sky and our feet as swift as hinds — we still could not thank You sufficiently ..." After expressing our paucity and total inadequacy in giving fitting praise to God, we then say, "Therefore, the organs that You set within us, and the spirit and soul that You breathed into our nostrils, and the tongue that You placed in our mouth — *all of them shall thank and bless, praise and glorify ... Your Name, our King.*" Is this not a reversal of what we had just said, that our human capacities can in no way address God properly?

One of the commentaries explained using a parable.

> *An officer of the king came to a town and told one of the citizens that the king was soon to visit the town, and they wished to set up a residence for the king in his home. The man was thrilled by the honor to accommodate the king, but said that there was no way he could possibly provide the furnishings and food appropriate for the king. He feared that whatever he did would be grossly inadequate and would actually be regarded as an offense against his majesty.*
>
> *The officer reassured the man. "We need only the use of your home," he said. "We will provide all the furnishings from the palace and the food from the royal kitchen. You will not have to provide anything of your own, and just serve the king with what is brought from the palace." With this, the man was greatly relieved.*
>
> *"This is what we say in Nishmas," the commentary continues. "Our own capacities would be too meager to give proper praise to God. However, it is with the organs that He set within us, the spirit and soul that He breathed into our nostrils and the tongue that He placed in our mouth, it is with these that we thank and bless, praise and glorify His Name. We serve Him with the 'provisions from the palace.' Hence we need not consider our inadequacies in addressing God."*

I must confess that although I had been saying this prayer for years, its full impact did not strike me until I heard a person recovering from alcoholism say, "I have been sober or four years. I wish I could tell you that they have been happy years. My company downsized and I have been unable to find another job. My wife is suing for divorce and custody of the children. I was unable to pay the mortgage and they foreclosed on my house. Last week my car was repossessed. But I can't believe that God brought me all this way only to walk out on me now."

The following Shabbos I said in *Nishmas*, "You redeemed us from Egypt, our God, and liberated us from the house of bondage. In famine You nourished us and in plenty You sustained us; From sword You saved us; from plague You let us escape; and from severe and enduring diseases You spared us. *Until now Your mercy has helped us, and Your kindness has not forsaken us. Do not abandon us, Hashem, our God, forever.*" I realized that I had never given adequate thought to these precious words. After all the ordeals in life which God has enabled me to survive, how foolish it would be to think that He might now abandon me!

Nishmas is one of the strongest reinforcements of our faith and trust in God.

Our Praise Reflects Our Awareness

When something extraordinary happens, we are more likely to recognize the hand of God. When things progress more or less normally, we may not be aware of the Divine kindness. The Psalmist says, "To Him Who alone performs great wonders" (*Psalms* 136:4), upon which the Talmud remarks that God alone knows His miraculous works. The recipient of a miracle is likely to be unaware that he was saved by a miracle, assuming that what happened was but a natural phenomenon (*Niddah* 31a).

The degree to which a person praises God is indicative of how much awareness he has of God's kindness. As the Haggadah says, "The more a person elaborates on the miracles of the Exodus, the more praiseworthy he is."

The Maggid of Dubnow explained with a parable. A ship had sprung a leak and began taking on water. The crew desperately searched for the hole but could not find it, and some of the crew began preparing the lifeboats to abandon ship. The passengers all prayed fervently, and suddenly a shout of triumph was heard. The leak had been discovered and could be sealed. Had this not happened, the passengers would have landed on shore with only their clothes on their backs.

The passengers gave thanks to God for their salvation. Those who had few belongings were not too ecstatic. They could have reached shore on the lifeboats. Those passengers who had considerable merchandise and valuables were profuse in their expression of gratitude. Whereas their lives could have been saved even if they had had to abandon ship, they would have suffered a grave loss because they could not have taken their belongings into the lifeboats.

The Psalmist says, "Let every *neshamah* praise God" (*Psalms* 150:6). The Midrash reads the word *neshamah* as *neshimah* (breath), and interprets the verse to mean that one should praise God for each breath one takes (*Bereishis Rabbah* 14:11). Little does the average person realize that each breath is a new gift of life. One who appreciates the constant kindness of God is likely to be profuse in his praise and gratitude.

Regardless of how much we thank God, "we still could not thank You sufficiently." This is stated in the prayer *Nishmas kol chai*, or as the Midrash would say, *Neshimos kol chai* — we should praise God for every breath which enables us to remain alive.

The Sanctity of Time

יְהִי רָצוֹן מִלְּפָנֶיךָ, ה׳ אֱלֹקֵינוּ וֵאלֹקֵי אֲבוֹתֵינוּ, שֶׁתְּחַדֵּשׁ עָלֵינוּ אֶת הַחֹדֶשׁ הַזֶּה לְטוֹבָה וְלִבְרָכָה...

May it be Your will, Hashem, our God and the God of our forefathers, that You inaugurate this month upon us for goodness and for blessing ...

On the first day of a new month, most people simply flip the page on the calendar. Time flows along automatically. Yesterday was February, today is March. Yesterday was September, today is October. That's all there is to it.

The prayer for inauguration of the new month conveys a radically different concept of time. Time is not merely a passive happening. *Time is what we make it.*

In the days of the Temple, there were no calendars. On the thirtieth day of the month the High Court was in session. If two witnesses testified that they saw the new moon the previous evening, the High Court declared the thirtieth day as the first day of the next month. If the new moon was not seen, the court declared the thirty-first day as the first day of the new month.

The Midrash states that when the angels asked God, "When is Pesach?" God responded, "We must wait for the declaration of the High Court." Pesach is on the fifteenth day of Nissan, and Nissan does not begin until the High Court declares the onset of the new month.

We commemorate the ritual of the High Court by announcing the beginning of the new month on the preceding Shabbos. Like the High Court, we announce when the new month will begin.

On the festivals, we recite the blessing to God, "Who has hallowed Israel and the times (festivals)." The message is that time is dependent on us. It is, as it were, our own creation.

It would appear that the secular world, too, values time. This would seem to be the reason for our interest in so many "time-saving" devices. We have jet planes, fax machines, instant foods, and microwave ovens. But what do many people do with the precious time they save? A business traveler may find the fastest way to get to his destination, and then check in to his hotel and turn on the television for several hours in order "to kill time." If time is indeed so valuable that one wishes to save it, why kill it? Is it not indicative of the devaluation of time that the single greatest industry is one which enables people to while away their leisure time?

We announce the new month with a prayer that God help us make the coming month productive. We indeed pray that it be one of health and wealth, but with the ultimate goal that there will be "fear of heaven and fear of sin," and that it will be "devoid of shame and humiliation and with love of Torah."

The prayer for the new month is unique to Judaism. It is a philosophical statement of our concept of time. Only a fool would destroy what he creates. We should be wise and cherish time.

Do We Know What Is Truly Good?

חַיִּים שֶׁיְּמַלֵּא ה׳ מִשְׁאֲלוֹת לִבֵּנוּ לְטוֹבָה. אָמֵן, סֶלָה.

A life in which our heartfelt requests will be fulfilled for the good. Amen, Selah.

We pray to God to grant our requests, but we qualify this prayer. "Fulfill only those prayers that are for the good." In other words, if we pray for something that is actually not beneficial, don't give it to us. But is it necessary to tell God not to give us something that is harmful to us?

The Psalmist says, "The will of those who fear Him He will do, and their cry He will hear, and save them" (*Psalms* 145:19). One of the commentaries states that God is not only a loving parent, but actually an indulgent parent. A child may plead with his parent for candy, and the parent will tell him that he has already had more than enough sweets. But if the child persists in tearfully asking for more, the parent may yield to the child's entreaties. When the child later complains of a stomachache, the parent will not say, "Too bad! I warned you not to eat more candy. You insisted, now suffer!" Rather, the parent will do everything possible to relieve the child's pain.

When we pray for something that is actually to our disadvantage, God will not give it to us. But if we persist in pleading for it, God may act much like a human parent. He may give in to our entreaties, and He may grant our request. When we later discover that what we desired was really not good for us and complain to God, He again responds like a loving parent, and tends to our distress. "The will of those who fear Him He will do, and their cry He will hear, and save them." He responds to our will, and later saves us when we cry for help.

We are frequently incapable of knowing what is really to our advantage. We may see things as real, even though they are illusory. Our psychological perception is so limited that we may not perceive that many things are illusory. If more light were shed on the subject, we might recognize the truth.

> *R' Yehudah Leib Chasman tells of a villager who visited the big city, and wanted to bring home something that was unavailable in the village. He was fascinated by a powerful flashlight, and thought that it would be very helpful in the poorly lit streets of his town.*
>
> *After he bought the flashlight, he was enticed to go to a movie. He had never been in a theater before, and when he came into the dark room, he put on his flashlight. Suddenly there was a cry of demands that he put out the light, because the screen appeared blank in the light.*
>
> *"All the objects on the screen appeared to be real only because there was darkness," R' Yehudah Leib said. "The presence of light revealed that the objects on the screen were not real."*
>
> *"So it is with our desires," R' Yehudah Leib said. "We want some things only because we are spiritually 'in the dark.' If we had spiritual brightness, we would realize that many of the things we want are nothing but illusions."*

If we recognize the limitations of our understanding, we are less likely to be attracted to illusions.

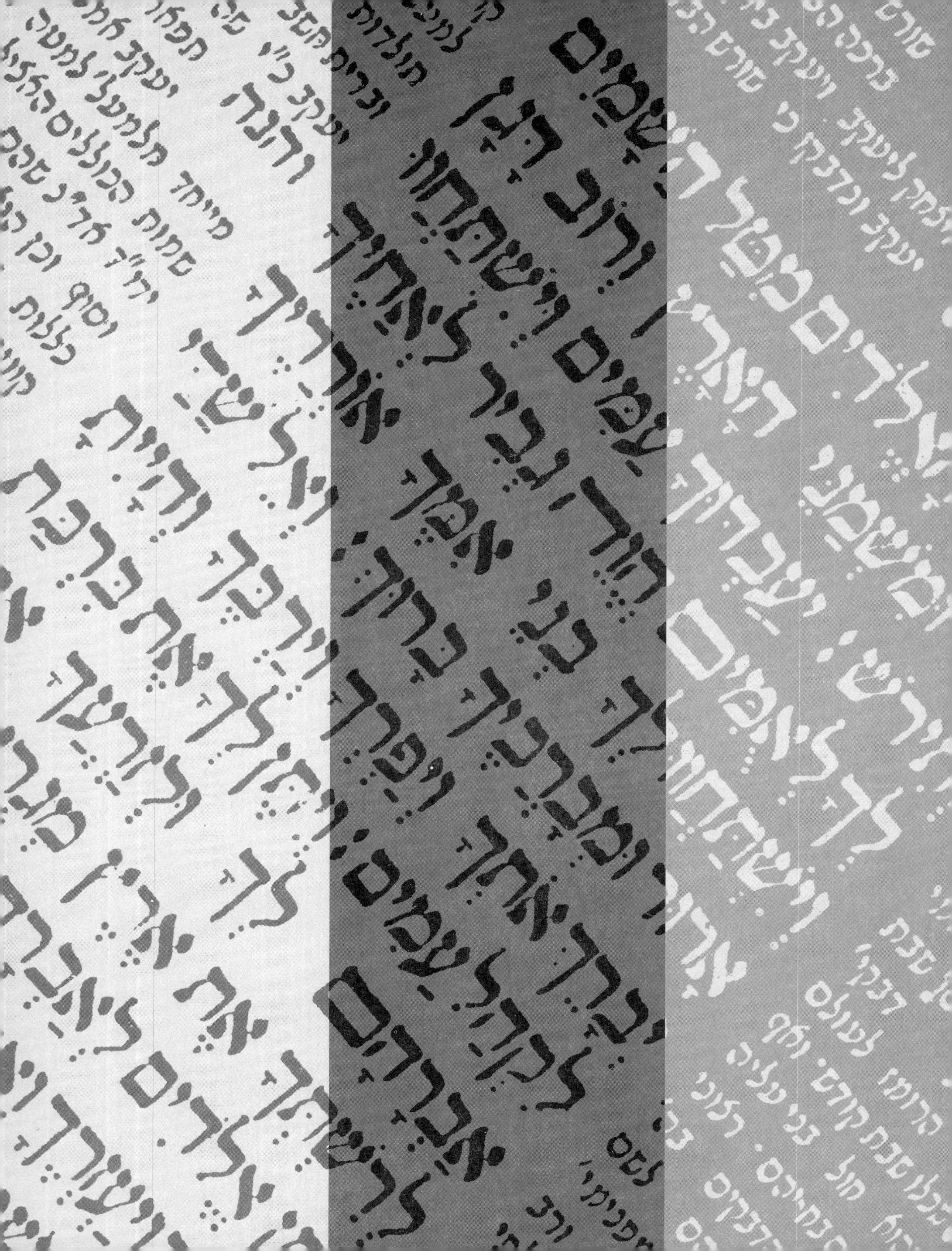

Motza'ei Shabbos - The Conclusion of the Sabbath

הִנֵּה קֵל יְשׁוּעָתִי אֶבְטַח וְלֹא אֶפְחָד...

וְיִתֶּן לְךָ הָאֱלֹקִים מִטַּל הַשָּׁמַיִם וּמִשְׁמַנֵּי הָאָרֶץ...
...וְהֵסִיר ה׳ מִמְּךָ כָּל חֹלִי...

... אוּן דִיא וָואךְ זָאל אוּנְז קוּמֶען צוּ חֶסֶד, אוּן צוּ מַזָל, אוּן צוּ בְרָכָה, אוּן צוּ הַצְלָחָה, אוּן צוּ גֶזוּנְט, אוּן צוּ עוֹשֶׁר וְכָבוֹד, אוּן צוּ בָּנֵי חַיֵי וּמְזוֹנֵי, לָנוּ וּלְכָל יִשְׂרָאֵל. אָמֵן.

Behold! God is my salvation, I shall trust and not fear...

And may God give you of the dew of the heavens and of the fatness of the earth ... God shall remove from you all illness ...

... May this week arrive for kindness, for good fortune, for blessing, for success, for good health, for wealth and honor, and for children, life and sustenance, for us and for all Israel. Amen.

On Shabbos eve we brought closure to the past week. Shabbos was a day of freedom from all worries. Now this sacred day has passed, and we confront the reality of the workweek. Experience has taught us that there are not only many stresses in the workweek, but that there may also arise unexpected difficulties. Approaching the workweek may be fraught with anxiety.

The prayers at the close of Shabbos inspire us with strength, hope and courage. "God is my salvation, I shall trust and not fear ... And may God give you of the dew of the heavens and of the fatness of the earth ... God shall remove from you all illness." And the beautiful prayer *Gut fun Avraham,* composed in Yiddish by R' Levi Yitzchok of Berditchev: "May this week arrive for kindness, for good fortune, for blessing, for success, for good health, for wealth and honor, and for children, life and sustenance, for us and for all Israel. Amen.

Halachah requires that the Shabbos should be accompanied by a meal, *Melaveh Malkah* (escorting the Shabbos Queen), as she takes leave of us. This is known as "the meal of King David," and we sing of the promise of the Redemption, heralded by the prophet, Elijah.

Just as the traditional *farfel* on Friday night helps bring closure to the past week, the tradition of telling stories about the lives of our great *tzaddikim* and their faith and trust in God reinforces our hope and courage for the coming week.

> *The Baal Shem Tov was seeking someone from whom to learn unwavering bitachon (trust) in God. It was revealed to him that he was to learn this from a simple person in a distant village whose trust in God is so firm that he is free of worry.*
>
> *The Baal Shem Tov traveled to meet this person, who welcomed him and invited him to a meal. At the meal, the Baal Shem Tov asked, "How much rent do you pay the poritz (feudal lord) for this house?"*
>
> *"Three thousand gulden a year," the man answered.*
>
> *"Do you pay this in installments?" the Baal Shem Tov asked.*
>
> *"No," the man answered. "I must pay it in one lump sum at the beginning of the rental year."*
>
> *"And when is that?" the Baal Shem Tov asked.*
>
> *"In about one week. I am required to pay the whole amount on that day, otherwise the poritz will evict me."*
>
> *"Do you have much of that sum now," the Baal Shem Tov asked, "or do you anticipate additional income during the next week?"*
>
> *"I don't have a single gulden at the moment. No one owes me any money, and I do not have any transactions pending that can bring me that amount."*
>
> *"Then how do you expect to pay the rent in one week?"*
>
> *The man's composure was one of calmness and tranquility. "I trust in God," he said. "He has stood by me through all life's ordeals, and I know he will not abandndon me now."*
>
> *Wishing to test the sincerity of the man's bitachon, the Baal Shem Tov said, "But what if you do not have the money by the date? The poritz is very cruel and will promptly send his troops to evict you. Why don't you try to borrow the money during the next week?"*

The man responded, "The verse says, 'Do not put your trust in humans' (Psalms 146:3), and that it is better to trust in God than in people. I know God will not forsake me."

The Baal Shem Tov decided he would remain to see what transpired. Two days before the due date, an agent of the poritz came demanding the rent money, threatening to evict the man if he defaulted. "Why are you bothering me now?" the man said. "The due date is two days away."

On the morning of the due date the agent returned. "The poritz is demanding his money, Jew. Woe unto you if you do not deliver it."

The man responded, "Go tell your master that our agreement is that I pay before the end of the day. Until that time, I don't want to be pressured."

The Baal Shem Tov said to him, "You have only a few hours left. Go into the city; I'm certain you will find people willing to lend you the money."

"That is God's worry, not mine," the man said. He proceeded to pray and eat as if there were no problem.

Late in the afternoon three people came in. "We are grain merchants," they said, "and we wish to buy the entire harvest of the poritz. We understand that he is a difficult person to deal with. We know that he trusts you as an honest person. We would like you to negotiate the deal for us. We are willing to pay a reasonable price, even a bit more than the current rate, and we will pay you 500 gulden to negotiate the deal for us."

"I think I can get a better price for you, but my fee is 3,000," the man said.

"Three thousand gulden!" the merchants said. "That is too steep. We'll pay you a thousand gulden."

The man responded calmly, "I'm sorry. You may negotiate the deal yourselves. My fee is 3,000 gulden, paid in advance."

The merchants huddled in a brief discussion and said, "Then we will look elsewhere to buy grain."

"As you wish," the man said.

The merchants left, and the Baal Shem Tov looked at the man with wonderment. He did not appear the least bit perturbed.

As dusk fell, the agent of the poritz returned. "Where is the money, Jew?"

The man said, "Just wait a bit." At that point there was a knock on the door. The merchants returned, saying, "All right, you can have 3,000 gulden. But get us a good price."

The man took the 3,000 gulden, gave them to the poritz's agent and said, "Please tell the poritz that I will come shortly to make a very profitable deal for him."

The Baal Shem Tov said, "I am grateful to God for providing me with a lesson in bitachon."

Just as the Baal Shem Tov prayed for *bitachon*, we may do so, too.

It was stories like this that enabled us to face the challenges of the new week with the proper equanimity.

The Divine Humility

בָּרוּךְ אַתָּה ה׳, אֱלֹקֵינוּ מֶלֶךְ הָעוֹלָם, אֲשֶׁר בְּמַאֲמָרוֹ בָּרָא שְׁחָקִים, וּבְרוּחַ פִּיו כָּל צְבָאָם. חֹק וּזְמַן נָתַן לָהֶם שֶׁלֹּא יְשַׁנּוּ אֶת תַּפְקִידָם. שָׂשִׂים וּשְׂמֵחִים לַעֲשׂוֹת רְצוֹן קוֹנָם, פּוֹעֵל אֱמֶת שֶׁפְּעֻלָּתוֹ אֱמֶת. וְלַלְּבָנָה אָמַר שֶׁתִּתְחַדֵּשׁ, עֲטֶרֶת תִּפְאֶרֶת לַעֲמוּסֵי בָטֶן, שֶׁהֵם עֲתִידִים לְהִתְחַדֵּשׁ כְּמוֹתָהּ, וּלְפָאֵר לְיוֹצְרָם עַל שֵׁם כְּבוֹד מַלְכוּתוֹ. בָּרוּךְ אַתָּה ה׳, מְחַדֵּשׁ חֳדָשִׁים.

Blessed are You, Hashem, our God, King of the Universe, Who with His utterance created the heavens, and with the breath of His mouth all their legion. A decree and a schedule did He give them that they not alter their assigned task. They are joyous and glad to perform the will of their owner — the Worker of truth Whose work is truth. To the moon He said that it should renew itself as a crown of splendor for those borne [by Him] from the womb, those who are destined to renew themselves like it, and to glorify their Molder for the Name of His glorious kingdom. Blessed are You, Hashem, Who renews the months.

Saturday night appears to be a particularly propitious time to reflect on humility. In one of the evening prayers we quote a passage from the Talmud: "Wherever you find the greatness of God, there you find His humility" (*Megillah* 31a). Humility is so important a trait that God wishes to teach it to us by demonstrating His own humility. For example, God sought the counsel of the angels before He created man. Obviously, God does not need anyone's advice. He did this to teach us that regardless of how great a person is, one should not hesitate to take advice from a lesser person (*Rashi, Genesis* 1:26).

It is customary to say the prayer of "Sanctification of the Moon" on Saturday night. Here we find an even greater teaching of humility. In the above prayer we speak of the restoration of the brightness of the moon to its state before it was diminished. The Midrash states that at the time of Creation, the sun and the moon were equally bright. The moon said, "There cannot be two coequal rulers." God responded, "You are right. You must become smaller," and He reduced the brightness of the moon

Our calendar is regulated by the lunar cycle. On the first day of the new month, a special sin-offering is brought, as prescribed in the Torah, "and one sin-offering to God" (*Numbers* 28:15). Rashi (ibid.) quotes the Talmudic interpretation, "one sin-offering *for* God." God said, "Bring a sin-offering to achieve forgiveness for Me for having reduced the brightness of the moon."

God does not err and God does not sin. This is but another way in which He wishes to teach us that a person should not think of himself as being without sin, and no person should think of himself as being so great that he cannot ask for forgiveness. This is a powerful teaching. As we begin a new month, a new segment of life, this prayer reminds us not to deny our mistakes, and to ask forgiveness when we have done wrong.

ויתיצב עמו ... אל ... נצר
ויקרא ... ואמת ... וסלחת
ורב־חסד ... ונקה ... כי חטאנו
ופשע וחטאה ... סלח לנו אבינו ... וסלח ורב
ונחלתנו ... כי אתה ... טוב וסלח
כי פשענו ... לכל־קראיך

הש"ץ אומר קדיש ... ולאח"כ ... אחרי תחלה מתחיל לצבור הפלים

ועתה יגדל־נא כח אדני כאשר דברת לאמר: זכר רחמיך ה' וחסדיך

יתגדל ויתקדש שמה רבא ... בעלמא די
וימליך מלכותה בחייכון וביומיכון
ישראל בעגלא ובזמן קריב ואמרו
יהא שמה רבא מברך לעלם ולעלמי

Selichos

The Insanity Plea

סְלַח לָנוּ אָבִינוּ, כִּי בְּרוֹב אִוַּלְתֵּנוּ שָׁגִינוּ, מְחַל לָנוּ מַלְכֵּנוּ, כִּי רַבּוּ עֲוֹנֵינוּ.

Forgive us, our Father, for in our abundant folly we have erred; pardon us, our King, for our iniquities are many.

It would appear that when asking for forgiveness, we should try to minimize the gravity of our sins rather than exaggerating them. Why, then, do we say "... for our iniquities are many"?

We find something similar to this in Moses' prayer for forgiveness after the worship of the Golden Calf. Moses said to God. "I implore! This people has committed a grievous sin and made themselves a god of gold" (*Exodus* 32:31). Why did Moses accentuate the sin in his plea for forgiveness?

Even sin must have some logic. A person who is meticulously observant of Torah may conceivably forget to check that his coat pockets are empty before leaving the house on Friday evening, and it is possible that he may find a coin in his pocket on Shabbos. It is indeed a sin to handle money on Shabbos, but it is understandable that this could happen. However, if this same person would eat in a non-kosher restaurant on Yom Kippur, we would conclude that something must have happened that caused him to take leave of his senses. This is something that he could never have done if he were in his right mind.

This man does not need to be reprimanded. Rather, he needs the services of a psychiatrist to restore him to sanity.

This was Moses' plea for the Israelites. They had witnessed the miracles of Egypt, the dividing of the waters of the Reed Sea, and the Revelation at Sinai. For them to worship a Golden Calf as a god is so absurd that it can hardly be considered a sin. It could only be that something caused them to lose their sanity. They need to be helped rather than punished.

The Talmud says that a person would not sin unless he was overtaken by a spirit of insanity (*Sotah* 3a). This is our defense before God. The sins we did were so grievous that we could not possibly have done them if we were in our right minds. It can only be that the *yetzer hara* so overwhelmed us with desire that we were not fully sane when we committed our sins.

This is a powerful argument and it may indeed mitigate the severity of the sinful act. However, once we had satisfied our desire, that stress was gone, and we could again think rationally. Why did we not do *teshuvah* for our sins. Failure to do *teshuvah* is not defensible and may be a greater transgression than the sinful act itself.

If we do proper *teshuvah* in these days of penitence, we may merit total forgiveness. The sinful act itself occurred when the *yetzer hara* made us bereft of logical thinking, and realizing that we acted in folly, we do *teshuvah*. We may, therefore, confidently ask God for forgiveness.

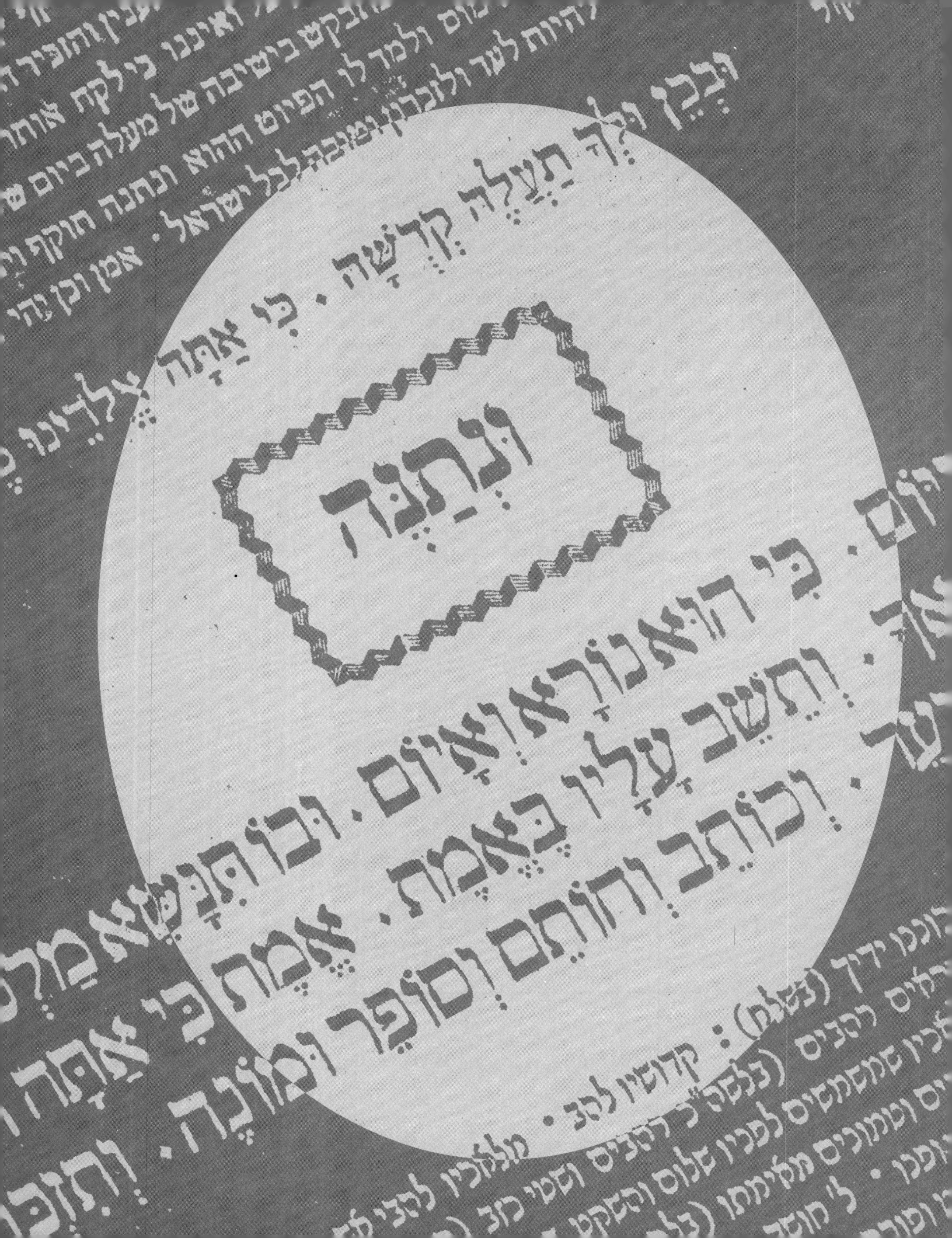
ובכן
ולך תעלה קדשה. כי אתה אלהינו
ונתנה
כי הוא נורא ואיום. ובו תנשא
ותשב עליו באמת. אמת כי אתה
וכותב וחותם וסופר ומונה.

The High Holy Days

The True "Happy New Year" Greeting: A Prayer

לְשָׁנָה טוֹבָה תִּכָּתֵבוּ וְתֵחָתֵמוּ לְאַלְתַּר, לְחַיִּים טוֹבִים וּלְשָׁלוֹם.

For a good year may you be inscribed and sealed, immediately, for a good life and for peace.

Let us compare how a new year is inaugurated by the Jewish people as opposed to the secular world.

On December 31, there are gatherings for merriment, some held in homes, some in banquet halls. Everyone awaits the magic moment of the arrival of the new year. Invariably, they prepare themselves for this great moment by consuming copious amounts of alcohol, and are in a state of inebriation when they shout "Happy New Year" at the top of their lungs.

As an expert on alcoholism, I can tell you that alcohol has only one major effect on the mind. *Alcohol is an emotional anesthetic.* People may feel relieved and relaxed when they drink because alcohol anesthetizes their minds and numbs them to whatever unpleasant feelings may be disturbing them. It is understandable why people may wish relief from unpleasant feelings, but it makes no sense whatever to anesthetize oneself to pleasant feelings. If you really feel happy, you want to savor every moment. You would hardly wish to anesthetize yourself to avoid feeling good.

Why, then, do so many people drink to bring in the new year, if it is such a happy occasion?

As a rule, we do not pause too often to make a reckoning of what we have achieved in the past and what we plan to do in the future. We generally plod along without taking a personal inventory. But there are times when one may be inspired to do so. One such time is the beginning of a new year. "In just several hours it is going to be 2001! How can that be? I've just gotten accustomed to dating the checks 2000 instead of 1999. You mean a whole year has passed? Heavens! What do I have to show for that year? Am I any healthier? No. Am I any wiser? No. Am I better off financially? No way! I owe more money than ever before. All that has happened is that I am a year older. And what prospects are there that this next year is going to be much better? None, really."

This is a most depressing thought. Anyone who feels this way can hardly celebrate the new year with joy. Not unless they anesthetize themselves with alcohol. It is only when their depressed mood has been relived by alcohol that they can exclaim, "Happy New Year."

Rosh Hashanah is so, so, different. During the preceding month we do some serious soul-searching and discover those things about ourselves that we need to change. In the days immediately preceding Rosh Hashanah we recite the extra prayers for forgiveness. We become more spiritual. We reassert our *bitachon* (trust) in God and become more secure in the knowledge that He will help us do what is best for us. If the past year had its downside, our *emunah* (faith) in God's benevolence enables us to accept it. We need not be depressed about the year that has passed and we can have hope for success in the coming year. There is no need to drown away any misery in drink.

In the Rosh Hashanah prayers we say, "Our Father, Our King, inscribe us for a year of good life, of redemption and salvation, of sustenance and support, of merits, forgiveness and pardon."

We joyously greet one another with the wish and prayer, "May you be inscribed for a good year."

Making Our Rosh Hashanah Prayers More Effective

זָכְרֵנוּ לְחַיִּים, מֶלֶךְ חָפֵץ בַּחַיִּים, וְכָתְבֵנוּ בְּסֵפֶר הַחַיִּים, לְמַעַנְךָ אֱלֹקִים חַיִּים.

Remember us for life, O King Who desires life, and inscribe us in the Book of Life — for Your sake, O Living God.

Let's face it. There are many shuls which are sparsely populated all year round and are full only on Rosh Hashanah and Yom Kippur. While God welcomes everyone at any time, our prayers for His blessings would be more effective if we visited His dwelling place more often.

This is hardly a modern-day phenomenon. The Maggid of Dubnow commented on this some 200 years ago with this parable.

A merchant suffered a disastrous loss when his business burned down, destroying all his merchandise. He was uninsured and owed his supplier a huge sum of money. There was no way he could possibly raise enough money to pay the debt, and he became very depressed. His friends advised him to go to his supplier and tell him what had happened. Surely the supplier would be considerate and arrange reasonable terms for payment of the debt.

The merchant accepted this advice and traveled to the city of the supplier. However, when he approached the supplier's office and realized that he was in such terrible straits that he had to beg for mercy, he was overcome with depression and began to cry. The supplier, hearing someone weeping, went to investigate. Seeing one of his best customers in tears, he invited him into his office. When the merchant calmed down, he told the supplier what had happened, and asked if he could make some accommodation so that he could repay the debt.

The supplier was deeply moved by the merchant's plight. He said, "My friend, do not worry about repayment now. Of course I will sharply reduce the debt. Furthermore, I will lend you 2,000 rubles and give you enough merchandise so that you can go into business again. Eventually you will make enough profit to repay me." He encouraged and comforted the merchant and wished him well.

Upon returning to the inn where he was lodging, the merchant was in high spirits and told some of the other guests about his good fortune. Hearing this story, one of the guests went to the supplier's office and began crying aloud. When the supplier asked him why he was crying, he said that his business had failed and that he was in need of funds to start up again. The supplier gave him a donation of two rubles.

"Two rubles is all you are giving me?" the man asked. "Why, I know that you gave another merchant 2,000 rubles and a huge supply of merchandise."

The supplier said, "You fool! That merchant has been doing business with me for twenty years. During that time, I made considerable profit transacting with him. Now that he has fallen upon hard times, it is only fair that I help him. But you! I have never seen you before. I have never profited a single cent from you. What right do you have to expect me to do for you what I did for him?"

The Maggid continued. "When a Jew who has been going to shul to pray every day and has done his best to obey God's will makes his moral inventory before Rosh Hashanah and realizes how derelict he was in serving God properly, he comes to shul and tearfully asks God for forgiveness. God feels this person's broken heart, and gladly forgives him, blessing him with a year of prosperity. He knows this merchant will do his utmost to repay the debt. But those who are negligent in observing God's commandments and come to shul only once a year, they are much like the person who expects a handsome donation from the supplier with whom he never did any business. Is it not a chutzpah that they make unreasonable requests from God?"

R' Yechezkel of Kuzhmir used the above parable to explain the prayer, "Remember us for life, O King Who desires life, and inscribe us in the Book of Life — for Your sake, O living God." What is meant by "for Your sake"?

R' Yechezkel explained that the supplier knows that the only way he will ever get his money back is if he enables the merchant to go into business again. He is, therefore, motivated by personal interest to help the merchant get back on his feet. Similarly, we say to God, "Even though we have been derelict in Your service, please give us a year of life so that we can rectify our errors and serve You properly." We appeal to God that it is "for His sake" that we ask for life.

True, God is merciful to all. However, it is only logical that His response to those who "transacted" with Him all year round will be more favorable. Those who have not done so may still merit abundant kindness by sincerely promising to come to shul more often.

Simple but Sincere

Prior to Rosh Hashanah, R' Levi Yitzchok of Berditchev announced that he was seeking someone to blow the shofar. A number of learned scholars applied, and R' Levi Yitzchok asked them what their kavannah (intention) would be when they sounded the shofar. The scholars, who were well versed in the Kabbalah, told R' Levi Yitzchok about the highly complex esoteric Appellations of God which they would think of. R' Levi Yitzchok was not impressed.

One of the candidates was a very simple, unlearned but devout man. When R' Levi Yitzchok asked him about his kavannah, he replied, "Rabbi, I know nothing about the Kabbalah. I have three daughters of marriageable age, but I cannot afford a dowry, and they have not been able to find shidduchim. My kavannah would be, 'Dear God, I am doing Your will by blowing the shofar. I ask You to have compassion on me and do my will. Please give me the means that I may marry off my three daughters.'"

R' Levi Yitzchok was elated. "You are the person I am looking for."

The learned scholars' kavannah was much more sophisticated. The unlearned person's kavannah was simple but would be put forth with all his heart. Its simplicity and sincerity made it superior to all the others.

Earlier I related several stories about the effectiveness of sincere prayer, even the prayer of people who hardly knew the meaning of the words they were reciting. I wish to share two additional stories with you.

> *On a visit to Israel, I attended a meeting of recovering alcoholics in Jerusalem. One man related his life's story, a rather typical story of the deterioration resulting from drinking and the refusal of the alcoholic to recognize the problem and accept help. As a rule, one does not do so until one has reached a crisis, referred to as "rock bottom."*
>
> *What impressed me about this man's story was that he had never been religious. "I was an atheist," he said. "I had never set foot into a synagogue. Prayer was out of the question.*
>
> *"My drinking cost me my job and my friends. The grocer told me to please make my purchases one time for the entire week and to come first thing in the morning. He said some of his patrons would avoid coming in to his store if I was there.*
>
> *"I finally reached my bottom," he continued. "My wife threw me out of the house. I had nowhere to go. I walked along the beach, thinking about whether I should just walk into the sea and get it over with. Then I lifted my eyes to the sky and I shouted, 'If You are really up there, then help me!' And you know, He helped me! I am now six years sober, and I am back with my family. I never could have made it on my own. I now pray every day."*

When I heard this story, the verse of psalm 145 flashed through my mind. "God is close to all who call upon Him — to all who call upon Him sincerely."

My favorite story of the effectiveness of the sincere prayer of simple folk is the following.

> *A chassid of R' Menachem Mendel of Lubavitch (Tzemach Tzedek) returned from a trip to Eretz Yisrael. He told the Rebbe that he was disappointed because he had expected to find more profoundly spiritual people in the Holy Land.*
>
> *"What makes you think that you are a mayven on spirituality?" the Rebbe asked. "Let me tell you about a spiritual person in the Holy Land.*
>
> *"There was a very simple, unlearned but pious man who owned a small farm. He could read Hebrew but did not understand the words. The degree of his ignorance was such that he could not grasp the order of the daily prayers for the days of the week. Once each week he would come into town, and*

the Rabbi would write down for him the prayers for Monday, Tuesday, Wednesday, etc., and the prayers for special days.

"One time he told the Rabbi that he would be unable to come into town for several weeks, and could the Rabbi please write the instructions for the daily prayers for the month. The Rabbi did as he was asked.

"Two weeks later the man happened to come into town and went to the Rabbi's house. The Rabbi's wife told him that the Rabbi was in shul because this was a fast day and one of special prayers. 'But that can't be,' the man said. 'The Rabbi did not mark today as a fast day, and I ate today!' He rushed off to the synagogue where people had gathered in fervent prayer.

" 'Rabbi,' he said. 'Why didn't you tell me that today is a fast day? I did not know what special prayers to say, and I ate today.'

"The Rabbi said, 'There was no way I could have known about this two weeks ago. You see, today is not a regularly scheduled fast day. We are in the midst of a severe draught, and the Rabbis in Jerusalem decreed today as a fast day with special prayers for rain. I did not know this when I wrote your instructions.'

"The man appeared bewildered. 'But why do you have to fast for rain? Why, I just go out to the field and I say, "Father, You always give me my food. My field needs rain. Please give me rain." That is all that is needed.'

"The Rabbi said, 'Can you pray that way for us as well?'

" 'Of course,' the man said. He then went out of the synagogue, lifted his eyes to heaven and said, 'Father, Your children need food. They need rain to make their food grow. Please give them rain.'

"Shortly afterward," R' Menachem Mendel continued, "gray clouds appeared on the horizon, and soon there was abundant rain.

"Now tell me," R' Menachem Mendel said to the chassid, "if you saw this simple man, would you have thought of him as being particularly spiritual?"

Fathers respond positively to a child's request. If only we truly felt that God was a loving father!

Rosh Hashanah Shacharis

God, the King

הַמֶּלֶךְ יוֹשֵׁב עַל כִּסֵּא רָם וְנִשָּׂא.

O king Who is sitting upon a high and lofty throne!

Although we regularly refer to God in our *berachos* as "King of the Universe," we emphasize His sovereignty in the ten days that span Rosh Hashanah and Yom Kippur. For example, in place of "the holy God" in the *Amidah*, we say "the holy King." This is to remind us that these are days of judgment in which the Divine conduct as King is dominant.

The main part of the morning service begins with the *chazzan* chanting *HaMelech* (the King), which appears in the *machzor* (holiday prayer book) in large, bold letters, again to emphasize that these are days in which we stand in judgment before God.

> *The Chassidic master, R' Aaron of Karlin, fell into a swoon when he heard the chazzan chant "HaMelech. "When he was revived, he explained that he was reminded of an episode related in the Talmud (Gittin 56a). During the Roman siege of Jerusalem, R' Yochanan ben Zakkai managed to exit the city and come before Vespasian, who was then a Roman general. R' Yochanan addressed him as "Your Majesty." Vespasian said that this salutation is used solely to address an emperor. R' Yochanan replied that the emperor had died and that the Roman*

senate had appointed Vespasian in his place. Shortly afterward, a messenger delivered the news that Vespasian had indeed been named as emperor.

Vespasian then said to R' Yochanan, "If you knew I was emperor, why did you not come to me before this?"

R' Aaron said, "When I heard the chazzan chant 'HaMelech,' it was as if God were saying to me, 'If you knew I am the King, why have you not come before Me earlier?' I realized how derelict I was in not being aware of the complete ramifications of God as King."

In some *machzorim* this story is given as a commentary to *HaMelech*, with the addendum, "If this great *tzaddik* felt he was derelict in the awareness that God is King, what can we say for ourselves?"

Shortly after *HaMelech*, Psalm 130 is recited in many congregations: "From the depths I called to you, God." The depths may be referring to our anguish over the paucity of our recognition of God as King. We pray for Divine mercy and consideration: "If You preserve iniquities, God, who could survive?" You created us with the frailty of human understanding. We are so vulnerable to our physical nature obscuring our perception of the truth. Why, even the great *tzaddik*, R' Aaron, felt that he was derelict in his awareness of Your sovereignty. But our hopes are high, because "with God there is kindness, and with Him is abundant salvation."

...מן אלהי המלך
...ישראל היום ברחמים אמן :

עלה אלהים בתרועה יהוה בקול שופר

...ומזומן לקיים המצוה שצונו בוראנו לתקוע בשופר היום הזה כמו שכתוב בתו...
לכם · ואני מכוון להוציא בתקיעתי כל השומעים קול תקיעתי :

אתה ... אלהינו מלך העולם אשר קד...
וצונו לשמוע קול שופר :

...אתה ... אלהינו מלך העולם שהח...
והגיענו לזמן הזה :

תקיעה : שברים

תקיעה : שברים : תרועה : תקיעה :

תקיעה : שברים : תרועה : תקיעה :

שברים : תרועה : תקיעה :

שב

...אלדי ואלדי אבותי שתקיעת תשר"ת שאנחנו תוקעים היום תעשה ממנו עט...
...) להיות עולה ולישב בראש אלהי ויעשה עמנו אות לטובה וימלא עלינו רחמים
אתה בעל הרחמים :

תקיעה : שברים : תקיעה :

תקיעה : שברים : תקיעה

Shofar Service

לַמְנַצֵּחַ לִבְנֵי קֹרַח מִזְמוֹר...

For the Conductor, by the sons of Korach, a song …

עָלָה אֱלֹקִים בִּתְרוּעָה, ה׳ בְּקוֹל שׁוֹפָר...

God has ascended with a blast, Hashem, with the sound of the shofar …

Many interpretations have been given to the shofar. Perhaps the most profound is that the shofar presents a sound without words. As rich and varied as our vocabulary may be, words are very limited in what they can convey. The most poetic description of a sunset falls far short of its grandeur. There are some concepts in prayer which cannot be expressed in words. The non-verbal sound of the shofar allows us to imbue it with our feelings. The power of the shofar is depicted in Psalm 47, which we recite seven times before the shofar is sounded. "God has ascended with the sound of the shofar." Whatever it is that is meant by the phrase "God has ascended," it is clear that the sound of the shofar is extremely powerful.

One of the terms of prayer is צְעָקָה which is a cry of anguish. The *Zohar* states that צְעָקָה is the highest degree of prayer and is closer to God than other forms of prayer. צְעָקָה is a cry without words, as is written, "Their *heart* cried in anguish (צָעַק לִבָּם) to God (*Lamentations* 2:18). The wordless sound of the shofar may represent this profound heartfelt emotion.

The Torah refers to Rosh Hashanah as a day of *teruah* (shofar sounding). The *teruah* is the series of broken sounds, which the Talmud states is reminiscent of the sounds of weeping. On the other hand, the term *teruah* is used as an expression of gladness, as "Sing to Him a new song, sing well with *teruah* (*Psalms* 33:3).

Rosh Hashanah is a most solemn day, a day of judgment, a day on which all of mankind passes before God and their actions are scrutinized. However, solemn does not mean sad. On Rosh Hashanah the prophet Nehemiah said, "This day is sacred to God. Do not be sad, for to be glad before God is your strength" (8:30). With proper *teshuvah*, we may be secure that we will be inscribed in the Book of Life.

Teshuvah requires a firm resolution that we will not repeat our sins and errors. Unless we fully understand the gravity of transgressing the will of God, the resolution is nothing but lip service. If this understanding does not move us to tears, it is lacking in depth. The weeping sound of the shofar should express our emotions in *teshuvah.*

But the shofar is also a sound of triumph. The shofar is sounded on the Yom Kippur of the Jubilee year, declaring the emancipation of slaves and the return of land to its original owner. This sounding of the shofar is to "proclaim freedom throughout the land" (*Leviticus* 25:10).

The weeping sound of the shofar yields to the proclamation of freedom. With proper *teshuvah* and a resolve to observe the Divine will we liberate ourselves from the tyranny of our physical drives for indulgence that threaten to override our logic and deprive us of spirituality. The solemnity of the day precludes festive behavior, but the promise of the day should eliminate all sadness.

> *The Chassidic master, R' Dov of Radoshitz, lodged in an inn. In the morning he asked the proprietor, "Where did you get that clock? Every time it chimed I felt an urge to get up and dance."*
>
> *"That clock was left as a pledge by a guest who did not have money to pay his bill," the proprietor said.*
>
> *"Was this man perhaps related to the Seer of Lublin?" R' Dov asked.*
>
> *"I cannot say that," the proprietor said, "But now that you mention it, I did hear him speak about the Seer of Lublin."*
>
> *"Of course!" R' Dov exclaimed. "Now I understand it. You see, a clock is really a depressing instrument. Every time it chimes it reminds you that another segment of your life is irretrievably gone. But the clock of the Seer was different. Each chime meant that we are just a bit closer to the Redemption of Mashiach. No wonder I felt the urge to dance!"*

The shofar, like the clock of the Seer, can convey a feeling of exaltation. It heralds a new segment of life. We can begin the year with a clean slate, with hope for spiritual achievement.

The Shofar: A Plea for Compassion

וַיְהִי קוֹל הַשּׁוֹפָר הוֹלֵךְ וְחָזֵק מְאֹד, מֹשֶׁה יְדַבֵּר וְהָאֱלֹקִים יַעֲנֶנּוּ בְקוֹל.

And the sound of the Shofar became increasingly stronger, Moses would speak and God would respond to him with a voice (Exodus 19:19).

The Chassidic master, R' Levi Yitzchok of Berditchev is known for his advocacy of Israel before God. With regard to the verse, "And the sound of the shofar became increasingly stronger, Moses would speak and God would respond to him with a voice" (*Exodus* 19:19), which is recited in the Rosh Hashanah *Mussaf* prayers (*Shofros*), R' Levi Yitzchok had this to say.

A king once went on a fox hunt accompanied by his courtiers. He chased a fox into the forest and was separated from his courtiers. His efforts to rejoin them only led him farther and farther into the forest. When night fell, he was alone and frightened. After aimless wandering he saw a dim light and followed it to a hut, inhabited by a hermit dressed in shabby clothes. He told the hermit that he was the king, and the hermit allowed him to spend the night. He provided the king with food and a straw mattress on which to sleep. In the morning, he led the king out of the forest, and the king asked him to accompany him to the palace.

The courtiers, who had been concerned for the king's welfare, rejoiced at his return. The king told them that the hermit had saved him, and that he wished to reward him with a royal office. The hermit gladly accepted the reward.

Years went by, and the hermit foolishly allowed himself to become part of a palace intrigue against the king. When the plot was exposed, all the conspirators were sentenced to death. They were given one last request, and the hermit asked to be allowed to put on the shabby clothes he had worn in his earlier days and stand before the window where the king could see him. When the king saw the hermit in his shabby clothes, he recalled the incident many years earlier when he had been lost in the forest, and the hermit had provided food and shelter and showed him the way out of the forest. The king was overcome with gratitude and compassion and promptly pardoned the hermit.

R' Levi Yitzchok then addressed God. "Many years ago, You were unknown to the world. You offered the Torah to the pagans, but they rejected both You and the Torah. It was Israel that accepted You as their King at Sinai, and proclaimed Your sovereignty to the world. The Revelation at Sinai was accompanied by the sound of the shofar. Perhaps we have deviated from Your commandments, but let the shofar remind You of the earlier days, when Israel was the only nation that acknowledged You as their King. This should arouse Your mercy, so that you may grant us forgiveness."

But just as we pray that the shofar earn us Divine mercy, let us remember that it heralded our acceptance of God's rule. On Rosh Hashanah, just as at Sinai, we should rededicate ourselves to the service of God.

Rosh Hashanah Mussaf

זֶה הַיּוֹם תְּחִלַּת מַעֲשֶׂיךָ...

הַיּוֹם הֲרַת עוֹלָם, הַיּוֹם יַעֲמִיד בַּמִּשְׁפָּט כָּל יְצוּרֵי עוֹלָמִים.

"This day is the beginning of Your doings ..."

"This day is the birth (day) of the world. On this day all Your creations stand in judgment."

It is generally assumed, as the above verses seem to indicate, that Rosh Hashanah commemorates the beginning or first day of Creation. That is not the case. Rosh Hashanah represents the *sixth* day of Creation, the day on which God created man. This day is referred to as the beginning of Creation because the first five days were essentially a prelude, necessary precursors to man. Man was the object of Creation.

But it was not merely the human animal that was the purpose of Creation. The Talmud says that it was the *human being that would fulfill the Divine will* that was the goal of Creation. God said, "If no one accepts the Torah, I will return the universe to its original state of nothingness" (*Shabbos* 88a).

"On this day all creations stand in judgment." It is only by the merit of man that all creations exist, and it is only by the merit of *man who is subservient to God* that all creations exist. The birthday of man is, therefore, the birthday of the world.

In the chapter "Prayer — An Instrument for Change" we noted the Baal Shem Tov's observation that God created man as a being who was to participate in his own creation. Nascent man was nothing other than *homo sapiens*, a hominoid with intellect. This was an unfinished product. It is only when man rises above his animal status and subjugates his animal body to the rule of the *neshamah*, the Divine spirit within him, that he becomes true *man*.

On this day, man stands before God to be judged as to whether he has participated in his own creation, whether he has become the being that God desired. These verses of prayer should arouse us to a painstaking self-examination.

There are several traits that clearly distinguish man from other living things. Intellect is indeed important, but it does not constitute the whole of man.

Man has the ability to learn from the history of past generations, to emulate their laudable deeds and to avoid their mistakes. No animal can do this. Man is unique in having the ability to think about the purpose of his existence. Man has the ability to reflect on how he may improve himself and implement the changes that will make him a better person. Man has the ability to look ahead and consider the future consequences of his actions. Man has the ability to postpone gratification. Man is unique in being truly free. In contrast to animals that function under the tyranny of their bodily drives, man can defy a bodily urge and make moral and ethical decisions that may deny the body what it craves. Man is the only living being that can do *chesed* (acts of kindness), sacrificing his personal comfort and giving of himself and of his possessions to help others.

The sum total of all the traits that are unique to man comprise the human *spirit*. These traits may lie fallow, in which case man remains the *homo sapiens* that was formed on the sixth day of Creation, or he may develop these traits and become the true *man* that was the ultimate goal of Creation.

The judgment we undergo on Rosh Hashanah is whether we have indeed participated in our own creation. Have we learned from the history of the past? Have we reflected on the purpose of our existence? Have we seriously endeavored to improve ourselves? Have we considered the long-term consequences of our actions? Have we delayed gratification? Have we acted according to morals and ethics rather than according to our bodily urges? Have we given of ourselves in order to help others? To the extent that we have implemented these unique human abilities, to that extent we are *man*.

R' Shneur Zalman was once asked to describe his teacher, the Maggid of Mezeritch. He did not mention the Maggid's erudition in Talmud and Kabbalah, nor any of the other superlatives of this extraordinary *tzaddik*. He responded, "He was an *adam hashaleim* (a complete human being)." Could he not have accorded his great teacher a more complimentary description? However, the greatest level a person can achieve is to be an *adam hashaleim*, to become the being that God wanted man to be.

Our self-examination on this day, our birthday, should consist of determining how far we have progressed toward becoming an *adam hashaleim*.

וּנְתַנֶּה תֹּקֶף קְדֻשַּׁת הַיּוֹם, כִּי הוּא נוֹרָא וְאָיֹם. וּבוֹ תִנָּשֵׂא מַלְכוּתֶךָ, וְיִכּוֹן בְּחֶסֶד כִּסְאֶךָ, וְתֵשֵׁב עָלָיו בֶּאֱמֶת. אֱמֶת כִּי אַתָּה הוּא דַיָּן וּמוֹכִיחַ, וְיוֹדֵעַ וָעֵד, וְכוֹתֵב וְחוֹתֵם (וְסוֹפֵר וּמוֹנֶה), וְתִזְכּוֹר כָּל הַנִּשְׁכָּחוֹת. וְתִפְתַּח אֶת סֵפֶר הַזִּכְרוֹנוֹת, וּמֵאֵלָיו יִקָּרֵא, וְחוֹתָם יַד כָּל אָדָם בּוֹ. וּבְשׁוֹפָר גָּדוֹל יִתָּקַע, וְקוֹל דְּמָמָה דַקָּה יִשָּׁמַע. וּמַלְאָכִים יֵחָפֵזוּן, וְחִיל וּרְעָדָה יֹאחֵזוּן, וְיֹאמְרוּ הִנֵּה יוֹם הַדִּין, לִפְקֹד עַל צְבָא מָרוֹם בַּדִּין, כִּי לֹא יִזְכּוּ בְעֵינֶיךָ בַּדִּין. וְכָל בָּאֵי עוֹלָם יַעַבְרוּן לְפָנֶיךָ כִּבְנֵי מָרוֹן. כְּבַקָּרַת רוֹעֶה עֶדְרוֹ, מַעֲבִיר צֹאנוֹ תַּחַת שִׁבְטוֹ, כֵּן תַּעֲבִיר וְתִסְפּוֹר וְתִמְנֶה, וְתִפְקֹד נֶפֶשׁ כָּל חָי, וְתַחְתּוֹךְ קִצְבָה לְכָל בְּרִיּוֹתֶיךָ, וְתִכְתּוֹב אֶת גְּזַר דִּינָם.

Let us now relate the power of this day's holiness, for it is awesome and frightening. On it Your Kingship will be exalted; Your throne will be firmed with kindness and You will sit upon it in truth. It is true that You alone are the One Who judges, proves, knows, and bears witness; Who writes and seals (and counts and calculates); Who remembers all that was forgotten. You will open the Book of Chronicles — it will read itself, and everyone's signature is in it. The great shofar will be sounded and a still, thin sound will be heard. Angels will hasten, a trembling and terror will seize them — and they will say, "Behold, it is the Day of Judgment, to muster the heavenly host for judgment!" — for they cannot be vindicated in Your eyes in judgment. All who are in the world pass before You like members of the flock. Like a shepherd pasturing his flock, making sheep pass under his staff, so shall You cause to pass, count, calculate, and consider the soul of all the living; and You shall apportion the fixed needs of all Your creatures and inscribe their verdict.

The Divine Tribunal

This is an awe-inspiring prayer, depicting the Divine review of every person's activities. Record books are opened, and the facts speak for themselves. Each person's actions are confirmed by the seal of his own hand. The testimony is undeniable. God is both the witness and the judge, and He judges with compassion.

"All who are in the world pass before You like members of the flock." This is undoubtedly a description of the review process, but it may contain another meaning.

As we noted, Rosh Hashanah marks the day man was created. The Talmud states that man was created as a single individual to teach us that one person is as important as an entire world (*Sanhedrin* 37a). It may also teach us that each person should be an individual and not a non-entity. We need to be taught by our teachers, and we need Torah authorities to answer our questions. However, our decisions should be our own. We should not relinquish our individuality to become part of a herd.

Today, more than ever, we are in danger of losing our individuality. Our minds are molded by huge educational institutions, and our opinions are often formed by the mass media. Asserting one's individuality may label a person as a maverick. Let us remember that the Patriarch Abraham was an iconoclast refusing to accept the paganism of his environment.

We may think that by complying with the masses we can avoid the responsibility of making decisions. This is a mistake. Divesting oneself of making decisions is in itself a decision for which one is held responsible.

A common defense is, "But everyone is doing it." This defense does not hold up before the Divine tribunal.

Rambam states that if a person lives in an immoral and corrupt environment, he should relocate. If he cannot find a community free of immorality and corruption, then he should move to a cave in the woods. One should not expose himself to the danger of herd mentality.

"All who are in the world pass before You like members of the flock." This may be part of our judgment. We are held responsible if we allow ourselves to be a herd rather than an individual.

בְּאֵין מֵלִיץ יֹשֶׁר מוּל מַגִּיד פֶּשַׁע, תַּגִּיד לְיַעֲקֹב דְּבַר חֹק וּמִשְׁפָּט, וְצַדְּקֵנוּ בַּמִּשְׁפָּט, הַמֶּלֶךְ הַמִּשְׁפָּט.

In the absence of an advocate against the one who reports transgression, may You testify for the sake of Jacob'[s offspring] regarding [their observance of Your] decrees and ordinances; thereby may You vindicate us in the judgment, O King of judgment.

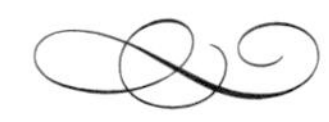

The Midrash states that prior to the creation of man, God took counsel with the angels whether or not man should be created. Some angels opposed man's creation, because, they said, man will be too prone to sin. On various occasions, when human beings have attained extraordinary spiritual heights, God says to the heavenly angels, "Look at the creature I created" (*Bereishis Rabbah* 12). These superior human beings were not necessarily the outstanding *tzaddikim*.

R' Levi Yitzchok of Berditchev's advocacy for Israel was unparalleled. He would extol the many virtues and merits of Jews. One year, prior to Rosh Hashanah, R' Levi Yitzchok's demeanor was extremely somber. It was clear that he felt unable to find adequate merits to assure a favorable judgment for his people on Rosh Hashanah.

One evening, R' Levi Yitzchok was walking the streets of Berditchev, absorbed in profound meditation. As he passed a small hut, he felt an aura of holiness. He knocked on the door, and a young woman emerged. Upon seeing the Rabbi she began crying. It was known that before Rosh Hashanah R' Levi Yitzchok would visit people who had sinned, urging them to do teshuvah. "I know the Rabbi has come to prod me to do teshuvah. I know my sin, but I do not know what more I can do for teshuvah."

"No, my child," the tzaddik said. "It has not a sin that brings me here. To the contrary, you must have done something very meritorious. I sensed a holiness here."

"I don't know about anything meritorious I have done. I can only tell you about myself," the woman said.

"I lived with my parents on a farm we leased from the poritz," the woman continued. "When my parents died, I went to the poritz to ask him to let me continue working the farm. I was young and beautiful, and when the poritz saw me he made advances toward me. He spoke such obscene words that I was frightened. When he saw that I was going to run away, he said, 'Have no fear. I shall not harm you. You may continue working the farm, and I will even lower the rent. Just allow me to kiss your beautiful curls.' With that, he grabbed my hair and kissed it.

"I ran home in a panic. I chastised myself for not having fled promptly, and I felt contaminated. I took scissors and cut my curls. I did not feel safe on the poritz's land. The next morning I packed a few belongings and abandoned the farm. I moved to the city and supported myself as a domestic. I married a fine man, but he died a year ago. I feel that he may have died because I did not deserve him."

"And what did you do with your curls?" R' Levi Yitzchok asked.

"I threw them away, all except one," she said. "I keep that one so that when I bewail my sorry plight and feel resentment toward God for my fate, I can take out the curl. It reminds me of my sin — that I allowed that vulgar poritz to touch me. My resentment disappears because I realize that I am being justly punished for my sin."

That Rosh Hashanah, R' Levi Yitzchok led the services with a tone that betrayed his anguish. He had evidently not been able to overcome Satan's condemnation of the Jews for their sins. The congregants intensified their prayers for Divine mercy.

Just as they were preparing to sound the shofar, R' Levi Yitzchok said, "Master of the universe! If our sins are so many that they warrant a harsh judgment, I ask You to take the lock of hair of that woman as a forgiveness offering. She had been orphaned, and sought to support herself by working the farm. Seeing the poritz's passion, she could easily have received the farm as a gift if she would have allowed him to embrace her. But instead she tried to escape, knowing that she would forfeit her means of a livelihood. When the poritz kissed her hair, she felt that she had been defiled. She left the farm to avoid any possible contact with him, and worked as a domestic to support herself. She was left a poor widow. Others would have been angry at You for such repeated hardships. But not this woman! She would rather feel that she had sinned than to question Your judgment. She saved the lock of hair to remind her of her 'sin' so that she could justify her suffering.

"Heavenly father! B'ayn melitz yosher, if we have nothing else in our defense, taggid l'Yaakov dvar chok u'mishpat. See how the children of Jacob cherish your judgment, how this woman castigates herself rather than impart any injustice to You. We have no Temple and no High Priest to bring sin-offerings for us. I, Levi Yitzchok son of Sara Sosha plead before You to accept this woman's lock of hair as a sin-offering, and grant us forgiveness."

As he finished his plea, R' Levi Yitzchok's face brightened. He had once again championed the cause of his people.

The Inverse Remembrance

אֱלֹקֵינוּ וֵאלֹקֵי אֲבוֹתֵינוּ, זָכְרֵנוּ בְּזִכָּרוֹן טוֹב לְפָנֶיךָ, וּפָקְדֵנוּ בִּפְקֻדַּת יְשׁוּעָה וְרַחֲמִים מִשְּׁמֵי שְׁמֵי קֶדֶם ... כִּי זוֹכֵר כָּל הַנִּשְׁכָּחוֹת אַתָּה הוּא מֵעוֹלָם, וְאֵין שִׁכְחָה לִפְנֵי כִסֵּא כְבוֹדֶךָ. וַעֲקֵדַת יִצְחָק לְזַרְעוֹ הַיּוֹם בְּרַחֲמִים תִּזְכּוֹר. בָּרוּךְ אַתָּה ה׳, זוֹכֵר הַבְּרִית.

Our God and the God of our forefathers, remember us with a favorable remembrance before You, recall us with a recollection of salvation and mercy from the primeval, loftiest heavens ... For it is You Who eternally remembers all forgotten things, and there is no forgetfulness before Your Throne of Glory, and may You mercifully remember today the Akeidah of Isaac for the sake of his offspring. Blessed are You, Hashem, Who remembers the covenant.

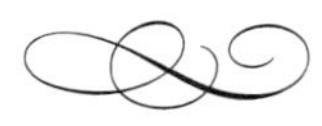

R' Moshe Leib of Sassov said, "What man remembers, God forgets. What man forgets, God remembers."

R' Moshe Leib explained that there is nothing as dear to God as humility. "I will rest among the downtrodden" (*Isaiah* 57:15). There is nothing God despises as much as vanity. "He who is haughty of eye ... him I will not tolerate" (*Psalms* 101:5).

If a person who performs a mitzvah retains conscious memory of it, it is because he thinks of himself as being a *tzaddik* who is most deserving. This is a mitzvah which is shrouded in vanity, and God turns away from it. On the other hand, if he forgets the mitzvah because he thinks he has not done enough, this is very dear to God.

Just the reverse is true of sin. If a person forgets that he has sinned, it means that he does not appreciate the gravity of his action. On the other hand, if he remembers that he has sinned and he agonizes over it, this is humility, which is dear to God. Hence, what man forgets, God remembers, and vice versa.

This is indeed true, but with some qualification. If a person remembers the sweetness of a mitzvah and this stimulates him to do additional mitzvos, this is meritorious and is not vainglory. On the other hand, once a person has done adequate *teshuvah*, he should not carry the burden of his sin. He should trust and accept God's forgiveness. The only reason to remember the sin is to recognize his vulnerability to such an act so that he may be on the alert not to repeat it.

The one exception where God will remember that which we remember is the merit of the Patriarch Isaac who willingly offered himself as a sacrifice to God. This devotion of Isaac is a symbol of *mesiras nefesh*, because it indicates that fulfilling the Divine will is dearer than life itself. We merit Divine mercy if we emulate the Patriarch.

This is the sequence of the above prayer. In regard to our actions, God will remember that which we forget, but insofar as the *mesiras nefesh* of Isaac is concerned, God will remember this if we do.

כמוך נושא עון
ועובר על פשע

Tashlich

To the Bottom of the Sea

מִי קֵל כָּמוֹךָ נֹשֵׂא עָוֹן וְעֹבֵר עַל פֶּשַׁע לִשְׁאֵרִית נַחֲלָתוֹ לֹא הֶחֱזִיק לָעַד אַפּוֹ כִּי חָפֵץ חֶסֶד הוּא. יָשׁוּב יְרַחֲמֵנוּ יִכְבֹּשׁ עֲוֹנֹתֵינוּ וְתַשְׁלִיךְ בִּמְצֻלוֹת יָם כָּל חַטֹּאתָם. (וְכָל חַטֹּאת עַמְּךָ בֵּית יִשְׂרָאֵל, תַּשְׁלִיךְ בִּמְקוֹם אֲשֶׁר לֹא יִזָּכְרוּ, וְלֹא יִפָּקְדוּ, וְלֹא יַעֲלוּ עַל לֵב לְעוֹלָם.)

Who, O God, is like You, Who pardons iniquity and overlooks transgression for the remnant of His heritage; Who has not retained His wrath eternally, for He desires kindness. He will again be merciful to us; He will suppress our iniquities, and cast into the depths of the sea all their sins. (And all the sins of Your nation, the House of Israel, cast away to a place where they will neither be remembered, considered, nor brought to mind — ever.)

It is widely assumed that with the *Tashlich* prayer we get rid of our sins by throwing them into the water. This is a rather juvenile concept. The only way we can divest ourselves of our sins is by sincere *teshuvah*. This is a much more demanding task than taking a pleasant walk to the park pond or to the seashore and reciting a few sentences.

I believe that the significance of *Tashlich* lies in the reinforcement of a concept that we discussed in the chapter "Abundant in Forgiveness," namely, that once we have done proper *teshuvah*, we should let go of our sins and not ruminate over them. This concept is contained in the *Tashlich* prayer: "He will again be merciful to us. He will suppress our iniquities, and cast into the depths of the sea all their sins. And all the sins of Your nation, the House of Israel, *cast away to a place where they will neither be remembered, considered, nor brought to mind — ever.*" We do not throw our sins into the water. Rather, we make a gesture which should teach us that with proper *teshuvah*, God will dispose of our sins in a way that they will never be remembered, considered, nor brought to mind.

Why the ritual of going to the water's edge? Why not simply say this prayer in shul? It is because symbolic actions can make a deeper impression on us than mere words. This is why we beat our chest when confessing our sins. The quality of confession does not depend on how forcefully we strike the chest, but on our understanding that we must sincerely regret the mistakes we made as a result of yielding to the desires of the heart.

Rosh Hashanah has other symbolisms. On the first night we eat certain foods such as honey to symbolize our hope and prayer for a sweet new year, or foods whose names lend themselves to particular prayers. For example, the Yiddish word for carrots is *mehren*, which also means "abundance." We recite a prayer before eating the sweet carrots, "May it be Your will that our merits be abundant."

We should bear in mind that many of the things we pray for require initiation on our part.

> *A chassid once asked R' Yechezkel of Shinov to pray for him that he may do proper teshuvah. R' Yechezkel closed his eyes as if in profound meditation, then said to the chassid, "I prayed for you, and God has accepted my prayer. He is fully agreeable that you should do proper teshuvah and has agreed to accept it. Now the rest is up to you."*

We pray that we have many merits. God may provide us with the opportunity to earn merits, but we must do the meritorious deeds. We indeed pray for God to bless us with a sweet year, but there is much that we can do to make it sweet. We can avoid shouting, control our anger, and speak in a soft tone. We can divest ourselves of resentments against others. We can be considerate and do acts of kindness for others. We can do as the Talmud states, "Greet every person with a pleasant countenance" (*Ethics of the Fathers* 1:15).

If we do our share in implementing the symbols, God will bring them to fruition.

Shabbos Shuvah

A Plea for Forgiveness

שׁוּבָה יִשְׂרָאֵל עַד ה׳ אֱלֹקֶיךָ כִּי כָשַׁלְתָּ בַּעֲוֺנֶךָ: קְחוּ עִמָּכֶם דְּבָרִים וְשׁוּבוּ אֶל ה׳ אִמְרוּ אֵלָיו כָּל תִּשָּׂא עָוֺן וְקַח טוֹב וּנְשַׁלְּמָה פָרִים שְׂפָתֵינוּ.

Return, O Israel, to Hashem, your God, for you have stumbled through your iniquity. Take words with you and return to Hashem; say to Him, "Forgive every sin and accept goodness, and let our lips substitute for bulls." (Hosea 14:2-3).

This chapter of the Scriptures is read on the Shabbos of *teshuvah* between Rosh Hashanah and Yom Kippur. The Talmud notes that the Hebrew word for transgression, עָוֺן refers to a deliberate sin, whereas "stumbled" indicates an unintentional act.

One of the Chassidic masters cited the verse, "And it shall be forgiven to the entire assembly of Israel and to the proselyte who sojourns among them, for it happened to the entire people unintentionally" (Numbers 15:26). He said, "Master of the Universe! In order for a mitzvah to be done with proper intent (kavannah) we preface it by saying, 'I am hereby ready and prepared to fulfill the commandment of my Creator.' Dear Heavenly Father! I can assure you that the worst sinner has never prefaced a sin by saying, 'I am hereby ready and prepared to transgress the commandment of my Creator.' All sins are, therefore, lacking in intent, and must be considered unintentional."

This is what the prophet means. Even your פְּשָׁעִים (deliberate sins) can be considered unintentional.

We should indeed feel deep remorse for any sins we have committed. However, it is possible that the *yetzer hara* may try to sabotage our efforts at *teshuvah* by saying, "How dare you ask for forgiveness! You sinned in brazen defiance of God. There is no forgiveness for deliberate sins." At such times we must invoke the defense of the Chassidic master. We never had any intent of defying the will of God. Even if we knowingly committed a sin, it was because the *yetzer hara* so incited our physical urges that we somehow rationalized our behavior. We should ask for forgiveness and be confident that God will grant it to us.

The words in the prayers for forgiveness are powerful indeed. We may recite them with profound feelings of remorse. However, it may happen that these words remain in the shul. When we return to the outside world, we may forget the anguish we felt for having behaved improperly. The prophet, therefore, cautions us, "Take these words with you." If we carry these words with us, we are certain to return to God.

אל לקחת בעי"כ עופות לכפרה וכו' • ולוקין

שאמר אם יהיו חטאיכם כשנים כשלג ילבינו

ם ישבי חשך וצלמות. אסירי עני וב

חשך וצלמות ומוסרותיהם ינתק:

ומענתיהם יתענו: כל-אכל תתע

מות: ויזעקו אל-יי בצר להם

רי מות: וירפאם וימלט מ

שלח דברו וירפאם: אם יש

ישלח ... לבני אדם: ו

רו ונפלאותיו לבני אדם ישרו: ו

מני-אלף להגיד לאדם ישרו כו

מרדת שחת מצאתי כו

ואחר כך יסבב התרנגול ג' פעמים על ר

זה חליפתי. זה תמורתי. זה כפרתי. זה התרנגול

לחיים טובים ארוכים ולש

חליפתי ... בני אד

יאמר פסוקים המזכירים ... ואם מסבב

Ten Days of Repentance

Emulate God, but Not All the Way

ה׳, ה׳, קֵל, רַחוּם, וְחַנּוּן, אֶרֶךְ אַפַּיִם, וְרַב חֶסֶד, וֶאֱמֶת, נֹצֵר חֶסֶד לָאֲלָפִים, נֹשֵׂא עָוֹן, וָפֶשַׁע, וְחַטָּאָה, וְנַקֵּה.

Hashem, Hashem, God, Compassionate and Gracious, Slow to anger, and Abundant in Kindness and Truth. Preserver of kindness for thousands of generations, Forgiver of iniquity, willful sin, and error, and Who cleanses.

We recite the Thirteen Attributes of God numerous times in the Ten Days of Repentance. The Talmud states that when God revealed these attributes to Moses (*Exodus* 34:6), He said, "Whenever Israel sins, let them perform before Me this order of prayer and I shall forgive them" (*Rosh Hashanah* 17b). Alshich notes that forgiveness requires *enacting* these attributes, not merely reciting them. Lip service is not enough.

If we compare the verse in the prayer book with that in the Scriptures, we note one striking discrepancy. In the prayer book the verse ends with "Who cleanses," whereas in the Torah it continues "but does not cleanse completely." The reason for this is that only God has the right to determine how much to forgive, because His judgment is perfect. He knows when someone does not merit "complete cleansing." Humans cannot judge how far forgiveness should go. Therefore, we should completely forgive those who have offended us. We should not emulate God in withholding total forgiveness.

If we totally forgive others, we can be deserving of complete forgiveness by God. Even if our *teshuvah* is incomplete, the attribute of *middah keneged middah* (that God acts toward us as we act toward others) goes into effect. We can then merit "complete cleansing."

The reason for this is that if we can so develop our character that we can be totally forgiving, eliminating every trace of resentment towards others, we will have achieved a level of spirituality that constitutes *teshuvah.*

We find something similar in the Midrash. "If a person observes Shabbos properly, even if he had been an idol worshiper, he is forgiven" (*Koheles Rabbah* 4). This apparently means that he is forgiven even if he has not done proper *teshuvah.* The reason for this is that proper observance of Shabbos will bring a person to a level of spirituality that will make idol worship impossible.

There are some character traits that cannot coexist with others. If we attain perfection in some desirable traits, this may automatically eliminate some undesirable traits. It follows that "even a small amount of light can banish a great deal of darkness."

If we emulate the Divine Attributes, we can be deserving of "complete cleansing."

Let Us Exchange Forgiveness

בְּנֵי אָדָם יֹשְׁבֵי חֹשֶׁךְ וְצַלְמָוֶת, אֲסִירֵי עֳנִי וּבַרְזֶל. יוֹצִיאֵם מֵחֹשֶׁךְ וְצַלְמָוֶת, וּמוֹסְרוֹתֵיהֶם יְנַתֵּק.

זֶה חֲלִיפָתִי, זֶה תְּמוּרָתִי, זֶה כַּפָּרָתִי. זֶה הַתַּרְנְגוֹל יֵלֵךְ לְמִיתָה [זֶה הַכֶּסֶף יֵלֵךְ לִצְדָקָה], וַאֲנִי אֶכָּנֵס וְאֵלֵךְ לְחַיִּים טוֹבִים אֲרוּכִים וּלְשָׁלוֹם.

Children of Man, who sit in darkness and the shadow of death, shackled in affliction and iron. He removed them from darkness and the shadow of death, and broke open their shackles.

This is my exchange, this is my substitute, this is my atonement. This rooster will go to its death [this money will go to charity] while I will enter and proceed to a good long life, and to peace.

One of the disciples of the Chassidic master, Rabbi Elimelech of Lizhensk, asked the master for the concealed meaning of the Kaparos ritual. What is really meant by "This is my exchange"? Rabbi Elimelech told him to travel to a particular inn and to observe the innkeeper, who would teach him how the "exchange" achieves forgiveness.

The disciple arrived at the inn, and did not get the impression that the proprietor was very much of a spiritual person. He noted that he would hurry through his morning prayers, and spend the day serving his customers, with whom he engaged in petty conversation. At first he was certain that the innkeeper was one of the holy tzaddikim who must conceal their true identity. But the more he observed him, the more he realized this could not be the case. He could not see what it was that the master expected him to learn from this simple person.

Yom Kippur was approaching, and the disciple was frustrated that he had not learned anything about the way Kaparos contributes to forgiveness.

On the night before the eve of Yom Kippur, after the inn was closed for the night, the disciple noticed that the innkeeper fetched two huge ledgers. From the first he began reading a list of things he had done wrong. As he read his misdeeds, he would heave a sigh of remorse. When he finished his litany, he opened the second ledger and began reading: "On this day a cask of wine turned rancid, and I took a heavy loss. On this day a hail storm tore off part of my roof. On this day my wife fell and broke her leg. On this day one of my cows died. On this day a group of bandits came by, and did not pay for their food or drink." He continued to recite all the bad things that had happened to him that year.

When he finished, he closed both ledgers and said, "Master of the Universe! I know I have done many wrong things this year. But You have also done many things that have hurt me. Inasmuch as tomorrow night is Yom Kippur, let us exchange forgiveness. You forgive me for what I did wrong, and I will forgive You for the things You did to me."

When the disciple returned to Rabbi Elimelech, the master said, "A person must learn how to forgive God. When people suffer adversity they may harbor resentments against God: Why did You do this to me? What did I do that I deserved this? This is actually a lack of faith in Divine justice. If we achieve a true faith and trust in God and believe that He is absolutely benevolent, we can accept that everything that God does is just and good, even though we cannot understand it. That constitutes 'forgiving' God. The achievement of this purity of faith is what can merit our being forgiven."

Yom Kippur is all about forgiveness. We have to forgive others, we have to accept being forgiven and we have to "forgive" God.

ועל דעת
אנו מתירין
עם העבריינים
וְקוֹנָמֵי
על נפשתנא
ג' פעמים
שֶׁל מטה
המקום
וְשְׁבוּעוֹת
וְלָא אֱסָרָא
וְלָא שְׁבוּעוֹת
בְּנֵי יִשְׂרָאֵל
הָעָם בִּשְׁגָגָה
הָעוֹלָם

Yom Kippur Eve

A Return to His People

עַל דַּעַת הַמָּקוֹם וְעַל דַּעַת הַקָּהָל, בִּישִׁיבָה שֶׁל מַעְלָה, וּבִישִׁיבָה שֶׁל מַטָּה, אָנוּ מַתִּירִין לְהִתְפַּלֵּל עִם הָעֲבַרְיָנִים.

With the approval of the Omnipresent and with the approval of the congregation; by the authority of the heavenly tribunal and by the authority of the earthly tribunal, we hereby grant permission to pray together with those who have transgressed.

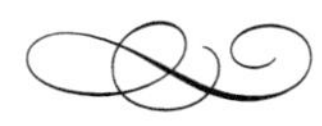

"For none shall be cast away" (II Samuel 14:14).

The Chassidic master, R' Leib son of Sarah, devoted his life to redeeming Jews who had been thrown into dungeons by feudal lords. His travels, often by foot, took him to a wide variety of places, but he never failed to pray all three daily services with a minyan. One time he had to free an imprisoned Jew from a debtor's prison in a small village. This was just before Yom Kippur, and by the time he arranged for the man to be set free, it was too late for him to travel, and he had to remain in the village for Yom Kippur. He was greatly distressed that he was stranded and could not be in the company of many tzaddikim on this holiest of days.

R' Leib was told that there were seven Jews in the village. He was the eighth, and three people generally came from a nearby village to make up the minyan. R' Leib found a nearby pond where he could immerse in a mikveh. Late in the afternoon, when they gathered for Minchah, one of the men from the nearby village came and said that he was the only one who could come. They were short one man for a minyan.

"Isn't there any other Jew in the area who can join us?" R' Leib asked. The villagers said that there were none. They would simply have to pray without a minyan.

To R' Leib this was unthinkable. Never in his life had he missed a single weekday prayer without a minyan, and now he would not have a minyan for Yom Kippur!

"Is there, perhaps, a Jew who has abandoned his Jewishness for another faith?" R. Leib asked. "If there is, I am ready to plead with him to join us. A Jew never ceases to be a Jew even if he has rejected his faith."

The villagers exchanged glances. "Yes," one said. "The poritz of our area is a convert to Christianity. As a young man, he was very handsome and made deliveries to the previous poritz. The poritz's one and only daughter was infatuated with him, and the poritz told him he could marry her if he converted. He would then be the sole heir to the entire fiefdom. At first he resisted, but he could not overcome the lure of wealth. It is over forty years that he has been a devout Christian."

"Does he have children?" R' Leib asked.

"No," the villagers said. "He is childless, and his wife died two years ago."

"Then I must go to him," R' Leib said.

"Heaven forbid!" the villagers said. "His guards will let the dogs loose on you."

But there was no stopping R' Leib. He removed his tallis and kittel and headed for the palace. He knocked on the palace door and promptly pushed it open, and soon found himself face to face with the poritz. There they stood in a confrontation, the tzaddik whose every move was devoted to God and a person who had rejected the faith of his fathers. The poritz's eyes blazed with fury at this intruder who had dared to enter his palace without permission, and he was about to call his servants to throw R' Leib out. But R' Leib's countenance was calm, and the trace of a smile disarmed the poritz. "What are you doing here?" he asked.

"My name is Leib the son of Sarah," R' Leib said. "I was privileged to know the Baal Shem Tov, for whom many of your fellow poritzim had great respect. The Baal Shem Tov said that every person should pray the words of King David, 'Hatzileni medamim Elokim (Rescue me from the guilt of bloodshed, O God)' (Psalms 51:16). Damin, blood, can also be translated as money; therefore the verse can mean, 'Save me that money should not become my god,' that I should not reject God in favor of wealth.

"My mother was a very beautiful young woman, and the local poritz fell in love with her. In desperation, she married an elderly melamed, to be beyond the reach of the poritz. My father died soon after I was born, and she remained a widow for life. She had the courage that you lacked.

"But there is nothing that stands in the way of teshuvah," R' Leib continued. "A person can redeem himself at any point in his life. You can rectify your sin. Tonight is Yom Kippur and we lack one person for a minyan. You can be the tenth person. The Torah says, 'The tenth one shall be holy unto God' (Leviticus 27:32)."

Meanwhile, the villagers were reciting Tehillim, praying for R' Leib's safety. How astonished they were when R' Leib entered accompanied by the poritz! R' Leib handed the poritz a tallis, in which he wrapped himself with trembling hands. R' Leib then began the prelude to Kol Nidrei, and in a heartrending voice said, "With the approval of the Omnipresent and with the approval of the congregation; by the authority of the heavenly tribunal and by the authority of the earthly tribunal, we hereby grant permission to pray together with those who have transgressed." A cry of pain that penetrated into the hearts of all the worshipers was emitted by the poritz.

Throughout the evening service and all day of Yom Kippur the poritz stood on his feet, following all the prayers, periodically bursting into tears that moved the entire congregation. When the final service of Ne'ilah came to a close, the poritz bent into the aron kodesh (ark of the Torah), embraced the Torah and cried out, "Shema Yisrael," in a heartrending tone. He then stood upright and began reciting seven times, "Hashem, He is the true God!" with steadily increasing fervor, each time elevating his voice. As he completed the phrase the seventh time, he collapsed to the floor, lifeless.

R' Leib addressed the congregation. "The Talmud says that a person can acquire Gan Eden in one hour's time (Avodah Zarah 10b). This man died a tzaddik." R' Leib then began the evening service, "He, the Merciful One, is forgiving of iniquity ..."

R' Leib was no longer distressed that he had been stranded in this tiny village on Yom Kippur. He had freed yet another Jew from captivity.

כָּל נִדְרֵי, וֶאֱסָרֵי, וּשְׁבוּעֵי, וַחֲרָמֵי, וְקוֹנָמֵי, וְקִנּוּסֵי, וְכִנּוּיֵי,
דְּאִנְדַּרְנָא, וּדְאִשְׁתַּבַּעְנָא, וּדְאַחֲרִמְנָא וּדְאָסַרְנָא
עַל נַפְשָׁתָֽנָא. מִיּוֹם כִּפּוּרִים שֶׁעָבַר עַד יוֹם כִּפּוּרִים זֶה, וּמִיּוֹם
כִּפּוּרִים זֶה עַד יוֹם כִּפּוּרִים הַבָּא עָלֵינוּ לְטוֹבָה, בְּכֻלְּהוֹן
אִחֲרַטְנָא בְהוֹן.

All vows, prohibitions, oaths, consecrations, konam-vows, konas-vows, or equivalent terms that we may vow, swear, consecrate, or prohibit upon ourselves — from the last Yom Kippur until this Yom Kippur, and from this Yom Kippur until the next Yom Kippur, may it come upon us for good — regarding them all, we regret them henceforth.

That Yom Kippur is the holiest day of the Jewish year is beyond question. It is a day of intense soul-searching and praying for forgiveness in an atmosphere where a person is separated from physical gratification. Indeed, on Yom Kippur Jews are considered to have the purity of the heavenly angels.

What is not clear is the awesome solemnity that characterizes *Kol Nidrei*. This prayer is essentially a declaration of annulment of personal vows one has made in the past or will make in the future. What is so significant about this ritual that gives it an ambience of solemnity that exceeds that of all other occasions?

One well-known theory is that *Kol Nidrei* can be traced to the Spanish Inquisition, when Jews were forced to renounce Judaism and accept Christianity. Their vows of conversion were made under the most fearful oaths. Many of these converts, referred to as Marranos, secretly practiced Judaism. On Yom Kippur eve they gathered clandestinely and expressed their remorse for having taken vows to embrace Christianity, praying for forgiveness for making these vows under duress and declaring them to be null and void. It is said that the traditional somber melody of *Kol Nidrei* originated with the Marranos.

Another theory ascribes the prominence of *Kol Nidrei* as a way of emphasizing the authority of the Oral, Rabbinic Law. During the Middle Ages, there was a faction of Jews, known as Karaites, who rejected the Oral Law, abiding by the literal words of the Pentateuch. According to the Pentateuch, the only way annulment of vows can be effected is by a father or husband (*Numbers* 30:2-17). The Sages established annulment of vows by a *beis din*, if it could be demonstrated that the vow was made on erroneous premises. The Karaites strongly objected. In order to emphasize and reinforce the validity of the Oral Law, the declaration of annulment of vows was assigned to Yom Kippur eve, when the largest number of Jews would assemble in the synagogues.

According to either theory, *Kol Nidrei* expresses important principles of Judaism; namely, that a Jew can never abdicate his Judaism, and that authentic Judaism is that which is based on the Oral Law and the rabbinic interpretation of the Written Law. Acceptance of these fundamentals of Judaism is a most appropriate way to inaugurate the day of forgiveness.

שְׁמַע ׀ יִשְׂרָאֵל, ה׳ ׀ אֱלֹקֵינוּ, ה׳ ׀ אֶחָד:
בָּרוּךְ שֵׁם כְּבוֹד מַלְכוּתוֹ לְעוֹלָם וָעֶד.

Hear, O Israel, Hashem is our God, Hashem, the One and Only.

Blessed is the Name of His glorious kingdom for all eternity.

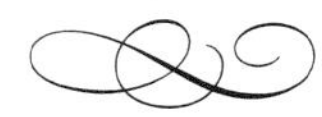

More Privileged Than Angels

When we recite the *Shema,* the verse, "Hear O, Israel, Hashem is our God, Hashem, the One and Only," is followed by the verse, "*Baruch Shem* ... Blessed is the Name of His glorious kingdom for all eternity." This second verse is said silently. One of the reasons given for this practice is that Moses heard this prayer from the angels and taught it to the Israelites. In order not to arouse the envy of the angels, we say it silently.

Yom Kippur is an exception. Inasmuch as we fast on Yom Kippur and deprive ourselves of physical pleasures, we are sufficiently similar to angels that we may openly voice their praise of God.

We may not only approach the spirituality of angels but also surpass them. The Talmud says that angels are not permitted to pronounce the Divine Name until they have said *three* words, "Holy, holy, holy." We are more privileged in that we may pronounce the Divine Name after the *two* words, *Shema Yisrael*" (*Chullin* 91b).

In *Angels Don't Leave Footprints*, I pointed out that the enormous holiness of the heavenly angels notwithstanding, they are holy only because they were created holy. Man was formed from a clump of earth. He has a physical and essentially animal body that craves everything that is antithetical to holiness. Man becomes spiritual only by sheer effort, by a lifelong struggle against his animalistic drives and temptation by the *yetzer hara*. Angels have no difficulty in bonding with God. Man must remove all the impediments to spirituality that are inherent within his physical being so that he may bond with God

Is it not paradoxical that in the same service that we claim so great a spirituality we confess a list of many sins that are hardly angelic?

Avoidance of sin is enhanced by the appreciation of the spirituality that can be ours. If you have a fine silk garment, you take great caution to protect it from being the least bit stained. You would not take such precautions if you were wearing work clothes that are soiled by grime and grease. If a silk garment was accidentally smudged, you would try to carefully remove the stain to retain the beauty of the garment.

We say the *Baruch Shem* aloud to remind us that we have the capacity to attain a level of purity akin to that of the heavenly angels, and that we may be even dearer to God than angels because we achieve our purity by the sweat of our brow. This purity dare not be marred by sin. This realization should enable us to say the confession with the sincerity that constitutes true *teshuvah*.

Our Absolute Dependence

כִּי אָנוּ עַמֶּךָ, וְאַתָּה אֱלֹקֵינוּ. אָנוּ בָנֶיךָ, וְאַתָּה אָבִינוּ . . . אָנוּ צֹאנֶךָ, וְאַתָּה רוֹעֵנוּ. אָנוּ כַרְמֶךָ, וְאַתָּה נוֹטְרֵנוּ. אָנוּ פְעֻלָּתֶךָ, וְאַתָּה יוֹצְרֵנוּ . . . אָנוּ קְשֵׁי עֹרֶף, וְאַתָּה אֶרֶךְ אַפַּיִם. אָנוּ מְלֵאֵי עָוֹן, וְאַתָּה מָלֵא רַחֲמִים.

For we are Your people and You are our God. We are Your children and You are our Father ... We are Your sheep and You are our Shepherd. We are Your vineyard and You are our Watchman. We are Your handiwork and You are our Shaper ... We are obstinate, but You are slow to anger. We are filled with iniquity, but You are filled with mercy.

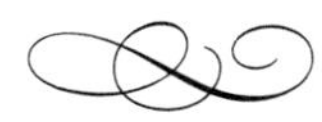

We have noted that the reason we repeat the praises to God is not because He needs them, but to remind us of our *existential* dependence on Him. We are often subjected to the intense pressure of the *yetzer hara* to act in ways that the Torah has forbidden. If we are aware that our bonding with God is nothing less than the oxygen of life, we are unlikely to do anything that would jeopardize this relationship.

One of the tactics of the *yetzer hara* is to make us forget this dependency. We noted in the chapter "Accepting the Yoke," R' Grodzinski's comment on the dialogue between R' Yehudah HaNasi and Antoninus with regard to the initial influence of the *yetzer hara*. The primary thrust of the *yetzer hara,* R' Grodzinski says, is not as many think — gratification of physical desires. *The primary drive of the yetzer hara is to be free of all restraint.* The *yetzer hara* cannot accept being restricted or confined.

This is an important observation. We have an innate impulse to resist anything that resembles control, even if being free is to our detriment. The *yetzer hara*, therefore, tries to make us oblivious of our dependence upon God, so that we should feel free to do as we please. Indeed, Moses warned the Israelites that this tendency is so strong that they are at risk of forgetting the Divine miracles of the Exodus and their dependence on God for their daily food and water during the forty years of sojourn in the desert. "You may come to think, 'My strength and the might of my own hand have given me all this wealth' " (*Deuteronomy* 8:17). This is why we must remind ourselves many times during the day that we are totally dependent on God.

The above prayer reinforces our awareness of our utter dependence on God. In whatever way we may think of ourselves, we are totally dependent on Him, whether we see ourselves as His people, His children, His servants, His congregation, His flock, or His vineyard.

This prayer precedes the *Vidui* (Confession of sins), which is the prerequisite for *teshuvah*. It is only if we realize that causing ourselves to be separated from God by sinful behavior is lethal to our spiritual existence that we will be motivated to do proper *teshuvah*.

The prayer closes with a plea for forgiveness, throwing ourselves upon God's infinite mercy. "We are filled with iniquity, but You are filled with mercy."

> *R' Levi Yitzchok of Berditchev gave this verse a charming interpretation. "Master of the universe!" he said. "It is true, I am full of sin. But how big is Levi Yitzchok altogether? How much sin can fit into this little person? But You, God, are infinite. Inasmuch as You are full of mercy, Your mercy is infinitely great. In proportion to Your immense mercy, the quantity of my sin is infinitesimally small. Your overwhelmingly great mercy can easily overcome the finite quantity of my sins."*

This, too, follows the earlier theme. If we are truly aware of God's infinite greatness, we will realize that we cannot exist apart from Him.

For the Sins We Have Committed

עַל חֵטְא שֶׁחָטָאנוּ לְפָנֶיךָ בְּאֹנֶס וּבְרָצוֹן,
וְעַל חֵטְא שֶׁחָטָאנוּ לְפָנֶיךָ בְּאִמּוּץ הַלֵּב . . .

. . . יְהִי רָצוֹן מִלְּפָנֶיךָ, ה׳ אֱלֹקַי וֵאלֹקֵי אֲבוֹתַי, שֶׁלֹּא אֶחֱטָא עוֹד וּמַה שֶּׁחָטָאתִי לְפָנֶיךָ מְחוֹק בְּרַחֲמֶיךָ הָרַבִּים, אֲבָל לֹא עַל יְדֵי יִסּוּרִים וָחֳלָיִם רָעִים.

For the sin that we have sinned before You under duress and willingly; and for the sin that we have sinned before You through hardness of the heart.

May it be Your will, Hashem, my God and the God of my forefathers, that I not sin again; and what I have sinned before You, may You cleanse with Your abundant mercy, but not through suffering or serious illness.

In this lengthy confession we enumerate many sins. We may feel that we are innocent of a number of them, but we must nevertheless confess them because the confession is expressed in the plural: for the sin *we* have committed. This is in keeping with the principle of interdependence and mutual responsibility. To some degree, we are held responsible for the sins of other people. In an ideal community where every person was law abiding and there was no tolerance whatsoever of violation of the law, crime would hardly exist. Fire cannot burn in the absence of oxygen, and crime cannot occur in a community that does not, in some way, condone crime. *I* may not have committed a particular sin, but I must share in the responsibility for those sins that *we* committed.

It is noteworthy that a number of sins are ascribed to parts of the body, literally: "with the expression of the lips, with the speech of the mouth, with the thoughts of the heart, with the force of the hand, with the evil of the tongue, with the haughtiness of the neck, with the glance of the eye, with an arrogant forehead, with the running of the feet to do harm." Perhaps this is intended to indicate that we realize that while we have allowed our physical body to act improperly, the real "self," the *neshamah*, remains pure and untainted. This should prevent us from becoming despondent over our misdeeds and from becoming discouraged of being forgiven.

This may also be the meaning of the sin בְּאִמּוּץ הַלֵּב, "through hardness of the heart." Our falling prey to sin is invariably because we allow our emotions to override our intellect. Logically we know that we should not be doing a given act, but we allow our emotions to distort our judgment. We rationalize that what we wish to do is permissible. We have the ability to exercise our intellect and not allow ourselves to be duped by our desires. This realization enables us to sincerely resolve that we will avoid repeating our sins by applying "the might of the mind."

The literal Hebrew of the "hardness (might) of the heart" is generally translated to mean "with obstinacy." While we may invoke in our defense our inability to withstand temptation, we have no defense for not having done *teshuvah* after we sinned and the intense lust was quelled. This hesitancy is no longer due to temptation but to the unwillingness to admit that we were wrong, We, therefore, confess our dereliction in failing to do *teshuvah*.

The term "with the expression of the lips" is especially relevant. It is possible that *the very act of confession may be a sin!* If all we do is read the confession from the prayerbook and not put our heart into sincere regret and *teshuvah*, then this "lip service" is a sin.

We may delude ourselves into thinking that by reciting the words and beating our breast we have done adequate *teshuvah*. If we are not sincere in remorse, we are essentially lying to God by saying that we regret our sins when in fact we do not.

We might wonder about the verse, "the sins we committed with the *yetzer hara*." Are not all our sins the product of the *yetzer hara*?

We may understand this with a parable in the *Zohar*. A king wished to test the moral fiber of his son. He engaged a woman of ill repute to tempt the prince to sin. The woman did as she was instructed, but deep in her heart she hoped that the prince would resist the seduction.

The *Zohar* states that God assigned the *yetzer hara* the task of inciting people to sin. Out of obedience to God, the *yetzer hara* does its work faithfully, but secretly wishes that people would resist its seduction. When we succumb to the *yetzer hara*, we are actually doing something that *it does not want us to do*. Therefore, in committing sin we are actually offending the *yetzer hara*, and we must do *teshuvah* for this. Solomon says, "When a man's ways please God, even his enemies will be at peace with him" (*Proverbs* 16:7). The *yetzer hara*, the internal enemy, is actually pleased when we defy it and obey God's will.

One of the verses that follows the confession is enigmatic. "May it be Your will that I not sin again." What does it mean to pray that God should will that we not sin again? Of course that is His will. If we are praying that God eliminate the *yetzer hara* and the temptation to sin, that would be in opposition to the purpose of our existence. Rabbi Moshe Chaim Luzzatto states that man was put on earth to fulfill the Divine will by subduing the *yetzer hara* and earning the privilege to be in the Imminent Presence of God in *Gan Eden* (Paradise).

As noted, R' Shneur Zalman (author of *Tanya*) was once found to be crying, "Dear God! I do not want any reward in the eternal world. I do not want *Gan Eden*. I want only to be with You!"

Perhaps we are saying, "True. Without the struggle against the *yetzer hara* we would earn neither reward nor *Gan Eden*. We might suffer the humiliation of the privilege of being in the Divine Presence only by the *chesed* of God rather than by having earned it. But the danger of succumbing to the *yetzer hara* and separating ourselves from God is so great, that we prefer accepting this privilege as *tzedakah* rather than running the risk of losing it by struggling to earn it." If this is what we mean, it indicates our appreciation of bonding with God.

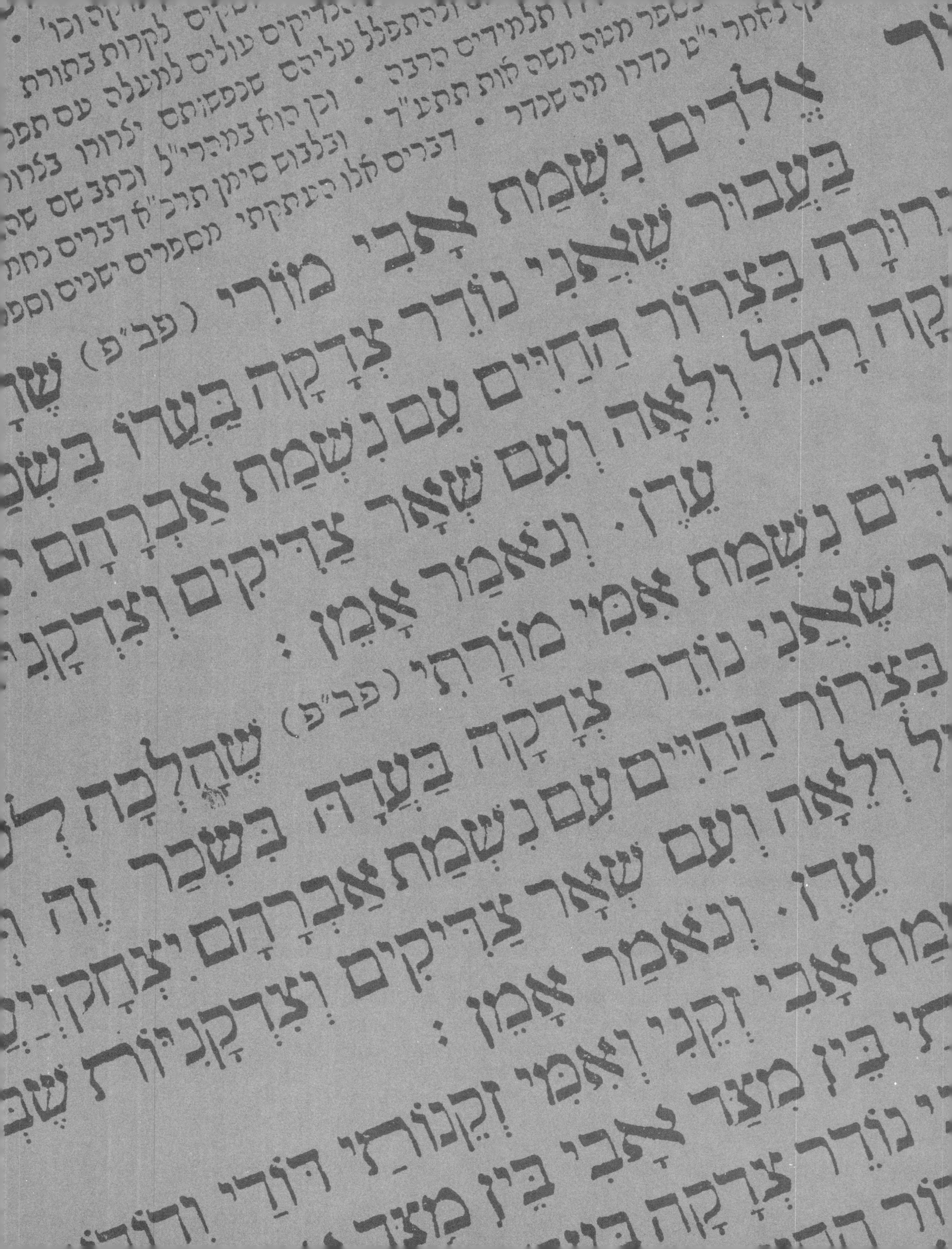
נשמת אבי מורי (פב"פ)
בעבור שאני נודר צדקה בעדו בשכר
בצרור החיים עם נשמת אברהם
רחל ולאה ועם שאר צדיקים וצדקניות
עדן. ונאמר אמן:
נשמת אמי מורתי (פב"פ) שהלכה
בעבור שאני נודר צדקה בעדה בשכר זה
בצרור החיים עם נשמת אברהם יצחק
ולאה ועם שאר צדיקים וצדקניות
עדן. ונאמר אמן:

Yizkor Service

The Essence of the Soul

יִזְכֹּר אֱלֹקִים נִשְׁמַת . . . תְּהֵא נַפְשׁוֹ צְרוּרָה בִּצְרוֹר הַחַיִּים, עִם נִשְׁמוֹת אַבְרָהָם יִצְחָק וְיַעֲקֹב, שָׂרָה רִבְקָה רָחֵל וְלֵאָה, וְעִם שְׁאָר צַדִּיקִים וְצִדְקָנִיּוֹת שֶׁבְּגַן עֵדֶן. וְנֹאמַר: אָמֵן.

May God remember the soul of ... May his soul be bound in the Bond of Life, together with the souls of Abraham, Isaac and Jacob; Sarah, Rebecca, Rachel and Leah; and together with the other righteous men and women in the Garden of Eden. Now let us respond: Amen.

In the *Yizkor* prayer we pledge to give *tzedakah* in memory of the departed. It is assumed that the departed person in his or her lifetime inspired us to give *tzedakah*. We invoke this merit in their memory.

However, the wording "May God remember" is somewhat confusing. In the Rosh Hashanah prayer we say, "There is no forgetfulness before Your Throne of Glory." God does not need to be reminded.

Perhaps we may exercise poetic license, and interpret this verse as a prayer, "May God help *me* remember the soul." But even this is somewhat odd. Certainly we do not forget our parents or other beloved relatives who have passed on.

No, we do not forget them. But the emphasis is on the word *neshamah*, the soul. *Yizkor* should remind us of the essence of the human soul. An understanding of what the *neshamah* is can help us in our efforts to live a spiritual life.

The Midrash states that at the time of conception, God instructs an angel to bring a particular neshamah from Gan Eden and He commands the neshamah to enter the newly formed cell that will develp into a human being.

The neshamah says, "Master of the universe: Since You created me and placed me in Gan Eden, I am pure and holy. Why are You asking of me to inhabit a mortal body?"

God responds, "The world to which I am sending you will be better for you than Gan Eden. When I created you, it was for this purpose, that you inhabit this mortal body. You must do so."

The angel then shows the neshamah the neshamos of the righteous in Gan Eden. "These neshamos inhabited mortal bodies. They observed the Torah and mitzvos and earned an eternal reward in Gan Eden. The bonding with God that they achieved is far superior to what you have experienced. If you live as they did, you too will earn this eternal reward" (Tanchuma, Pekudei).

We may not think that this world, which is so full of struggle and distress, is better than the *Gan Eden* where the *neshamah* has resided. But the words of God are unmistakable. "The world to which I am sending you will be better for you than *Gan Eden.*" Indeed, the Talmud says: "Better one hour of repentance and good deeds in This World than the entire life of the World to Come" (*Ethics of the Fathers* 4:22).

Yizkor is recited on Yom Kippur, the Day of Repentance, on Passover and on Succos (Shemini Atzeres), which are laden with special mitzvos, and on Shavuous, when we commemorate the giving of the Torah at Sinai. On these days *we* should be reminded of our transient sojourn in this world, and be inspired to make every effort to provide our *neshamah* with a return to a greater glory in *Gan Eden.*

Yom Kippur Minchah

Fleeing From Whom?

וַיְהִי דְּבַר ה׳ אֶל יוֹנָה בֶן אֲמִתַּי לֵאמֹר: קוּם לֵךְ אֶל נִינְוֵה הָעִיר הַגְּדוֹלָה וּקְרָא עָלֶיהָ כִּי עָלְתָה רָעָתָם לְפָנָי: וַיָּקָם יוֹנָה לִבְרֹחַ תַּרְשִׁישָׁה מִלִּפְנֵי ה׳ וַיֵּרֶד יָפוֹ וַיִּמְצָא אֳנִיָּה . . . וַיִּשְׂאוּ אֶת יוֹנָה וַיְטִלֻהוּ אֶל הַיָּם וַיַּעֲמֹד הַיָּם מִזַּעְפּוֹ: וַיִּירְאוּ הָאֲנָשִׁים יִרְאָה גְדוֹלָה אֶת ה׳ וַיִּזְבְּחוּ זֶבַח לַה׳ וַיִּדְּרוּ נְדָרִים:

And the word of Hashem came to Jonah son of Amittai saying: "Arise! Go to Nineveh, the great city, and call out against her, for their wickedness has ascended before Me." But Jonah arose to flee to Tarshish from before Hashem. He went down to Jaffa and found a ship ... So they lifted Jonah and heaved him into the sea, and the sea stopped its raging. Then the men felt a great fear of Hashem; they slaughtered a sacrifice to Hashem and took vows.

I can recall, as a child, being fascinated by the story of Jonah: the stormy sea, Jonah sleeping in the hold of the ship, the casting of lots to see whose sin was responsible for the storm, the casting of Jonah into the sea to be swallowed by a whale. I remember asking my teacher how a prophet could think that he could run away from God. Even as a child, I knew that God was everywhere. How could a prophet not know what I knew as a 8-year-old child? I do not remember what my teacher answered, probably because the answers were unsatisfactory.

As I grew older, I read the explanations given by Torah commentaries, and I realized that Jonah did not think he could run away from God. It was his mission that he was trying to evade, for what he felt were valid reasons. But yet, just like some juvenile ideas may not be totally eliminated when one matures, so did the question of my childhood continue to disturb me. How could a prophet try to run away from the mission God had commanded?

We read this story at *Minchah* of Yom Kippur to reassure us that nothing stands in the way of *teshuvah.* The decadent city, Ninveh, was spared because it did *teshuvah.* We should be confident that if our *teshuvah* on Yom Kippur it sincere, all our sins will be forgiven and we can begin the new year with a clean slate.

But there is another message in this dramatic epic. Perhaps the Torah is telling us the *virtue* of the prophet. This was the *only* time he sought to evade his mission. We are far inferior to Jonah, because we so often evade our mission. We often try to flee from God.

The Talmud tells us that before our *neshamah* descends to earth, it is given the charge, "Be a *tzaddik*!" That is our mission. But being a *tzaddik* is not easy. It is so restrictive. We must always be honest and truthful. We may not speak disparagingly of others. We must be respectful of others. We dare not insult anyone. We may not be vain. We must be humble. We must dedicate every free moment to Torah study. We must accept the adversities we experience as just. These and a host of pleasurable activities which are prohibited by the Torah may inconvenience us. We often succumb to the lure of the *yetzer hara* and fail to fulfill our mission of being a *tzaddik.* But we do believe the watchful eye of God is upon us, and we feel guilty for our failure. Like Adam in the Garden of Eden, we may try to hide from God. Like Jonah, we may try to flee from Him.

We may try to flee into work, into amusements, into indulgence or into chemicals that will anesthetize the distressing feeling of guilt or distract us from it. The existential question continues to eat away at us, subconsciously if not consciously: "Why do you think you are here? What is the purpose and goal in life? Why are you not pursuing that goal?" We try to flee, to escape the nagging question. But just like Jonah could not flee from God, neither can we.

The human being is comprised of a body and a *neshamah.* The body is essentially an animal body. Our uniqueness lies in the *neshamah.* Our real self is the *neshamah,* which very much wishes to fulfill its mission. When we succumb to the wiles of the *yetzer hara,* we are not only running away from God, but we are fleeing from our true self. Just as it is impossible to flee from God, so it is impossible to escape from one's own self. We take the self with us wherever we go.

In my work with alcoholics, I have seen how alcohol is used in an effort to escape. Escape what? Escape themselves! They continue this futile effort until it brings them down. They finally reach a point where they realize that the escape does not and cannot work. We refer to this as "hitting rock bottom." When they hit rock bottom, they can begin to recover.

The stormy sea which threatened to drown Jonah and all others on board was Jonah's "rock bottom." He recognized that he could not flee from his mission. The rest of the epic tells of Jonah's return and his carrying out his mission.

We need not experience a stormy sea nor anything like the rock bottom of the alcoholic. However, we should realize that escaping our mission is futile. We can then start our "recovery." We can stop our "running away" from ourselves. We can realize that our true self wishes to fulfill its mission, and we will allow it to do so.

...ינוּ · שֶׁאֵין
עַזֵּי פָנִים וּקְשֵׁי עֹרֶף · לוֹ...
אֱלֹהֵינוּ וֵאלֹהֵי אֲבוֹתֵינוּ צַדִּיקִים אֲנַחְ...
אֲנַחְנוּ חָטָאנוּ :
בָּגַדְנוּ · גָּזַלְנוּ · דִּבַּרְנוּ דֹפִי : הֶעֱוִינוּ ·
חָמַסְנוּ · טָפַלְנוּ שֶׁקֶר · יָעַצְנוּ רָע : כִּזַּבְנ...
...רַדְנוּ · עָוִינוּ · פָּשַׁעְנוּ · צָרַרְנוּ · קִשִּׁינוּ עֹ...
תִּעַבְנוּ · תָּעִינוּ · תִּעְתָּעְנוּ : סַרְנוּ מִמִּצְוֹ...
...א שָׁוָה לָנוּ : וְאַתָּה צַדִּיק עַל כָּל הַבָּא
...חְנוּ הִרְשָׁעְנוּ : מַה נֹּאמַר לְפָנֶיךָ יוֹשֵׁב
...שׁוֹכֵן שְׁחָקִים הֲלֹא כָּל הַנִּסְתָּרוֹת וְהַנִּגְ...
לַפּוֹשְׁעִים · וִימִינְךָ פְשׁוּטָה לְקַבֵּל שָׁבִ...
לְהִתְוַדּוֹת לְפָנֶיךָ עַל כָּל עֲוֹנוֹתֵינוּ לְמַעַן...
...נוּ בִּתְשׁוּבָה שְׁלֵמָה לְפָנֶיךָ כְּאִשִּׁים וּכְנִי...
...אַמְרַת אֵין קֵץ לְאִשֵּׁי...

Yom Kippur Ne'ilah

The Outstretched Hand

אַתָּה נוֹתֵן יָד לַפּוֹשְׁעִים, וִימִינְךָ פְשׁוּטָה לְקַבֵּל שָׁבִים...
וּמוֹתַר הָאָדָם מִן הַבְּהֵמָה אָיִן, כִּי הַכֹּל הָבֶל.

You extend a hand to transgressors, and Your right hand is stretched forth to receive the penitents ... and the pre-eminence of man over beast is nonexistent, for all is vain.

Although man initiates sin, it is a Divine kindness that he need not initiate *teshuvah*. The Talmud says that there is a Divine pronouncement from heaven that arouses a person and stimulates him to do *teshuvah* (*Chagigah* 15a). Not only is God's hand outstretched to receive the penitent, but He also activates within the person a desire to do *teshuvah*. The Seer of Lublin quoted the Talmud: "If a person desires to cleanse himself of sin, *they* will help him" (*Shabbos* 104a). Not only does God arouse a desire for *teshuvah* in the person, but He also provides others who can help the penitent.

The Seer of Lublin himself participated in helping a person do teshuvah. One time one of the Seer's chassidim complained that he had no money to provide his daughter with a dowry, as a result of which she might not find a shidduch (marriage match). "Go to Krushnik," the Seer said. "There you will find your needs."

The chassid was bewildered. He did not know a single soul in Krushnik. What was he to do there? But he had faith in the tzaddik's words, and went to Krushnik.

He checked into an inn. The proprietor of the inn appeared to be a very fine, pious person. For several days the chassid did nothing other than pray and study Torah. The proprietor, noting that the man obviously did not have business dealings in Krushnik, asked him what he was doing there. "I don't know myself," the man said. "The tzaddik of Lublin told me that my salvation would be here, so I am here and waiting."

Several more days passed. One midnight, when the chassid was reciting the midnight lamentations, he heard a knock at the door of the inn. Inasmuch as everyone in the household was asleep, the chassid opened the door. In walked a man who said, "I have noticed your presence here, and I must ask a favor of you.

"Many years ago," the man continued, "the proprietor of this inn engaged me as a tutor for his children. I discharged my duties faithfully, and I was respected by the whole family.

"One time the proprietor returned from a successful business trip, bringing a large sum of money. He concealed the money under one of the floorboards. I don't know what demon took possession of me, but I was overtaken by an uncontrollable urge to take the money. At night, when all were asleep, I removed the money from its hiding place. The next day, when the proprietor discovered that the money was gone, a hullabaloo took place. He searched all around the house, thinking that perhaps he had hidden the money elsewhere. They then thought that one of the customers might have noticed where the money was hidden, and somehow was able to steal it. Their trust in me was so great that it did not occur to them that I might be the guilty party.

"I had no means of returning the money without admitting my crime, and I could not get myself to do that. It hurt me to see the pain that I had caused, but I saw no way of rectifying the situation.

"Eventually I left the proprietor's employ, taking the money with me. Many years have passed, and I have simply not been able to find a way of returning the money without acknowledging my guilt. I just cannot bring myself to confess my heinous deed. But you are a total stranger here, you could never be personally implicated, and I see that you are a Torah scholar. Surely you can find a way of returning the

money without exposing me." With that, the man placed a bag of money on the table and left.

The following morning the chassid called the proprietor aside. "I have something important to tell you, but you must promise me that you will not ask me how I came upon this knowledge." The proprietor made the promise.

"Did you ever lose a large sum of money that was never recovered?" the chassid asked.

The proprietor thought for a moment, then said, "Yes, a large sum of money was stolen from me many years ago, but I have long since put that out of my mind. Why do you ask?"

The chassid then placed the bag with the money on the table. "Is this the money that was stolen?"

The proprietor recognized the bag, and removed the money from it. "Yes, this is it. But how did this come to you?"

The chassid smiled. "You must remember your promise," he said.

The proprietor counted the money. "It is all here, to the last kopek, as if untouched. Obviously the tzaddik of Lublin sent you here to be the instrument of my reclaiming my loss, and you should be appropriately rewarded. How much do you need for your daughter's dowry?" He then gave the chassid the required amount.

The chassid returned to the Seer, who said, "I indeed wished to help you get the money for your daughter's dowry, but my overriding concern was to enable the melamed (tutor) to return the money. He had been praying for God to show him a way to do teshuvah. His sincere desire to do teshuvah caused me great anguish and disturbed my sleep. When you told me your need, it occurred to me that you may be the instrument that God has chosen for this man's teshuvah.

The hand that God extends to transgressors is not empty. It contains a key to *teshuvah.*

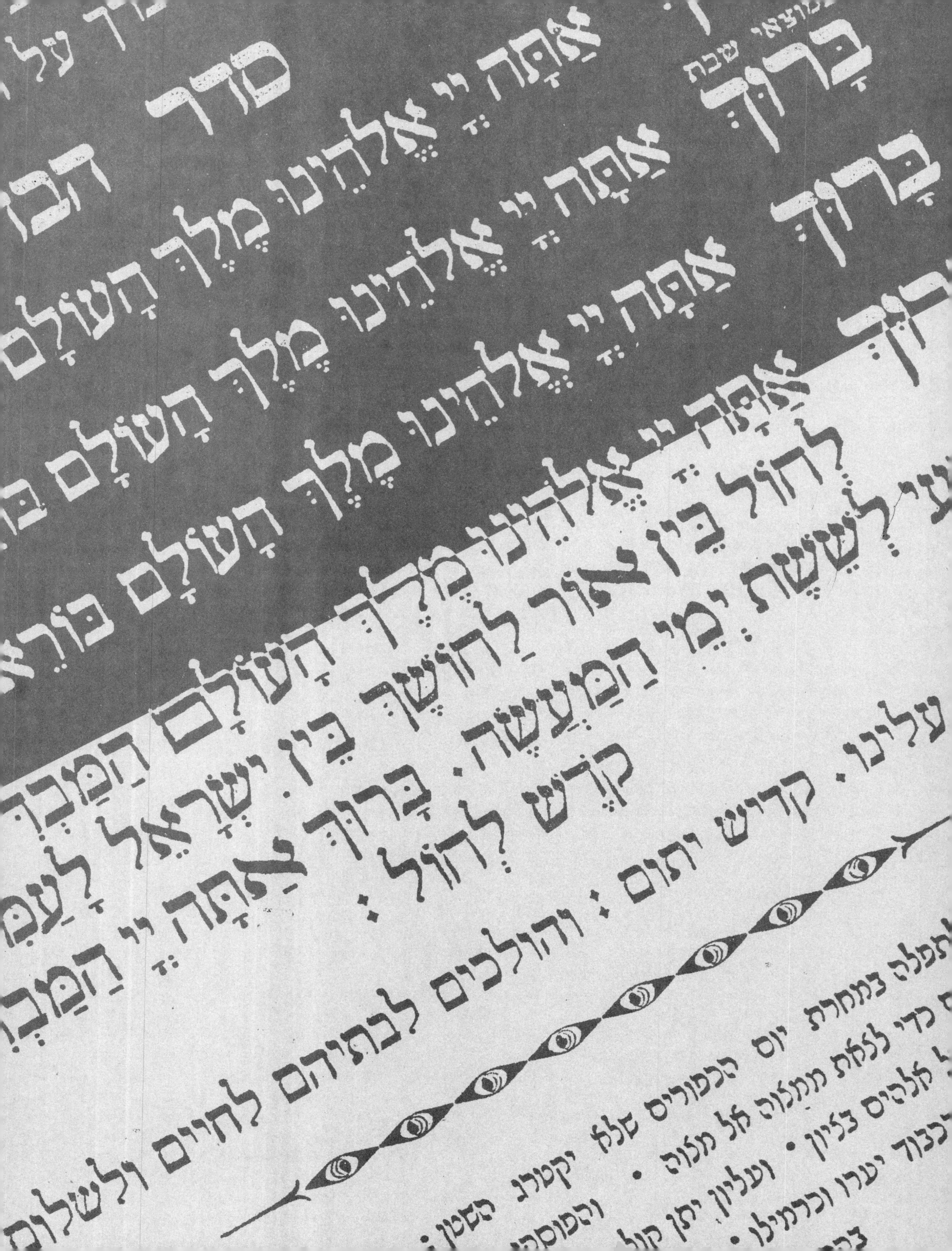

מוצאי שבת
ברוך
סדר הב
ברוך אתה יי אלהינו מלך העולם
אתה יי אלהינו מלך העולם
אתה יי אלהינו מלך העולם בו
אתה יי אלהינו מלך העולם בורא
אתה יי אלהינו מלך העולם המבד
לחול בין אור לחושך בין ישראל לעמ
עי לששת ימי המעשה. ברוך אתה יי המב
קדש לחול:
עלינו. קדיש יתום: והולכים לבתיהם לחיים ולשלום
תפלה במחרת יום הכפורים שלא יקטרג השטן
ם כדי ללכת ממצוה אל מצוה • והפוסקי
אלהים בציון • ועליון יתן קול
כבוד יערו וכרמילו •

Motza'ei Yom Kippur

Maintaining the Spirit

סְלַח לָנוּ אָבִינוּ כִּי חָטָאנוּ, מְחַל לָנוּ מַלְכֵּנוּ כִּי פָשָׁעְנוּ, כִּי מוֹחֵל וְסוֹלֵחַ אָתָּה. בָּרוּךְ אַתָּה ה׳, חַנּוּן הַמַּרְבֶּה לִסְלוֹחַ.

Forgive us, our Father, for we have erred; pardon us, our King, for we have willfully sinned; for You pardon and forgive. Blessed are You, Hashem, the gracious One Who pardons abundantly.

There is a witticism, "Why, in the evening *Amidah* at the close of Yom Kippur, do we say 'Forgive us, Our Father'? Inasmuch as all of our sins have been forgiven on Yom Kippur, and we have not yet even had an opportunity to sin, why are we asking for forgiveness?" The answer is that in our hurry to break the fast we rush through the evening service so rapidly that we may skip or mispronounce words, and we do not pray with the proper *kavannah*. For this we must ask forgiveness.

Although it is only a witticism, it does have a kernel of truth. One might think that after the spiritual uplift of Yom Kippur, we would say the evening prayer more slowly and with more *kavannah* than the rest of the year. But alas! It seems that nothing has changed.

A chassid complained to his rebbe that he had read that if a person fasts forty consecutive days, breaking his fast only at night, he would receive

Divine inspiration. "I have fasted forty consecutive days," he said, "and I have not received any Divine inspiration."

The Rebbe told him that Chassidic lore relates that the Baal Shem Tov's horses ran with miraculous speed, and would cover long distances in a short period of time. The Baal Shem Tov would tell his driver, Alexi, to turn with his back to the horses, and they would speed toward the destination.

When the horses passed an inn where they would normally be watered and fed, they wondered why they were not being watered and fed. "Perhaps we are not horses," they thought. "Perhaps we are human beings, and we only stop at an inn for meals." When they sped by several other inns without stopping, they thought, "Even human beings do not go this distance without eating. Perhaps we are really angels, and we do not need any food at all." When they arrived at the destination and were fed hay, they realized that they were horses after all.

"You see," the Rebbe said, "fasting forty days merits Divine inspiration if one progresses spiritually. When the forty days are over, one should no longer eat to please one's palate, but only to have the necessary nourishment that will allow one to study Torah and perform mitzvos. If, after the forty fast days, one returns to one's previous habit, then nothing has changed. If one has not become more spiritual by fasting, one can hardly merit Divine inspiration."

The Israelites at Sinai achieved unprecedented spiritual heights. God then said to Moses, "Tell them, 'Return to your tents'" (*Deuteronomy* 5:27). It is not enough to be spiritual at the Revelation at Sinai. One must carry the spirituality home.

On Yom Kippur we desist from all mundane pleasurable activities. This should enable us to have a more spiritual perspective on life. If, as soon as Yom Kippur has passed, one regresses to indulgence, then Yom Kippur has not accomplished much.

The Festivals

Pesach

The Haggadah

To Be Truly Free

עֲבָדִים הָיִינוּ לְפַרְעֹה בְּמִצְרָיִם, וַיּוֹצִיאֵנוּ ה׳ אֱלֹקֵינוּ מִשָּׁם בְּיָד חֲזָקָה וּבִזְרוֹעַ נְטוּיָה. וְאִלּוּ לֹא הוֹצִיא הַקָּדוֹשׁ בָּרוּךְ הוּא אֶת אֲבוֹתֵינוּ מִמִּצְרַיִם, הֲרֵי אָנוּ וּבָנֵינוּ וּבְנֵי בָנֵינוּ מְשֻׁעְבָּדִים הָיִינוּ לְפַרְעֹה בְּמִצְרָיִם. וַאֲפִילוּ כֻּלָּנוּ חֲכָמִים, כֻּלָּנוּ נְבוֹנִים, כֻּלָּנוּ זְקֵנִים, כֻּלָּנוּ יוֹדְעִים אֶת הַתּוֹרָה, מִצְוָה עָלֵינוּ לְסַפֵּר בִּיצִיאַת מִצְרָיִם. וְכָל הַמַּרְבֶּה לְסַפֵּר בִּיצִיאַת מִצְרַיִם, הֲרֵי זֶה מְשֻׁבָּח.

We were slaves to Pharaoh in Egypt, but Hashem, our God, took us out from there with a mighty hand and an outstretched arm. Had not the Holy One, Blessed is He, taken our fathers out from Egypt, then we, our children, and our children's children would have remained enslaved to Pharaoh in Egypt. Even if we were all men of wisdom, understanding, experience, and knowledge of the Torah, it would still be an obligation upon us to tell about the Exodus from Egypt. The more one tells about the Exodus, the more he is praiseworthy.

Passover is much more than an Independence Day. No country has a seven- or eight-day Independence Week. Certainly the arduous preparations for Passover and the extremely rigid prohibition of *chametz* (leavened products) are far beyond the celebration of political independence. In addition, we refer to the Sabbath and all the festivals as being זֵכֶר לִיצִיאַת מִצְרָיִם, in commemoration of the Exodus. Many of the mitzvos — *tefillin, tzitzis,* redemption of the firstborn — are in commemoration of the Exodus. Multiple daily references to the Exodus clearly indicate that Passover must be more than an Independence Day celebration.

In the Haggadah *From Bondage to Freedom* I shared an insight that I gained from my work in treating addiction. One young man, after experiencing a few months free of drugs, attended his father's *seder*. When his father read the portion of the Haggadah, "We were slaves unto Pharaoh in Egypt," the son remarked, "Father, can you truthfully say that you were a slave? It was your ancestors thousands of years ago who were slaves, but not you. *But I can say that I was a slave.* When I was in my drug addiction, the drugs were my taskmaster, and they were a vicious and uncompromising taskmaster. I had no freedom of choice. In order to get drugs I did things that I never could have imagined I would do. I did them because I was under the tyranny of drugs. The drugs were my Pharaoh. Today I know what it means to be free."

This is an important insight, and its implications extend far beyond drug addiction. Some people are in such intense pursuit of money or acclaim that they will do virtually anything to attain these. People who are compulsive eaters or compulsive gamblers will testify that although they realize that their eating or gambling is self-destructive, they feel helpless to stop it. *Any compulsive behavior is a type of slavery.* Inasmuch as we consider freedom of choice to be a precious human privilege, compulsive behavior deprives us of the most cherished human trait. This can be a mortal blow to one's self-esteem.

When we threw off the yoke of Pharaoh and acquired our freedom, we were given the Torah. Comprehensive observance of Torah should enable us to overcome compulsive habits. Of course, there are compulsive *diseases* which may require treatment. With the exception of these, compulsive habits may be overcome by Torah observance.

One might say, "I observe Shabbos, *kashrus*, and all the mitzvos, yet this does not help me overcome some compulsive habits." Whereas observance of the mitzvos is a *sine qua non* of Torah observance, it does not constitute *all* of Torah observance. The latter requires spiritual transformation of all our drives and urges. With the help of our many ethical works, this can be achieved. However, it is by no means an easy task. Implementation of all the steps to spirituality described in *Path of the Just (Mesillas Yesharim)* requires considerable work, effort and an unrelenting dedication to the goal.

The degree to which we attain total freedom will depend on how much we wish to sacrifice for it. Inasmuch as we are subject to compulsive habits many times during our daily life, the reason for frequently referring to the Exodus becomes clear. We thank God for giving us this festival of liberation. How much use we wish to make of this precious gift is up to us.

Prayer for Dew

Rebuilding Jerusalem With Brotherly Love

טַל תֵּן לִרְצוֹת אַרְצָךְ, שִׁיתֵנוּ בְרָכָה בְּדִיצָךְ, רֹב דָּגָן וְתִירוֹשׁ בְּהַפְרִיצָךְ, קוֹמֵם עִיר בָּהּ חֶפְצָךְ, בְּטַל.

Dew — give it to favor Your land; establish us for blessing in Your pleasure; with abundant grain and wine may You strengthen [us]; establish the city containing Your delight — with dew.

While we always include our wish for the rebuilding of Jerusalem and the Temple in all our prayers, the words "establish the city containing Your delight — with dew" is a bit difficult to understand. In what way can dew contribute to the rebuilding of Jerusalem?

The Talmud tells us that Jerusalem and the Temple were lost because of the baseless animosity that existed among Jews. It is evident that to merit the rebuilding of Jerusalem and the Temple, we must overcome this fault. We must join in brotherly love.

Rashi (*Deuteronomy* 32:2) explains the difference between dew and rain. Farmers are happy with rain because it helps their crops grow. However, travelers are hampered by the rain, and vinters who have pits full of wine are unhappy because the water may dilute the wine. The traveler and the vinter cannot feel happiness for their farmer, because while the rain is a blessing to him, it is detrimental to them.

Dew, on the other hand, causes everyone to be happy because it does not harm anyone. Dew is a universal blessing, and people can be happy for others as well as for themselves.

> *R' Naftali of Ropschitz said that he was put in his place by an unlearned person. On Simchas Torah, when everyone was rejoicing and dancing with the Torah, this person joined heartily in the festivities. R' Naftali asked him, "What cause do you have to celebrate? Do you know anything of the Torah that you are rejoicing with it?"*
>
> *The man answered, "No, Rabbi. I never had the opportunity to learn anything of Torah. But when my brother married off his daughter, I danced at the wedding. It was not my daughter who was getting married, but I had every reason to rejoice in my brother's simchah.*
>
> *"The same is true of Simchas Torah. I know nothing of Torah, but many of my Jewish brothers are Torah scholars. I am rejoicing in my brothers' simchah."*

R' Naftali always repeated how this person had taught him a valuable lesson.

We should be able to share in other people's joy much as if it were our own. Sharing in joy is symbolized by dew. Dew is beneficial to everyone, and in contrast to rain, there is nothing to deter a person from being happy for others, just as one participates in a brother's *simchah.*

It is with the blessing of dew, a feeling that we are all brothers, that Jerusalem and the Temple will be rebuilt.

The Counting of the Omer

One Day at a Time

רִבּוֹנוֹ שֶׁל עוֹלָם ... יְתֻקַּן מַה שֶּׁפָּגַמְתִּי בִּסְפִירָה (חֶסֶד, גְּבוּרָה, תִּפְאֶרֶת, נֶצַח, הוֹד, יְסוֹד, מַלְכוּת) וְאֶטָּהֵר וְאֶתְקַדֵּשׁ בִּקְדֻשָּׁה שֶׁל מַעְלָה, וְעַל יְדֵי זֶה יֻשְׁפַּע שֶׁפַע רַב בְּכָל הָעוֹלָמוֹת.

Master of the Universe ... may there be corrected whatever blemish I have caused in the sefirah. May I be cleaned and sanctified with the holiness of Above, and through this may abundant bounty flow in all the worlds.

Everyone knows that New Year's resolutions regularly fail to be upheld. "This year I will keep up my diet... This year I will quit smoking... This year I will control my temper." Several days into the new year, most resolutions are forgotten even though they may have been made with the utmost sincerity.

The reason for this is that assuming a change of behavior for a whole year is too big a bite to swallow. The twelve-step programs to overcome destructive addictions owe their success primarily to the principle of "one day at a time." A habitual drinker who pledges never to drink again quickly discovers that he has undertaken more than he can do. However, if he says, "I can get by without a drink *today*," that is manageable. What about tomorrow? That challenge can be dealt with tomorrow. There is no point in coping today with tomorrow's challenge. This brings the behavioral change down to bite-size. There are many stresses that we can deal with if it is only for one day.

One of the greatest miracles in history is the rapid transformation of a people who had been enslaved and dehumanized for centuries into a spiritual people, a "kingdom of priests and a holy nation" (*Exodus* 19:6). It was only seven weeks after the liberation from Egypt that the Israelites were given the Torah at Sinai. How could so radical a transformation have occurred in so brief a period of time?

The answer is that with the mitzvah of the Counting of the *Omer* the transformation took place one day at a time. True, the actual mitzvah of bringing the *Omer*-offering was not implemented until the Israelites had settled in the Promised Land. But just as today the counting of the *Omer* is accompanied by transformation of a particular character trait, this process occurred after the Exodus as well.

There are seven basic character traits: (חֶסֶד,) lovingkindness; (גְבוּרָה) fortitude and awe; (תִּפְאֶרֶת) beauty of behavior; (נֶצַח) triumph and durability; (הוד) glory; (יְסוֹד) moral purity; and (מַלְכוּת) royal dignity. Each of these can be subdivided; e.g., lovingkindness with fortitude and awe, awe with moral purity, triumph with royal dignity. All in all there are forty-nine specific character traits. Each day we are required to rectify one of these. Even though this may be a difficult task, it is not impossible nor formidable when we take it one day at a time. This is the way our ancestors were able to emerge from the status of downtrodden slaves, stripped of all human dignity, to become the recipients of the most advanced code of spirituality the world has known: the Torah.

Numerous times, Moses accompanies his Torah teachings with the words "this day." E.g., "If you will hearken to the mitzvos which I instruct you *this day*" (*Deuteronomy* 11:13). "You are standing before G-d *this day*" (ibid. 29:9). The repeated emphasis on "this day" is to teach us precisely this approach. The *yetzer hara* may attempt to lead us astray by telling us, "The demands of the Torah and its many prohibitions are unrealistic. There is no way you can observe them at all times. Why fight a losing battle?" Our answer should be, "It is not difficult for me to forego some desires and to observe Torah today. This is certainly within my ability. As far as the future is concerned, I will deal with it when it comes."

"Today is the seventh day of the *Omer*, which is one week. By counting this day, I will rectify any defects I may have in performing lovingkindness with dignity." As our ancestors did, we can prepare ourselves for renewing the receiving of the Torah on Shavuos by developing proper character traits one day at a time.

Shavuos

הגדלה והגבורה
והממלכה והמתנשא
רוממו
ירחם עם עמוסים
משאלותינו

Giving of the Torah

A Gift of Love

God created many living things, almost all of which are motivated by selfish desires. Except for pets that may adopt some human characteristics, animals are not altruistic. Mother animals care for their young, and there is a herd instinct that may unite animals against a predator, but acts of *chesed*, of sacrificing oneself to help another person, are uniquely human. God intended for animals to operate according to their innate drives and instincts, but He gave man a spirit wherewith a person could be master over his drives rather than be enslaved by them. In contrast to animals, man was meant to be a creature that acts according to morals and ethics. That is the purpose for which man was created.

The Talmud says that had we not been given the Torah, we would have been held responsible to learn morals and ethics from the observation of living things. For example, we would have been expected to learn respect of private property from observation of ants. It is known that if an ant leaves a crumb of food, no other ant will touch it. We would have been expected to learn faithfulness in marriage by observing doves, who are monogamous. We would have been expected to learn modesty by observing cats (*Eruvin* 100b). Had we failed to learn these proper behaviors, we would have been held culpable.

However, there is no assurance that we would have made the proper observations. It is possible that we might have learned rapaciousness from tigers and promiscuity from dogs. If we had properly exercised our human intellect, we would have indeed come to the conclusion that we were given our great intellect to elevate ourselves above the self-gratification that motivates most animal behavior. But it is also possible that we might have preferred the indulgence in pleasure to the intelligent life of spirituality. We would then have failed in our assignment to live as dignified humans.

To help us avoid the grave error of dereliction in achieving our humanity, God, in His great love for us, gave us the Torah. We need not be at risk of making the wrong decisions about our behavior. Much as a parent teaches his child to avoid running into the street or touching a hot surface, God gave us precise instructions to prevent us from acting foolishly and self-destructively.

Human intellect is indeed great, but it is fallible. We are adept at rationalization. Solomon says, "All a person's ways are right in his own eyes" (*Proverbs* 16:2). If we have a desire for something, we can find justification for it. People have been known to justify even the most abominable acts.

The Torah is a Divine gift. It is explicitly instructive. It tells us in great detail what we are to do and what we are not to do. It removes the danger of our judgment being distorted by our physical drives. The giving of the Torah is indeed a manifestation of God's love for us.

אקדמות מלין

ושריות שו
אולא שקלנא הרמן ורשו
בבי תרי ותלת דאפתח בנקשו
בברי דברי ושרי עדי לקשישו
גבורן עלמין לה ולא ספק פרישו
גויל אלו רקיעי קני כל חורשו
דיו אלו ימי וכל מי כנישו
דירי ארעא ספרי ורשמי רשו
ושליט ביבש

Akdamus

An Antidote to Assimilation

תָּאִין וּמִתְכַּנְּשִׁין, כְּחֵזוּ אִדְוָתָא.
תְּמֵהִין וְשָׁיְלִין לַהּ, בְּעֵסֶק אָתְוָתָא.
מְנָן וּמָאן הוּא רְחִימָךְ, שַׁפִּירָא בְּרֵיוָתָא.
אֲרוּם בְּגִינֵיהּ סָפִית, מְדוֹר אַרְיְוָתָא.
יְקָרָא וְיָאָה אַתְּ, אִין תַּעַרְבִי לְמַרְוָתָא.
רְעוּתֵךְ נַעֲבִיד לִיךְ, בְּכָל אַתְרְוָתָא.
בְּחָכְמְתָא מְתִיבָתָא לְהוֹן, קְצָת לְהוֹדָעוּתָא.
יְדַעְתּוּן חַכְּמִין לֵיהּ, בְּאִשְׁתְּמוֹדָעוּתָא.
רְבוּתְכוֹן מָה חֲשִׁיבָא, קֳבֵל הַהִיא שְׁבַחְתָּא.
רְבוּתָא דְּיַעְבֵּד לִי, כַּד מַטְיָא יְשׁוּעֲתָא.
בְּמֵיתֵי לִי נְהוֹרָא, וְתַחֲפֵי לְכוֹן בַּהֲתָא.
יְקָרֵיהּ כַּד יִתְגְּלֵי, בְּתָקְפָא וּבְגֵיוָתָא.
יְשַׁלֵּם גְּמֻלַּיָּא, לְסַנְאֵי וְנַגְוָתָא.

The wicked come and gather, appearing like sea waves,
With wonderment they inquire of Israel
regarding proofs:
"Whence and Who is your Beloved,
O nation of beautiful appearance,
That for His sake you perish in a lions' den?
Honored and comely would you be,
if you would blend into our dominion;
We would grant your wish in every place."
With wisdom she responds to them in part —
to let them know:
"If your wise men could but know Him
with full awareness!
What value has your greatness compared to His praise?
Of the great things He will do for me
when redemption shall arrive;
When He will bring me light,
and you will be covered with shame;
When His glory will be revealed
with power and with grandeur,
He will repay in kind to the haters and the isles."

*T**efillah* constitutes a bonding. It should, therefore, serve to prevent those things that threaten to sever the bond with God. One of the themes in the prayer *Akdamus* can serve this function, and suggests a method to preserve the bond.

Jews have suffered repeated persecutions throughout history: the Inquisition, the Crusades, the pogroms, the Holocaust. As devastating as these have been, we have stubbornly survived them. Ironically, persecution seems to stimulate our survival instinct.

However, there is a threat to Jewish existence which does not ignite the spark of survival and set it ablaze. This is when we lose our children in a peaceful manner to the epidemic of assimilation. Jews marrying out of the faith are invariably lost to Judaism. Whatever frail ties they may have retained are totally absent in their children, who may lack all Jewish identity.

How does desertion from Judaism occur at all? There is a popular aphorism, "No one flees from good." Why is it that young people fail to see the beauty and good in Judaism?

In the above prayer we hear the beckoning and seduction of forces that pull people away from their Jewishness: Why retain your Jewish identity and subject yourself to so much suffering? Just Who is this God for Whom you have so often chosen martyrdom rather than renounce Him? If you will divest yourself of your Jewishness and join us, we will provide you with peace and prosperity.

The wise person answers, "You speak this way only because you have no understanding of God. If you knew Him the way we do, you would be devoted to Him as we are. Yes, we have experienced much suffering, for reasons known only to Him. But there will be the great Redemption, at which time God will reveal Himself to us, and we will rejoice, basking in His glory."

This is the response of the wise person. But alas, so many lack this wisdom.

We recite the above prayer on Shavuos, when we commemorate and celebrate the receiving of Torah at Sinai. We were given the only source of true wisdom, the Torah, which is the Divine wisdom. Those who are well versed in Torah have the wisdom with which they can resist secular seduction and refute its spurious arguments.

But unfortunately, not all Jewish children are privileged to become well versed in Torah. Some well-meaning parents think that by sending their children to public or private secular schools where they will mix with non-Jewish children, they will be spared the discrimination of anti-Semitism. They feel that their children should have a secular education that will enable them to compete for admission to choice colleges. They view Torah education as being unimportant.

However, these parents do not seem to recognize that they are detaching their children from their nation, something that they really do not wish to do. One business executive who was not observant asked me to try and discourage his son from marrying a non-Jewish girl. "No one in our family has ever intermarried. I may not be religious, but I want to have Jewish grandchildren. I realize I made a grave error by not giving my son a Jewish education in a Jewish environment." I felt this man's pain as he cried, but there was little I could do.

I then understood what had been a puzzling passage in the Talmud. The Talmud relates an episode involving Elazar ben Doradia, who all his life had violated Torah. In his last days, he did *teshuvah*, and was so heartbroken about his past history that he cried incessantly, and died while crying. A voice from heaven declared, "Elazar ben Doradia has earned a place in Paradise." R' Yehudah HaNasi wept. "It is possible for a person to redeem an entire lifetime in just a single hour" (*Avodah Zarah* 10b).

Why did this cause R' Yehudah to weep? Is it not a heartening thought that a person can redeem an entire lifetime in a single hour? Yes, but although one can redeem *oneself*, one cannot reclaim the children that one had allowed to stray from Judaism.

The Jewish nation has survived throughout history against all odds. The secret of our survival is the Torah. We dare not allow our children to be lost to our people by depriving them of a Torah education.

שנה ארבעה עשר תמימים
ומנחתה ונסכה
במספרם כמשפט

Succos

Ushpizin

Welcoming the Succah Guests

אֲזַמֵּן לִסְעֻדָּתִי אֻשְׁפִּיזִין עִלָּאִין: אַבְרָהָם יִצְחָק יַעֲקֹב יוֹסֵף מֹשֶׁה אַהֲרֹן וְדָוִד.

I invite to my meal the exalted guests: Abraham, Isaac, Jacob, Joseph, Moses, Aaron and David.

There is a tradition that the seven Biblical *tzaddikim*, Abraham, Isaac, Jacob, Joseph, Moses, Aaron and David join us in the *succah*. They are referred to as the *ushpizin*, which is the Aramaic word for "guests." It is related that great *tzaddikim* were actually able to see the *ushpizin*. R' Mendel of Kotzk said, "I do not see them. I believe they are here, and believing can be an even stronger conviction than seeing."

These seven historical figures represent seven traits of character which we must develop. Abraham represents lovingkindness; Isaac, fortitude and awe before G-d; Jacob, beauty and behavior which is the synthesis of lovingkindness and fortitude; Joseph, the purity of morality; Moses, the triumph and eternity of Torah; Aaron, the glory of serving God; and David, the dignity of royalty.

While we may not be fortunate enough to see the *ushpizin*, nor do we have R' Mendel's depth of conviction of their presence, we should have the feeling of their being with us in spirit. This is possible only to the degree that we develop and perfect the trait with which each of the *ushpizin* is identified. This is illustrated by the following charming story.

The Chassidic master, R' Pinchas of Koritz, was very charismatic. He was beloved by all, and the townspeople constantly sought his advice and blessing. R' Pinchas felt that this distracted him from the study of Torah. He prayed to God to remove his charisma so that people would not desire his company. His prayer was answered, and he found himself free to spend his time studying Torah.

At times, R' Pinchas would have a minyan in his home, but now he found that no one wished to come to him. Nevertheless, he felt that having the time to study Torah was worth this sacrifice.

One day, R' Pinchas' wife said to him, "I don't know what has happened. When I used to go to the market, people would always greet me and talk to me. Now everyone turns away and shuns me. I did nothing to alienate people."

R' Pinchas explained to her that he had prayed to be uninviting to people, and that since she was his wife, his wish must have affected her as well. His wife was unhappy about this, but she said that if this was his wish, she would accept it.

Every Succos, people volunteered to put up the succah for R' Pinchas. On this Succos no one offered, and R' Pinchas had to put up his succah without anyone to assist him. On Succos night, he entered the succah, but had no guests. He felt that the ushpizin were not with him and he saw the Patriarch Abraham standing outside the succah. He invited the Patriarch to enter, but Abraham said, "I do not enter a succah where guests do not share in the meal. My home had doors in all the four walls, so that a wayfarer could find easy entrance. My entire being was dedicated to the love of other people. How can I enter a succah where someone has separated himself from his fellow Jews?"

R' Pinchas realized he had erred. He prayed that his charisma be returned to him, and soon his house was buzzing with visitors. He felt the presence of the ushpizin in the succah once again.

The all-encompassing principle of Torah is the love and consideration for others. Torah study is indeed precious, but a person should not isolate himself and be estranged from other Jews even for so lofty a purpose.

The spirit of Abraham will join us if we exhibit lovingkindness. The spirit of Isaac will be with us if we demonstrate fortitude in our dedication to God and stand in awe of His majesty. The spirits of all the *ushpizin* will join us if we emulate their traits.

העולם אשר קדשנו במצותיו וצונו לישב בסוכה
מלך העולם שהחיינו וקימנו והגיענו לזמ
מקיף חסד

The Blessing on Eating in the Succah

Succos: The Season of Our Rejoicing

בָּרוּךְ אַתָּה ה׳ אֱלֹקֵינוּ מֶלֶךְ הָעוֹלָם, אֲשֶׁר קִדְּשָׁנוּ בְּמִצְוֹתָיו וְצִוָּנוּ לֵישֵׁב בַּסֻּכָּה.

Blessed are You Hashem, our God, King of the universe, Who has sanctified us with His commandments and has commanded us to dwell in the succah.

The Torah refers to Succos as "the festival of harvest" (*Exodus* 23:16). Biblical Israel was an agricultural country. Harvest season was indeed a time when people were happy.

However, in prescribing the mitzvah of the *succah* the Torah says, "You shall dwell in the *succah* for seven days ... so that your generations should know that I had the children of Israel dwell in *succos* (huts) when I delivered them from Egypt" (*Leviticus* 23:43). While the festival indeed occurs at harvest time, its prime function is to commemorate the *succos* in which the nation dwelled following the Exodus.

The Talmud cites two opinions. R'Akiva says that the *succah* is to commemorate the thatched huts which housed the Israelites during their forty years in the desert. R' Eliezer states that by encircling us, the walls and roof of the succah commemorate the Clouds of Glory which encircled and protected the Israelites from the elements and wild beasts of the desert (*Succah* 11b).

The latter opinion is indeed adequate reason for celebration. We recall the protection that God provided for our ancestors, and we are strengthened in our belief that He will protect us as well. But what is so special about living in thatched huts in the desert that warrants commemoration for generations?

One of the human frailties is that we have some desires that are insatiable, one of these being the desire for wealth. The Midrash says, "A person never leaves this world with having satisfied even half of his desires. Whoever has a hundred gold pieces desires two hundred " (*Koheles Rabbah* 1:34). This is why the Talmud says that a truly wealthy person is one who is satisfied with whatever he has (*Ethics of the Fathers* 4:1).

A person cannot be truly happy as long as he feels he is lacking something. This is particularly true if he is envious of people who have more than he does. Solomon says that "Envy [brings] rotting of the bones" (*Proverbs* 14:30). Also, "Sweet is the sleep of the laborer ... but the satiety of the rich person does not let him sleep" (*Ecclesiastes* 5:11). Inasmuch as the rich person's happiness is dependent on his wealth, he is in a state of anxiety lest he lose some of his wealth. The person who has meager earnings and lives on what he earns can be tranquil and can rest without anxiety. It is only when a person is free of greed and envy that he can be happy.

Although the harvest season should be one of happiness, this joy may be far from universal. A person who has a large farm will have a much greater harvest than someone with a smaller farm. Neither may be happy. The wealthier farmer may be anxious, as Solomon says, lest he lose some of his wealth. The farmer who has less may be envious of the person with a much larger harvest.

In order for there to be happiness with one's harvest, we must emulate the words of *Ethics of the Fathers*, to be satisfied with whatever we have. This occurred in the desert, where all Jews were equal. Each person received precisely the amount of manna he could consume. There was no way of saving manna, for any excess rotted. Everyone lived in thatched huts. No one had a mansion, lavishly constructed and opulently furnished. There was no opportunity for greed or envy, and that is why there could be true happiness.

But at harvest time there was the danger that greed and envy might ruin the joy of receiving God's bounty. To remind us of what is necessary for true happiness, we leave our homes and live in the *succah* for a week. The wealthy person who owns a forty-four room mansion with costly furnishings, and the person who lives on a subsistence level, both live in a *succah* for seven days: no expensive imported wood, no marble staircase and no oriental carpets, just four walls and a thatched roof.

The opinions of R' Akiva and R' Eliezer are both right. We rejoice in our *succos* commemorating the Divine Clouds of Glory, but in order to rejoice with our harvest, we should recall how we lived in the desert, when there was neither greed nor envy to spoil our happiness.

הושענא
אֲדוֹנֵי הָאֲדוֹנִים
צוּר עוֹלָמִים
אֱלֹהֵי הָאֱלֹהִים
מוֹשֶׁל בַּכֹּל
למענך
הושענא
למען חסדך
למען כבודך
למען נצחך
למען פארך
למען רחמיך

Hoshanos

We Must Model for God

הוֹשַׁעְנָא, לְמַעַנְךָ אֱלֹקֵינוּ, הוֹשַׁעְנָא. הוֹשַׁעְנָא, לְמַעַנְךָ בּוֹרְאֵנוּ, הוֹשַׁעְנָא. הוֹשַׁעְנָא, לְמַעַנְךָ גּוֹאֲלֵנוּ, הוֹשַׁעְנָא. הוֹשַׁעְנָא, לְמַעַנְךָ דּוֹרְשֵׁנוּ, הוֹשַׁעְנָא.

Please save — for Your sake, our God! Please save! Please save — for Your sake, our Creator! Please save! Please save — for Your sake, our Redeemer! Please save! Please save — for Your sake, our Attender! Please save!

We often hear it said that some people behave in a manner of "Do as I say, not as I do." We know that effective teaching of proper behavior to children requires that parents model the desired behavior for them. Parents who lecture to their children about proper values but do not practice those values themselves will find their efforts unrewarding.

The Talmud tells us that we must model for God, too. God acts toward us *middah keneged middah.* I.e., He behaves toward us as we behave toward others. If we are kind and forgiving, we earn His kindness and forgiveness. If we are stern and unyielding, He deals with us in a similar manner.

The prayer "Please save – for Your sake, our God!" was initially invoked by Moses when the Jews sinned by worshiping the Golden Calf. To forestall God's destroying the Israelites, Moses pleaded that the Egyptians would claim that God took the Jews out of Egypt with the evil intent to annihilate them in the desert

(*Exodus* 32:12). When the Israelites accepted the account of the spies that the conquest of Canaan was impossible and wished to return to Egypt, Moses again pleaded, "The Egyptians will say that You lacked the ability to bring them into Canaan, and that is why You slaughtered them in the desert (*Numbers* 14:16). This plea invokes preserving the Divine honor. Anything that would cause disrespect of God must be avoided.

David, too, echoed this theme in Psalm 115. "Not for our sake, O God, not for our sake, but for Your Name's sake give glory." The idea is that although we may not be deserving of salvation, God should save us so that His Name is not desecrated when His nation, Israel, suffers. The *chillul Hashem* must be avoided. In the first of the *Hoshana* prayers, we cite many ways in which failure of our salvation would be an affront to the Divine honor. "Save us because of Your truth, Your covenant, Your greatness and glory, etc."

But as we invoke this powerful plea, we must ask ourselves: How cautious are we not to cause desecration of the Divine Name? If we are dishonest, if we are deceptive, if we are arrogant or in any way behave in an undignified manner, we are guilty of *chillul Hashem*. Inasmuch as God conducts Himself *middah keneged middah*, the plea that He should save us to avoid dishonor to His Name loses its potency. It is an effective plea only to the degree that we are cautious not to bring any dishonor to His Name.

Properly understood, the *Hoshana* prayer is an admonishment to us as well as a plea to God. It calls for us to examine our behavior and to see how cautious we are in bringing glory to God.

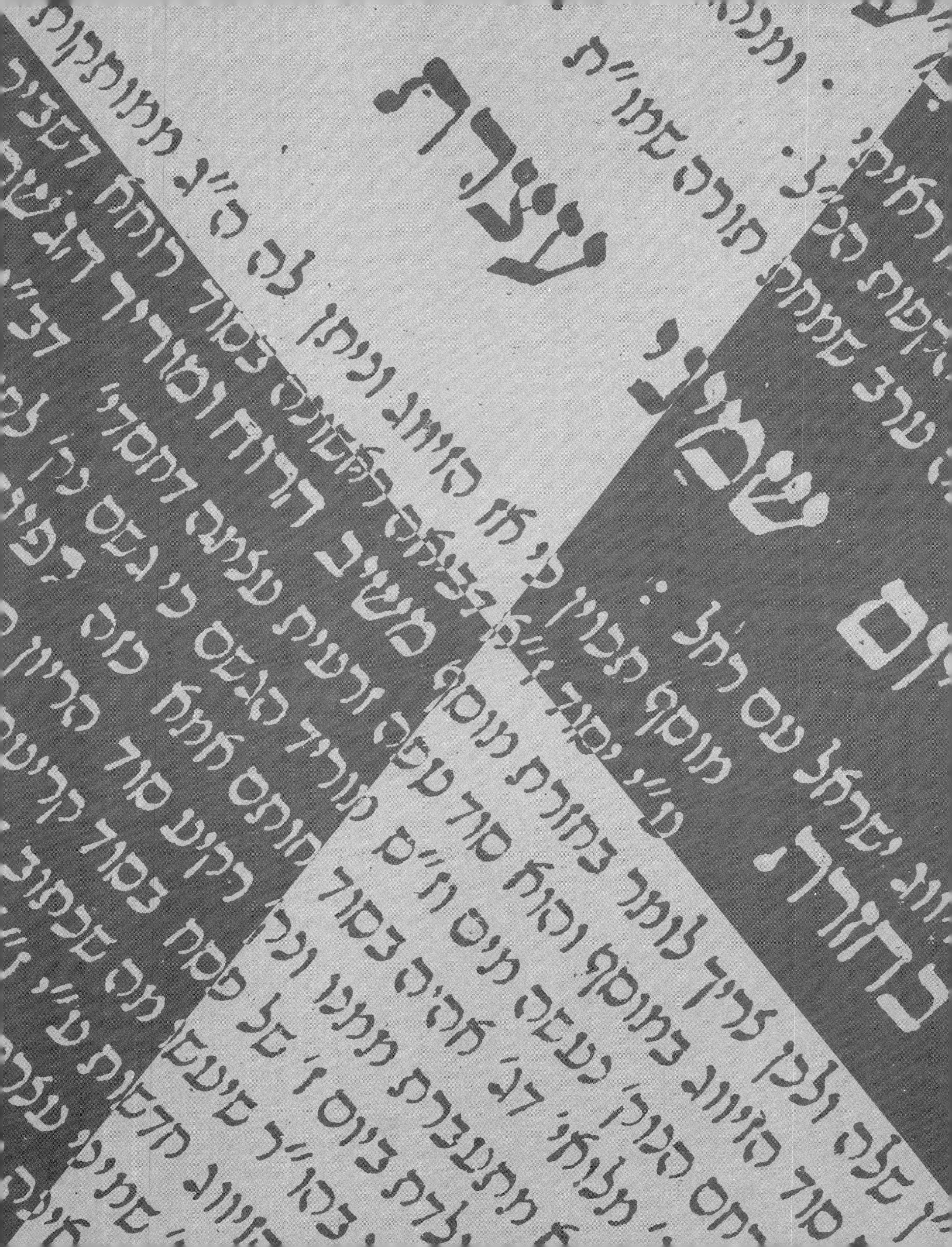

Shemini Atzeres and Simchas Torah

God's Love of Unity

Shemini Atzeres actually means "the eighth day of holding back." The Midrash gives the reason for this festival which is appended to Succos with a parable.

A king declared a holiday of seven days of festivities, during which people from all over the kingdom visited the palace. When the seventh day was over, the king said, "I so enjoyed all my subjects being here. Let us extend the holiday for one more day." So it is with Shemini Atzeres. Jews from all over Israel came to the Temple in Jerusalem for Succos. When Succos was over and everyone was about to leave for home, God said, "Your separation is too difficult for Me. Please stay another day" (See *Rashi* to *Leviticus* 23:36, *Numbers* 29:36). *Atzeres* is a "holding back" from returning home.

We generally assume that the separation God refers to is that of the Jews leaving Jerusalem and becoming more distant from Him. One of the Chassidic masters gave it an additional interpretation. During the seven days of Succos, Jews from all over

Israel came together. People who had not seen each other for some time could meet again. Friendships were renewed, and new friendships were formed. People who brought offerings would invite others, especially the poor, to join in their meals. The festival was a time for camaraderie.

But when everyone returned home, the closeness would fade. Great distances separated friends. The workweek precluded large get-togethers. Engaging in commerce was likely to cause dissension, either due to competition or to exploitation. Everyone pursued personal gain, which sometimes encroached on the properties of others. God, therefore, said, "Your separation *from each other* is difficult for Me to bear. Please remain one more day. Let there be another day of unity and brotherhood."

How happy parents are when their children come together and are close with each other! How distraught parents are when they see brothers and sisters quarreling and quibbling! We can easily understand how much it pleases God to see His children united, and how it must grieve Him to see them torn asunder.

The festivals are meant to provide us with reason to rejoice all year round. If we apply the teaching of Shemini Atzeres and do not allow our differences to cause divisiveness among us, we can bring great joy to God as well as to ourselves.

פנות ארץ
מזל שבט דלי
המזכירים מאמתי
מים

The Prayer for Rain

The Greatest Merit

זְכוֹר מָשׁוּי בְּתֵבַת גֹּמֶא מִן הַמַּיִם, נָמוּ דָּלֹה דָלָה וְהִשְׁקָה צֹאן מַיִם, סְגוּלֶיךָ עֵת צָמְאוּ לַמַּיִם, עַל הַסֶּלַע הָךְ וַיֵּצְאוּ מָיִם. בְּצִדְקוֹ חֹן חַשְׁרַת מָיִם.

Remember the one [Moses] drawn forth in a bulrush basket from the water. They said, "He drew water and provided the sheep with water." At the time Your treasured people thirsted for water, he struck the rock and out came water. For the sake of his righteousness, grant abundant water!

In our prayer for rain, we invoke the great merits of our ancestors who devoted their entire lives to G-d. When we mention Moses, we say that "he struck the rock, and out came water." The Torah relates that Moses erred in this, because God had told him to speak to the rock rather than strike it. Because of this misdeed, Moses was not permitted to enter the Promised Land (*Numbers* 20:12). Why would we mention this misdeed when we seek to invoke Moses' merits?

The Chassidic master, R' Baruch of Mezhibozh, once severely chastised a chassid publicly. He realized that other chassidim were stunned by this, because the Talmud says that if one humiliates a person publicly, he loses his portion in the eternal world. R' Baruch said, "I saw that there was a harsh decree on this person that he would have an early death. Inasmuch as the Talmud equates public humiliation with death, my action satisfied this decree and he will continue to live. I knew that by doing this I would forfeit my portion in the Eternal World. However, I am willing to forfeit it in order to prolong a person's life."

R' Mendel of Vorki said that Moses was aware that God had instructed him to speak to the rock. However, he knew that the Israelites were of a rebellious nature (*Deuteronomy* 9:24) and had repeatedly disobeyed God's commands. He reasoned that if he spoke to the rock and it delivered water, this would magnify the sin of the Israelites. Satan would argue that the inanimate rock obeyed verbal instructions, whereas the Israelites, who had witnessed the Revelation at Sinai, repeatedly disobeyed God's instructions. Moses, therefore, reasoned that in order to ameliorate the sins of the Israelites, he would smite the rock rather than speak to it. He knew that for doing this he would be punished, but he was willing to sacrifice himself and suffer punishment in order to mitigate the sins of the Israelites.

Just as we invoked the *mesiras nefesh* (self-sacrifice) of the Patriarch Isaac, we also invoke the *mesiras nefesh* of Moses.

This prayer should remind us that *mesiras nefesh* is the greatest of virtues. In *Dearer Than Life* I pointed out that *mesiras nefesh* does not require martyrdom. *Mesiras nefesh* means that nothing should be of grater importance than fulfilling the Divine will. This may require sacrifices. We may be required to sacrifice some comforts, conveniences and even some of our assets to observe the mitzvos. However, it is common to forego comforts and conveniences to attain something we strongly desire, and we may part with many of our assets to acquire what we want. This is the concept of *mesiras nefesh.*

For Moses, the preservation of his people was dearest to him. We should emulate Moses in making *ahavas Yisrael*, our love for our people, dearest to us.

בשמחת תו

...נעשות ז׳ הקפות בשמח׳ גדולה ומרקדים ומזמרים לפני

הראת לדעת כי ידוד הוא האלדים אין עוד מלבדו

נפלאות גדולות לבדו כי לעולם חסדו : אין כמוך

אין כמעשיך : יהי כבוד ידוד לעולם ישמח ידוד במעש

ברוך מעתה ועד עולם : יהי ידוד אלדינו עמנו כאש

אל יעזבנו ואל יטשנו : ואמרו הושיענו אלדי ישע

מן הגוים להודות לשם קדשך להשתבח בתהלתך : יד

ידוד ימלוך לעולם ועד : ידוד עז לעמו יתן ידוד יברך

ויהיו נא אמרינו לרצון לפני אדון כל : ויהי בנסע הארן

יד ויפוצו אויביך וינוסו משנאיך מפניך : קו

אתה וארון עזך : כהניך ילבשו צדק וחסידיך ירננו

אל תשב פני משיחך ואמר ביום ההוא הנה אלדינו זה ק

ידוד קוינו לו נגילה ונשמחה בישועתו : מלכותך מ

ממשלתך בכל דור ודור : כי מציון תצא תורה ודבר

מירושלים : אב הרחמים

הושיעה נא : אנא ידוד הצליחה נא : אלדי הרוחות הושיעה נא : בוחן לבבות הצליחה נא : אנא ידוד עננו

ביום קראנו : דובר צדקות הושיעה נא

ותיק וחסיד עננו ביום קראנו : זך וישר הושיעה נא

הצליחה נא : טוב ומטיב עננו ביום קראנו

הדור בלבושו הצליחה נא

הושיעה נא : לובש צדקות עננו ביום קראנו : יודע מחשבות הושיעה נא : חו

נאור ואדיר הצליחה נא : סומך נופלים עננו ביום קראנו

קדוש ונורא הושיעה נא : פודה ומציל הצליחה נא : מלך

ביום ...

The Joy of the Torah

The Joy of the Torah

שִׂישׂוּ וְשִׂמְחוּ בְּשִׂמְחַת תּוֹרָה.

Rejoice and be glad on Simchas Torah.

A more accurate translation of the Hebrew is "Rejoice and be glad *in the joy* of the Torah." This version has a significant implication.

R' Yosef Dov of Brisk noticed one of the congregants who was jubilant on Simchas Torah. He knew that this person was not a Torah scholar and not particularly observant of mitzvos. He called him aside and asked him, "Are you really so happy with the Torah that you are so jubilant?"

The man responded, "Rabbi, I don't know if anyone else is as happy with the Torah as I am.

"A year ago I borrowed money. There were no witnesses to the loan and I did not give a promissory note. When the lender demanded his money, I denied having borrowed it. He had no evidence, but he wanted to press a claim in court anyway.

"I don't know what the outcome in court would have been, but I convinced him to bring his claim before a beis din. Inasmuch as he had no evidence, the rabbis applied the law of the Torah, that I was to swear that I had not borrowed the loan. I swore, and the beis din dismissed his claim. The law of the Torah saved me much money. That is why I am happy with it."

R' Yosef Dov said, "You are making a grave error. Simchas Torah does not mean only that we rejoice with the Torah, but it also means 'the joy of the Torah.' The Torah must be as happy with us as we are with it. In your situation, you exploited the Torah in support of dishonesty. The Torah is not at all pleased with you, and it is an affront to the Torah that you dance with it."

Perhaps we were derelict in study of Torah and performance of mitzvos in the past year. However, during Rosh Hashanah, the ten days of *teshuvah,* and Yom Kippur we made a reckoning and resolved to do better in the coming year. On Succos we had the mitzvah of the *succah* and the four species. We began the year with *teshuvah* and with mitzvos. Inasmuch as we have dedicated ourselves to greater observance of Torah and mitzvos during the coming year, we can be certain that the Torah will be happy with us as we are with it. Simchas Torah can be a mutual joy of both ourselves and the Torah.

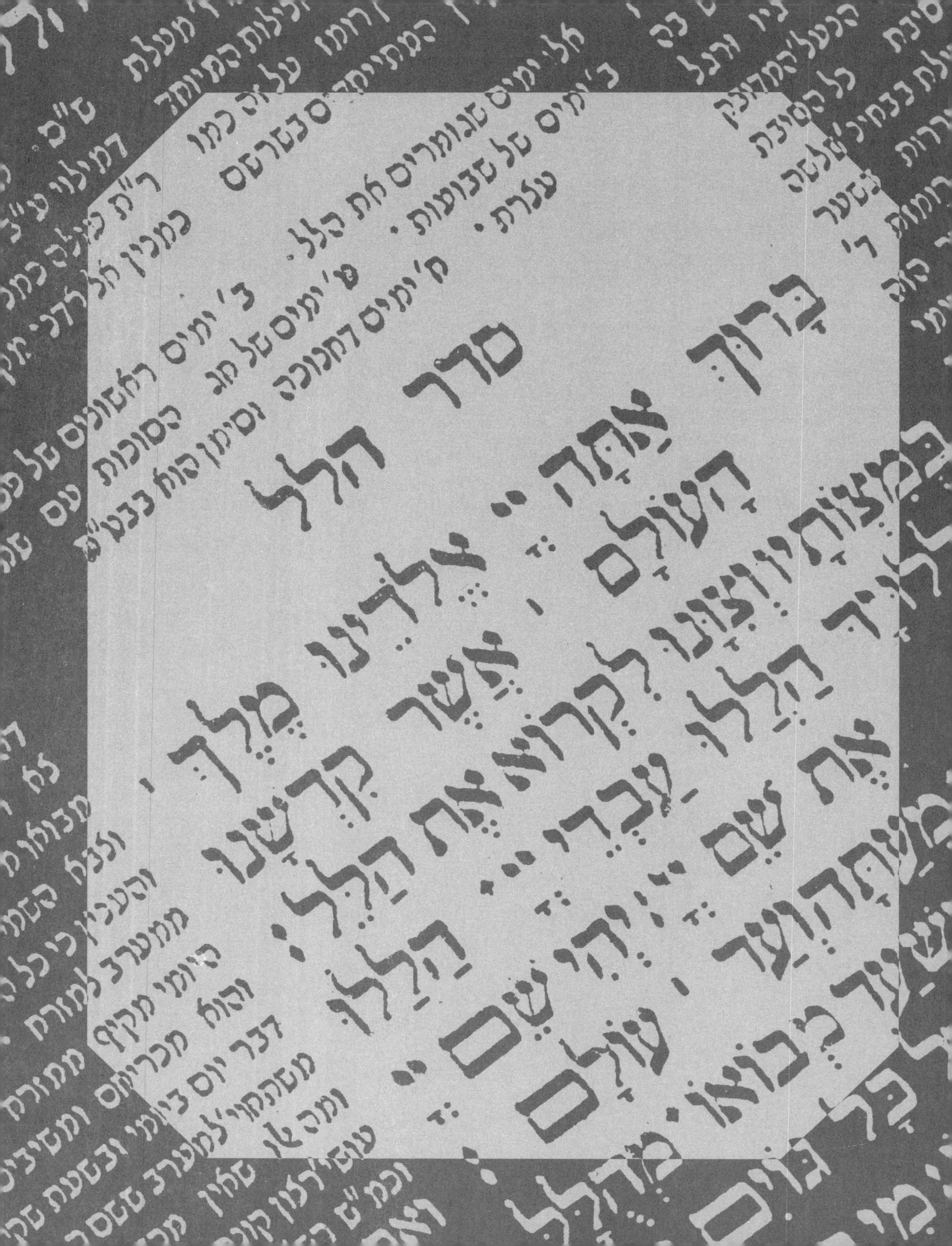
סדר הלל
ברוך אתה יי אלהינו מלך
העולם, אשר קדשנו
במצותיו וצונו לקרוא את הלל:
הללו עבדי יי. הללו
את שם יי. יהי שם
יי מבורך מעתה ועד עולם:

Hallel

הַלְלוּקָהּ הַלְלוּ עַבְדֵי ה׳, הַלְלוּ אֶת שֵׁם ה׳. יְהִי שֵׁם ה׳ מְבֹרָךְ, מֵעַתָּה וְעַד עוֹלָם. מִמִּזְרַח שֶׁמֶשׁ עַד מְבוֹאוֹ, מְהֻלָּל שֵׁם ה׳. רָם עַל כָּל גּוֹיִם ה׳, עַל הַשָּׁמַיִם כְּבוֹדוֹ. מִי כַּה׳ אֱלֹקֵינוּ, הַמַּגְבִּיהִי לָשָׁבֶת. הַמַּשְׁפִּילִי לִרְאוֹת, בַּשָּׁמַיִם וּבָאָרֶץ. מְקִימִי מֵעָפָר דָּל, מֵאַשְׁפֹּת יָרִים אֶבְיוֹן. לְהוֹשִׁיבִי עִם נְדִיבִים, עִם נְדִיבֵי עַמּוֹ. מוֹשִׁיבִי עֲקֶרֶת הַבַּיִת, אֵם הַבָּנִים שְׂמֵחָה, הַלְלוּקָהּ.

Halleluyah! Give praise, you servants of Hashem; praise the Name of Hashem! Blessed be the Name of Hashem, from this time and forever. From the rising of the sun to its setting, Hashem's Name is praised. High above all nations is Hashem, above the heavens is His glory. Who is like Hashem, our God, Who is enthroned on high — yet deigns to look upon the heaven and the earth? He raises the needy from the dust, from the trash heaps He lifts the destitute. To seat them with nobles, with the nobles of His people. He transforms the barren wife into a glad mother of children. Halleluyah!

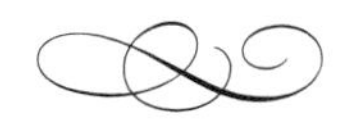

The six chapters of Psalms, 113-118, constitute the *Hallel*, which is recited on the festivals, on Chanukah, and on Rosh Chodesh, the first day of the new month. These six chapters epitomize the course of Jewish history, which parallels the life of King David.

Both King David and the Jews had humble origins. The Jews were initially oppressed as slaves, and had a sudden elevation at Sinai to become "a kingdom of priests and a holy nation" (*Exodus* 19:6). David was an outcast who for the first 23 years of his life was erroneously thought to be illegitimate. It was only when the prophet Samuel anointed him as king that his true identity was revealed. The first chapter, therefore, says of both, "He raises the needy from the dust, from the trash heaps He lifts the destitute" (*Psalms* 113:7).

Moses prayed that God forgive Israel lest their destruction result in dishonor to God (*Exodus* 32:12). David was relentlessly persecuted, first by King Saul, then by his enemies and even by his own son. The Israelites called to God in their anguish (ibid. 14:10), as did David (*Psalms* 116:3-4). Both the Israelites and David sang praises to God for His salvation (*Exodus* 15:1-19; *Psalms* 116:12-19); The Israelites rose from their humble origins to become a mighty kingdom, and David's statement, "The stone which the builders despised has become the [chief] cornerstone" (ibid. 118:22), refers to his ascending the throne after having been rejected as an outcast.

The Jewish nation, like King David, have survived unthinkable persecutions. The future of the Jewish nation will be like the glory of King David. Perhaps this similarity is responsible for the statement, "David, King of Israel, lives and exists."

The pivotal point of *Hallel* is in the first chapter. "High above all nations is God, above the heavens is His glory. Who is like Hashem, our God, Who is enthroned on high — yet deigns to look upon the heaven and the earth" (ibid. 113:4-6). Indeed, this is the theme of the entire Book of Psalms and is the basis for prayer. It is the statement of our belief in *hashgachah pratis* (Divine providence).

Rambam states that the worship of idolatry began with the erroneous belief that God was far too high and sublime to take an interest in earthlings. The ancients believed that God created the world, but because they thought it to be beneath His dignity to concern Himself with what transpires in the world, He retreated and left the management of the world to underlings. They, therefore, began to worship these underlings.

The fallacy in this thinking is that relative to infinity, both great and small are equal. Inasmuch as God is infinite, the heavenly angels and super galaxies are no more and no less significant than is mortal man. Either God is interested in nothing or in everything. Judaism teaches the latter.

This concept is expressed in the verses cited. God is high above all and His glory is above the heavens, yet He looks down on *both the heaven and the earth*. God's concern with the mighty heavens is a manifestation of His humility, which corresponds to His greatness (*Megillah* 31a). Just as His interest in the heavenly angels and in the expanse of the universe is due to His humility, so is His interest in mortal man. Without this belief, prayer would make no sense. There would be no point in praying to a disinterested God.

King David's life was filled with agony, yet he never despaired. His trust in God was unshakeable. David's unfaltering faith in God is the reason why we include so many of the psalms in our daily prayers, and why we turn to them for strength and comfort when we are in distress.

The Universal Appreciation of God

מִמִּזְרַח שֶׁמֶשׁ עַד מְבוֹאוֹ, מְהֻלָּל שֵׁם ה׳.

From the rising of the sun to its setting, Hashem's Name is praised.

"How can we say that God is universally praised, when there are so many faiths that worship idols?" asked the Maggid of Dubnow.

The Maggid called attention to a nuance in the verse. "Note that it does not say that *God* is universally praised, but that *the Name of God* is praised. He then offered this explanation with one of his inimitable parables.

> *In a far-flung corner of a vast empire, a man dressed himself in royal robes and said that he was the king. The people of the region, never having seen the king, had no way of knowing that this was an imposter. They paid homage to him and accorded him the honor due to a king.*
>
> *When word about this filtered back to the royal court, the officers expected that the king would fly into a rage and levy a penalty upon those who had paid homage to the imposter. To their surprise, the king was good-humored.*
>
> *"Why should I punish these people?" he said.*

"They meant well. They thought it was me whom they were honoring. They had no way of knowing that this man was an imposter. When they paid homage to him, their intention was to pay homage to the true king. They just have to be enlightened, not punished."

The Maggid continued, "So it is with nations who were never enlightened as to the true God. They may worship the sun or a mountain because they do not know any better. If they were only taught properly, they would worship the true God. The Psalmist says that the Name of God is universally praised. It is just that unenlightened people mistakenly misapply the Name of God."

This is why the prophet says that with the ultimate Redemption, all people in the world will be enlightened, and the knowledge of the true God will be universal and as widespread as the water that covers the bed of the sea (*Isaiah* 11:9).

No One Should Despair
of Spirituality

מְקִימִי מֵעָפָר דָּל, מֵאַשְׁפֹּת יָרִים אֶבְיוֹן.

He raises the needy from the dust, from the trash heaps He lifts the destitute.

This concept is recited before the *Amidah*: וּמַגְבִּיהַּ שְׁפָלִים: "He lifts the lowly to great heights." A person should never feel alienated from God and undeserving of a relationship with God. The "needy" and "destitute" refers also to those who are spiritually impoverished. They, too, may approach God in prayer. Even the spiritually lowly can achieve great heights. The Talmud says that if a person who is a profligate *rasha* enters a marriage contract with the specified condition that he is a perfect *tzaddik*, the marriage may be valid. It is possible that he had meditated on *teshuvah* (*Kiddushin* 49b). Think of it! A single moment of sincere *teshuvah* can change the status of a person from that of the worst *rasha* to the greatest *tzaddik*!

The Chafetz Chaim points out that this concept is stated in the third paragraph of the *Shema*. "That you do not deviate after your heart's desires and after the lusting of your eyes after which you stray. So that you may remember and perform all My commandments, and *be holy to your God*." Moses is delivering this message to those who are suspect of deviating toward idol worship and lust, and is telling them that God expects them to become holy! Not only can the worst sinners become observant, but they can achieve the status of *kedoshim*, the highest possible level of spirituality.

"God has distanced our iniquities from us as east is distant from west" (*Psalms* 103:12). One of the commentaries remarked, "If you are facing east and just turn around, you are already facing west." In other words, a change as radical as from east to west can be accomplished in even a single moment with a single action. Of course, the attitudinal change must be sincere, thorough and permeating every fiber of one's being.

"From the trash heaps He lifts the destitute, to seat them with nobles, with the nobles of His people." From the spiritual trash heaps to spiritual nobility. For this we say, "Halleluyah."

Don't Wait for a Brick

אָהַבְתִּי כִּי יִשְׁמַע ה׳, אֶת קוֹלִי תַּחֲנוּנָי. כִּי הִטָּה אָזְנוֹ לִי, וּבְיָמַי אֶקְרָא. אֲפָפוּנִי חֶבְלֵי מָוֶת, וּמְצָרֵי שְׁאוֹל מְצָאוּנִי, צָרָה וְיָגוֹן אֶמְצָא. וּבְשֵׁם ה׳ אֶקְרָא, אָנָּה ה׳ מַלְּטָה נַפְשִׁי. חַנּוּן ה׳ וְצַדִּיק, וֵאלֹקֵינוּ מְרַחֵם. שֹׁמֵר פְּתָאִים ה׳, דַּלּוֹתִי וְלִי יְהוֹשִׁיעַ. שׁוּבִי נַפְשִׁי לִמְנוּחָיְכִי, כִּי ה׳ גָּמַל עָלָיְכִי. כִּי חִלַּצְתָּ נַפְשִׁי מִמָּוֶת, אֶת עֵינִי מִן דִּמְעָה, אֶת רַגְלִי מִדֶּחִי. אֶתְהַלֵּךְ לִפְנֵי ה׳, בְּאַרְצוֹת הַחַיִּים. הֶאֱמַנְתִּי כִּי אֲדַבֵּר, אֲנִי עָנִיתִי מְאֹד. אֲנִי אָמַרְתִּי בְחָפְזִי, כָּל הָאָדָם כֹּזֵב.

I love [Him], for Hashem hears my voice, my supplications. As He has inclined His ear to me, so in my days shall I call. The pains of death encircled me, the confines of the grave have found me; trouble and sorrow I would find. Then I would invoke the Name of Hashem: "Please Hashem, save my soul." Gracious is Hashem and righteous, our God is merciful. Hashem protects the simple; I was brought low, but He saved me. Return, my soul, to your rest; for Hashem has been kind to you. For You have delivered my soul from death, my eyes from tears, my feet from stumbling. I shall walk before Hashem in the lands of the living. I have kept faith although I say, "I suffer exceedingly." I said in my haste, "All mankind is deceitful."

King David is describing an altogether too common phenomenon: praying to God only at times of distress. While the synagogue is certainly a place where one can find solace at times of distress, this is not the only time it should be visited.

In my work with people recovering from alcoholism, it is characteristic that an alcoholic does not come for help until some crisis forces him to do so. In the addiction field this is known as "hitting rock bottom." Unfortunately, much damage can be accrued while on the way to rock bottom.

Of course, we provide help when a person asks for it, but it would be so much better if one would not wait for a crisis. And God will certainly listen to prayers when one is in anguish, but it would be so much better if one developed a relationship with God before trouble arises.

> *There is a story about a man who was driving his new automobile, when it was suddenly hit by a rock thrown by a child. The man pulled his car over to the curb and was about to let loose his fury when the child said, "Please, mister, don't hit me. My brother fell off his wheelchair and I can't lift him up. I tried to flag down some cars, but nobody stopped to help me. I'm sorry I hit your car, but it was the only thing I could do to get help."*
>
> *The man lifted the boy onto the wheelchair. He never repaired the dent in the car. He wanted it to serve as a reminder to be alert to people's needs without waiting to get hit by a brick.*

This principle has wide applications. Not only should we always be alert to help others without waiting for a traumatic event, but we should also pray without being aroused to do so by a crisis.

In many areas of life, this principle can serve as a guide: Don't wait to get hit by a brick.

Our Help Comes From God

אָנָּא ה׳ הוֹשִׁיעָה נָּא. אָנָּא ה׳ הוֹשִׁיעָה נָּא. אָנָּא ה׳ הַצְלִיחָה נָא. אָנָּא ה׳ הַצְלִיחָה נָא.

Please, Hashem, save now! Please, Hashem, save now! Please, Hashem, bring success now! Please, Hashem, bring success now!

The Talmud says, "A person should not depend on miracles" (*Pesachim* 64b). A person may not place himself in a dangerous situation and expect that God will save him. Similarly, a person is required to do something to earn a livelihood. "God will bless you in all your handiwork that you may undertake" (*Deuteronomy* 14:29). But while we act rationally and responsibly, we should know that it is the providence of God and His blessing that protects and sustains us.

The theme of trust and dependence upon God is fully expressed in this psalm. David points out that reliance on humans is unwise. Whatever one does, one must pray for Divine help and know that his successes are due to God's blessing. David knows that his past triumphs are not an indication of his own might and provide no assurance of victory in the future. After expressing his profound gratitude for all that God has done for him, David exclaims, "Please, God, save now! Please, God, bring success now!" (*Psalms* 118:25).

A man came to the tzaddik R' Mendel of Kotzk, and told him of his plight. He had sustained a severe economic loss and could not even borrow any money. He needed a respectable sum to try and reestablish himself in business. R' Mendel gave him a letter addressed to his chassid, R' Moshe Chaim, who was very wealthy, in which he asked R' Moshe Chaim to help this man.

Wearily the man made his way to the town where R' Moshe Chaim lived. The latter received him graciously, and after reading the Rebbe's letter, took out a small bill from his purse and gave it to him.

The man felt crushed. This paltry donation hardly covered the cost of his trip. He was expecting a significant sum. But R' Moshe Chaim shrugged. "That is all I can give you," he said." Brokenhearted, the man left.

He was just a short distance away when he heard his name called. R' Moshe Chaim was running after him. Overtaking him, R' Moshe Chaim handed him a bundle of money.

"I don't understand," the man said. "If you were going to give me the money, why did you not give it to me in your home? Why did you put me through this agony?"

R' Moshe Chaim said, "It was evident to me that you had put all your trust in me. After all, the Rebbe had given you a letter of recommendation, and you were certain that I would help you. King David warns us against relying on humans. When I disappointed you, you realized that your help could come only from God. Now that you know that, I am pleased to help you."

It is easy to be deluded. We flip a switch and the light goes on. It was our action that made the light go on. We invest in a stock and it increases in value. It was our sharp investment acuity that enriched us, right? If we will only open our eyes, we will see that neither our own efforts nor our dependence on other people can guarantee success. "It is the blessing of God that enriches" (*Proverbs* 10:22).

ועל הנסים ועל הפרקן ועל הגבורות ועל התשועות ועל המלחמות שעשית לאבותינו בימים ההם בזמן הזה:
לחנוכה
בימי מתתיהו בן יוחנן כהן גדול חשמונאי
ולפורים
בימי מרדכי ואסתר בשושן הבירה כשעמד עליהם המן הרשע בקש להשמיד

Chanukah

Chanukah: A Spiritual Celebration

הַנֵּרוֹת הַלָּלוּ אֲנַחְנוּ מַדְלִיקִין עַל הַנִּסִּים וְעַל הַנִּפְלָאוֹת, וְעַל הַתְּשׁוּעוֹת וְעַל הַמִּלְחָמוֹת, שֶׁעָשִׂיתָ לַאֲבוֹתֵינוּ בַּיָּמִים הָהֵם בַּזְּמַן הַזֶּה, עַל יְדֵי כֹּהֲנֶיךָ הַקְּדוֹשִׁים. וְכָל שְׁמוֹנַת יְמֵי חֲנֻכָּה, הַנֵּרוֹת הַלָּלוּ קֹדֶשׁ הֵם. וְאֵין לָנוּ רְשׁוּת לְהִשְׁתַּמֵּשׁ בָּהֶם, אֶלָּא לִרְאוֹתָם בִּלְבָד, כְּדֵי לְהוֹדוֹת וּלְהַלֵּל לְשִׁמְךָ הַגָּדוֹל עַל נִסֶּיךָ וְעַל נִפְלְאוֹתֶיךָ וְעַל יְשׁוּעָתֶךָ.

These lights we kindle upon the miracles, the wonders, the salvations, and the battles which you performed for our forefathers in those days at this season, through Your holy priests. During all eight days of Chanukah these lights are sacred, and we are not permitted to make ordinary use of them, but to look at them in order to express thanks and praise to Your great Name for Your miracles, Your wonders and Your salvations.

Most nations commemorate great military victories with parades, fireworks and patriotic speeches. Chanukah does indeed commemorate a heroic military triumph of a handful of militiamen over the mighty Greek army. However, the emphasis of Chanukah is not on the military victory, but on the miracle of the Menorah, where a vial of oil sufficient for one night miraculously burned for eight days. We do not celebrate Chanukah by parades and dramatic fireworks, but by the soft glow of tiny flickering flames.

The miracles of Chanukah and Purim are commemorated differently. Purim is celebrated by feasts and by an exchange of gifts, while Chanukah is celebrated by kindling the lights and reciting psalms of praise (*Hallel*) to God. This is because the salvation of Purim was from the threat of physical destruction. Haman's decree was to annihilate the Jews. We, therefore, have a physical celebration, with feasts and gifts of food. The salvation of Chanukah, however, was from spiritual destruction. The Greeks did not threaten to kill the Jews. Their decree was to abolish observance of the Torah and replace it with a pagan religion. We, therefore, celebrate the miracle of Chanukah in a spiritual way.

"During all eight days of Chanukah these lights are sacred, and we are not permitted to make ordinary use of them, but to look at them in order to express thanks and praise to Your great Name." Most military triumphs are for personal gain, for expansion of the country's boundaries and for booty. The victory of Chanukah was to permit the Jews to restore the service in the Temple in Jerusalem and to allow them to observe all the mitzvos of the Torah. No personal gain was sought, hence we may not use the illumination of the Chanukah candles for personal needs.

Chanukah underscores the mission of Judaism to bring the light of the true God to the world. "(The nations will say:) let us go to the house of Jacob, by the light of God" (*Isaiah* 2:5). "And I will make you as a light for the nations" (ibid. 49:6). This is the charge we were given at Sinai.

The lights of Chanukah are indeed sacred.

There may be an additional message. The Shabbos candles, too, are sacred, but they are to be enjoyed and to be used as a source of illumination for the household. But we may not derive any benefit from the light of the Chanukah candles. Why?

The Syrian Greeks sought to impose Hellenism on Israel. The philosophies of Torah and Hellenism are at opposite poles. Hellenism is hedonistic. It teaches that a person should seek to maximize his pleasures, for this earthly world is the only world, and one should derive as much pleasure as possible during one's lifetime.

Torah teaches us that man was placed in this earthly world to fulfill a mission dictated by God. The ultimate existence is in the Eternal World, but in order to merit being in the Immanent Presence of God in the Eternal World, man must fulfill the mitzvos of the Torah. Man may certainly enjoy the earthly world, but his enjoyment must be within the parameters prescribed by Torah, and he must give praise to God for the pleasures he experiences. In sharp contrast to Hellenism, Torah teaches that pleasure is *not* the goal of life.

To emphasize the Torah principle, the lights of Chanukah, which represent the triumph of Torah over Hellenism, are sacred. In contradistinction to the Shabbos candles, one should *not* derive any benefit from the Chanukah lights. They are to be observed but not used. It is a symbolic expression that the goods of this world are not here primarily for our pleasure. We indeed partake of them, but only because they are a vehicle for achieving a spiritual goal.

Man Must Begin – God Will Complete

וְעַל הַנִּסִּים וְעַל הַפֻּרְקָן וְעַל הַגְּבוּרוֹת וְעַל הַתְּשׁוּעוֹת וְעַל הַמִּלְחָמוֹת שֶׁעָשִׂיתָ לַאֲבוֹתֵינוּ בַּיָּמִים הָהֵם בַּזְּמַן הַזֶּה.

בִּימֵי מַתִּתְיָהוּ בֶּן יוֹחָנָן כֹּהֵן גָּדוֹל חַשְׁמוֹנָאִי וּבָנָיו ... וְאַתָּה בְּרַחֲמֶיךָ הָרַבִּים, עָמַדְתָּ לָהֶם בְּעֵת צָרָתָם, רַבְתָּ אֶת רִיבָם, דַּנְתָּ אֶת דִּינָם, נָקַמְתָּ אֶת נִקְמָתָם. מָסַרְתָּ גִּבּוֹרִים בְּיַד חַלָּשִׁים, וְרַבִּים בְּיַד מְעַטִּים, וּטְמֵאִים בְּיַד טְהוֹרִים...

And for the miracles, and for the salvation, and for the mighty deeds, and for the victories, and for the battles which You performed for our forefathers in those days, at this time.
In the days of Mattisyahu, the son of Yochanan, the High Priest, the Hasmonean, and his sons ... You in Your great mercy stood up for them in the time of their distress. You took up their grievance, judged their claim, and avenged their wrong. You delivered the strong into the hands of the weak, the many into the hands of the few, the impure into the hands of the pure ...

"It is not incumbent upon you to complete the task, but you are not free to withdraw from it" (Ethics of the Fathers 2:21).

This message is contained in the Torah as well: "God will bless you in all that you do" (*Deuteronomy* 14:29). Without the help of God we can do nothing. But we are required to make an effort, and ask for His blessing to bring it to success.

This concept is underscored by the two miracles of Chanukah. The miracles of Passover were indeed great, but they were blatantly the hand of God. The Israelites did nothing to gain their freedom from Egypt. However, the miracles of Chanukah were initiated by us and were brought to completion by God.

The triumph of the Maccabees was indeed miraculous. "You stood up for them in the time of their distress ... You delivered the strong into the hands of the weak, the many into the hands of the few." But it was the few and the weak that initiated the battle with their trust that God would help them.

The miracle of the lights occurred in a similar vein. When only one vial of uncontaminated oil was found and the procurement of pure oil was eight days away, the Maccabees could have thrown up their hands in despair. There seemed to be no point in lighting the Menorah and then having to promptly discontinue the service. But rather than despair, they did the best they could, and the single vial miraculously burned for eight days.

It is also important to note that the oppression of the Syrian Greeks did not threaten our physical survival. They were perfectly willing to allow the Jews to live in peace if only they would renounce their faith in God and accept the paganism of Hellenism. The battle of the Maccabees was for our spiritual survival.

The prayers of Chanukah serve as a reminder that we are never to despair, and that we must struggle to maintain our devotion to God even against overwhelming pressures.

Purim

Unsung Miracles

בָּרוּךְ אַתָּה ה׳ אֱלֹקֵינוּ מֶלֶךְ הָעוֹלָם, אֲשֶׁר קִדְּשָׁנוּ בְּמִצְוֹתָיו, וְצִוָּנוּ עַל מִקְרָא מְגִלָּה.

בָּרוּךְ אַתָּה ה׳ אֱלֹקֵינוּ מֶלֶךְ הָעוֹלָם, שֶׁעָשָׂה נִסִּים לַאֲבוֹתֵינוּ, בַּיָּמִים הָהֵם, בַּזְּמַן הַזֶּה.

בָּרוּךְ אַתָּה ה׳ אֱלֹקֵינוּ מֶלֶךְ הָעוֹלָם, שֶׁהֶחֱיָנוּ, וְקִיְּמָנוּ, וְהִגִּיעָנוּ לַזְּמַן הַזֶּה.

Blessed are You, Hashem, our God, King of the universe, Who has sanctified us with His commandments and has commanded us regarding the reading of the Megillah.

Blessed are You, Hashem, our God, King of the universe, Who has wrought miracles for our forefathers, in those days at this season.

Blessed are You, Hashem, our God, King of the universe, Who has kept us alive, sustained us, and brought us to this season.

The Chassidic literature accords a unique status to Purim. It cites the Midrash that even after the coming of Mashiach, when all other festivals will fade, Purim will continue to be observed. What about Purim gives it so important a status? Were not the many miracles of the Exodus culminating in the dividing of the Reed Sea much greater?

In the thanksgiving (*Modim*) prayer of the *Amidah* we thank God "for Your miracles that are with us each day, and the wonders and kindnesses that are with us in every season – evening, morning and afternoon." We may take it for granted that it is "natural" that we can breathe and see, that tiny seeds produce giant trees, and that a microscopic single cell can absorb nutrients and transform them into a living human being. Because these things occur with regularity, we think of them as "natural" phenomena. Actually, all these are miraculous occurrences. It is just that we fail to recognize them as miracles. That is why we testify in the *Amidah* that we are constantly the beneficiaries of God's wonders, and that they are no less miraculous because they appear to be part of nature. This is a fundamental concept of our faith.

The miracle of Purim was not a supernatural phenomenon. It was the result of a series of events that could easily be considered "natural." A king became intoxicated, and when the queen defied his orders, he had her executed. He then chose a Jewess for a queen, but she concealed her national origin. A virulent anti-Semite rose to the prime-ministership and plotted to annihilate the Jews. A Jew in the royal court, who was the queen's uncle, discovered a conspiracy to assassinate the king, and reported it to the queen. He was accorded a royal tribute, much to the chagrin of the prime minister. The queen then revealed her Jewish identity, and that she and her uncle, who had saved the king's life, were under the threat of execution by the evil prime minister. The king had the prime minister put to death, and appointed the queen's uncle to his position. The Jews were then given the right to eliminate their enemies.

This does not seem to differ much from the many accounts of palace politics and intrigue. The fact is, however, that each event was engineered by Divine intervention. This served as an example that what might appear to us as "natural" is in fact a Divine miracle. Proper understanding of Purim teaches us to appreciate every "natural" phenomenon as an act of God.

Why were the miracles in the days of yore dramatically supernatural, whereas today's miracles are in disguise as natural events? The proprietor of an inn where he was lodging, whose belief in God seemed to be a bit fragile, posed this question to the Chafetz Chaim. The Chafetz Chaim said he would answer his question a bit later.

Later in the day, the innkeeper's young daughter returned home from school overjoyed. She had won first prize in the course on poetry, and she proudly displayed the certificate that she had received.

The Chafetz Chaim asked the child to recite her poetry, but the child refused. He then asked the innkeeper to tell the child to say her poem. Again the child refused and said to her father, "I have this certificate that attests to my proficiency in poetry. I don't have to prove it to everyone. That's what the certificate is for."

The Chafetz Chaim said to the innkeeper, "There you have the answer to your question. In ancient times, people did not have a belief in the true God. As a result of the many miracles, they came to realize that God is Master of the world. At Sinai, God gave us a 'certificate,' the Torah. He no longer has to prove to everyone that He is Master of the world. That is what the certificate is for."

This story explains the Talmudic statement that although Israel accepted the Torah at Sinai, they again accepted it after the miracle of Purim (*Shabbos* 88a). The acceptance at Sinai was preceded and accompanied by supernatural miracles. It was possible that subsequent generations who did not witness these miracles might have questioned their faith in God, just as the innkeeper did. After the miracle of Purim, they understood that even natural events are miracles, and that the Torah serves as the certificate of God's sovereignty.

Another Missing Berachah - Another Reprimand

שִׂמְחָה וּמִשְׁתֶּה וְיוֹם טוֹב וּמִשְׁלוֹחַ מָנוֹת אִישׁ לְרֵעֵהוּ.

An occasion of gladness, feasting and festival, and for sending delicacies to one another.

Earlier we noted the absence of what appears to be an important *berachah*. Upon arising in the morning, we thank God for all the faculties he has given us. However, we do not thank Him for giving us the ability to speak. The explanation offered is that the faculty of speech is so widely abused by *lashon hara* and speaking falsehood, that it is inappropriate to express gratitude for something which in some respect has unfortunately turned out to be so detrimental. The absence of a *berachah* for the unique human feature of speech is a pungent rebuke. We are responsible for the absence of this *berachah*.

A similar reprimand is effected by the prominent absence of a *berachah* on Purim. One of the important mitzvos on Purim is *mishloach manos*, sending a gift to another person. Like every other mitzvah, this mitzvah deserves a *berachah*. We recite a *berachah* for the reading of the *Megillah*. Why not for *mishloach manos*?

One of the commentaries provides an answer based on a precise translation of the verse in the *Megillah*, that Purim should be celebrated as "an occasion of gladness, feasting and festival, and for sending delicacies to one another" (*Esther* 9:19). He points out that the Hebrew words אִישׁ לְרֵעֵהוּ are generally translated as a figure of speech, "to one another." The literal meaning is "a person to *one's friend.*"

A person may send a gift of delicacies to another person whom he does not really like at all and whom he does not consider to be a true friend. The gift may be sent for ulterior motives. For example, he may be seeking a favor from the other person and wishes to ingratiate himself. He may feel obligated to send a gift for any one of several reasons, but in his heart he may wish that he were free of this obligation. If he were to recite a *berachah* for *mishloach manos* sent to anyone but a true friend, it would not be fulfilling the mitzvah appropriately. The *berachah* might be considered a *berachah levatalah* (pronouncing God's Name in vain). To avoid this, the *berachah is* omitted.

Is this not a sharp reprimand? How often do we dissimulate and lead someone to think that we are a devoted friend, when the truth is that we care little about him? Even if we are not Machiavellian, we may nevertheless be less than honest in our interpersonal relationships.

If we were genuine and thoroughly honest, we would have had the privilege of reciting a *berachah* for *mishloach manos.* The absence of this *berachah* should spur us to greater honesty.

כי אין תדפנו רוח כן הרשעים שעד קליפתם מן העולם
תדפנו רוח הטומאה אשר ברחו בהעוותם בתוך כף הק

כי לא דבר רק הוא מגולו דעת ולומר כי הנה
ים יחוסר בסור מרע ולמעלה הימנו אשר יחוסר

א אשרי

האיש אשר לא הלך בעצת רשעים ובדרך חטאים לא עמד ובמושב לצים לא ישב: ב כי אם בתורת ידוד חפצו ובתורתו יהגה יומם ולילה: ג והיה כעץ שתול על פלגי מים אשר פריו יתן בעתו ועלהו לא יבול וכל אשר יעשה יצליח: ד לא כן הרשעים כי אם כמוץ אשר תדפנו רוח: ה על כן לא יקמו רשעים במשפט וחטאים בעדת צדיקים: ו כי יודע ידוד דרך צדיקים ודרך רשעים תאבד:

ב א **למה** רגשו גוים ולאמים יהגו ריק: ב יתיצבו מלכי ארץ ורוזנים נוסדו יחד על ידוד ועל משיחו: ג ננתקה את מוסרותימו ונשליכה ממנו עבתימו: ד יושב

בשמים

תאמר הלא טוב
הנה לצדיקים בלבד
הרשעים יקומו לזכ
אומרים כי הגלחה
וגם כמה צדיקים
ישנו ויהיו רשעים ע
רשעים לא תחוש כי
ומוצלחים לא יקומו
בדין ולא ינצלו גם
צדיקים שלא ישנו
צדיקים יולאו מכ
לעשות רשעים (ו
על כן כו' הוא על כ
ומשפיע ה' דרך צדי
אלהים והוא כי לא
אותו ואין רשע בי
להסתר באיזה זמן וי
באופן לא יעברנו עו
מלשוב וגם הצדיקים
רשעים ברחותם ה
כי הלא ודרך רשעים
הוא יתברך מרחי
באופן שתאבד מהם
לבלתי יחטאו : (ד
הנה אמרתי שלא יוד
בעה"ז כל הצדיקים ר
בתורה כאומרי כי אם
הוא אשר כל אשר יע
לא כל יתר צדיקים
רשעים שמגיע אליהם
והסוף הוא הראוי כי
ומיטיב ה' לטובים

הרשעים אל' תחוש כי לא כן הרשעים בטובתם כטובת
חפצו שאמרתי וכל אשר יעשה יצליח כי אם כמוץ כמפור
ועל ייסורי הצדיקים ג"כ אל תתמה כי על כן שמתייסרים
הצדיקים לעתיד רשעים נדינים · והרשעים במשפט

הוא דבור וגם הוא מעשה היותו יגע בה יומם
כי והיה כעץ שתול כו' והתכ' הכתוב כי הנה
את אליו יתברך והיא בחינת סודה ויש
פשטה והנה השיג החדש הסוד לא כל אדם

Tehillim

The Potent Prayers

Except for the Five Books of Moses, no other book of the Scriptures has been as widely accepted, studied and read as the Book of Psalms. This book was authored primarily by King David, with just a few chapters contributed by Moses, the children of Korah, Asaph, Heman and Ethan the Ezrahite. Some of its chapters have become an integral part of the *siddur* and are recited daily.

One can find verses that express one's needs in the psalms. There are expressions of gratitude, cries of anguish, statements of hope and trust and prayers for salvation. No human emotion is overlooked in the psalms.

The effectiveness of praying the psalms sincerely is legendary. The psalms are variously divided into seven parts, one for each day of the week. There is also a division for each day of the month. Among some chassidim it is customary to recite the entire *Tehillim* on the Shabbos before the new month. Other chassidim do so every Shabbos morning.

Some psalms are designated as prayers for the sick. Others are recited as prayers at the grave site of a loved one. Reading the psalms can provide hope and solace, courage and strength.

There is a charming story that reflects feelings about the psalms.

A man who was childless after many years of marriage visited the Steipler Gaon for a berachah. When a son was born to him, he spread the word that the Steipler Gaon had performed a miracle, because doctors had given him no hope of having a child.

When the dean of the yeshivah of Ponevezh, the sage, R' Eliezer Shach, heard of this, he said to the Steipler Gaon, "I did not know that you have become a miracle worker."

The Steipler Gaon responded, "Heaven forbid! Let me tell you what happened.

"This man came to me, bitterly crying that doctors have given him no hope of having a child. I gave him a berachah that God should answer his prayers, and reassured him that God can override doctors' opinions.

"The man was not satisfied with a berachah. 'You must promise me that I will have a child,' he said. 'You must guarantee it.'

" 'How can you ask that of me?' I said. 'Do you think I have magical powers? I can give you my blessing, and that is all.'

"But this man would not take no for an answer. He sat there crying and said that he would not leave until I promised him a child. I tried to concentrate on studying the gemara, but this man kept nagging. In order to get rid of him so that I could continue my learning, I blurted out, 'All right! You will have a child. Now please leave!'

"After the man left," the Steipler Gaon continued, "it occurred to me — What have I done? How could I have said such a thing? This man is going to feel certain that my promise will be fulfilled. But when nothing happens, he will be disillusioned. It is my ill fortune that people think I am some kind of a tzaddik. What can I do if they are so deluded? If this man does not have a child, he may lose faith, and it will have been my fault. I was afraid I would be the cause of a chillul Hashem (desecrating the Divine Name).

"I was in great anguish and did not know what to do. So I took the Tehillim and prayed that God should bless this man with a child so that I should not be the cause, God forbid, of a chillul Hashem."

Upon hearing the Steipler Gaon's defense, R' Shach said, "Oh, so you prayed by saying Tehillim. Well, then that is no miracle. Tehillim is an effective prayer."

I think this story is one of the most beautiful I have ever heard, especially since I was privileged to know the Steipler Gaon. He was the Torah authority and *tzaddik* of our generation, yet his humility was genuine. He was in true anguish that people though of him as a *tzaddik*. One time he wrote to me, "Please do not address me with lavish titles that do not befit me at all. Our Sages taught, 'One who praises another, attributing to him that which is untrue, causes that person's embarrassment' (*Zohar Vayechi* 232b). I am a victim of people's delusions about me."

R' Shach did not consider the potency of the Steipler Gaon's prayers to be a miracle. He was right. If I were to hit a home run, it would be the greatest miracle of all times. If a "home-run king" hits a home run, it is just a natural act. The Steipler Gaon's *Tehillim* resulting in the man's wish for a child being fulfilled was not really a miracle!

We cannot compare ourselves to the great *tzaddikim*, but we must not dismiss the potency of praying the *Tehillim*. We may not understand in what way our prayers are effective. We may be disappointed that our wishes may not have been fulfilled the way we had hoped. But let the *Tehillim* be your companion. Every chapter is an appropriate prayer for all occasions.

Let us look at some of the verses in *Tehillim*, and learn how we can use them to express our feelings.

A Spiritual Analgesic

תְּהִלִּים כב

Psalm 22

לַמְנַצֵּחַ עַל אַיֶּלֶת הַשַּׁחַר, מִזְמוֹר לְדָוִד. קֵלִי קֵלִי לָמָה עֲזַבְתָּנִי, רָחוֹק מִישׁוּעָתִי דִּבְרֵי שַׁאֲגָתִי. אֱלֹקַי, אֶקְרָא יוֹמָם וְלֹא תַעֲנֶה, וְלַיְלָה וְלֹא דוּמִיָּה לִי. וְאַתָּה קָדוֹשׁ, יוֹשֵׁב תְּהִלּוֹת יִשְׂרָאֵל. בְּךָ בָּטְחוּ אֲבֹתֵינוּ, בָּטְחוּ וַתְּפַלְּטֵמוֹ. אֵלֶיךָ זָעֲקוּ וְנִמְלָטוּ, בְּךָ בָטְחוּ וְלֹא בוֹשׁוּ. וְאָנֹכִי תוֹלַעַת וְלֹא אִישׁ, חֶרְפַּת אָדָם וּבְזוּי עָם. כָּל רֹאַי יַלְעִגוּ לִי; יַפְטִירוּ בְשָׂפָה, יָנִיעוּ רֹאשׁ. גֹּל אֶל ה׳ יְפַלְּטֵהוּ, יַצִּילֵהוּ כִּי חָפֵץ בּוֹ. כִּי אַתָּה גֹחִי מִבָּטֶן, מַבְטִיחִי עַל שְׁדֵי אִמִּי. עָלֶיךָ הָשְׁלַכְתִּי מֵרָחֶם, מִבֶּטֶן אִמִּי קֵלִי אָתָּה. אַל תִּרְחַק מִמֶּנִּי כִּי צָרָה קְרוֹבָה, כִּי אֵין עוֹזֵר. סְבָבוּנִי פָּרִים רַבִּים, אַבִּירֵי בָשָׁן כִּתְּרוּנִי. פָּצוּ עָלַי פִּיהֶם, אַרְיֵה טֹרֵף וְשֹׁאֵג. כַּמַּיִם נִשְׁפַּכְתִּי, וְהִתְפָּרְדוּ כָּל עַצְמוֹתָי; הָיָה לִבִּי כַּדּוֹנָג, נָמֵס בְּתוֹךְ מֵעָי. יָבֵשׁ כַּחֶרֶשׂ כֹּחִי, וּלְשׁוֹנִי מֻדְבָּק מַלְקוֹחָי; וְלַעֲפַר מָוֶת תִּשְׁפְּתֵנִי. כִּי סְבָבוּנִי כְּלָבִים; עֲדַת מְרֵעִים הִקִּיפוּנִי, כָּאֲרִי יָדַי וְרַגְלָי. אֲסַפֵּר כָּל עַצְמוֹתָי, הֵמָּה יַבִּיטוּ יִרְאוּ בִי. יְחַלְּקוּ בְגָדַי לָהֶם, וְעַל לְבוּשִׁי יַפִּילוּ גוֹרָל. וְאַתָּה ה׳ אַל תִּרְחָק, אֱיָלוּתִי לְעֶזְרָתִי חוּשָׁה. הַצִּילָה מֵחֶרֶב נַפְשִׁי, מִיַּד כֶּלֶב יְחִידָתִי. הוֹשִׁיעֵנִי מִפִּי אַרְיֵה, וּמִקַּרְנֵי רֵמִים עֲנִיתָנִי. אֲסַפְּרָה שִׁמְךָ לְאֶחָי, בְּתוֹךְ קָהָל אֲהַלְלֶךָּ. יִרְאֵי ה׳ הַלְלוּהוּ, כָּל זֶרַע יַעֲקֹב כַּבְּדוּהוּ, וְגוּרוּ מִמֶּנּוּ כָּל זֶרַע יִשְׂרָאֵל. כִּי לֹא בָזָה וְלֹא שִׁקַּץ עֱנוּת עָנִי, וְלֹא הִסְתִּיר פָּנָיו מִמֶּנּוּ; וּבְשַׁוְּעוֹ אֵלָיו שָׁמֵעַ. מֵאִתְּךָ תְהִלָּתִי בְּקָהָל רָב, נְדָרַי אֲשַׁלֵּם נֶגֶד יְרֵאָיו. יֹאכְלוּ עֲנָוִים וְיִשְׂבָּעוּ, יְהַלְלוּ ה׳ דֹּרְשָׁיו; יְחִי לְבַבְכֶם לָעַד. יִזְכְּרוּ וְיָשֻׁבוּ אֶל ה׳ כָּל אַפְסֵי אָרֶץ, וְיִשְׁתַּחֲווּ לְפָנֶיךָ כָּל מִשְׁפְּחוֹת גּוֹיִם. כִּי לַה׳ הַמְּלוּכָה, וּמֹשֵׁל בַּגּוֹיִם. אָכְלוּ וַיִּשְׁתַּחֲווּ כָּל דִּשְׁנֵי אֶרֶץ, לְפָנָיו יִכְרְעוּ כָּל יוֹרְדֵי עָפָר, וְנַפְשׁוֹ לֹא חִיָּה. זֶרַע יַעַבְדֶנּוּ, יְסֻפַּר לַה׳ לַדּוֹר. יָבֹאוּ וְיַגִּידוּ צִדְקָתוֹ, לְעַם נוֹלָד כִּי עָשָׂה.

For the Conductor, on the Ayeles HaShachar, a psalm by David. My God, my God, why have You forsaken me; why so far from saving me, from the words of my roar? O my God! I call out by day — and You answer not; and by night — but there is no respite for me. Yet You are the Holy One, enthroned upon the praises of Israel! In You our fathers trusted, they trusted and You delivered them. To You they cried out and they were rescued, in You they trusted and they were not shamed. But I am a worm and not a man, scorn of humanity, despised of nations. All who see me, deride me; they open wide with their lips, they wag their heads. One who casts [his burden] upon Hashem — He will deliver him! He will save him, for He desires him! For You are the One who drew me forth from the womb, and made me secure on my mother's breasts. You have provided for me from my birth, from my mother's womb You have been my God. Be not aloof from me for distress is near, for there is none to help. Many bulls surround me, Bashan's mighty ones encircle me. They open their mouths against me like a tearing, roaring lion. I am poured out like water, and all my bones became disjointed; my heart is like wax, melted within my innards. My strength is dried up like baked clay, and my tongue cleaves to my palate; in the dust of death You set me down. For dogs have surrounded me; a pack of evildoers has enclosed me, like a lion's prey are my hands and my feet. I can count all my bones — they look on and gloat over me. They divide my clothes among themselves, and cast lots for my clothing. But You, Hashem, be not far from me. O my Strength, hasten to my assistance! Rescue my soul from the sword, my only one from the grip of the dog. Save me from the lion's mouth as You have answered me from the horns of the reimim. I will proclaim Your Name to my brethren; in the midst of the congregation I will praise You. You who fear Hashem, praise Him! All of you, the seed of Jacob, glorify Him! Be in awe of Him, all you seed of Israel. For He has neither despised nor loathed the supplication of the poor, nor has He concealed His face from him; but when he cried to Him, He heard. From You is my praise in the great congregation; I will fulfill my vows before those who fear Him. The humble will eat and be satisfied, those who seek Hashem will praise Him — your hearts will live forever. All the ends of the earth will remember and turn back to Hashem; all the families of nations will bow before You. For the kingship belongs to Hashem, and He rules the nations. All the fat of the land will eat and bow down, all who descend to the dust will kneel before Him, but He will not revive his soul. About the seed of those who have always served Him, it will be told of the

Lord to the latter generation. They will come and relate His righteousness, to the newborn nation that which He has done.

This psalm may provide comfort and encouragement in moments of great distress and anguish, at times when a person may feel that God has abandoned him and he cries out, "My God, My God, why have You forsaken me" (ibid. v. 2)? Some commentaries say that David composed this psalm during one of his many moments of anguish, perhaps when he was being relentlessly pursued by King Saul who was determined to kill him. Others say that this was composed prophetically for Israel when it would suffer the destruction of Jerusalem and be driven into exile. It would appear that this psalm is saying that it is not heresy for one to complain that God has abandoned him.

While we cannot fathom the Divine wisdom and understand why God permits such great suffering, our faith should be sufficiently secure that we should know that God never abandons us. I often point out the example of a mother who has the doctor administer a painful injection to protect her child from dreaded diseases. She does this because of her love of her child. God is a loving parent and our trust in Him should be such that we know that God never abandons us, even at times when, like the child, we feel that He is allowing us to be hurt.

It is important to note that even in the moments of great anguish during which David composed this psalm, his trust in God never faltered. David was certain that ultimately God will save him. After all the expressions of fear and anguish, David says, "I will proclaim Your Name to my brethren; in the midst of the congregation I will praise You [with songs proclaiming Your mighty acts]" (ibid. v. 23). Amidst his very suffering, David is certain of God's salvation.

R' Samson R. Hirsch has a penetrating insight into this psalm. Citing the interpretation that *ayeles hashachar* refers to the morning star, R' Hirsch translates the opening verse "upon the strengthening of day's dawning." It is proverbial that it is darkest just before dawn, yet one knows that this darkness will soon be displaced by the light of dawn, which will increase in intensity. Thus, the theme of Divine salvation which begins in verse 23 is foreshadowed in the opening verse.

R' Hirsch continues his interpretation by noting that the word *lamah* does not mean "why," but rather *le'mah,* "for what reason." David is not questioning, "Why have you forsaken me" in the sense of a complaint. Rather, he knows that when God allows a person to experience suffering, it is for a valid reason, something that is to the person's ultimate advantage. Just as it is easier to tolerate a painful surgical procedure when one understands what it will accomplish, so it is easier to tolerate suffering if one could know what its purpose is. Seen in this way, the psalm is not one of complaint of abandonment, but rather one of trust in God and a desire to understand.

Yet, the tone of the psalm does sound like a complaint of abandonment. "In You our fathers trusted, they trusted and You delivered them. To You they cried out and they were rescued, in You they trusted and they were not shamed" (ibid. vv. 4-6). That sounds very much like, "And why are You not helping me the way You helped them?" Is it because "I am a worm," not deserving of Your help? (ibid. v. 7). But immediately the Psalmist recognizes that like his forefathers, he, too, trusts in God. "You have provided for me from my birth" (ibid v. 11).

Although the theme of the psalm, as pointed out, is one of hope rather than despair, the tone serves a purpose. It conveys the idea that it is not a sin to complain. The Talmud says that a person is not held culpable for what he says when he is distressed (*Bava Basra* 16b). Furthermore, it should be obvious that a statement, "You helped my ancestors. Why are You not helping me?" is an affirmation that one believes in God and that God is all-powerful. Such an affirmation of faith, even in the form of a complaint, can hardly be considered a sin. Indeed, the prophet said: "The righteous person shall live through his faith" (*Habakkuk* 2:4). One should address God with great reverence, but complaining is not disrespectful. R' Levi Yitzchok of Berditchev never complained about any personal distress, but he often protested as to why God allowed His people to suffer. R' Levi Yitzchok said, "You can be for God, or even against God. You just cannot be without God."

Whichever way one conceptualizes this psalm, it is a soothing balm at times of distress.

The Psalm of Serenity

תהלים כג

Psalm 23

מִזְמוֹר לְדָוִד, ה׳ רֹעִי, לֹא אֶחְסָר. בִּנְאוֹת דֶּשֶׁא יַרְבִּיצֵנִי, עַל מֵי מְנֻחוֹת יְנַהֲלֵנִי. נַפְשִׁי יְשׁוֹבֵב, יַנְחֵנִי בְמַעְגְּלֵי צֶדֶק לְמַעַן שְׁמוֹ. גַּם כִּי אֵלֵךְ בְּגֵיא צַלְמָוֶת, לֹא אִירָא רָע כִּי אַתָּה עִמָּדִי; שִׁבְטְךָ וּמִשְׁעַנְתֶּךָ הֵמָּה יְנַחֲמֻנִי. תַּעֲרֹךְ לְפָנַי שֻׁלְחָן נֶגֶד צֹרְרָי; דִּשַּׁנְתָּ בַשֶּׁמֶן רֹאשִׁי, כּוֹסִי רְוָיָה. אַךְ טוֹב וָחֶסֶד יִרְדְּפוּנִי כָּל יְמֵי חַיָּי, וְשַׁבְתִּי בְּבֵית ה׳ לְאֹרֶךְ יָמִים.

A psalm by David. Hashem is my shepherd, I shall not lack. In lush meadows He lays me down, beside tranquil waters He leads me. He restores my soul. He leads me on paths of justice for His Name's sake. Though I walk in the valley overshadowed by death, I will fear no evil, for You are with me. Your rod and Your staff, they comfort me. You prepare a table before me in view of my tormentors. You anointed my head with oil, my cup overflows. May only goodness and kindness pursue me all the days of my life, and I shall dwell in the House of Hashem for long days.

Ideally, parents should not have a favorite child. They should love all their children equally. And ideally, one should not have a favorite portion of Torah. But the fact is that some parents do have a favorite child, and some people do have a favorite portion of Torah. Psalm 23 has endeared itself to many people. If there is a psalm which many people know by heart, it is Psalm 23.

David, the shepherd, had experienced a relationship with his flock of sheep. He was devoted to them, he provided them with grass and water and he sacrificed himself to protect them from predators. "And David said to Saul, 'Your servant shepherded his father's sheep, and a lion and a bear carried off a sheep from the flock. I went after him and smote him, and saved it from his mouth' " (*I Samuel* 17:34-35). He felt the flock's trust in him. They followed him wherever he led them. It was this feeling that David transferred to the relationship between God and man, and he enriched our lives with this psalm.

"Because God as my shepherd cares for all my needs, I lack for nothing. I do not miss what I do not have. If I really needed something, God would have provided it for me."

R' Samson R. Hirsch points out that the word יְשׁוֹבֵב denotes "returning repeatedly to a former state or condition." Therefore, "Again and again he restores my soul." Life is not one smooth journey. There are obstacles and rough spots along the way. There are periods of distress and agitation. But each time, God restores my soul and leads me beside the peaceful waters. I do not have constant tranquility, but with the knowledge that God is my shepherd, I can have serenity even when I am in distress. "Though I walk in the valley overshadowed by death, I will fear no evil, for You are with me." David could feel the security and trust his flock had in him. If there can be such trust in a mortal, how much more so should one have trust in Omnipotent God.

"You anointed my head with oil" undoubtedly refers to the prophet Samuel anointing him as the future king of Israel (*I Samuel* 16:13). But this led to David's greatest period of anguish, as he was relentlessly hunted by Saul. Nevertheless, even during this precarious period when his life was in danger, David was content. "My cup overflows."

David's faith and trust in God is absolute. He is essentially saying, "Whatever life may bring me, I know that everything that happens to me is goodness and kindness."

No wonder this psalm has become a favorite.

The Chafetz Chaim was lodging at an inn, and a man asked the innkeeper if he could have a few moments with the sage. The Chaftez Chaim was dining at the time, and the man sat patiently at the table.

It was the Chafetz Chaim's practice to recite Psalm 23 at each meal. He said the psalm with his characteristic kavannah, pausing a bit toward the end. Then the Chafetz Chaim said to the man, "As I was saying this kapitel (chapter), it occurred to me that the verse 'May only goodness and kindness pursue me all the days of my life' is a bit strange. 'Pursuit' generally refers to running after someone to harm him, and one flees from a pursuer. But why would one flee from goodness and kindness? How could goodness and kindness be pursuers?

"I paused to reflect on this. It occurred to me that sometimes a person does chesed – he gives tzedakah, makes free loans, visits the sick, attends to community needs – and he may begin thinking that doing chesed is quite expensive. He could save some of the money he gives away and could spend the time he gives to community causes to promote his own affairs. He may see goodness and kindness as being detrimental to him, as pursuers. To this person David says, 'Even if you should think that goodness and kindness are pursuers, don't discontinue doing them. To the contrary, pray that God should enable you to continue doing chesed and to be "pursued" by these all your life.' "

Abruptly the man rose and left. The innkeeper said to him, "I thought you wished to discuss something with the Chafetz Chaim. You haven't said a word to him."

The man responded, "I don't need to. He answered my question without my asking it.

"Several years ago," the man continued, "I established a free-loan fund for people in need. I sit on the committee which dispenses the money from this fund. It now takes up so much of my time that my wife feels I am neglecting my business, and that I should give over management of the fund to someone else. This did not appeal to me, and we agreed to speak to the Chafetz Chaim and abide by his opinion.

"The Chafetz Chaim said that even if goodness and kindness appear to be pursuers, one should nevertheless continue doing them. I already have the answer to my question."

I recall my father raising the question of the apparently inappropriate use of the phrase "being pursued by goodness and kindness." He quoted an explanation by one of the Torah commentaries, who gave the following parable.

A king was once conducting a public audience, and a disgruntled citizen in the crowd threw a rock at him. The guards quickly subdued the offender and imprisoned him. The court sentenced him to a long prison term. However, the king not only pardoned the man, but also ordered that he be given a job at the palace with good pay.

The man could not grasp this. "Why would the king reward me when I tried to harm him?" When he received his pay, he thought, "How could I have been so vile as to throw a rock at a king who is so benevolent?" His self-recriminations tormented him. The king then had him promoted, and his torment increased. Each time the king rewarded him in some way, he became increasingly anguished.

My father said, "This demonstrates that kindness can be a more severe punishment than a regular penalty. This is what David said. 'I know that I have sinned and deserve to be punished. But You can punish me with goodness and kindness. Let them be the method of chastisement You utilize. Let goodness and kindness be my pursuers.' "

I must now share a personal story with you.

When I was a medical intern, I was called to administer an intravenous injection of antibiotics to a patient. This was a person who had undergone orthopedic surgery, and in the midst of the operation his heart had stopped beating. The surgeon quickly opened the man's chest and began contracting the heart manually. The heartbeat soon returned to normal and the surgery was completed.

The nurse told me that the patient was very depressed and it was difficult to get him to comply with the doctor's instructions. After I administered the medication the patient said, "Are you a rabbi?" I said that I was.

"I'm not Jewish," the patient said, "but can you say a prayer with me?"

"Of course," I said, and began thinking about what prayer might be familiar to him. I said, "Let's say the 23rd psalm."

We began saying the psalm, and when we reached, "Though I walk in the valley overshadowed by death, I will fear no evil, for You are with me," the patient began crying. I stayed with him for a few minutes after we finished the prayer, and I told him I would come by the following day.

When I next visited him, the nurse told me that he had undergone a dramatic change. His mood was upbeat and he was doing the required exercises. As I walked in, he greeted me with a broad smile.

"When I woke up after the surgery and found that my chest was bandaged, I learned what had happened. I began

worrying. What happens if my heart stops again when there is no one around to get it started? I was afraid of dying.

"When we said the prayer, 'Though I walk in the valley overshadowed by death … You are with me,' it struck me that he was talking about me! When my heart had stopped, I was really in the valley overshadowed by death. Afterward I thought: I had been a police officer and then a sergeant for many years. I did my work honestly and treated people fairly. I think I helped people. I lived a decent life and I think that when I die, God will be with me.

"I'm 67 now. I may have one more year or ten more years. Who knows? But I am no longer afraid of dying."

Then he smiled and said, "That prayer was more powerful than the antibiotic!"

The antibiotic was certainly necessary, but what turned this patient around and gave him the will to live was a prayer.

Psalm 23 is recited on various occasions. It is always appropriate.

Denial of Our Mortality

תהלים מט

Psalm 49

לַמְנַצֵּחַ לִבְנֵי קֹרַח מִזְמוֹר. שִׁמְעוּ זֹאת כָּל הָעַמִּים, הַאֲזִינוּ כָּל יֹשְׁבֵי חָלֶד. גַּם בְּנֵי אָדָם, גַּם בְּנֵי אִישׁ; יַחַד עָשִׁיר וְאֶבְיוֹן. פִּי יְדַבֵּר חָכְמוֹת, וְהָגוּת לִבִּי תְבוּנוֹת. אַטֶּה לְמָשָׁל אָזְנִי, אֶפְתַּח בְּכִנּוֹר חִידָתִי. לָמָּה אִירָא בִּימֵי רָע, עֲוֹן עֲקֵבַי יְסוּבֵּנִי. הַבֹּטְחִים עַל חֵילָם, וּבְרֹב עָשְׁרָם יִתְהַלָּלוּ. אָח לֹא פָדֹה יִפְדֶּה אִישׁ, לֹא יִתֵּן לֵאלֹקִים כָּפְרוֹ. וְיֵקַר פִּדְיוֹן נַפְשָׁם, וְחָדַל לְעוֹלָם. וִיחִי עוֹד לָנֶצַח, לֹא יִרְאֶה הַשָּׁחַת. כִּי יִרְאֶה חֲכָמִים יָמוּתוּ, יַחַד כְּסִיל וָבַעַר יֹאבֵדוּ, וְעָזְבוּ לַאֲחֵרִים חֵילָם. קִרְבָּם בָּתֵּימוֹ לְעוֹלָם, מִשְׁכְּנֹתָם לְדוֹר וָדֹר; קָרְאוּ בִשְׁמוֹתָם עֲלֵי אֲדָמוֹת. וְאָדָם בִּיקָר בַּל יָלִין, נִמְשַׁל כַּבְּהֵמוֹת נִדְמוּ. זֶה דַרְכָּם כֵּסֶל לָמוֹ, וְאַחֲרֵיהֶם בְּפִיהֶם יִרְצוּ סֶלָה. כַּצֹּאן לִשְׁאוֹל שַׁתּוּ, מָוֶת יִרְעֵם; וַיִּרְדּוּ בָם יְשָׁרִים לַבֹּקֶר, וְצוּרָם לְבַלּוֹת שְׁאוֹל מִזְּבֻל לוֹ. אַךְ אֱלֹקִים יִפְדֶּה נַפְשִׁי מִיַּד שְׁאוֹל, כִּי יִקָּחֵנִי סֶלָה. אַל תִּירָא כִּי יַעֲשִׁר אִישׁ, כִּי יִרְבֶּה כְּבוֹד בֵּיתוֹ. כִּי לֹא בְמוֹתוֹ יִקַּח הַכֹּל, לֹא יֵרֵד אַחֲרָיו כְּבוֹדוֹ. כִּי נַפְשׁוֹ בְּחַיָּיו יְבָרֵךְ, וְיוֹדֻךָ כִּי תֵיטִיב לָךְ. תָּבוֹא עַד דּוֹר אֲבוֹתָיו, עַד נֵצַח לֹא יִרְאוּ אוֹר. אָדָם בִּיקָר וְלֹא יָבִין, נִמְשַׁל כַּבְּהֵמוֹת נִדְמוּ.

For the Conductor, by the sons of Korach, a psalm. Hear this all you peoples, give ear all you dwellers of decaying earth. Sons of Adam and sons of man alike; together — rich man, poor man. My mouth shall speak wisdom, and the meditations of my heart are insightful. I will incline my ear to the parable, with a harp I will solve my riddle. Why should I have to fear in days of evil, when the injunctions that I trod upon will surround me? Those who rely on their possessions, and of their great wealth they are boastful — yet a man cannot redeem a brother, nor give to God his ransom. Too costly is their soul's redemption and unattainable forever. Can one live eternally, never to see the pit? Though he sees that wise men die, that the foolish and boorish perish together and leave their possessions to others — [nevertheless,] in their imagination their houses are forever, their dwellings for generation after generation; they have proclaimed their names throughout the lands. But as for man — in glory he shall not repose, he is likened to the silenced animals. This is their way — folly is theirs, yet of their destiny their mouths speak soothingly, Selah! Like sheep, they are destined for the Lower World, death shall consume them; and the upright shall dominate them at daybreak, their essence is doomed to rot in the grave, each from his dwelling. But God will redeem my soul from the grip of the Lower World, for He will take me, Selah! Fear not when a man grows rich, when he increases the splendor of his house. For upon his death he will not take anything, his splendor will not descend after him. Though he may bless himself in his lifetime, others will praise you if you improve yourself. It shall come to the generation of its fathers — unto eternity they shall see no light. Man is glorious but understands not, he is likened to the silenced animals.

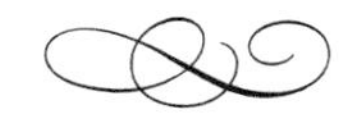

Solomon says, "It is better to go to the house of mourning than to go to a house of feasting, for that is the end of all man, and the living should take it to heart" (*Ecclesiastes* 7:2).

People may be most familiar with this psalm since it is recited in the prayers at the house of a mourner during *shivah*. Its theme is most important. Living a life of delusion is so foolish! "Make believe" is a juvenile game. Mature people should live in reality. This psalm emphasizes man's mortality. "Can one live eternally, never to see the pit? ... the foolish and boorish perish together and leave their possessions to others — [nevertheless,] in their imagination their houses are forever" (*Psalms* 49:10-12). If people realized that their sojourn on earth is limited, perhaps they would give more serious thought as to what they should be doing with their allotted years.

One might think that so important a concept would have been included in the daily prayers rather than at an infrequent condolence visit. Would it not have been more effective to recite this prayer each morning, so that one would conduct the day in the spirit of this insight?

Our sages were wise. They understood the words of Solomon, "... for that is the end of all man, and the living should *take it to heart.*" One could repeat this psalm many times a day, and it would have little impact on one's behavior. At the very best, one might achieve an intellectual grasp. Solomon knew that when intellect conflicts with desire, the latter most often triumphs. It is only in the house of a mourner, where the phenomenon of death is a stark reality, that a person might take the awareness of human mortality *to heart.*

We generally deny our mortality. Yes, we give it lip service. We know that a person does not live forever. Yet, is it not amazing that this knowledge notwithstanding, we live our lives not only as though we will never die, but as though we will never grow old and frail! The human psyche has formidable powers. It can prevent a person from becoming aware of something that is very unpleasant.

Several years ago I was asked to participate in a series of lectures for people between 40 and 50, to help them make plans for their retirement years. The lectures were to cover physical health, financial planning, estate planning, and psychological preparation for the leisure time of retirement. The program was well promoted, but the enrollment was meager. Most people simply put the subject out of their minds. Why, when their working years are over, they will play golf, take trips, go fishing, catch up on their reading and do all the things for which they had no time during the years when work occupied most of their lives. But what would they do if the wear-and-tear diseases of the later years precluded their capability of doing many of these things? What will they do with all the free time that had previously been occupied by work? Will these many hours not weigh heavily on them? That was not a consideration.

Working with alcoholics has given me an understanding of *denial.* Everything in the life of the alcoholic may be disintegrating before his very eyes – marriage, family, job, health, friends – and he has repeatedly been told by everyone that alcohol is his undoing, but it has no impact whatsoever on him. He believes that his wife and family will stay with him forever, that his job is secure, that his health is fine and that his friends are as devoted as ever. The doctor's warning that his liver is impaired is dismissed. His dependence on alcohol is so great that anything that threatens to deprive him of alcohol is completely blocked out of his awareness.

In regard to our mortality, many people are as much in denial as the alcoholic. "Man — in glory he shall not repose, he is likened to the silenced animals" (ibid. v. 13). Animals do not contemplate the end of their lives, nor do some people.

"This is their way – folly is theirs" (ibid. v. 14). Unlike animals, people do have the capacity to contemplate on their mortality, but they do not do it. The wicked could be aware of the destructiveness of their behavior, but their greed blinds them to it.

Psalm 49 emphasizes the futility of pursuing material wealth. Spending most of one's time and energy on the accumulation of earthly possessions does not befit a wise person. We all know that "you can't take it with you," but so many people behave as if they could.

> *There is an anecdote about two people who disputed the ownership of a piece of land. They brought the case before a rabbi, and each one tried to convince the Rabbi that the land belonged to him. Neither agreed to a settlement. After hearing their arguments, the Rabbi said he wanted to see the property in question.*
>
> *The two litigants took the Rabbi to the disputed property. The Rabbi said, "I will ask the land to whom it really belongs," and put his ear to the ground. After a few moments he arose and said, "The land said that it does not belong to either of you. To the contrary, both of you belong to it, and one day it will claim both of you."*

One may think that realizing one's mortality can be so depressing that it would make a person dysfunctional. Just the reverse is true. On a number of occasions during the year, we wear a *kittel* at services. The *kittel* ultimately serves as a shroud, and is worn as a reminder that it will one day be our final garment. There are many people who wear a *kittel*, and many of them are highly functional. Just as the alcoholic's life would greatly improve if he became aware of what he does not want to believe, so it is with our mortality.

Both as a physician and as a rabbi, I have been with people in the last days of their lives. Many people have expressed regret for having squandered away their years. Interestingly, no one has ever said, "My one regret is that I did not spend more time at the office."

It is unfortunate that such realization may occur when there is no longer an opportunity to implement it. Our lives would be so much richer if we could overcome our denial while there was still time to do something about our lifestyle.

In the house of the mourner, one sees the reality of death. This is the time when the message of Psalm 49 has a better chance of penetrating the psychological defense of denial and entering one's heart.

תהלים נא

Psalm 51

Psalm of Teshuvah

לַמְנַצֵּחַ מִזְמוֹר לְדָוִד. בְּבוֹא אֵלָיו נָתָן הַנָּבִיא, כַּאֲשֶׁר בָּא אֶל בַּת שָׁבַע. חָנֵּנִי אֱלֹקִים כְּחַסְדֶּךָ, כְּרֹב רַחֲמֶיךָ מְחֵה פְשָׁעָי. הֶרֶב כַּבְּסֵנִי מֵעֲוֹנִי, וּמֵחַטָּאתִי טַהֲרֵנִי. כִּי פְשָׁעַי אֲנִי אֵדָע, וְחַטָּאתִי נֶגְדִּי תָמִיד. לְךָ לְבַדְּךָ חָטָאתִי, וְהָרַע בְּעֵינֶיךָ עָשִׂיתִי; לְמַעַן תִּצְדַּק בְּדָבְרֶךָ, תִּזְכֶּה בְשָׁפְטֶךָ. הֵן בְּעָווֹן חוֹלָלְתִּי, וּבְחֵטְא יֶחֱמַתְנִי אִמִּי. הֵן אֱמֶת חָפַצְתָּ בַטֻּחוֹת, וּבְסָתֻם חָכְמָה תוֹדִיעֵנִי. תְּחַטְּאֵנִי בְאֵזוֹב וְאֶטְהָר, תְּכַבְּסֵנִי וּמִשֶּׁלֶג אַלְבִּין. תַּשְׁמִיעֵנִי שָׂשׂוֹן וְשִׂמְחָה, תָּגֵלְנָה עֲצָמוֹת דִּכִּיתָ. הַסְתֵּר פָּנֶיךָ מֵחֲטָאָי, וְכָל עֲוֹנֹתַי מְחֵה. לֵב טָהוֹר בְּרָא לִי אֱלֹקִים, וְרוּחַ נָכוֹן חַדֵּשׁ בְּקִרְבִּי. אַל תַּשְׁלִיכֵנִי מִלְּפָנֶיךָ, וְרוּחַ קָדְשְׁךָ אַל תִּקַּח מִמֶּנִּי. הָשִׁיבָה לִּי שְׂשׂוֹן יִשְׁעֶךָ, וְרוּחַ נְדִיבָה תִסְמְכֵנִי. אֲלַמְּדָה פֹשְׁעִים דְּרָכֶיךָ, וְחַטָּאִים אֵלֶיךָ יָשׁוּבוּ. הַצִּילֵנִי מִדָּמִים, אֱלֹקִים אֱלֹקֵי תְּשׁוּעָתִי, תְּרַנֵּן לְשׁוֹנִי צִדְקָתֶךָ. ה׳ שְׂפָתַי תִּפְתָּח, וּפִי יַגִּיד תְּהִלָּתֶךָ. כִּי לֹא תַחְפֹּץ זֶבַח וְאֶתֵּנָה, עוֹלָה לֹא תִרְצֶה. זִבְחֵי אֱלֹקִים רוּחַ נִשְׁבָּרָה; לֵב נִשְׁבָּר וְנִדְכֶּה, אֱלֹקִים לֹא תִבְזֶה. הֵיטִיבָה בִרְצוֹנְךָ אֶת צִיּוֹן, תִּבְנֶה חוֹמוֹת יְרוּשָׁלָיִם. אָז תַּחְפֹּץ זִבְחֵי צֶדֶק, עוֹלָה וְכָלִיל; אָז יַעֲלוּ עַל מִזְבַּחֲךָ פָרִים.

For the Conductor, a song by David. When Nathan the Prophet came to him, when he came to Bath Sheba. Show me favor, O God, according to Your kindness, according to Your vast compassion erase my transgressions. Abundantly cleanse me from my iniquity, and from my sin purify me. For I recognize my transgressions, and my sin is before me always. Against You alone did I sin, and that which is evil in Your eyes did I do; therefore, You are justified when You speak, and faultless when You judge. Behold, I was begotten with the capacity to sin, and in sin did my mother conceive me. Behold, the truth which You desire is in the concealed parts, and in the covered part is the wisdom which You teach me. Purge me of sin with hyssop and I shall be pure, cleanse me and I shall be whiter than snow. Make me hear joy and gladness, may the bones which You crushed exult. Hide Your face from my sins, and erase all my iniquities. A pure heart create for me, O God, and a steadfast spirit renew within me. Cast me not away from Your Presence, and Your Holy Spirit take not from me. Restore to me the joy of Your salvation, and with a generous spirit sustain me. I will teach transgressors Your ways, and sinners shall repent unto You. Deliver me from blood-guilt, O God, God of my salvation, let my tongue sing joyously of Your righteousness. My Lord, open my lips, that my mouth may declare Your praise. For You do not desire a sacrifice — else I would give it, a burnt-offering You do not want. The sacrifices God desires are a broken spirit; a heart broken and humbled, O God, You will not despise. Do good in Your favor unto Zion, build the walls of Jerusalem. Then You will desire the sacrifices of righteousness, burnt-offering and whole-offering; then will bulls go up upon Your altar.

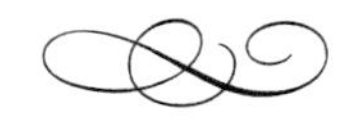

Earlier I commented on this psalm. It is of such importance that it should be read in its entirety. It is the text of *teshuvah*, par excellence.

No one is free of sin. "For there is no person in the land so righteous who does good and never sins" (*Ecclesiastes* 7:20). We are all in need of *teshuvah*.

The prophet Nathan rebuked David sharply for the incident with Bath Sheba (*II Samuel* 12). David was king, and it is not in the nature of powerful monarchs to admit they sinned. At the very least, they try to minimize their sin with any one of many mitigating factors. But David's confession was prompt and without any attempt to defend himself. His contrition was so immediate and sincere that the prophet told him that his death sentence would be commuted. Yet, he was to suffer punishment, because it must be made clear that God does not play favorites. Scoffers must know that God is just. Even His beloved minstrel would have to pay for his sin. David accepted this. The world must know that "You are justified when You speak, and faultless when You judge (*Psalms* 51:6)."

Today's rulers might say, "Let's put this personal event behind us and go on with the serious business of running the country." But not David. "My sin is before me always. There is nothing I can do to eradicate it. Only You, God, can cleanse me."

David does not invoke a defense of irresistible impulse. True, "I was begotten with the capacity to sin." A person does indeed have powerful sensual drives as part of his physiologic composition, but he has the spiritual capacity to be master over these drives.

As terrible as sin is, there is something even worse: the depression and despair that it can bring in its wake. One might say, "What is the use of my trying to be spiritual? I am beyond redemption." David avoids this pitfall. "A pure heart create for me ... Cast me not away ... Restore to me the joy of Your salvation" (ibid. vv. 12-14). David wishes to make an example of himself, accepting his punishment and showing that there is hope for the sinful. "I will teach transgressors Your ways, and sinners shall repent unto You" (ibid v. 15).

David closes with a powerful teaching for all generations. *Teshuvah* is not a ritual. Just beating one's chest and reciting the *al cheit* (Confession of sins) is not adequate. Even bringing offerings in the Temple is insufficient. It is only a broken and contrite heart and sincere regret that can allow one to come close to God again.

The Talmud says that David's sin was actually designed in order to teach people that no one should consider himself beyond the vulnerability to sin, and no one should consider himself beyond *teshuvah*. David was a good teacher. Psalm 51 is a superb lesson.

תהלים עט

Psalm 79

מִזְמוֹר לְאָסָף; אֱלֹקִים בָּאוּ גוֹיִם בְּנַחֲלָתֶךָ, טִמְּאוּ אֶת הֵיכַל קָדְשֶׁךָ, שָׂמוּ אֶת יְרוּשָׁלַיִם לְעִיִּים. נָתְנוּ אֶת נִבְלַת עֲבָדֶיךָ מַאֲכָל לְעוֹף הַשָּׁמָיִם, בְּשַׂר חֲסִידֶיךָ לְחַיְתוֹ אָרֶץ. שָׁפְכוּ דָמָם כַּמַּיִם, סְבִיבוֹת יְרוּשָׁלָיִם, וְאֵין קוֹבֵר. הָיִינוּ חֶרְפָּה לִשְׁכֵנֵינוּ, לַעַג וָקֶלֶס לִסְבִיבוֹתֵינוּ. עַד מָה ה׳ תֶּאֱנַף לָנֶצַח, תִּבְעַר כְּמוֹ אֵשׁ קִנְאָתֶךָ. שְׁפֹךְ חֲמָתְךָ אֶל הַגּוֹיִם אֲשֶׁר לֹא יְדָעוּךָ; וְעַל מַמְלָכוֹת, אֲשֶׁר בְּשִׁמְךָ לֹא קָרָאוּ. כִּי אָכַל אֶת יַעֲקֹב, וְאֶת נָוֵהוּ הֵשַׁמּוּ. אַל תִּזְכָּר לָנוּ עֲוֹנֹת רִאשֹׁנִים; מַהֵר יְקַדְּמוּנוּ רַחֲמֶיךָ, כִּי דַלּוֹנוּ מְאֹד. עָזְרֵנוּ אֱלֹקֵי יִשְׁעֵנוּ עַל דְּבַר כְּבוֹד שְׁמֶךָ, וְהַצִּילֵנוּ וְכַפֵּר עַל חַטֹּאתֵינוּ לְמַעַן שְׁמֶךָ. לָמָּה יֹאמְרוּ הַגּוֹיִם: אַיֵּה אֱלֹקֵיהֶם; יִוָּדַע בַּגּוֹיִם לְעֵינֵינוּ, נִקְמַת דַּם עֲבָדֶיךָ הַשָּׁפוּךְ. תָּבוֹא לְפָנֶיךָ אֶנְקַת אָסִיר; כְּגֹדֶל זְרוֹעֲךָ, הוֹתֵר בְּנֵי תְמוּתָה. וְהָשֵׁב לִשְׁכֵנֵינוּ שִׁבְעָתַיִם אֶל חֵיקָם, חֶרְפָּתָם אֲשֶׁר חֵרְפוּךָ, ה׳. וַאֲנַחְנוּ עַמְּךָ וְצֹאן מַרְעִיתֶךָ, נוֹדֶה לְּךָ לְעוֹלָם; לְדוֹר וָדֹר נְסַפֵּר תְּהִלָּתֶךָ.

A psalm of Asaph: O God! The nations have entered into Your inheritance, they have defiled the Sanctuary of Your holiness, they have turned Jerusalem into heaps of rubble. They have given the corpse of Your servants as food for the birds of the sky, the flesh of Your devout ones to the beasts of the earth. They have shed their blood like water round about Jerusalem, and there is none who buries. We became an object of disgrace to our neighbors, of mockery and scorn to those around us. Until when, Hashem, will You be ceaselessly angry, will Your jealousy burn like fire? Pour out Your wrath to the nations that know You not, and upon the kingdoms that do not call upon Your Name. For it has devoured Jacob, and they have desolated his habitation. Do not recall against us former iniquities. Speedily let Your mercy come to meet us for we have become exceedingly impoverished. Help us, O God of our salvation, for the sake of Your Name's glory, rescue us and grant us forgiveness for our sin, for Your Name's sake. Why should the nations say, "Where is their God"? Let Him be acknowledged among the nations before our eyes by avenging the blood of Your servants that has been spilled. Let the groan of the prisoner come before You; as befits the greatness of Your power — spare those condemned to die. And repay our neighbors sevenfold into their bosom — their disgrace with which they have disgraced You, O Lord. As for us, Your nation and the sheep of Your pasture, we shall thank You forever; for generation after generation we shall relate Your praise.

The Talmud asks, "Why is this psalm referred to as a "Song of Asaph?" Inasmuch as it refers to the destruction of the Temple, it would more appropriately be called "a lamentation of Asaph." The Talmud explains that the idolatry of the Jews at that time warranted a most severe punishment, as when they worshiped the Golden Calf, when God said to Moses, "Desist from Me. Let My anger flare up against them and I shall annihilate them" (*Exodus* 32:10). At that time, Moses interceded and achieved a measure of forgiveness that restrained the Divine wrath. When the Jews later reverted to idolatry, there was no Moses to intercede for them, and the Divine wrath would have resulted in their annihilation. In His mercy, God commuted their sentence, and punished them by allowing the Temple to be destroyed. The loss of the Temple thus spared the lives of the nation. This is why Asaph saw fit to refer to this psalm as a "song" rather than as a "lamentation." Bitter as it was, the loss of the Temple could be considered a "blessing in disguise" (*Kiddushin* 31b, *Rashi*).

The Midrash offers another explanation. Asaph was a descendant of Korach, whose rebellion against Moses resulted in his being swallowed up by the earth (Numbers 16:31). The Midrash gives a parable about a maidservant who was fetching water from a well, and her pitcher fell into the well. There was no way she could retrieve it, and she wept, anticipating that her master would punish her. One of the king's servants came along with a gold pitcher to fetch water, and that pitcher, too, fell into the well. The maidservant was overjoyed. "I had no way of getting my pitcher. However, someone will surely go down to retreive the gold pitcher, and will bring up my pitcher as well."

Asaph said, "'The gates of Jerusalem have sunk into the earth' (*Lamentations* 2:9). Surely God will bring up the gates of Jerusalem, and along with them He will bring up Korach" (ibid. *Maharsha*).

The psalm that would appear to be a lamentation is a song. The message is that when a person suffers adversity, he should bear in mind that God's benevolence is infinite.

When Job suffered his enormous tragedies, he denied that God was managing the world. A just and benevolent God would never have allowed such calamities to befall him. His friends tried to explain to him why God would allow such occurrences, but their explanations fell on deaf ears. Job rebutted all their arguments. Finally God said to Job, "And where were you when I created the world?" (*Job* 38:4). In other words, God has a master plan for the world. This plan makes sense only in its entirety, which requires a knowledge of infinite time and space. Only God has such knowledge. Man has no way of understanding how isolated incidents fit into the master plan.

When a person experiences a loss, it is difficult to see that it has any redeeming features. One feels only the God, and realize that although our limited intelligence does not enable us to see what good might come of this, God is benevolent in ways which we cannot understand.

תהלים קד

Psalm 104

בָּרְכִי נַפְשִׁי אֶת ה׳; ה׳ אֱלֹקַי גָּדַלְתָּ מְּאֹד, הוֹד וְהָדָר לָבָשְׁתָּ.
עֹטֶה אוֹר כַּשַּׂלְמָה, נוֹטֶה שָׁמַיִם כַּיְרִיעָה. הַמְקָרֶה בַמַּיִם
עֲלִיּוֹתָיו; הַשָּׂם עָבִים רְכוּבוֹ, הַמְהַלֵּךְ עַל כַּנְפֵי רוּחַ. עֹשֶׂה
מַלְאָכָיו רוּחוֹת, מְשָׁרְתָיו אֵשׁ לֹהֵט. יָסַד אֶרֶץ עַל מְכוֹנֶיהָ, בַּל
תִּמּוֹט עוֹלָם וָעֶד. תְּהוֹם כַּלְּבוּשׁ כִּסִּיתוֹ, עַל הָרִים יַעַמְדוּ מָיִם. מִן
גַּעֲרָתְךָ יְנוּסוּן, מִן קוֹל רַעַמְךָ יֵחָפֵזוּן. יַעֲלוּ הָרִים, יֵרְדוּ בְקָעוֹת,
אֶל מְקוֹם זֶה יָסַדְתָּ לָהֶם. גְּבוּל שַׂמְתָּ בַּל יַעֲבֹרוּן, בַּל יְשׁוּבוּן
לְכַסּוֹת הָאָרֶץ. הַמְשַׁלֵּחַ מַעְיָנִים בַּנְּחָלִים, בֵּין הָרִים יְהַלֵּכוּן.
יַשְׁקוּ כָּל חַיְתוֹ שָׂדָי, יִשְׁבְּרוּ פְרָאִים צְמָאָם. עֲלֵיהֶם עוֹף הַשָּׁמַיִם
יִשְׁכּוֹן, מִבֵּין עֳפָאיִם יִתְּנוּ קוֹל. מַשְׁקֶה הָרִים מֵעֲלִיּוֹתָיו, מִפְּרִי
מַעֲשֶׂיךָ תִּשְׂבַּע הָאָרֶץ. מַצְמִיחַ חָצִיר לַבְּהֵמָה, וְעֵשֶׂב לַעֲבֹדַת
הָאָדָם; לְהוֹצִיא לֶחֶם מִן הָאָרֶץ. וְיַיִן יְשַׂמַּח לְבַב אֱנוֹשׁ, לְהַצְהִיל
פָּנִים מִשָּׁמֶן, וְלֶחֶם לְבַב אֱנוֹשׁ יִסְעָד. יִשְׂבְּעוּ עֲצֵי ה׳, אַרְזֵי לְבָנוֹן
אֲשֶׁר נָטָע. אֲשֶׁר שָׁם צִפֳּרִים יְקַנֵּנוּ, חֲסִידָה בְּרוֹשִׁים בֵּיתָהּ. הָרִים
הַגְּבֹהִים לַיְּעֵלִים, סְלָעִים מַחְסֶה לַשְׁפַנִּים. עָשָׂה יָרֵחַ לְמוֹעֲדִים,
שֶׁמֶשׁ יָדַע מְבוֹאוֹ. תָּשֶׁת חֹשֶׁךְ וִיהִי לָיְלָה, בּוֹ תִרְמֹשׂ כָּל חַיְתוֹ
יָעַר. הַכְּפִירִים שֹׁאֲגִים לַטָּרֶף, וּלְבַקֵּשׁ מֵקֵל אָכְלָם. תִּזְרַח הַשֶּׁמֶשׁ
יֵאָסֵפוּן, וְאֶל מְעוֹנֹתָם יִרְבָּצוּן. יֵצֵא אָדָם לְפָעֳלוֹ, וְלַעֲבֹדָתוֹ עֲדֵי
עָרֶב. מָה רַבּוּ מַעֲשֶׂיךָ | ה׳, כֻּלָּם בְּחָכְמָה עָשִׂיתָ, מָלְאָה הָאָרֶץ
קִנְיָנֶךָ. זֶה הַיָּם, גָּדוֹל וּרְחַב יָדָיִם; שָׁם רֶמֶשׂ וְאֵין מִסְפָּר, חַיּוֹת
קְטַנּוֹת עִם גְּדֹלוֹת. שָׁם אֳנִיּוֹת יְהַלֵּכוּן, לִוְיָתָן זֶה יָצַרְתָּ לְשַׂחֶק בּוֹ.
כֻּלָּם אֵלֶיךָ יְשַׂבֵּרוּן, לָתֵת אָכְלָם בְּעִתּוֹ. תִּתֵּן לָהֶם, יִלְקֹטוּן;
תִּפְתַּח יָדְךָ, יִשְׂבְּעוּן טוֹב. תַּסְתִּיר פָּנֶיךָ יִבָּהֵלוּן; תֹּסֵף רוּחָם
יִגְוָעוּן, וְאֶל עֲפָרָם יְשׁוּבוּן. תְּשַׁלַּח רוּחֲךָ יִבָּרֵאוּן, וּתְחַדֵּשׁ פְּנֵי
אֲדָמָה. יְהִי כְבוֹד ה׳ לְעוֹלָם, יִשְׂמַח ה׳ בְּמַעֲשָׂיו. הַמַּבִּיט לָאָרֶץ
וַתִּרְעָד, יִגַּע בֶּהָרִים וְיֶעֱשָׁנוּ. אָשִׁירָה לַה׳ בְּחַיָּי, אֲזַמְּרָה לֵאלֹקַי
בְּעוֹדִי. יֶעֱרַב עָלָיו שִׂיחִי, אָנֹכִי אֶשְׂמַח בַּה׳. יִתַּמּוּ חַטָּאִים מִן
הָאָרֶץ, וּרְשָׁעִים עוֹד אֵינָם, בָּרְכִי נַפְשִׁי אֶת ה׳, הַלְלוּקָהּ.

Bless Hashem, O my soul. Hashem, my God, You are very great; You have donned majesty and splendor;

covering with light as with a garment, stretching out the heavens like a curtain. He Who roofs His upper chambers with water; He Who makes clouds His chariot; He Who walks on winged wind. He makes the winds His messengers, the flaming fire His attendants. He established the earth upon its foundations, that it falter not forever and ever. The watery deep, as with a garment You covered it; upon the mountains, water would stand. From Your rebuke they flee, from the sound of Your thunder they rush away. They ascend mountains, they descend to valleys, to the special place You founded for them. You set a boundary they cannot overstep, they cannot return to cover the earth. He sends the springs into the streams, they flow between the mountains. They water every beast of the field, they quench the wild creatures' thirst. Near them dwell the heaven's birds, from among the branches they give forth song. He waters the mountains from His upper chambers, from the fruit of Your works the earth is sated. He causes vegetation to sprout for the cattle, and plants through man's labor, to bring forth bread from the earth; and wine that gladdens man's heart, to make the face glow from oil, and bread that sustains the heart of man. The trees of Hashem are sated, the cedars of Lebanon that He has planted; there where the birds nest, the chassidah with its home among cypresses; high mountains for the wild goats, rocks as refuge for the gophers. He made the moon for festivals, the sun knows its destination. You make darkness and it is night, in which every forest beast stirs. The young lions roar after their prey, and to seek their food from God. The sun rises and they are gathered in, and in their dens they crouch. Man goes forth to his work, and to his labor until evening. How abundant are Your works, Hashem; with wisdom You made them all, the earth is full of Your possessions. Behold this sea — great and of broad measure; there are creeping things without number, small creatures and great ones. There ships travel, this Leviathan You fashioned to sport within. All of them look to You with hope, to provide their food in its proper time. You give to them, they gather it in; You open Your hand, they are sated with good. When You hide Your face, they are dismayed; when You retrieve their spirit, they perish and to their dust they return. When You send forth Your breath, they are created, and You renew the surface of the earth. May the glory of Hashem endure forever, let Hashem rejoice in His works. He looks toward the earth and it trembles, He touches the mountains and they smoke. I will sing to Hashem while I live, I will sing praises to my God while I endure. May my words be sweet to Him — I will rejoice in Hashem. Sinners will cease from the earth, and the wicked will be no more — Bless Hashem, O my soul. Halleluyah!

Someone said that it is worthwhile to learn Hebrew just to be able to read Psalm 104 in the original. During his early years, David was a shepherd, and this brought him into intimate contact with nature. David was a keen observer and extremely sensitive. He appreciated the marvels of nature and recognized the handiwork of God in everything he saw. After describing both the animate and inanimate components of nature, and how everything was in exquisite harmony, David exclaimed, "How abundant are Your works, God, with wisdom You made them all. The earth is full of Your possessions" (ibid. 104:24)! I have the feeling that this was an exclamation which burst forth from David when he could not contain his admiration for the Creator and the grandeur of nature.

Let me share with you my association to this. We are familiar with how joyously we dance on Simchas Torah. I have memories of my father on Simchas Torah. He would hold the Torah and stand quietly, swaying just a bit while everyone was singing the joyful melodies. Then abruptly he would break into a dance with the Torah. It was clear that he was experiencing the happiness of Torah while he was standing still, and began to dance when the level of joy had reached a point where it could not be contained, and moved him to dance. This is how I envision David's exclamation.

> *The Chassidic master, R' Leib son of Sarah, used to go from village to village, seeking to rescue Jews who had been thrown into the dungeons by the poritz because they had been unable to pay the rent. He often made his way by foot because he could not afford transportation.*
>
> *One time, R' Leib was walking in the fields on a bright and beautiful day. He was overcome with the beauty of nature and said, "Master of the universe! How can I possibly thank You and praise You for all the goodness and kindness, the beauty and grandeur that You have shown me? After the sweet minstrel of Israel, Your servant David, has said 'Bless God, O my soul. Hashem, my God, you are very great. You*

have donned majesty and splendor' (ibid. v. 1), what is there that I can add?

"But, my heavenly Father, this is what I can tell You. Leib son of Sarah has so good a life. He is healthy and strong. Which of the wealthiest people can compare himself to him? The wealthy may have gold, silver, houses and properties. All these have their limits. But to Leib the son of Sarah You have given unlimited riches. Leib has seen wealthy people with ornate chariots and many servants, but he has never yet seen a wealthy person who is truly happy. The terrible anxiety that they have that they may lose their wealth! The envy that another person is wealthier than they are! They have no tranquility during the day and no peace at night. They need guards and dogs to protect them.

"But what am I, Leib the son of Sarah, lacking? Nothing! Heavenly Father, You have so blessed me. Your whole world is my home. The bright sunlight is mine, the beautiful trees, the colorful and fragrant flowers. You have given all of these for Leib to enjoy, and I thank You for them. Wherever I travel, wherever I go, I am welcomed. My brethren greet me and are happy to see me.

"Leib the son of Sarah is more than wealthy. He is a king, a king without ministers and armies. The backpack he carries is worth more than the gold of kings. It is not just a backpack; it is storehouse of hearts, containing the good hearts of Jews, all their compassion for their fellow Jews. I collect tzedakah for the needy, the orphaned and widows, and for ransoming Jews from the dungeons. No one has refused Leib the son of Sarah, whether poor or wealthy. One gives more, one gives less, what difference does it make? How much money Leib has made, a king's fortune! It needs no guards. None of it can be stolen. It is safely invested in the poor and homeless, and in the ransomed prisoners, and the return on the investment is guaranteed unto eternity. Leib is so rich!

"And if Leib's wealth is not enough, You have shown him Your beautiful world in all its splendor. Who can compare himself to Leib? Leib is full of joy! Master of the universe, grant Leib that he should always be as happy as he is now." And with that, R' Leib broke into a dance, singing "Hashem is our Father! Hashem is our Father! Ashrenu, ma tov chelkenu (We are fortunate, how good is our portion)."

In my imagination, I see R' Leib becoming increasingly elated as he expresses his gratitude to God. I see him, like my father on Simchas Torah, breaking into a dance because he could not contain his joy. He did not lift his feet to dance. It was his feet that lifted him. As one of the Chassidic masters said, when one dances one detaches from the earth and becomes just a bit closer to heaven. It was this kind of dance to which he was referring.

I sometimes think, when reciting the verse *Ashrenu ma tov chelkenu* in the morning service, "Why am I not dancing like R' Leib? Have I not just recited *berachos* thanking God for giving me my sight, my strength, my clothes, my ability to move, to walk about? I have thanked Him for returning to me my *neshamah*, pure and clean, regardless of how I may have carelessly stained it. I have said a *berachah* thanking God for hallowing me with His mitzvos. I can see the beautiful world which David extolled. What is wrong with me that I am so unappreciative? Why do I not feel overjoyed when I say *Ashrenu*?"

David said, "Let my *neshamah* bless God." I, too, have a *neshamah*. The Talmud says that David uses the expression *borchi nafshi* five times, because the *neshamah* resembles God in five ways. Just as God occupies the entire universe, the *neshamah* occupies the entire body. Just as God sees but cannot be seen, so the *neshamah* sees but cannot be seen. Just as God nourishes the entire world, so the *neshamah* nourishes the entire body. Just as God is pure, so is the *neshamah* pure. Just as God is concealed, so is the *neshamah* concealed.

The *neshamah* is Godlike. Certainly my *neshamah* is appreciative and grateful, just as David's and R' Leib's. What is it that stifles its expression?

Is it because I have some worries on my mind, problems that depress me? I had similar worries years ago, things that I thought were major problems. I can't recall any of them now. In just a few days or weeks or months, the problems that I think are monumental today will have disappeared from my memory. And it is these ephemeral annoyances that I allow to suppress the rapture of my *neshamah*. I should be ashamed of myself.

When I put on my *tallis*, I recite the opening phrase of Psalm 104, "Bless God, O my *nefesh* (soul). Hashem, my God, You are very great; You have donned majesty and splendor." Did I not hear what I was saying? After wrapping myself in the *tallis*, I say, "How precious is Your kindness, God. The sons of man take refuge in the shadow of Your wings. May they be sated from the abundance of Your house, and may You give them to drink from the stream of Your delights" (ibid. 36:8-9). Am I so indifferent and insensitive?

> *Human nature is strange. There is some truth in the anecdote of the mother whose child was torn from her and swept out to sea by a sudden storm. She began screaming, "Dear God, have mercy! Save my child! Give me back my*

child!" Then a huge wave came ashore and set the child before her, safe and sound. She embraced and kissed the child, and with tears of gratitude said, "O, thank You, God! How can I ever thank You!" After a few minutes she looked up to heaven and said, "God, he was wearing a hat!"

This is more than an amusing story. It is a reflection on human nature. R' Leib was appreciative. David, whose life was so full of agony that the Midrash says he did not have a single good day in his 70 years, could nevertheless be ecstatic with joy. It was only his body that was in anguish. His *neshamah* was unfettered. It marveled at the grass-covered mountains, at the trees in which birds nested, at the streams, at the crevices in the rocks that provided a haven for animals, at the way in which God provided sustenance for all living things.

David bequeathed us a priceless psalm. We should read it slowly, savoring every word. David begins this psalm with, "Bless God, O my soul." He then goes on to tell why, and closes with, "I will sing to God while I live ... May my words be sweet to Him ... I will rejoice in God. Sinners will cease ... Bless God, O my soul. Halleluyah!" (ibid vv. 33-35). We, too, can sing our praises to God. David has provided us with the method. If we eliminate the character defects that suppress the *neshamah*, we, too, will say *Borchi nafshi* and allow our souls to bless God.

Security in God

תהלים קכא
Psalm 121

שִׁיר לַמַּעֲלוֹת; אֶשָּׂא עֵינַי אֶל הֶהָרִים, מֵאַיִן יָבֹא עֶזְרִי. עֶזְרִי מֵעִם ה׳, עֹשֵׂה שָׁמַיִם וָאָרֶץ. אַל יִתֵּן לַמּוֹט רַגְלֶךָ, אַל יָנוּם שֹׁמְרֶךָ. הִנֵּה לֹא יָנוּם וְלֹא יִישָׁן, שׁוֹמֵר יִשְׂרָאֵל. ה׳ שֹׁמְרֶךָ, ה׳ צִלְּךָ עַל יַד יְמִינֶךָ. יוֹמָם הַשֶּׁמֶשׁ לֹא יַכֶּכָּה, וְיָרֵחַ בַּלָּיְלָה. ה׳ יִשְׁמָרְךָ מִכָּל רָע, יִשְׁמֹר אֶת נַפְשֶׁךָ. ה׳ יִשְׁמָר צֵאתְךָ וּבוֹאֶךָ, מֵעַתָּה וְעַד עוֹלָם.

A song to the ascents. I raise my eyes upon the mountains; whence will come my help? My help is from Hashem, Maker of heaven and earth. He will not allow your foot to falter; your Guardian will not slumber. Behold, He neither slumbers nor sleeps — the Guardian of Israel. Hashem is your Guardian; Hashem is your Shade at your right hand. By day the sun will not harm you, nor the moon by night. Hashem will protect you from every evil; He will guard your soul. Hashem will guard your departure and your arrival, from this time and forever.

The Midrash states that the first two verses were said by the Patriarch Jacob when he fled from his brother, Esau. At his father's behest, Eliphaz, Esau's son, pursued Jacob to kill him. Jacob pleaded for his life, and finally gave everything he had to Eliphaz. "You may feel that you have indeed fulfilled your father's command. Having taken everything from me, you may truthfully say that you 'killed' me."

Left with nothing, Jacob said, "*Me'ayin yavo ezri*" (ibid. 121:1). This is generally translated as "whence will come my help." However, the word *ayin* also means "nothingness." The phrase can then be a question: "Can my help come from nothingness, when I have been left with nothing?" The next verse is then an appropriate answer. "My help is from God, Maker of heaven and earth." God created the world out of nothingness, *yesh me'ayin,* something out of nothing. Since God is my Source of help, my being bereft of everything does not discourage me. God can bring me help from nothing, just as He created the world out of nothingness.

One cannot avoid the question, "If God is our eternal protector, why have we suffered so many disasters throughout our history?" Of course, if one reads the dire warnings in *Deuteronomy* (28:15-68), one may understand that from the time our forefathers were driven into exile because of the bitter divisiveness and the senseless animosity among Jews, we have never rectified this defect. The Midrash says that if we were united, we would merit the Redemption. God is willing to forgive everything if His children would join together in harmony and love (*Bamidbar Rabbah* 11:16).

I must repeat here what I have said elsewhere. I was in a pediatrician's waiting room, where a mother was holding a cheerful infant. As soon as the white-clad doctor emerged, the child emitted a sharp wail and threw its arms around his mother. He knew what was about to happen, having experienced the pain of an injection twice previously. The mother took the child into the treatment room and restrained him. The child fought the mother, trying to free himself from her grip. After the doctor administered the injection, the child again threw his arms around his mother and held on for dear life.

While the mother was restraining the child, he must have thought, "What is happening here? My mother is the one who loves me. She feeds me and protects me. Why has she turned against me? Why is she collaborating with this villain to hurt me?" There was no way this child could understand that the pain he was being put through would save him from crippling and even fatal diseases.

But why did the child cling to the mother after the injection? Hadn't she just participated in hurting him? How could he now rely on her for protection? The answer is that although the child could not possibly understand why his mother was doing this, he nevertheless knew that she loved him and that she was his source of security.

Like the infant, we cannot understand why God has allowed us to suffer so many disasters. But like the infant, He is the One to Whom we turn for help and protection.

Yes, God is our eternal Protector. The Talmud says, "How powerful must be a Shepherd Who can protect a lone sheep who is surrounded by seventy hungry wolves" (*Yoma* 69b). Jews have always been a minority. We have always been surrounded by overt and covert enemies. That we have nevertheless survived is testimony that "the Guardian of Israel neither slumbers nor sleeps."

Afterword

In the Footsteps of the Patriarchs

The Talmud states that the three daily prayers were formulated by the Patriarchs. Abraham established *Shacharis* (the morning service), Isaac established *Minchah* (the afternoon service) and Jacob established *Maariv* (the evening service; *Berachos* 26b). It is rather unlikely that whereas we pray three times a day, the Patriarch Abraham prayed only once. Abraham undoubtedly prayed many times during the day. However, his prayers were in the character of *Shacharis*, the early morning.

Abraham was born into a world of spiritual darkness. His father, brothers, and everyone in his environment were pagans. As a child, Abraham realized the folly of idolatry, and began searching for the true God. There are varying versions in the Midrash as to how old Abraham was when he came to the awareness of the truth. This was a breakthrough from spiritual darkness into the light of truth. Abraham's prayers were, therefore, prayers of *Shacharis*, the light of dawn.

Isaac was born to Abraham and Sarah. From his first day, he was bathed in the light of spirituality. His life was rather free of distress. Although he had a deviant son, Esau, he never lost hope of reclaiming him. His life might be likened to the steady brightness of the midday sun. Isaac's prayers were, therefore, of *Minchah* character.

Jacob's prayers were of the onset and progression of darkness. Even before his birth, he was in strife with Esau. He had to flee to save his life from Esau's murderous intentions. For twenty years he suffered from the guile of Laban. He grieved for twenty-two years for his beloved son, Joseph. "Few and bad have been the days of the years of my life," he said to Pharaoh (*Genesis* 47:9). Jacob's prayers reflected the distress and darkness of his life. Jacob prayed many times during the day, but his prayers reflected the darkness he experienced. Jacob's prayers were of the *Maariv* character.

While we pray *Shacharis* in the morning, *Minchah* in the afternoon, and *Maariv* at night, we should reflect that the character of these prayers corresponds to various times in our lives. Regardless of what our circumstances are, we should pray to God for His help and be grateful for the kindness He has done for us.

There are times we feel we have had a breakthrough from darkness to light. Whether in our personal, professional or business lives, we may have emerged from a very difficult period into one of comfort and success. Our prayer at such a time should be that of Abraham, one of emerging from darkness to light. We may be in a state of relative freedom from distress, and our prayer at this time should be like that of Isaac. And if we happen to experience adversity and we feel that darkness is descending upon us, we should pray with the hope and trust of Jacob.

The relationship of our prayers to life's circumstances is not only to phases of our lives, but even to changes within the day. We may experience diverse conditions in any one day. We should be aware that the Patriarchs provided us with appropriate ways in which we can relate to God under all conditions and in every circumstance.